TIGERS IN NORMANDY

WOLFGANG SCHNEIDER

STACKPOLE
BOOKS
Essex, Connecticut
Blue Ridge Summit, Pennsylvania

STACKPOLE BOOKS
An imprint of The Globe Pequot Publishing Group, Inc.
64 South Main Street
Essex, CT 06426
www.globepequot.com

Distributed by NATIONAL BOOK NETWORK

First Stackpole Books paperback edition published 2025

Originally published in German in 2004 as *Tiger im Kampf: Die Einsätze in der Normandie*.

British Library Cataloguing in Publication Information available

Library of Congress Cataloging-in-Publication Data

Schneider, Wolfgang, Oberleutnant.
[Tiger im Kampf. English]
Tigers in Normandy / Wolfgang Schneider.
p. cm.
Includes bibliographical references.
1. World War, 1939–1945—Campaigns—France—Normandy. 2. World War, 1939–1945—Tank warfare. 3. Tiger (Tank) I. Title.
D756.5.N6S3713 2011
940.54'21421—dc23

2011027976

ISBN 9780811776950 (pbk.)

CONTENTS

FOREWORD

The two-volume series entitled *Tigers in Combat*, encompassing nearly 1,000 pages, has presented a nearly seamless overview of the fate of all of the armored formations equipped with the *Tiger*. It goes without saying that this could only be accomplished by using an abbreviated style that was reminiscent of that used in military daily logs.

The desire for a more comprehensive treatment has been voiced. This has been accomplished in a number of battalion histories—*schwere Panzer-Abteilung 503, schwere Panzer-Abteilung 507, schwere Panzer-Abteilung 508* and *schwere SS-Panzer-Abteilung 101* come to mind—but the first detailed analysis of a combat area of operations from the viewpoint of *Tiger* operations is to be found here.

The 60th anniversary of the Allied landings in Normandy in June 1944 provided the impetus for this effort. When one looks at the literature and evaluates the sources, one gains the impression that the *Tiger* must have played a decisive role in those combat operations. Both British and Canadian accounts create that impression, inasmuch as they continually reference how much that particular model of tank caused shock and fear.

The tank's debut in Normandy at Villers-Bocage on 13 June 1944 was a spectacular one and has been the subject of many accounts.

This book will determine whether these claims accurately reflected reality and the *Tiger* actually played such a significant role. In the face of an oppressive numerical superiority—especially in the air—and the small numbers of *Tigers* employed, doubts seem in order.

All of the engagements are analyzed with the help of accounts from both sides—German and Allied—so that it is possible to provide comparisons. In tank-versus-tank engagements, the *Tigers* had no competitors on the Western Allied side at that point in the war, but the *Tiger* crews had a number of demands placed on them that ultimately affected combat effectiveness.

✠

Some of the unique characteristics of the terrain also played a major role. For that reason, numerous current images of the battlefields have been added, as well as detailed maps. Therefore, this book also functions as a battlefield guide. It is hoped that the reader will be encouraged to visit these locations himself. On each of the current terrain photos, the cardinal direction of the compass is indicated for the direction in which the viewer is oriented, e.g., N = north. Furthermore, for every major area of operation of the *Tiger* battalions, a sketch map is provided that shows these differing perspectives from a bird's-eye view.

✠

This degree of detail is only possible through the assistance of competent historians whose research in the recent past has been extraordinary in tracing the developments of the fighting. In this regard, Henri Marie, Bruno Renoult and Philippe Wirton deserve special mention, since their work is worthy of the highest praise. It was primarily through their help that it was possible to determine and verify the individual fate and final location of almost all of the tanks.

✠

The accounts provided by individual soldiers have intentionally not been edited and, as a result, reflect personal sensitivities and viewpoints.

✠

It has not been simple to find contemporary photographs, since the holdings in the available archives are small and almost all of the images are already well known. During the last few weeks of operations, there are generally only images of abandoned tanks. In addition, the quality of those photographs often leaves much to be desired. One exception was the photographs provided by Gotthold Wunderlich, a former member of the battalion, who provided the images of the *3./schwere Panzer-Abteilung 503* at Camp Mailly and in Paris.

✠

In addition to the previously mentioned individuals, I would like to thank Thorsten Brandt for the production of the situation maps, my daughter, Kristine, for the design of the cover (German edition) and my family for their patience.

CHAPTER 1

Movement of the Tiger Formations to Normandy

Introduction

The formations equipped with the *Tiger* armored fighting vehicle have found special mention in the literature that comes from the side of the former Allies concerning the fighting in Normandy in the summer of 1944. A considerable amount of successful German defensive efforts in the course of the exhaustive fighting to break out of the beachhead are ascribed to these formations. Many firsthand accounts mention the superiority in battle of these tanks or the constant panic that was unleashed by them on the Allied side.

Up to this point, there has been no substantiated analysis of whether these claims accurately reflected reality or whether the *Tiger* actually played such a significant role. What is uncontested is the fact that in a tank-versus-tank engagement, it was greatly superior to all opposing tanks thanks to its superior armament and its superior ballistic protection. Did this superiority carry over to the tactical and operational levels, however?

This question will be examined in the following book. The operations in which *Tiger* tanks participated will be portrayed as well as their direct influence on the subsequent outcome. It will quickly become clear to the reader that there has been a series of incorrect interpretations in the available literature up to this point. Likewise, he will also receive a number of new and interesting insights.

While all of this will lead to a conclusion on the part of the author, which, in the end, is subjective, it is also intended to invite further discussion.

In order to keep this book within manageable proportions, it will be assumed that the reader is already familiar with a number of facts. This is particularly true with regard to the overall strategic framework. This is quite important, since the *Tiger* was never at any time omnipresent on the battlefield. Initially, it was only used against the British and Canadian forces in the greater area of Caen. Even then—as will be demonstrated—it was only employed in certain areas.

In the case of all the fighting portrayed, both sides will be presented. This is thanks to an extensive evaluation of all the available literature. As a result, a large amount of factual detail has been faithfully captured. Many facts that have heretofore been presented incorrectly or incompletely have now been set right, verified and unequivocally proven.

This book also serves another purpose. It is intended to pique the reader's curiosity so that he might also personally explore the areas where the fighting occurred and form his own impressions. To this end, the terrain directly influencing the fighting has also been discussed and illustrated with photographs.

Tiger Formations in Normandy

The first question that needs to be answered is how many formations participated in the fighting after the beginning of the Allied invasion of Normandy. It is also necessary to know how many *Tigers* were actually in those formations. It is perhaps surprising to discover that on the day of the invasion, there was not a single *Tiger* formation on the scene! Only *one* formation was on its approach march, and it was still far away, in fact, east of Paris. We are talking about *schwere SS-Panzer-Abteilung 101*. Due to the extensive damage to the railway network northwest of Paris, the main body of the battalion was detrained as far away as Versailles and started on a difficult land march in the direction of the front. As a consequence of Allied air superiority, the battalion was forced to move in individual groups and not until after the onset of darkness.

Similar circumstances applied to the second *Tiger* formation, *schwere SS-Panzer-Abteilung 102*, which reached the greater area of Paris more than a week later. This battalion also had to engage in the painful odyssey of a land march to the northwest.

In addition to the constant threat from the air, which caused initial losses, there was a special problem. The tanks were put to an extreme test on their long marches; there were a number of tanks temporarily disabled by mechanical problems. In addition, there was the considerable fuel consumption of the tanks. Just for the tanks to get to their areas of operations required that they cover distances of up to 300 kilometers under their own power. In fact, all of the vehicles—in most cases, several times—suffered mechanical problems that required repair. The maintenance personnel were correspondingly stretched to the limit when they had distances of some 50 kilometers or even more between the sites of the disabled vehicles.

The same dynamic applied to the logistics personnel, who had to bring forward fuel and oil products as well as urgently needed repair parts, all the while exposed to the constant danger of low-level aerial attack. As a result, the battalions reached their areas of operation in dribs and drabs, and the personnel and the equipment were only conditionally operational.

Adding difficulty to the situation was the fact that both of these battalions had only recently been formed. In each case, the cadre was formed from remaining personnel from a single *Tiger* company, which had previously been in the respective divisions—*SS-Panzer-Division "Leibstandarte SS Adolf Hitler"* and *SS-Panzer-Division "Das Reich."* As a result, no cohesiveness had been formed in many of the sub-units and the weapons system had not been sufficiently mastered by all crews. Only *schwere SS-Panzer-Abteilung 101* had been able to conduct larger-scale formation-level training in Belgium in May.

At the start of Operation "Overlord," a third formation was in the process of reconstitution within the borders of the *Reich*. This was *schwere Panzer-Abteilung 503*, the most senior *Tiger* battalion of them all. In contrast to the two *Waffen-SS* heavy tank battalions, this was a combat-experienced formation with great cohesion. It was not deployed until more than two weeks after 6 June 1944. It did not reach its area of operations east of Caen until 7 July 1944, after suffering problems similar to the ones experienced by the aforementioned battalions.

In the interest of completeness, a fourth element must be mentioned, whose formation took place under extremely poor conditions and, in the end, must be considered inadequate. This was a radio-controlled unit, that is, an element whose purpose was to steer radio-controlled demolitions carriers into valuable targets and then blow them up. The control vehicles for these were tanks or assault guns. This special-purpose unit was being considered for a time for deployment with *Panzer-Grenadier-Division "Großdeutschland."* It was designated *Panzer-Kompanie 316 (Fkl)* and was issued five *Tigers* as part of its table

TIGER BATTALIONS IN NORMANDY

Date	503	316	SS-101	SS-102
		Overlord		
7 June 1944			Versailles	
8 June 1944			Vimoutiers (*1./SS-101*); Argentan (*2./SS-101*); Paris (*3./SS-101*)	
9 June 1944			Argentan (*2./SS-101*)	
10 June 1944			Falaise (*2./SS-101*)	
11 June 1944				Tilburg–Breda
		Perch		
12 June 1944			Villers-Bocage (*1.* and *2./SS-101*)	Arras
13 June 1944			Villers-Bocage (*1.* and *2./SS-101*)	Lens
14 June 1944			Cahagnes (*1./SS-101*); Evrecy (*3./SS-101*)	
15 June 1944				
16 June 1944			Cahagnes	Laon
17 June 1944				
18 June 1944			Held in reserve in the vicinity of the Caen–Villers-Bocage road	
19 June 1944				Reims
20 June 1944				Reims
21 June 1944				Versailles
22 June 1944				
23 June 1944				Joue-du-Bois
		Epsom		
24 June 1944				
25 June 1944				Rambouillet
26 June 1944	Nancy		Rauray	Maintenon
27 June 1944			Corps rear area	Chateau neuf-en-Thymerais
28 June 1944	Melun		Grainville / Verson	Longny-aux-Perche
29 June 1944	Drieux		Maltot / Hill 112	
30 June 1944	Versailles			
1 July 1944				Joue-du-Bois (*2./SS-102*)
2 July 1944			Hill 112	Segrie Fontaine
3 July 1944			1 Company to Paderborn	Cauville
4 July 1944	Argentan			Cauville
5 July 1944			No operational tanks	Cauville
6 July 1944	Mezidon			Vacognes

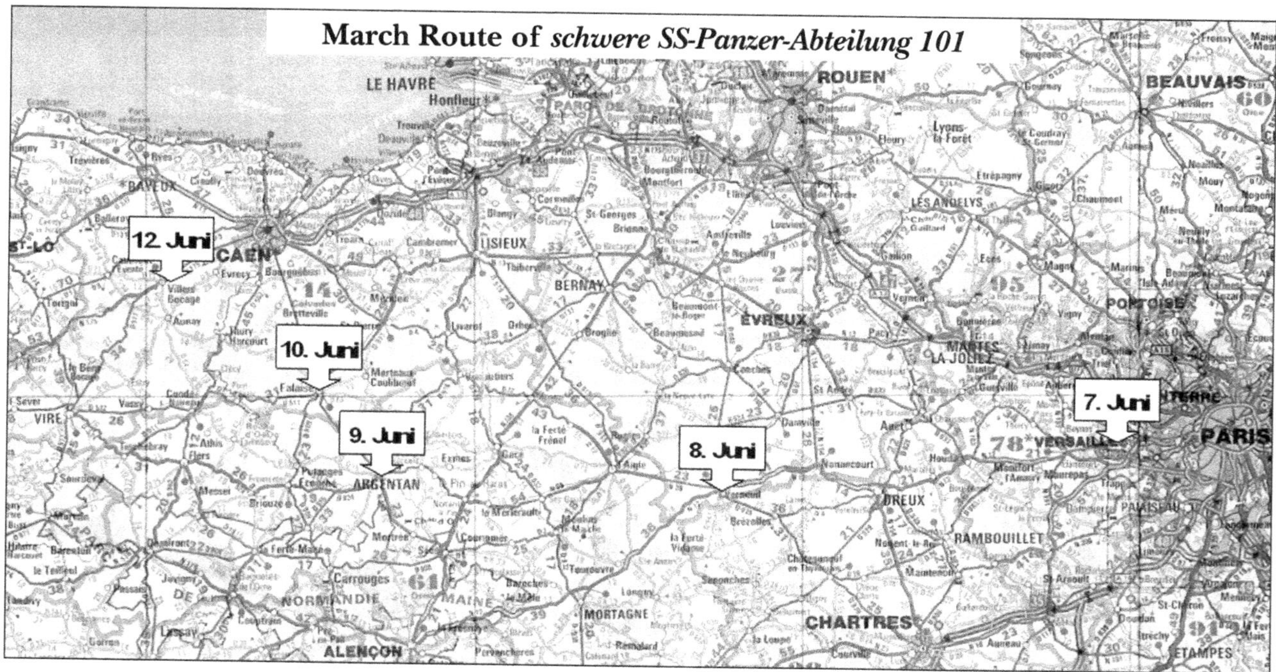

The date markers on the map indicate how slow the daily progress of *schwere SS-Panzer-Abteilung 101* was in its march from Paris to its initial area of operations in Normandy in the area to the southwest of Caen. Nearly a week was needed for the nearly 250 kilometers (Juni = June).

of organization and equipment.[1] These tanks were the very first *Tiger II's*—later known unofficially as the *Königstiger* or King Tiger. Even upon their arrival, these vehicles were not mechanically operational. They were later "consumed" in the local defense of Chateaudun on 15 and 16 August 1944.

Although this action will also be covered, we will concentrate on the operations of the three *Tiger* battalions.

One other item should also be mentioned. At the time of the invasion, there was another *Tiger* battalion in France, *schwere Panzer-Abteilung 504*. The battalion had completed its reconstitution efforts in the area around Poitiers and was in the process of being deployed to Italy, a rail movement that started on 3 June 1944. Even after the Allied landings became known, this movement was not stopped.

In conclusion, it can be said that at the time of the Allied landings, there were no *Tiger* formations that could have been committed to the fighting. It was only six days after the landings had started that the first two *Tiger* companies of *schwere SS-Panzer-Abteilung 101* finally assembled east of Villers-Bocage.

✠

On 6 June 1944, this battalion was due north of Beauvais, some 70 kilometers north of Paris. During the night of 6–7 June 1944, it started its road march towards the west. The tanks moved through Gournay-en-Bray initially and then the woods around Lyons and Morgny. There was an air attack on 7 June 1944, but there were no casualties.

1. *Fkl* = *Funklenk* = Radio Control

Because the bridge at Les Andelys was badly damaged, the tanks had to move through Paris. In an effective bit of propaganda, the battalion marched along the Champs-Elysées. That night, there was a large-scale aerial attack in the woods around Versailles, causing losses among the 3rd Company and the battalion's maintenance company.

The tanks continued their march to Falaise through Dreux, Verneuil and Argentan. The march was constantly disrupted by low-level attacks, resulting in personnel casualties. After passing through Epinay-sur-Odon, the 2nd Company reached the area around Villers-Bocage on 12 June 1944 and the 1st Company the area around Noyers. The battalion command post was established at Baron-sur-Odon.

Of its theoretical strength of fourteen tanks, the 1st Company ended its long march with eight tanks; its sister company, the 2nd Company, arrived in its area of operations with six. The rest of the battalion would dribble in over the course of the next few weeks. The same thing applied to the sister battalion, *schwere SS-Panzer-Abteilung 102*. At the outset, it was inconceivable to employ an entire battalion at once. Moreover, the situation that developed was so volatile that there could be no waiting for such a thing to happen. Consequently, the tanks were deployed split up into the smallest of sections. In the beginning, they were also unaware of the overall situation.

It therefore comes as no surprise that the first employment of *Tigers* in Normandy can be ascribed more to chance than design.

A crew replaces worn drive sprockets on its tank.

Schwere SS-Panzer-Abteilung 101 had been moved in the middle of January 1944 to Maisieres in Belgium (near Mons). The activation of the battalion was not completed until the end of March. At the beginning of April, the battalion was moved to the Gournay-en-Bray area. These photographs show the rail movement of the battalion.

In the middle of May, *schwere SS-Panzer-Abteilung 101* conducted a battalion-level training exercise east of Amiens. During the course of the exercise a series of propaganda photographs was taken, which have been frequently published. In the lower photograph, *SS-Sturmbannführer* Westernhagen, the battalion commander, looks on as *SS-Obersturmführer* Raasch, the commander of the 3rd Company, issues his orders to his assembled tank commanders. These photographs as well as those on the next two pages are courtesy of the German Federal Archives (*Bundesarchiv = BA*).

One day after the Allied landings, the battalion started its long road march to the Normandy region. In these images, the 2nd Company can be seen in the vicinity of Morgny. Commanding *Tiger 205* is *SS-Obersturmführer* Wittmann; *Tiger 221* is commanded by *SS-Obersturmführer* Hantusch, the 2nd Platoon Leader. These photographs are also courtesy of the *BA*.

On the road marches to the front, the threat from the air was ever present. During maintenance halts, the vehicles pulled off of the roads and into the nearby wooded areas. Thanks to that measure, the battalion did not suffer any losses during its movement. The distance covered was so great, however, that the tanks were subjected to a great deal of wear and tear, frequently breaking down and arriving at their staging area in poor mechanical condition. (*BA*)

The slow march through Morgny by the 1st Company can be seen on both of these pages. On some vehicles, both the radio operator and the gunner sit on the front slopes of the vehicles to serve as air guards. (*BA*)

GUVERBURG

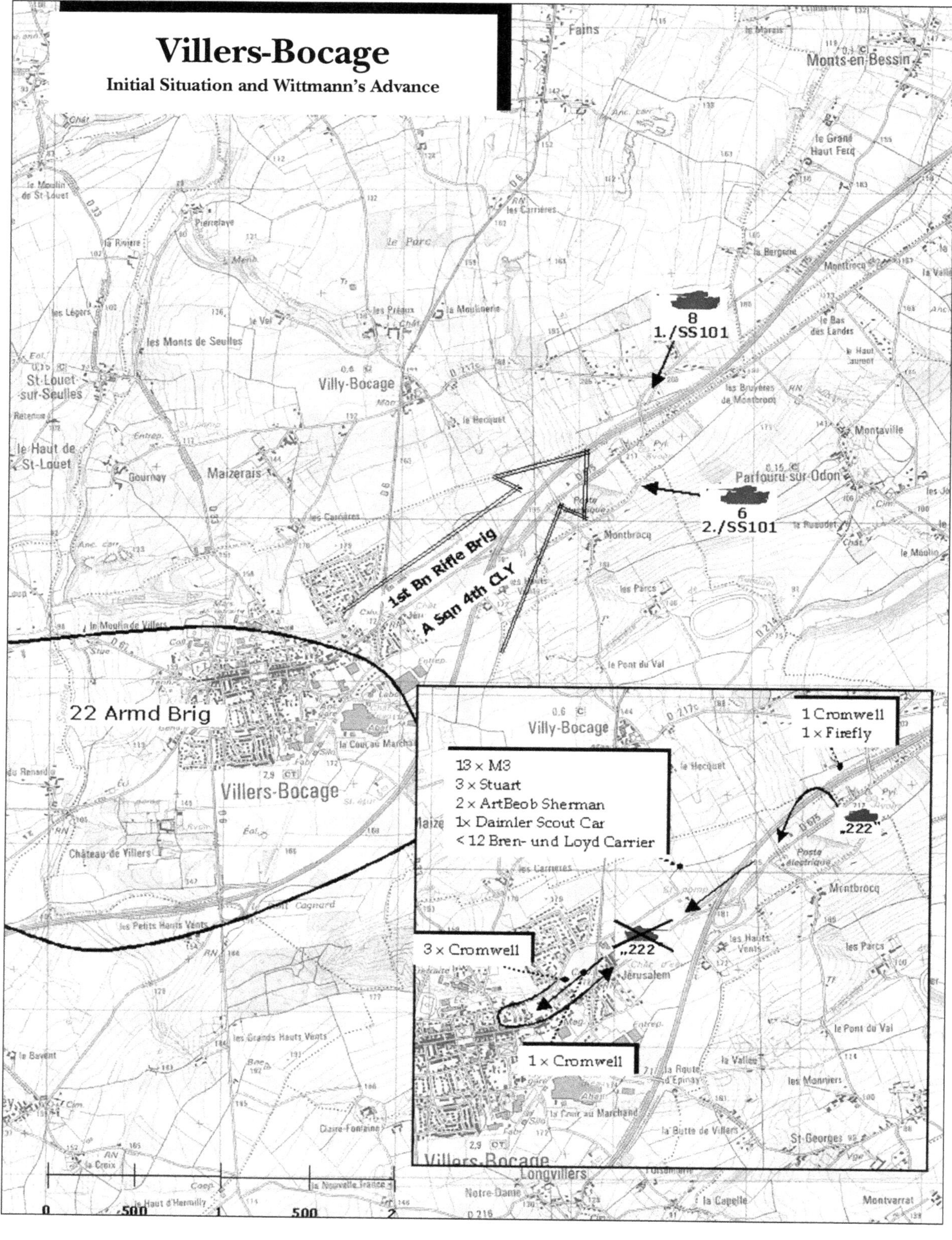
Villers-Bocage
Initial Situation and Wittmann's Advance
8
1./SS101
6
2./SS101
1st Bn Rifle Brig
A Sqn 4th CLY
22 Armd Brig
1 Cromwell
1 × Firefly
13 × M3
3 × Stuart
2 × ArtBeob Sherman
1x Daimler Scout Car
< 12 Bren- und Loyd Carrier
„222"
„222
3 × Cromwell
1 × Cromwell
Villers-Bocage
Villy-Bocage
Montbrocq
Parfouru-sur-Odon
Monts-en-Bessin
St-Louet-sur-Seulles
Maizerais
0
500
1
500
2

CHAPTER 2

The Mystery of Villers–Bocage

Probably everyone who is interested in the employment of the *Tiger* tank is familiar with the countless portrayals of this action of the "most successful tank commander" of the war, *SS-Obersturmführer* Michael Wittmann. Unfortunately, the vast majority is unaware that almost all of the accounts pertaining to it are completely incorrect! The conclusions drawn afterwards are also in pressing need of critical evaluation. It has been possible to do the latter for some time now since the events that transpired at Villers-Bocage have been verified down to the last detail.

✠

Let us look at the events of 12 June 1944 . . .

It was intended for *schwere SS-Panzer-Abteilung 101* to be staged for commitment on the left wing of the *I. SS-Panzer-Korps.* To this end, it was assigned a tactical assembly area directly east of Villers-Bocage. This coincided with the preparations of the British and the Canadians for Operation "Perch." The objective of this operation was to move around Caen to the northwest and take possession of the Odon River. On the night before, heavy artillery fire was initiated. The arriving tanks had to change their assembly area three times. The 2nd Company occupied the southern foothills of Montbroq Hill with six tanks in a defile some 100 meters south of National Road 175. This was two kilometers east of Villers-Bocage and about 500 meters southwest of Hill 213. The eight tanks of the 1st Company were somewhat farther to the northeast in a tactical assembly area on the other side of the National Road.

Although the aforementioned defile provided good concealment, it did not allow all tanks to move out simultaneously to the side. In addition, one of the tanks—that of *SS-Oberscharführer* Lötzsch—had track damage and was not operational. At the very front was the tank of *SS-Unterscharführer* Stief, which had engine problems.

After the tanks had occupied their positions, *SS-Obersturmführer* Wittmann, the company commander, had left the location for the purpose of establishing contact with other elements and leading other tanks forward. He returned during the night. The crews were completely exhausted as a result of the night marches that had taken many days. On each tank, there was a crewmember who stayed on watch. During his shift, the other crewmembers rested. It was intended to conduct absolutely essential maintenance the next day.

Among other forces, the British 7th Armoured Division, the famous "Desert Rats," had started to move out as part of Operation "Perch" at 0500 hours.

Here is what proceeded to happen . . .

A march group of the British 22nd Armoured brigade advanced in column along the road from Caen to Villers-Bocage. Still not deployed for combat, it stopped just before Point 213. Unnoticed, the brigade had exploited a gap between the *352. Infanterie-Division* and the *Panzer-Lehr-Division.*

The commander of the 2nd Company received a report in the aforementioned defile alerting him that tanks—probably British—were moving on the road and heading east. From a vantage point, *SS-Obersturmführer* Wittmann was able to observe the enemy column. He jumped into the first tank. He told the commander, *SS-Unterscharführer* Stief, to go to the other tanks and alert them. The driver received orders from Wittmann to move out. After 20 to 30 meters, the crew was able to make Wittmann understand that the engine was not running properly. The company commander dismounted and ran up to the next vehicle that was approaching from out of the defile. It was *Tiger 222* of *SS-Unterscharführer* Sowa. Wittmann had him dismount and took over the tank himself.

SS-Obersturmführer Wittmann attacked the lead elements of the British forces ahead of his company, which was still not ready to engage in combat. It was A Squadron of the 4th City of London Yeomanry and elements of the 1st Rifle Brigade. Firing in the direction of Caen, he initially knocked out a Cromwell and then a Firefly of A Squadron, which were already at Point 213. He then moved parallel to the road to Villers-Bocage, where he knocked out most of the 1st Rifle Brigade's vehicles from pointblank range. These consisted of thirteen M3 halftracks, three Stuart reconnaissance tanks, two forward-observer Shermans, the Daimler scout car of the brigade's intelligence officer, and the M3 halftrack of the brigade surgeon as well as more than a dozen Bren and Lloyd carriers (some belonging to the antitank battery).

At the edge of the town, he destroyed three of the four Cromwells of the regimental command group of the 4th City of London Yeomanry. He then moved by himself into enemy-occupied Villers-Bocage, where he was followed by the fourth Cromwell, which had designs on knocking him out from the rear. In the town, *SS-Obersturmführer* Wittmann was intercepted by tanks of B Squadron of the 4th City of London Yeomanry, including one which was dangerous for the *Tiger*—the Sherman Firefly. He turned around and headed for an exit point from the town. On his way back, Wittmann knocked out the Cromwell that had been following him. Although the Cromwell had fired two rounds from a distance of only 50 meters, both of them ricocheted off. A few hundred meters farther on, the *Tiger* was immobilized by an antitank round to its running gear. The crew abandoned the tank and fought its way back to the command post of the *Panzer-Lehr-Division* at Orbois-Sermentot.

The three remaining operational tanks of the 2nd Company took up position east of Villers-Bocage after their commander had taken off. South of the National Road, they knocked out two additional Cromwells (*SS-Unterscharführer* Sowa) and three Shermans (*SS-Oberscharführer* Brandt). In addition, approximately 230 soldiers surrendered.

Attack of the *1./schwere SS-Panzer-Abteilung 101*

Starting at 0800 hours, eight *Tigers* of the 1st Company under *SS-Hauptsturmführer* Möbius also attacked along the N 175 to Villers-Bocage. Five Cromwells located north of the town were abandoned by their crews without firing a shot. Several *Panzer IV's* of the *Panzer-Lehr-Division,* which were in Parfouru-sur-Odon, also participated in the attack. Two *Tigers* and one *Panzer IV* advanced along the main street of Villers-Bocage, the Rue Pasteur. The trail tank—*Tiger 112* of *SS-Oberscharführer* Ernst—was knocked out by a Firefly of B Squadron of the City of London Yeomanry, which fired through two corner windows. During the course of the further advance, the *Panzer IV* was knocked out by an antitank gun, when the tank changed position. The lead tank—*Tiger 121* of

SS-Untersturmführer Lukasius—was also knocked out from the rear by a Firefly. These three tanks were later set on fire by the British.

Five other *Tigers* advanced along roads farther to the south. One *Tiger* was knocked out in the Rue Emile Samson by an antitank gun. Two other *Tigers* were immobilized after being hit, one at the corner of Rue Jeanne Bacon and Boulevard Joffre by a 57mm antitank gun of the 7th Queens Lancers.

During the fighting in the village, *SS-Unterscharführer* Wendt's *132* had remained on the outskirts of the town. That night, *Tiger 132* took up position on Hill 213; four other *Tigers* of the 1st Company established positions south of Villers-Bocage. The 2nd Company went back to its positions in the defile parallel to the N 175.

The battalion lost three noncommissioned officers and seven enlisted personnel killed on this day. Three *Tigers* of the 1st Company were lost. It was intended to recover Wittmann's tank in the village, but the recovery operation was never carried out. The British lost a total of twenty-six tanks, fourteen M3's, eight Bren carriers and eight Lloyd carriers.

In the meantime, the remaining company of the battalion—the 3rd Company—reached Falaise.

Tactical Evaluation

On the next day, the commanding general of the *I. SS-Panzer-Korps*, *SS-Obergruppenführer* Dietrich, recommended *SS-Obersturmführer* Wittmann for the award of the Oak Leaves with Swords to the Knight's Cross of the Iron Cross.

The decoration was awarded on 22 June 1944 along with a simultaneous promotion to *SS-Hauptsturmführer*. The following statements in the award recommendation are worthy of note:

- "*Kompanie Wittmann* . . . was . . . ready for combat . . . at Point 213"
- "Wittmann was unable to issue any more orders to his men, who were separated from him"
- "Eliminated . . . all vehicles in range . . . " (in Villers-Bocage after he had to dismount due to his vehicle being immobilized)
- "Advanced once again on Villers-Bocage [after reaching the command post of the *Panzer-Lehr-Division* and] . . . employed it [meaning the *1./ schwere SS-Panzer-Abteilung 101*]"
- The number of tank "kills" was listed as twenty-five.

So much for the facts.

When evaluating these events, we should not take the easy way out. The following should be considered:

- Wittmann was liked by his subordinates and recognized by his superiors. First in the Balkan campaign and then especially later on the Eastern Front, he had fought bravely and knocked out numerous enemy tanks with his assault gun and, later, his tank.
- The situation on the morning of 12 June 1944 was anything but clear.
- The decision to attack the enemy, who was about to effect a decisive breakthrough, was proper.
- The personal actions of Wittmann were dynamic and courageous.

Nonetheless, a number of critical questions are raised. The easiest thing to pass judgment on is the award recommendation submitted by *SS-Obergruppenführer* Dietrich. All of the statements cited above are false. The reader can easily determine for himself the number of "kills": there were seven. Even if we were to count the forward-observer tanks that were "armed" with a dummy main gun made out of wood and the light Stuarts, the numbers still do not add up to twenty-five.

Nevertheless, the fact remains that a "serious threat" was turned back as a result of Wittmann's courageous actions. Normally, the separate levels of the Knight's Cross were awarded for individual deeds that "decided battles" and not for knocking out many enemy vehicles. We will come back to this later.

I would like to initiate my critical remarks with a series of observations that take into consideration the operational principles of armored forces.

- Tanks are to be displaced in an assembly area in such a manner that their freedom of movement is left as unrestricted as possible.
- The tactical leader always maintains detailed knowledge on the combat readiness of his vehicles and his crews.
- An area is to be secured in such a manner that the enemy cannot approach unnoticed.
- Tanks are always to be concentrated for an operation.

With regard to these points, the reader can draw his own conclusions from the events that are presented above.

It is difficult to assess after the fact whether there was enough time to wait for the remaining three tanks of the company to attain complete combat readiness. The fact that the tank of *SS-Unterscharführer* Sowa was able to follow out of the defile immediately indicates that it would have only taken a few minutes, however.

If the British had not been so ill prepared for combat and careless, Wittmann would have still been able to knock out several enemy vehicles. It is also highly likely, however, that he would have been stopped, at the very least through damage to his running gear. The engagement distances were so short that even the normally "toothless" Cromwell would have been able to achieve those types of hits.

Had Wittmann taken this into consideration, he might have then taken up a position to observe, wait for his tanks to close up and then move out against the enemy with considerably more combat power and mutual fire protection.

Even if several enemy tanks had continued on over Hill 213 in the direction of Caen, they would have run into the tanks of the 1st Company.

Beyond all discussion is Wittmann's decision to move into an enemy-occupied built-up area all by himself. The reader is left asking what he intended to accomplish by doing that.

The attack into Villers-Bocage that followed by elements of the *Panzer-Lehr-Division* and almost all of the *1./schwere SS-Panzer-Abteilung 101* without infantry support also does not correspond to basic principles of armor employment: Built-up areas are to be bypassed by tanks as much as possible. Painful losses were suffered almost immediately.

In conclusion, it must be noted that the danger of a decisive breakthrough on the part of the British was deflected by the actions of the two *Tiger* companies (together with forces of the *Panzer-Lehr-Division* in some cases). The critical questions concerning how this was done remain, as does the point whether Wittmann's actions were decisive to the fighting.

The Initial Losses of the *3./schwere SS-Panzer-Abteilung 101*

In the days that followed, there was additional fighting for Cahagnes involving *schwere SS-Panzer-Abteilung 101.* Its 3rd Company closed up at Evrecy. This took place before the British had to temporarily call off their attack in the direction of the Odon.

In this situation, the counterattack of the battalion's 1st Company in the areas between Villers-Bocage and Cahagnes on 14 June 1944 remained without effect under the concentrated fires of the enemy artillery (160 guns). The tank of *SS-Obersturmführer* Philipsen was hit and immobilized; it was repaired enough during the night to be able to move under its own power back to the German lines.

During the night of 15 June 1944, the 3rd Company was hit in its assembly area at Evrecy by a heavy bombing attack. *SS-Sturmmann* Ernst Kufner, a radio operator in the company at the time, wrote this firsthand account concerning the strike:

> All at once, the trees were burning, the grass between the tanks, the buildings and church of Evrecy. Aircraft dropped phosphorous bombs first, then fragmentation bombs. I woke up the crews that were sleeping underneath the tanks. All of us jumped into the tanks. During a break, I heard the company commander cry out: "Start up! Get the tanks out of here!"
>
> Our driver attempted to start the engine. The starter failed. We had to stay there with our tank. We could observe everything through our vision ports and had to watch as everything next to us and in front of us was burning.
>
> It was twin-engine aircraft that were dropping their loads of bombs on us and on Evrecy. It lasted about 20–30 minutes, until everything was over. It took all our strength to open the tank's hatches. When we had them opened, it was very quiet all around us. There was a layer of earth on the tank that was some 20 centimeters thick. The buildings in Evrecy were still burning. There was nothing to be seen or heard of our comrades.
>
> We moved the tank—the starter was not defective after all—as far as the war memorial. After moving just 100 meters, the engine became hot. The cooling fans were plugged with dirt. Next to our location were bomb craters that were big enough that a *Tiger* could have fit inside them.
>
> We looked for our comrades during the morning hours. As I recall, the assistant armorer showed up. His overcoat was in tatters. He had sought protection in a bomb crater and was lucky. We didn't see any of our comrades from the trains any more.
>
> The other *Tigers* were damaged and not operational. The *Tiger* of *Untersturmführer* Günther had received a direct hit and had burned out completely. There was nothing left of the crew except carbonized bits and pieces of uniforms, buttons and shards of bones.
>
> The tank of the company commander, *Obersturmführer* Raasch, had been hit on the gun barrel. The three men in the turret were affected by it and all of them had burns; the driver and the radio operator were dead.
>
> A third *Tiger* had moved into the open and crashed into a six- to seven-meter-deep defile after about 300 meters. This crew was also dead.
>
> In all, there were 18 dead and 11 wounded in the company; the civilian population suffered 130 dead.

Conclusion of the Fighting around Villers-Bocage

On the morning that followed, three *Tigers* of the 1st Company, including *Tiger 132* of *SS-Oberscharführer* Wendt, attacked into the withdrawing British. Five enemy tanks were knocked out; *SS-Oberscharführer*

Wendt's tank was also knocked out at the Greland farm, but the crew was able to dismount.

On 16 June 1944, four *Tigers* of the 1st Company counterattacked at Cahagnes. *Tiger 111* of the platoon leader, *SS-Obersturmführer* Philipsen, was set on fire by a hit from an antitank gun. The driver and the radio operator were killed; after bailing out, the platoon leader was also killed.

In the days that followed, the battalion was designated as a reserve and occupied positions on both sides of the Caen–Villers-Bocage road. It was possible to perform maintenance that was urgently needed.

On 22 June 1944, the award of the "Swords" to *SS-Obersturmführer* Wittmann was approved. As previously mentioned, he was simultaneously promoted to *SS-Hauptsturmführer.* He was presented the award at Hitler's retreat at Berchtesgaden on 29 June 1944.

On 23 June 1944, several tanks of the 3rd Company under *SS-Untersturmführer* Amselgruber were in position on the N 175 and turned back a reconnaissance effort on the part of the British. Five enemy tanks were knocked out.

On 24 June 1944, *SS-Unterscharführer* Warnecke knocked out seven addition enemy tanks in his *Tiger 332,* while the latter were carelessly being refueled.

A *Tiger* that was recovered from Villers-Bocage was deemed incapable of being repaired. As of this date, the strength of the battalion had sunk from forty-five prior to the start of the decisive breakthrough efforts on the part of the British to thirty-four.

One of the many knocked-out vehicles was this Cromwell. The divisional insignia of the British 7th Armoured Division, the famed "Desert Rats," can be seen in the middle of the front slope.

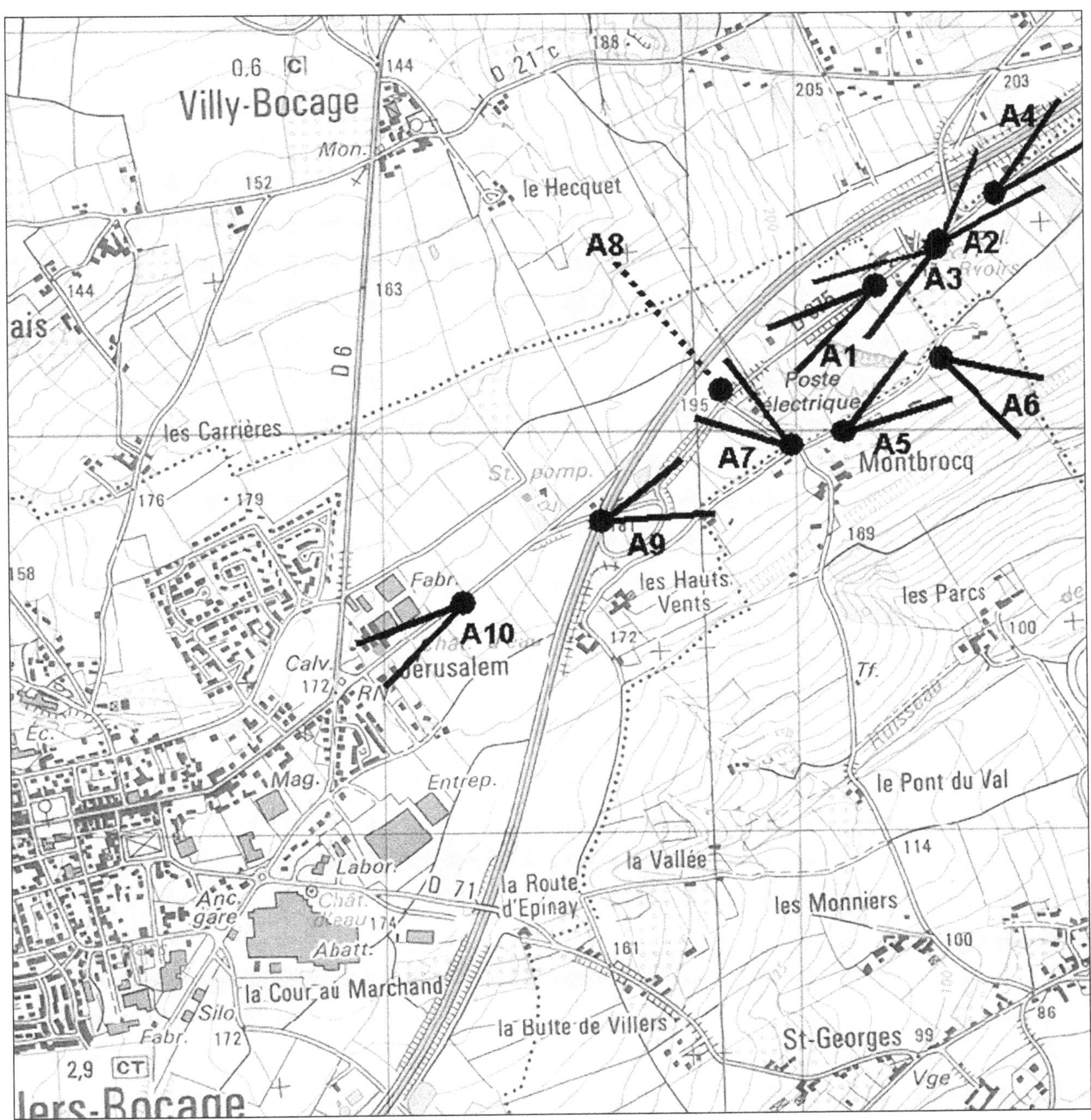

This map is marked with the standpoint from which the following photographs were taken. A5 shows the area where the lead elements of the 2nd Company had bivouacked. At A8, Wittmann turned onto what was then the main road. A2 and A3 show the view towards Hill 203 and away from it (towards Villers-Bocage). A9 shows the approach route of *Tiger 222.* A10 shows the present-day entrance to the village.

This view from Hill 213 in the direction of Villers-Bocage shows how the British probably imagined themselves concealed through the reverse slope and thus moved along the road without adequate security. It was along this road that Wittmann left behind a trail of destruction (lower left previous page and upper right). The lower photograph shows the crossroads on the crest of Hill 213. The 1st Company of *schwere SS-Panzerabteilung 101* had assembled in the area directly behind the crossroads to the viewer's left. Note: SW = Southwest, NE = Northeast.

SW

Views from Hill 213 (A3 above) in the direction of Villers-Bocage and towards Caen (A4 below). The 1st Company on the hill was not in a position to report the advancing British early. It was only able to report the arrival of the British lead elements on the hill. At that point, the 2nd Company reacted. A view to the east convincingly demonstrates what great opportunities the British would have had for an advance on Caen.

NE

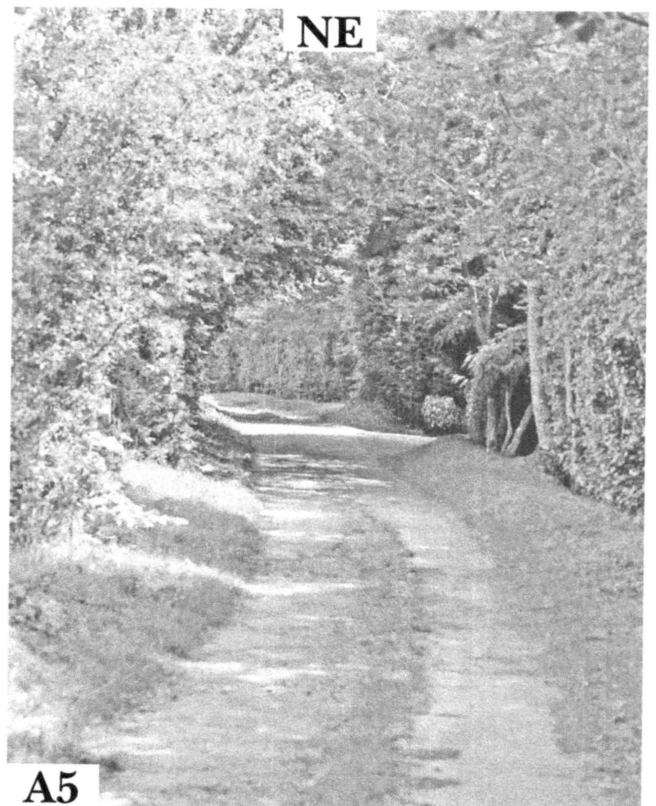

The start of the defile, where the 2nd Company was bivouacked (left). About 300 meters farther on, the woods opened up to the right (south) and offered good observation (right). The photograph below shows the last tank in the column. The restricted opportunities for movement can clearly be seen. The photograph to the right below shows the location of the lead elements of the company at the entryway to the main road leading from Villers-Bocage to Caen, which starts at the yield sign. It becomes clear that the wooded defile, which runs parallel to the main road, is on the other side of the hill. The British could not see Wittmann's company. At the same time, the *Tiger* crews were not in a position to see the enemy armored vehicles in a timely manner. (*BA*)

SE

A6

NW

A7

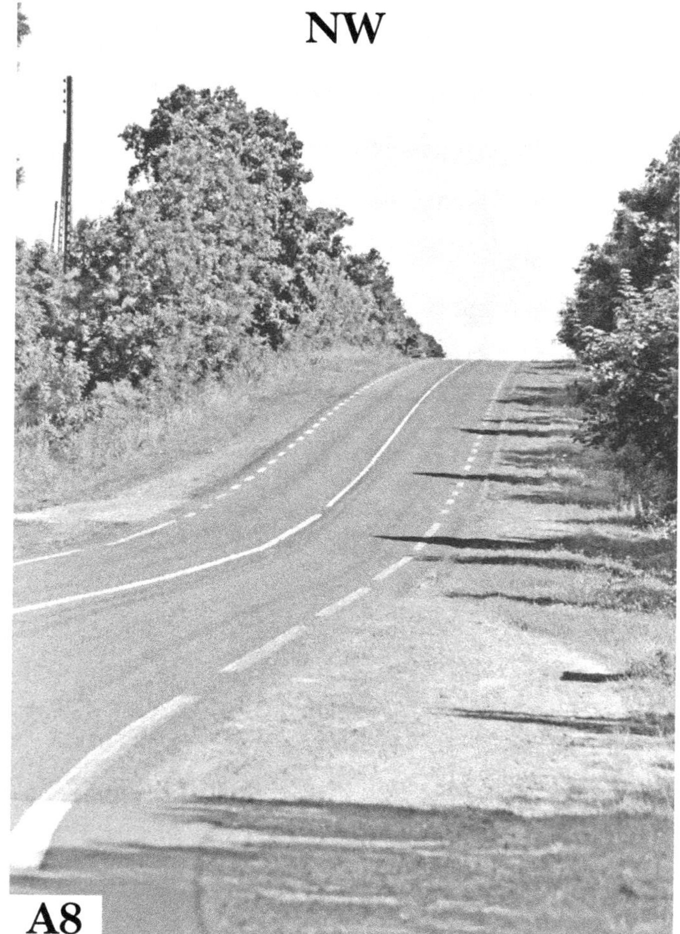

Once he arrived on the main road, Wittmann initially oriented to the right in the direction of Hill 213 and knocked out several vehicles there before he turned around and moved along the British column in the direction of Villers-Bocage. The lower photograph shows the entrance to Villers-Bocage at the time. No experienced armor commander would enthusiastically enter that type of built-up area.

The entrance to Villers-Bocage is now marked by a traffic circle. In the background, the main road and Hill 213 can be seen. In 1944, the road led straight to the village. The lower photograph shows how the road into the village continues to drop off. Wittmann moved into the village along the main road, the Rue Pasteur, followed by a Cromwell. Wittmann knocked out the British tank—after he had turned—just beyond the curve in the road on the rise (light-colored bus).

NW

This was the view that presented itself to Wittmann as he approached the center of the village. He was unable to see the Sherman Firefly at the end of the street, since it dropped again after about 400 meters. This is made clear when looking at the photograph below, which shows the main street from the viewpoint of the Firefly tank commander. The Firefly fired at Wittmann's tank when it was on the rise, but the British tank missed the *Tiger*. At that short of a range, even a *Tiger* would not have had a chance.

After evading the dangerous Firefly, Wittmann encountered the Cromwell of Captain Dyas, whose tank had moved around the upper curve of the Rue Pasteur in the meantime. Despite the short range, his main gun proved ineffective, and Wittmann then knocked out Dyas's tank. A short while later, a hit to Wittmann's running gear immobilized his tank. (*BA*) The lower photograph shows the location of the Cromwell at the time (the same place where the rear car is parked).

After the conclusion of the fighting, two *Waffen-SS* soldiers stroll towards the *Tiger* that Wittmann had used for his bold attack. (*BA*) The lower photograph shows the same location today.

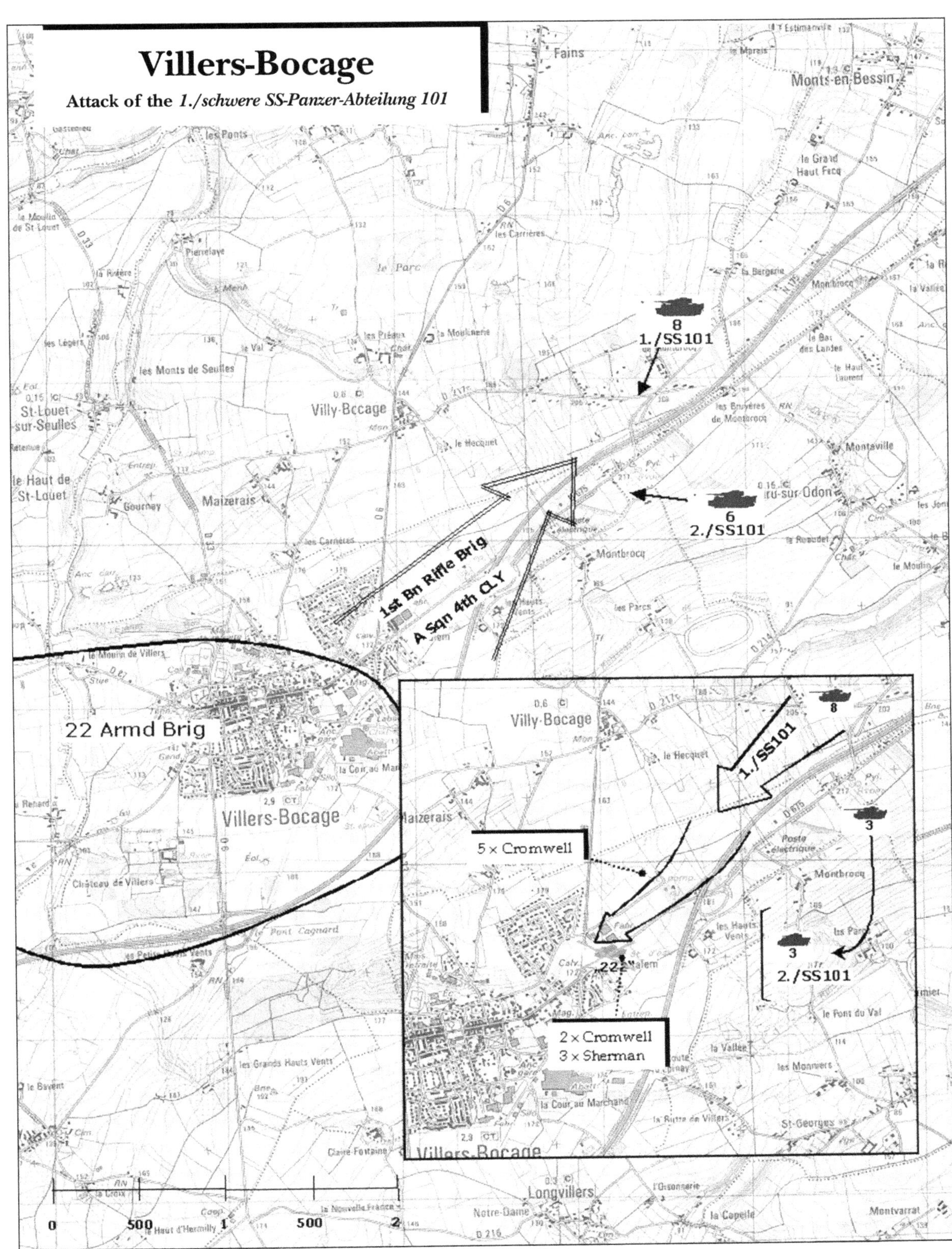
Villers-Bocage
Attack of the 1./schwere SS-Panzer-Abteilung 101
8
1./SS101
6
2./SS101
1st Bn Rifle Brig
A Sqn 4th CLY
22 Armd Brig
1./SS101
5 × Cromwell
3
3
2./SS101
2 × Cromwell
3 × Sherman
0
500
1
500
2

Three Cromwells, a Sherman Firefly and a 6-pounder set up an ambush position on city-hall square (*mairie* on the map). When the second *Tiger* rolled past, the Firefly opened fire. It missed, however, with its round going just over the *Tiger*. The *Tiger* continued rolling forward. It had started to traverse its turret to the left, when it was hit by the second round and destroyed. The lower photograph shows the knocked-out tank, *Tiger 112*. A while later, a *Panzer IV* attempted to roll past it, when it was hit from the rear and knocked out by the 6-pounder on city-hall square.

The same scene as viewed from the front. The lower photograph shows the same location on the Rue Pasteur today.

Tiger 121, moving ahead, was hit by the Sherman Firefly from the rear and continued rolling a few meters forward. It came to a stop by a butcher's. It was later set alight by the British. (*BA*) The photograph on the left shows the same location today.

Looking to the left of *Tiger 121* and down the street, we see the knocked-out *Panzer IV* and *Tiger 122.* Rubble caused by artillery shelling and several air attacks can be seen along the street. The rear deck of *Tiger 121* is also covered with debris.

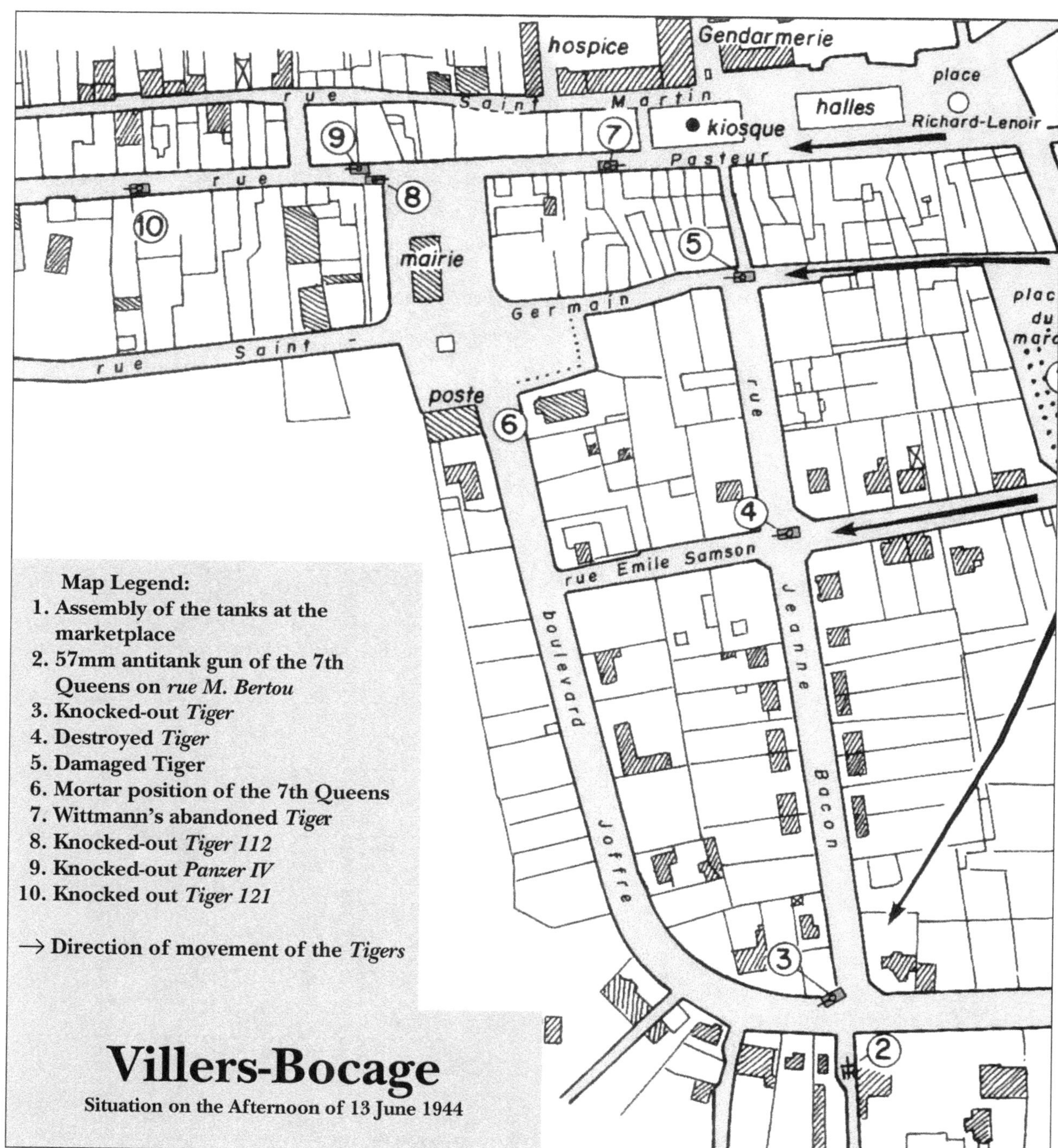

The above sketch has been taken from the excellent book by Henri Marie, *Villers-Bocage, Normandy 1944* (Editions Heimdal, 2003). It shows the locations of the *Tigers* at the conclusion of the fighting and puts the reader in the position of being able to correctly place the photographs. The first action took place with Wittmann, when he moved down the Rue Pasteur from the west (right) into the middle of the village and then turned, when he received fire from a Sherman Firefly at the end of the street. Moving back, he knocked out a Cromwell at pointblank range and then became immobilized because of a hit to the running gear. The crew had to dismount and flee on foot. Shortly afterwards, the 1st Company of *schwere SS-Panzer-Abteilung 101*, together with elements of the *Panzer-Lehr-Division*, attacked into the village.

The images on this page and the next show a recovery operation conducted the next day with *Tiger 232* towing *Tiger 231* to the maintenance facility. The platoon leader, *SS-Untersturmführer* Hantusch, is seen in the motorcyclist's overcoat. (*BA*)

The photographs on this page and the next show the tank wrecks after the British took back the village. Prior to that, a devastating aerial attack had destroyed much of Villers-Bocage. Only pieces of the *Panzer IV* can be seen. Apparently, the Germans had emplaced antitank mines prior to leaving. The British engineers used them to prepare *Tiger 121* for demolition. (IWM)

This *Tiger* was knocked out at the intersection of Rue Emile Samson and Rue Jeanne Bacon—number 4 on the sketch map—by flanking fires from a British antitank gun.

The last to arrive in the area of operations was the 3rd Company and the battalion command section. Heavy camouflage against air attack is evident. Below and right: *Tigers 008* and *009* can be seen refueling after arrival.

SS-Untersturmführer Günther's tank after a devastating air attack. (IWM)

This photograph shows the village of Evrecy today and the ridgeline behind it. Farther to the viewer's left, but not visible in the photograph, is Hill 112.

Tiger 111 of the platoon leader, *SS-Obersturmführer* Philipsen, knocked out by an antitank gun at Cahagnes on 16 June 1944. The driver, radio operator and the platoon leader were killed.

SS-Hauptsturmführer Michael Wittmann being presented the award of the Swords to the Knight's Cross of the Iron Cross at Hitler's retreat at Berchtesgaden on 29 June 1944.

Wittmann, who was made into one of the best-known war heroes of the *Waffen-SS*, was used many times for propaganda purposes. In April 1944, he addressed the assembly-line workers at the Henschel *Tiger* plant in Kassel.

There are a number of propaganda images of Wittmann. In this one, he is seen standing next to his gunner, *SS-Oberscharführer* Woll, who had also received the Knight's Cross, an unusual occurrence for a tank gunner. It is known that there were a number of officers and noncommissioned officers in the armored forces and antitank forces of the Army who had similar numbers of "kills" to their credit—in a few cases, even more—who were not recipients of the Knight's Cross. But the legend of Wittmann being the "most successful" tank commander of World War II continues to this day. It is incontestable that he was a brave officer who was respected by his men, but he was also made into an "idol" by the leadership of the *Waffen-SS*.

CHAPTER 3

The Fighting for Hill 112

The fighting for Caen and the surrounding area is inextricably bound with this unimposing hill. The fighting raged there for more than two weeks with very little interruption. At this time—the start of the second half of June 1944—it is important to know that the Germans still very much intended to launch a decisive offensive to eliminate the Allied bridgehead. This was to be done with newly brought-up armored formations—the *II. SS-Panzer-Korps*—as well as armored divisions that were to be pulled from elsewhere out of then-current front lines. It was to this end that the three *Tiger* battalions were introduced. It was intended for the main effort to advance west past Caen on both sides of Tilly towards Bayeux and Arromanches. The purpose was to split the Allies. Following the destruction of the U.S. formations, the British forces were to be eliminated.

It was therefore essential that the terrain northwest of the Orne remain in German hands. Both the Orne River and its southeast banks restricted movement considerably. For their part, the British and the Canadians needed to take this sector in order to keep their operational options open, that is, to be able to continue the attack to the right (west) past Caen, since their attack had bogged down east of it.

General Montgomery started his Operation "Epsom" in the middle of the German preparations. One day prior to this—25 June 1944—was the attack of the 49th West Riding Division (Operation "Martlet"). Its objective was to take the smaller Odon River, which ran parallel to and north of the Orne to a certain extent, along with the dominant ridgeline on both sides of Rauray. It was also intended for this attack to force the Germans to prematurely commit their reserves in this sector, rendering them unable to commit them against the 15th Scottish Division to the east. Although the Operation "Martlet" attack caused a crisis within the *Panzer-Lehr-Division,* it did not achieve its day's objective by a long shot.

In fact, the countermeasures employed by elements of the *12. SS-Panzer-Division "Hitlerjugend,"* together with tanks of the *3./schwere SS-Panzer-Abteilung 101,* stabilized the situation to the west of Rauray on 26 June 1944. The attack by the 147th Infantry Brigade in the woods between Tessel and Bretteville and at Rauray was blocked by one of the division's mechanized infantry regiments. At Grainville, *SS-Untersturmführer* Amselgruber destroyed three enemy tanks together with an additional *Tiger* of his 3rd Company and brought the infantry attack there to a standstill. A single *Tiger* eliminated four Shermans of the 23rd Hussars at Mouen. New positions were occupied along a line running Marcelet—high ground southeast of Cheux—Rauray—Vendes. After losing nine tanks, the 9th Royal Tank Regiment had to pull back towards evening.

The fighting on 26 June 1944 has been impressively portrayed in an autobiography written by Stuart Hills—*By Tank into Normandy*—concerning his operations with the 8th Armoured Brigade:

> Meanwhile A Squadron had begun moving up from Fontenay, the plan being that they would come through us and thrust towards Rauray. John Semken was Squadron Leader and he had already heard from C Squadron that there were tanks about, so his gun loader put an AP shell up the spout, just in case. As they cleared Fontenay, they were suddenly confronted by an enormous tank coming round the bend in front. It was hard to know who was more surprised, but John shrieked, "Fire, it's a Hun," and they loosed off about ten rounds into the smoke. As this cleared away, it was observed that the crew were baling out as small flames came from inside the tank. It was a Tiger of 12th SS Panzer, the first Tiger to be captured in Normandy, and made an impressive sight at close quarters as both its size and the thickness of its armour became apparent. Although the range had been only sixty yards, not one Sherman shell had penetrated that armour. The fire in the Tiger, we discovered, had instead been caused by a shot hitting the side of the driver's observation visor and showering white-hot splinters into the tank. The driver had screamed that he had been hit and the commander had obligingly ordered his crew out.
>
> A Squadron squeezed past the Tiger and into a field on the right where they deployed. During the next two hours they systematically shot up every hedgerow as they advanced. Some of John Semken's tanks were Sherman Fireflies, and they started knocking out one German tank after another. Sergeant Dring claimed no less than four himself, and a Panther was shot up by the whole squadron as it drove across our front, its crew baling out as it was still moving. The German infantry started to surrender, leaping out of the ground under the noses of the tanks, while our own infantry came up to finish things off. It had been a great day. Thirteen Panzer Mark IVs had been knocked out, along with a Tiger and a Panther. The enemy tank force defending Rauray had been eliminated and their infantry overrun. Aggressive tactics had paid off, and at relatively small cost to ourselves. C Squadron had lost two tanks, with two dead and two wounded. I felt encouraged by the way each squadron had performed and this was reflected in the general morale of my troop, in spite of the casualties. We had won a tank battle against significant opposition, and this gave our confidence an important boost.

On the next day, *SS-Unterscharführer* Warmbrunn's tank was knocked out during a reconnaissance mission at Cheux, where it was destroyed by a 57-millimeter antitank gun of the 119th Battery and several Shermans. The battalion's eighteen operational tanks were scattered over the entire corps sector.

During the failed defense against the enemy attack on Grainville on 28 June 1944, *Tiger 331* of *SS-Untersturmführer* Amselgruber was knocked out after it had destroyed two Shermans. Despite severe leg wounds, Amselgruber remained with his troops. *SS-Hauptsturmführer* Möbius succeeded in knocking out six enemy tanks before a round jammed in his main gun that could not be extracted. He was then knocked out by some ten enemy tanks.

The remaining *Tigers* turned back other enemy advances south and southeast of Verson. *Tiger 334* was abandoned in Rauray proper. This was also described by Stuart Hills in his book:

> The next day, June 27, it was B Squadron's turn to take the lead. They sent out two troops to investigate the situation in Rauray but ran into several Panthers which must have been brought up during the night. Three Shermans were destroyed, and Troop Leader Ray Scott and the experienced Sergeants Biddell and Green were killed. By midday Rauray had been cleared and in it were found about eight German tanks, all damaged to some extent, and one Tiger, which seemed to be in perfect working order. We tried to incorporate it into our ranks, but unfortunately High Command wanted it to be taken back to England. Later that afternoon B Squadron ran into more trouble around Rauray, and by the end of the day only had seven tanks still serviceable out of their usual sixteen.

A view towards Tessel from the direction of Fontenay-le-Pesnel shows the dominant ridgeline in the distance that is located between the Orne and Odon Rivers.

The knocked-out *Panther* at the intersection of the *D139* and the *D173*. The still-smoking *Tiger*, hit several times, can be seen behind it. The photograph below shows the same intersection today. (IWM)

W

E

The view from the immobilized and abandoned *Tiger* shows that the British were attacked in the flank at precisely the moment that they were attempting to take the open terrain. The lower photograph shows that the British were able to start the *Tiger* and move it towards the intersection in the direction of Fontenay. The hits to the turret and the front slope caused the crew to abandon it in panic.

This page and the three following: Various views of *Tiger 334* in Rauray. (IWM)

The dead German soldier is probably a *Waffen SS* despatch rider from the *12. SS-Panzer-Division*

S

The lower photograph shows the approach route to Grainville from the north. This vantage point demonstrates how the terrain climbs to the north bank of the Odon, thus favoring the defense. The German counterattack aimed past Rauray (viewer's left), but it was only partially successful.

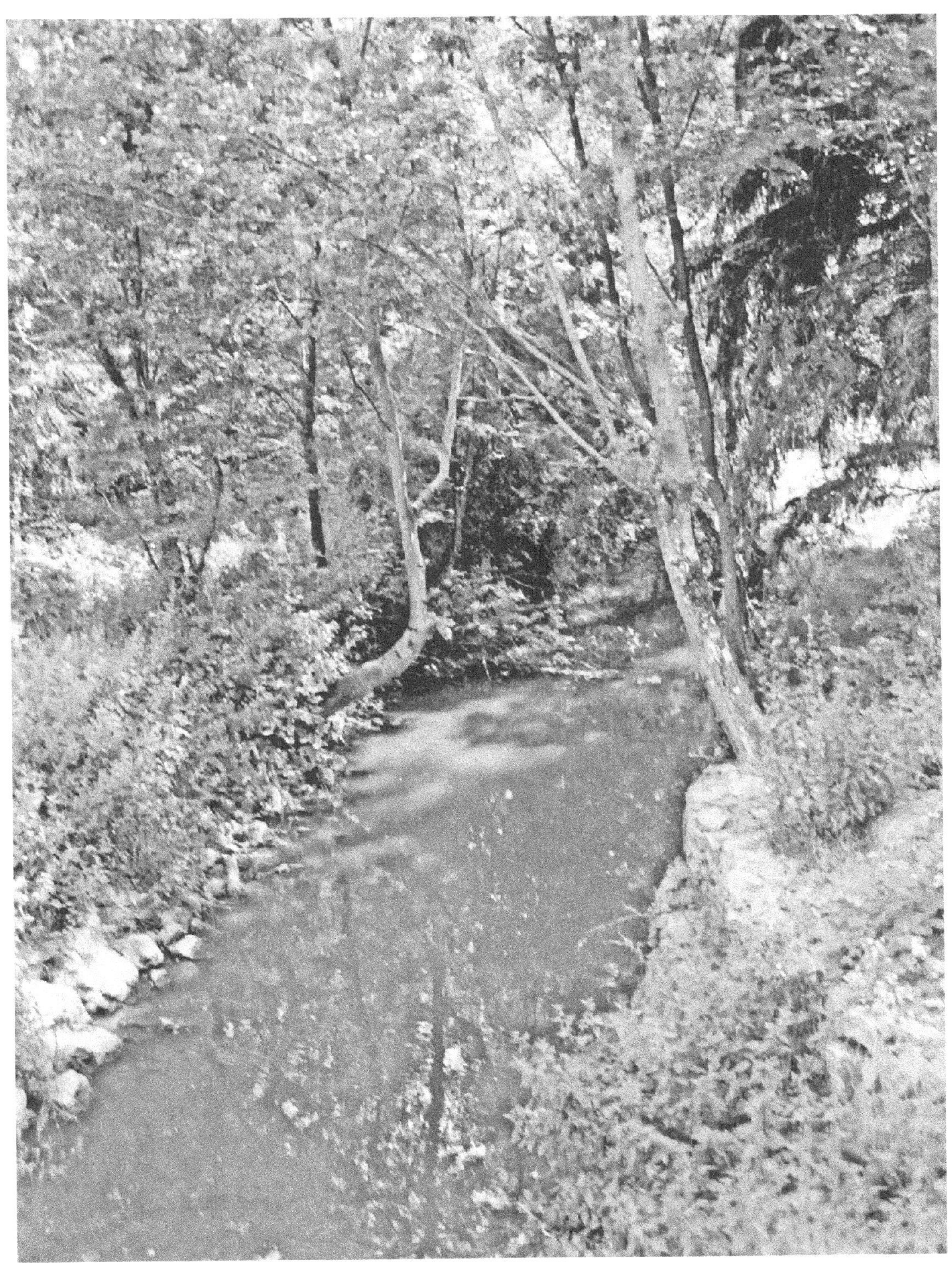

The Odon is only two meters wide and not very deep, but it runs through a deep cut. As a result, the British needed a great deal of fascines to establish crossing points. For that reason, the capture of the bridge at Tourville intact was even more important.

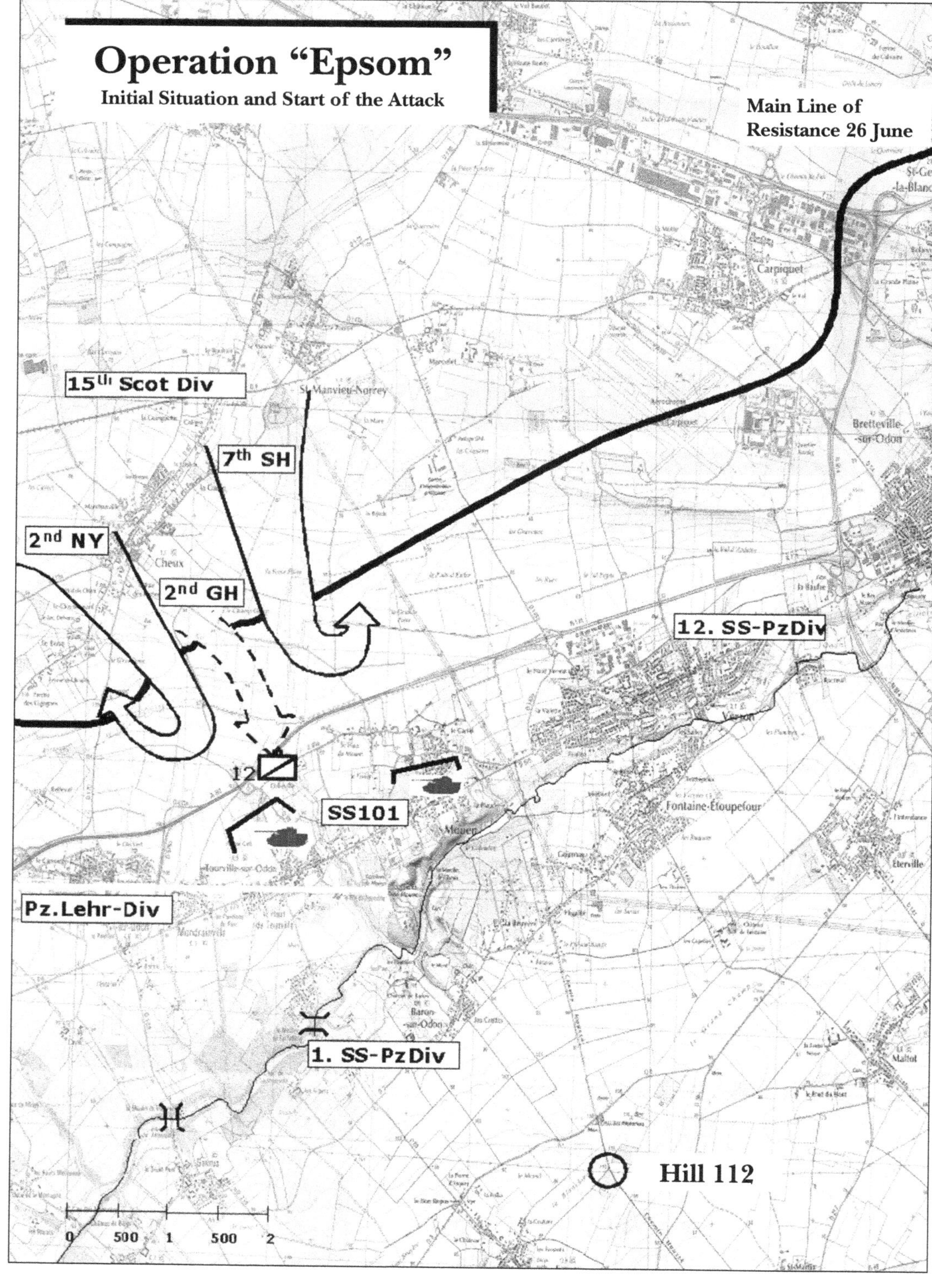
Operation "Epsom"
Initial Situation and Start of the Attack
Main Line of Resistance 26 June
15th Scot Div
7th SH
2nd NY
2nd GH
12. SS-PzDiv
12
SS101
Pz.Lehr-Div
1. SS-PzDiv
Hill 112
Carpiquet
Cheux
Fontaine-Étoupefour
Baron-sur-Odon
0 500 1 500 2

CHAPTER 4

Operation "Epsom"

From the very beginning, this operation was born under an unlucky star. Although the constant rain had stopped by the early light of 26 June 1944, thick fog took its place. As a consequence, the planned immense support from the air from England—for the first time since D-Day—was not possible. Only the fighter-bombers that were already based in Normandy were able to fly sorties. Although 500 were flown, they were likewise appreciably hindered by the fog. The artillery support from some 736 artillery pieces partially fell among friendly ranks.

Passing Cheux on both sides, the 15th Scottish Division and then the 11th Armoured Division fought their way forward towards the Odon in the direction of Mondrainville while sustaining heavy casualties. At this point, six *Tigers* from *schwere SS-Panzer-Abteilung 101* attacked, however. From positions south of Colleville, the *Tigers* engaged the left flank of the 2nd Northamptonshire Yeomanry and drove it back. The 7th Seaforth Highlanders experienced a similar fate. Their frontal advance on Colleville was stopped by *PaKs* as well as *Tigers* in positions at Mouen. The British infantry had to attack again. Late in the afternoon, the 2nd Gordon Highlanders succeeded in penetrating into Colleville for a period of time. Half of the seventeen Churchills of C Squadron of the 7th Royal Tank Regiment that were supporting the attack were knocked out; the rest were forced to pull back. The forces in Colleville were encircled; most were taken prisoner.

That evening, the 15th Scottish Division was ordered to advance to the Odon the next day. Following that, the 11th Armoured Division was to move on to the actual objective, the Orne. This was an ambitious plan, as will be seen later. It is even more astounding inasmuch as this was the very first combat operation for most of the British formations involved.

Difficulties were preordained because the three tank brigades were crammed together in an area of only around 7 square kilometers (about 4.3 square miles) and then only a few kilometers away from the German lines. There was not enough room to deploy and develop any type of offensive punch. The 10th Highland Light Infantry Regiment, which was employed south of Cheux, got bogged down in the Germans' heavy defensive fires. That evening, the commander said the following to his officers and senior noncommissioned officers:

> I am very disappointed with you all. You've shown me what you're made of; you're yellow, practically the whole bloody lot of you! I am ashamed of you. There will be some changes made and they won't be very nice, I can tell you. I've never seen such a

> bloody awful performance, it really was stinking. (Tim Saunders, *Operation Epsom*)

Several soldiers were reduced in rank the same day. From the German standpoint, such actions were truly incomprehensible.

The 2nd Gordon Highlanders were finally able to dislodge the defending *SS-Panzer-Aufklärungs-Abteilung 12* from Colleville after sustaining heavy casualties. It was then intended for the 29th Armoured Brigade to finally take the banks of the Odon. Several *Tigers* of *schwere SS-Panzer-Abteilung 101* offered combat, but they were unable to do anything against the numerical superiority and the heavy artillery fire. A *Tiger* was knocked out by the 3rd Royal Tank Regiment at Mouen; another one was lost at Colleville. The *SS* reconnaissance soldiers had to pull back in a hurry; towards 1700 hours, the 2nd Argyll & Sutherland Highlanders succeeded in capturing the bridge at Tourmauville intact. The bridge at Gavrus was also lost. The enemy expanded his bridgehead that same evening and sent tanks across. As a result of the enemy's success, the German counterattacks originally planned for this day were overcome by events.

In his book concerning the 11th Armoured Division, *Monty's Marauders,* Patrick Delaforce recounts the events of the day as follows:

> The 2nd Fife and Forfarshire took casualties but fought their way towards Grainville, where, despite heavy fire plans and attacks by 15th Scottish supported by Churchill tanks, the German defences held firm. 119 Battery 75 A/Tank claimed one Tiger and five Panthers, put out of action round Cheux for the loss of Sergeant Hancock's M-10. At Norrey-en-Bessin 118 Battery had a troop under command of 4 KSLI, 1st Herefords and 3rd Mons. On the left (east) the 23rd Hussars battled their way on. Two Honeys were knocked out by a single AP shot near Cheux and another by an SP gun from Mouen down at the railway. B squadron pushed through Mouen to a position north-west of Mondrainville and picked off targets on the far side of their objective, the River Odon. Their Belgian Major, Henri Le Grand, DSO, was killed in action when four 23rd Hussar tanks were brewed up by 88s east of Mouen. Mondrainville was like a wasps' nest full of Panthers and snipers, and was then only partially "smoked out." The main Caen-Villers road was straight and well covered by 88s and German tanks. "Mondrainville was a blackened mass of ruin," wrote Rifleman Norman Habertin. "Burning tanks were poking out of doorways, enemy guns were overturned; in fact it was like most of the other villages in Normandy."
>
> When the depleted Argyll and Sutherland Highlanders seized an unblown bridge over the River Odon at Tourmauville, C squadron swept through and crossed the river at about 1730 hrs. By 1900 hrs two squadrons of 23rd Hussars were across the river and H Company 8 RB [Rifle Brigade] were guarding the precious Odon bridge. But on the west bank the German counter-attack towards Mondrainville took its toll, and half a dozen tanks were lost. During the 27th, 23rd Hussars lost twenty-four killed, twenty-four wounded and five, including two officers, were taken prisoner. It had been a tough and dangerous day.
>
> The divisional artillery fired "Uncle" targets against Tiger tanks on the east side of the river. Later on 2nd Fife and Forfarshire

Yeomanry crossed, followed by the infantry of the Herefords and 4 KSLI. Unfortunately 3rd Mons set off in the dark, wandered offline and found themselves in the village of Mouen, south-east of Cheux. Leaving C Company to hold Mouen, 3rd Mons moved south, took Colleville and Mondrainville and arrived on the north bank of the River Odon by dawn. The Germans counter-attacked at Mouen and captured or killed all but fourteen of C Company. Despite a chaotic briefing by the 159 Infantry Brigade CO, 4 KSLI made their way from Odon, missed the covering artillery barrage, marched cross country through the night, crossed the River Odon, captured their objective, Baron, and were well dug in by dawn. A superb effort.

Starting early on the morning of 28 June 1944, elements of the 8th Rifle Brigade advanced as far as Hill 112.

The British offensive was successfully able to fend off a counterattack by *Kampfgruppe Weidinger*—with several *Tigers* in support—that was launched in the direction of Grainville (north of the Odon). It also turned back an attack from the east on Bretteville by *Kampfgruppe Frey*. The enemy was immediately turned out of Mouen, however, and Colleville was also attacked. The British corridor to the Odon was becoming progressively smaller. In addition, six *Tigers* of the *1./schwere SS-Panzer-Abteilung 101* attacked from Maltot in the direction of Hill 112. Although the German attack wavered, an advance by elements of the 3rd Royal Tank Regiment from the northwest side of Hill 112 in the direction of Esquay was turned back.

On 29 June 1944, the forces in the bridgehead were reinforced by the 129th Infantry Brigade and the good weather conditions enabled devastating bombing attacks by the Allies. But the arrival of the *9. SS-Panzer-Division "Hohenstaufen"* and the *10. SS-Panzer-Division "Frundsberg"* made the situation for the British considerably worse. Although the attacks of the total of five *SS* armored divisions only made slow progress, the position of the British became untenable.

In order not to be cut off, the forces on the far side of the Odon pulled back. The first attempt to take Hill 112 had been turned back.

In Patrick Delaforce's book *The Black Bull*, the day is described as follows:

> 3 RTR [Royal Tank Regiment] were in action most of the day with 13 RHA FOOs [Royal Horse Artillery Forward Observation Officers] bringing down divisional barrages and Typhoon fire on Tigers dug into the woods.
>
> At Gavrus 119 Battery 75 A/tank destroyed five tanks including one Tiger, lost two of their M-10s and two officers were killed, a third on the 30th. At 1800 hrs the expected major counter-attacks started coming to cut the Villers-Bocage-Caen road and the road from Noyers to Cheux. On Hill 112 Noel Bell saw:
>
> At last light some eight tanks reported as Tigers together with about 150 infantry advancing from the west. Very lights were going up and machine gunning broke out. Artillery support was enlisted—time was urgent—and a devastating barrage was brought to bear on the advancing infantry. The gunners succeeded in wreaking complete havoc on the enemy on the ground. The tanks finding their ground

support virtually liquidated . . . withdrew. With darkness now complete we awaited our next call to action.

"We were more concerned about survival on Hill 112 than the Orne bridges," remarked Bill Close, 3 RTR.

We knew there was only a narrow corridor behind us back to the Odon and were afraid of being cut off or attacked in the rear . . . We lost about a dozen tanks in all . . . five from my squadron.

Before dawn:

We move slowly up to the crest. Suddenly there is a flash on my left and an 88 whistles in front of my tank. We swing round and fire at him. Meanwhile Tiger tanks are reported advancing on our position. They are engaged, orders to withdraw to our new position are given, and the last but one my troop is told to go. The little stone bridge over the Odon has stood, thank God, and with my corporal towing a broken down tank in front we rumble over.

Just over an hour before dawn we were again ordered to withdraw. With most of the vehicles already gone, it was once more a case of climbing on to anything that moved. Through the night we made our way back to an area south-west of Norrey-en-Bessin (6 miles north of the Odon bridge). Even God never knew how good it was for us to see the sun again.

At the end of Operation "Epsom," VIII Corps had 4,020 casualties. 15th Scottish suffered most with 2,331, and 11th Armoured and 43rd Division lost 1,256.

In the days that followed, the few operational *Tigers* of *schwere SS-Panzer-Abteilung 101* were sporadically committed west of Maltot. The 1st Company transferred its seven remaining *Tigers* to the 3rd Company; its personnel then moved to Paderborn on 9 July 1944 to be issued the new *Tiger II*. This company would never return to the Normandy area of operations.

Although Operation "Epsom" proved in the final analysis to be a miscalculation, it had also negated the German intent of deliberately regrouping for a major attack. When the *II. SS-Panzer-Korps* launched its counterattack, it had also proven problematical that the zone of attack was still within range of the large-caliber naval artillery, which was able to effectively intervene in the ground combat. Both *Generalfeldmarschall* Rommel and *Generalfeldmarschall* von Runstedt—the latter particularly so—had attempted to stress this fact upon Hitler when they met with the *Führer* at Margival (vicinity of Soissons) on 17 June 1944. Another meeting with the *Führer*—this time at Berchtesgaden on 29 June 1944—reinforced their impression that Hitler was somewhat in the dark on how critical the entire situation was. When the Commander-in-Chief of *Panzergruppe West*, *Generaloberst* Geyr von Schweppenburg, recommended on the following day that the portions of Caen on the far side of the Orne be abandoned and that this recommendation was expressly supported by *Generalfeldmarschall* von Runstedt, it was all too much for Hitler. He ordered all current positions be held where they were and replaced *Generalfeldmarschall* von Runstedt with *Generalfeldmarschall* von Kluge. On 3 July, *Generaloberst* Geyr von Schweppenburg was replaced by *General der Panzertruppen* Heinrich Eberbach.

✠

On 8 and 9 July 1944, the British and the Canadians finally took Caen in heavy fighting, at least what was left of it.

In the meantime, *schwere SS-Panzer-Abteilung 102* had also entered this sector, and it was positioned southwest of Caen at St. Honorine du Fay right before the start of the new British offensive across the Odon on the evening of 9 July 1944, Operation "Jupiter." On 7 and 8 July, the officers of the battalion had an opportunity to conduct leaders' reconnaissance of their new area of operations. This was one of the reasons for the successes of the next few days.

This is view the attacking British had of the dominant piece of terrain, Hill 112. It demonstrates how difficult it was to assault across terrain that was practically without cover or concealment.

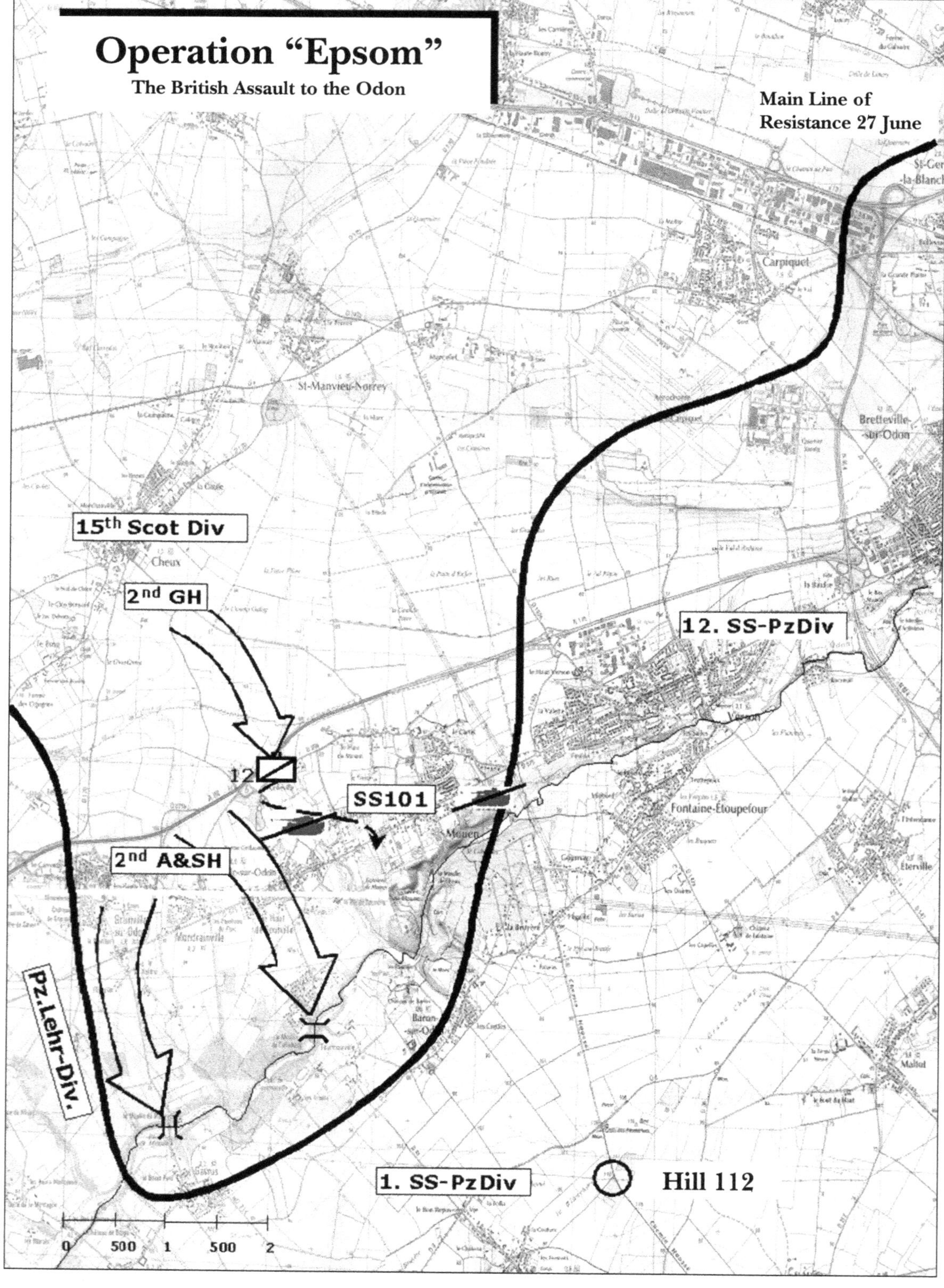
Operation "Epsom"
The British Assault to the Odon
Main Line of Resistance 27 June
15th Scot Div
2nd GH
12
SS101
12. SS-PzDiv
2nd A&SH
Pz.Lehr-Div.
1. SS-PzDiv
Hill 112
Carpiquet
St-Manvieu-Norrey
Cheux
Bretteville-sur-Odon
Fontaine-Étoupefour
Verson
Mouen
Eterville
Maltot
0 500 1 500 2

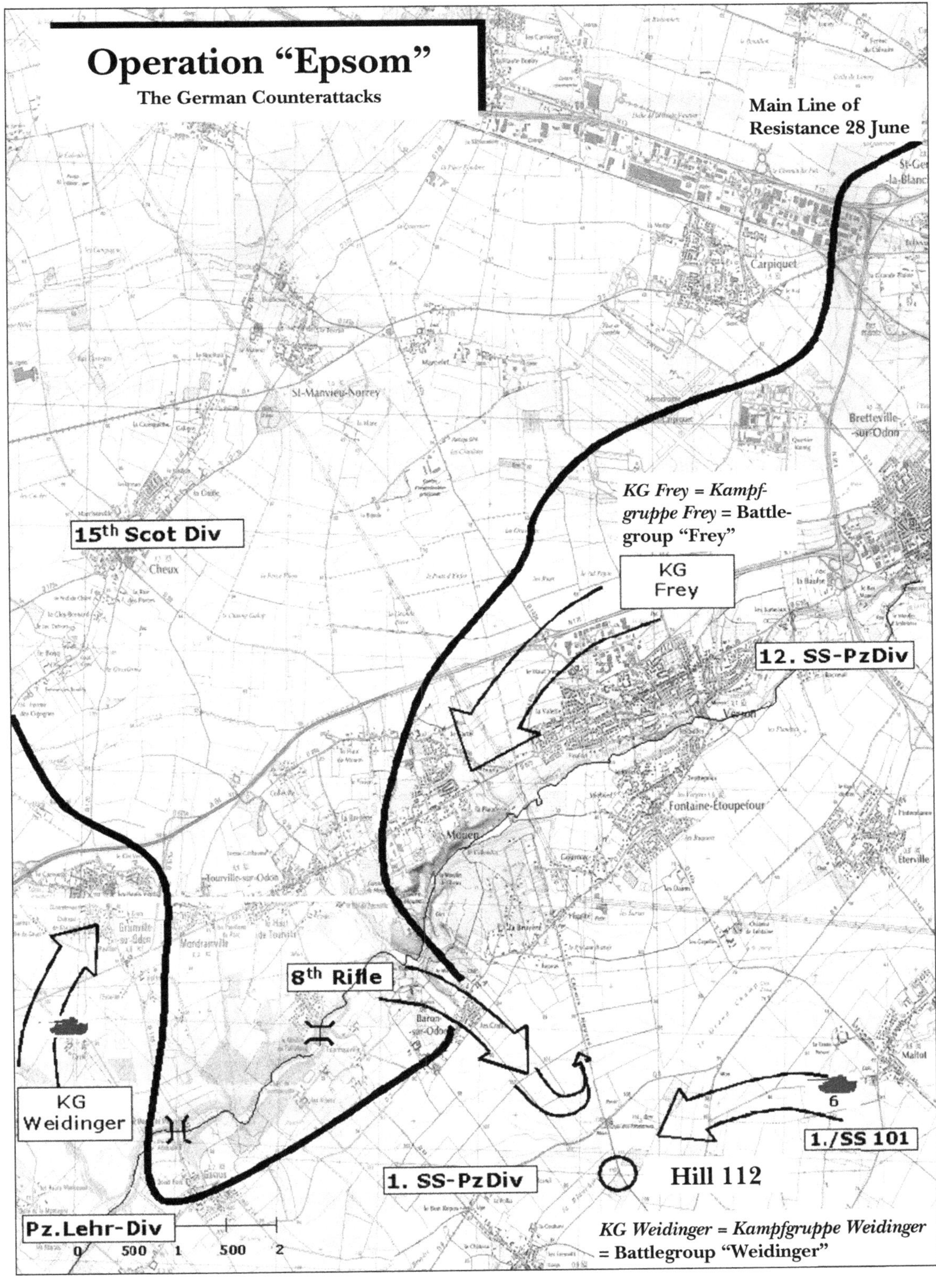
Operation "Epsom"
The German Counterattacks
Main Line of Resistance 28 June
KG Frey = Kampf-gruppe Frey = Battle-group "Frey"
KG Frey
12. SS-PzDiv
15th Scot Div
8th Rifle
KG Weidinger
1./SS 101
1. SS-PzDiv
Hill 112
Pz.Lehr-Div
0 500 1 500 2
KG Weidinger = Kampfgruppe Weidinger = Battlegroup "Weidinger"
Carpiquet
St-Manvieu-Norrey
Cheux
Bretteville-sur-Odon
Fontaine-Etoupefour
Mouen
Tourville-sur-Odon
Mondrainville
Baron-sur-Odon
Eterville
Maltot

S

B2

View from Mondrainville to the south. The vegetation in the middle marks the location of the Odon. It can be clearly seen that the terrain climbs steadily behind the river line and, in addition, offers little in the way of cover or concealment. It was therefore especially important for the British not to lose any momentum in their attack.

The newly activated *schwere SS-Panzer-Abteilung 102* prepared for its future operations at the Dutch training area at Wezep. For the road march to Normandy that followed, the battalion needed nearly three weeks.

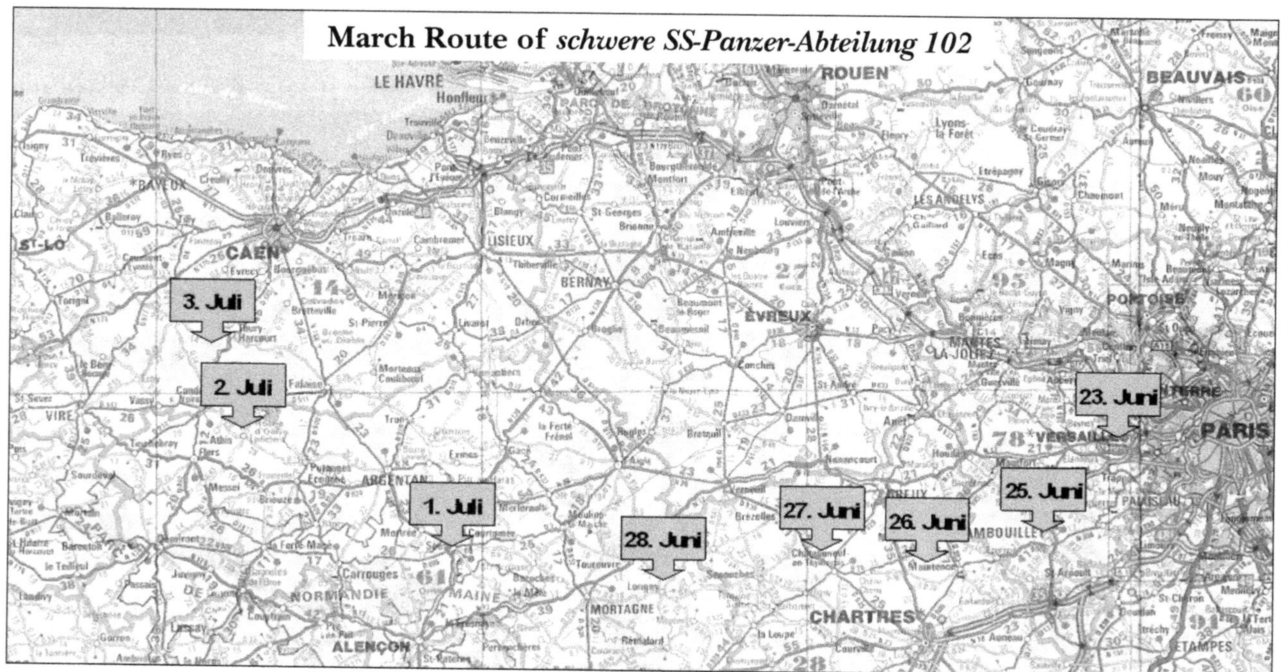

Juli = July; Juni = June

The battalion's road march to Normandy took nearly two weeks after passing through Paris. Camouflaged with vegetation, the tanks resembled moving bushes in an effort to disguise themselves from Allied air activity. As a result of the extensive camouflage efforts, the tanks were only infrequently discovered by fighter-bombers. Like its sister battalion, *schwere SS-Panzer-Abteilung 102* suffered no casualties from the air during its long road march.

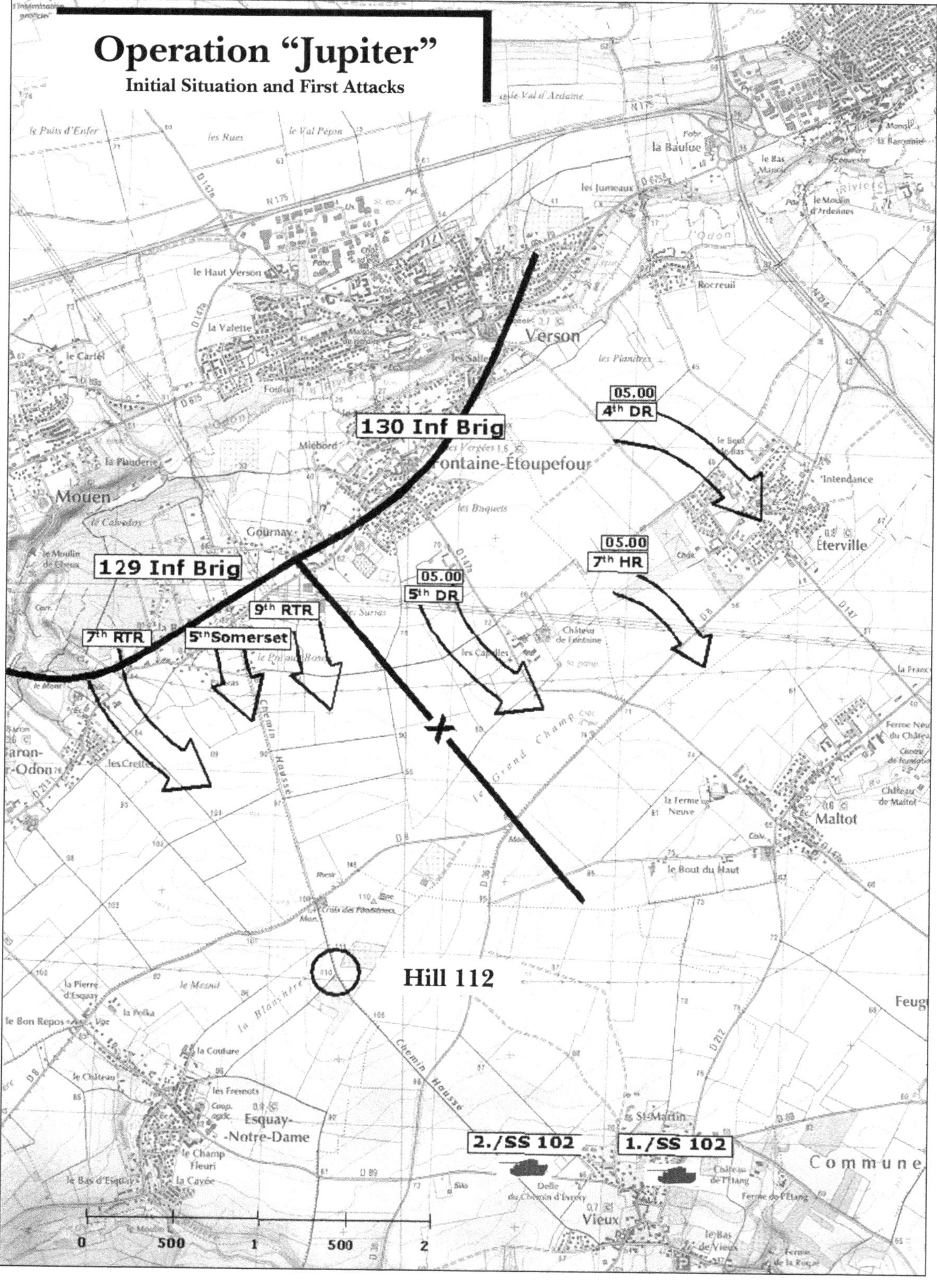
Operation "Jupiter"
Initial Situation and First Attacks
130 Inf Brig
129 Inf Brig
05.00
4th DR
05.00
7th HR
05.00
5th DR
9th RTR
7th RTR
5th Somerset
Hill 112
2./SS 102
1./SS 102
Verson
Mouen
Fontaine-Étoupefour
Éterville
Maltot
Esquay-Notre-Dame
Vieux
0
500
1
500
2

CHAPTER 5

Operation "Jupiter"

This time, the 43rd Scottish Division received the mission of finally taking Hill 112 and creating the prerequisites for the continued advance over the Orne. At 0445 hours on 10 July 1944, the British fifteen-minute artillery preparation was started from more than 1,000 guns, including naval artillery. When it was over, the lead battalions of the 129th and 130th Infantry Brigades moved out. Eterville was rapidly taken by the 4th Dorsetshire Regiment with assistance from Crocodile flamethrower tanks. The village was then subjected to counterattacks the entire day.

After tough fighting, the area northwest of Maltot was taken in the afternoon, some two kilometers east of Hill 112. Even the open terrain to the high ground was almost crossed, when the counterattack launched by *schwere SS-Panzer-Abteilung 102* in the direction of Hill 112 as well as Maltot started to show effect. For the time being, the situation at Maltot stabilized for the Germans. The *Tigers* intervened at just the moment when the British wanted to start their decisive push to the Orne.

✠

On the day before the British attack, *schwere SS-Panzer-Abteilung 102* had received orders shortly after 2000 hours to move to the northern outskirts of St. Martin (northeast of Vieux). The road march started at 2230 hours and proceeded via Maiset and Amayé-sur-Orne. *Tiger 211* became disabled along the way. The two companies of the battalion—the 3rd Company had not yet closed into the area of operations—received the following mission: Attack Hill 112 (2nd Company) and the area east of it (1st Company). In all, some twenty-seven *Tigers* were operational.

As it dawned on 10 July 1944, there was an aerial attack, whereby two *Tigers* were destroyed.

The 7th Hampshire Regiment was receiving fire not only from the front but also from several *Tigers* of the 1st Company in an elevated position some 1,000 meters northeast of St. Martin. Four *Tigers* under *SS-Oberscharführer* Baral reached Maltot the same time as the Scots did. They moved through the village, went into position on the northern outskirts and then saw several Churchills in front of them.

With the *Tigers* racing across from St. Martin was *SS-Unterscharführer* Will Fey:

> Our four tanks led the reconnaissance into Maltot. We had to protect the flank of our Tiger tanks on Hill 112. Off we went at top speed over the open fields. We reached the edge of the village. Wasting no time, we pushed through the hedges. There, in front of us, were four Sherman tanks [Churchills]. Two rounds finished off the one on the left;

the one next to him suffered the same fate, and the platoon leader pushed forward to knock out a third. The fourth sought safety in racing back along the road. It was a great boost for our young tank crew. (J. J. How, *Hill 112*. English translation of the German original corrected.)

To state it mildly, the British had reported the capture of Maltot at 0915 hours a bit prematurely. The 5th Dorsetshire Regiment, which was moving on Maltot from the right, received such strong fire that it had to pull back to the Chateau de Fontaine. By this time, one British tank after another was being knocked out in Maltot. The situation was becoming critical for the Scots. It was only through artillery barrage fire and large swarms of Typhoon fighter-bombers that the German attacks against Maltot could be held up. At 1600 hours, the 4th Dorsetshire Regiment was also moved to Maltot so as to reinforce the remnants of the Hampshire Regiment. These forces were decimated on the way there. That night, the first British forces were withdrawn from Maltot. Both battalions had lost approximately 50 percent of their personnel on this one day.

✠

The fighting developed as follows on the forward slope of Hill 112: At 0530 hours—using German time, which was two hours ahead of British time—the attack of the battalion's two tank companies started with two operational platoons. The 3rd Platoon of *SS-Untersturmführer* Rathmann was on the left; the 1st Platoon of *SS-Untersturmführer* Schroif was on the right. A meeting engagement against the 7th Battalion of the Royal Tank Regiment (northeast of Baron) and the 9th Battalion of the Royal Tank Regiment (on both sides of the Fontaine Etoupefour–Maltot road) started from a movement to contact. The so-called "Patch of Woods of Half Trees" (*Wäldchen der halben Bäume*)—so named because of what the artillery fire had done to it—hard northwest of Hill 112 was taken. *Tiger 213* of *SS-Unterscharführer* Piller received a hit from an antitank gun of the 4th Wiltshire Regiment and had to return to the rear. Three enemy tanks and an antitank gun were knocked out.

The following account of the British attack to the northwest past Hill 112 is found in J. J. How's book, *Hill 112*:

A nasty surprise was awaiting the men of Wessex. At a quarter to three in the morning a battalion of new Tiger tanks arrived on the German side of the hill and moved into the village of St. Martin. These fifty-six ton Tigers were Germany's most feared weapon. Neither the British nor the Americans had anything to compare with them. There were never more than three battalions of them fighting in Normandy, and all fought in the British sector. The 102 SS Heavy Tank Battalion was the Tiger battalion of the IInd SS Panzer Corps. It had been eighteen days on the road from Holland. It should have been in the IInd SS Panzer Corps counter-attack on the Scottish corridor. It was just as well for the British that they had failed to turn up, for had these "Kings of the Battlefield" been present at Cheux and le Valtru, who knows what the outcome might have been.

As dawn streaked the sky in the east the British bombardment suddenly flashed brighter in the sky above Hill 112. The distant sound of the guns was followed by a scream and howl as shells crashed down amongst the Tiger tanks in the orchards of St. Martin.

> The Tiger tanks that had early that morning arrived in St. Martin had joined the battle. Two companies, about twenty [tanks] in number, had first moved up the German slope and halted at the hedge facing the little wood from the east. They were above the morning mist; the sun was trying to break through. Allied aeroplanes suddenly swooped out of the sky, dropped their bombs, circled and dived with all machine-guns firing. It was the 10th SS Panzer Grenadiers who suffered the casualties. The noise deadened the senses. The hilltop was being pounded by shellfire. Nothing of the fierce battle raging there could be seen.
>
> Commanding the 2nd Company was Hauptsturmfuehrer (Captain) Endemann. His wireless wasn't working. He was transmitting orders by hand signal. He took the company past the little box-shaped wood and on to the plateau. Corporal Piller's Tiger was immediately hit and had to pull back. Rathsack fired and knocked out a British tank. Untersturmfuehrer (Lieutenant) Schroif knocked out two more and an anti-tank gun. Endemann disappeared into the smoke and dust and was not seen or heard of again.

The 3rd Company moved on to the eastern side of the plateau. Hans Richter was a Tiger commander with this company:

> A solid armour-piercing shot went clean through the turret. It took with it the head of the gunner, Hans Kruckner. It took also my left forearm and smashed my right one. It peppered my chest with bits of metal and sent a splinter into my right eye. That was the end for us. I was sure that I would bleed to death. "Reverse!" I shouted. The gun-loader tore at my headphones. He tied the cable around my left upper arm to stop the bleeding. I was getting weaker. But I managed to get out of the turret. This is it, I thought, as I staggered across an open field in a din of crashing shellfire. Another Tiger came roaring past. It stopped. "We'll take you!" Strong arms lifted me up. First onto the back of the [tank], and then, when the firing got worse, into the turret. I lay semi-conscious on the turntable [turret floor]. I remembered an ambulance—doors open—the entrance to a village. I heard someone say: "Main artery! Take him! Quickly!"

Little wonder that for the Churchills of the 7th Royal Tank Regiment, which were supporting the Somersets, things got steadily worse:

> Lieutenant Colonel Gaisford blinded in one eye and Major Fleming killed in his tank, "C" Squadron suffered terribly, losing six tanks. . . . The Somersets were decimated.
>
> The Somersets would be lucky to hold on to what they had won. Of the sixteen rifle company officers who had moved up the hill, only four remained. One company was under the command of a Sergeant. The carrier platoon commander, who was to have arrived with his men to help clear the plateau, was dead. The surviving Churchill tanks had pulled back to hull-down positions. And it was there, on the reverse slope hidden by the crest, that the Somersets were digging in. They had left only lightly manned observation posts higher up along the line of the road.
>
> Plotting the progress of the British offensive in his battle headquarters was

the commander of the 10th SS Frundsberg Division, [*SS-Oberführer*] (Brigadier) Harmel:

Whilst our divisional and the corps artillery, together with the mortars of the 8th Werfer Brigade, brought down a heavy curtain of fire to prevent the British from developing their attack on the top of Hill 112, the armoured [personnel carrier] battalion of the 21st SS Panzer Grenadier Regiment and the 10th SS Reconnaissance Battalion were moved forward to counter-attack at Maltot with the support of Tiger tanks from the 102 SS Heavy Battalion.

Meanwhile the Hampshires had fought their way through Maltot and were digging in four hundred yards further south. The company on the left flank of the advance was missing. Then comes an entry in the battalion war diary: "0955 hours . . . Imperative to withdraw—Tiger tanks and infantry attacking from the south-east and the south-west."

Infantry pushing forward from Château Fontaine to try to make contact with the Hampshires ran into three more Tigers in a little wood west of Maltot. Captain "Crasher" White, "in a soft cap and brandishing a cane," rushed forward with two anti-tank guns. He was not seen again. These men of the 5th Dorsets could do nothing about those impregnable monsters. They were forced to retire leaving many dead in the corn.

The commander of the *2./schwere SS-Panzer-Abteilung 102*, *SS-Hauptsturmführer* Endemann on *Tiger 221*, whose radio set had become disabled, moved too far to the right in rolling terrain and has been missing ever since. Heavy British fire with smoke rounds and aerial attacks forced the open terrain to be abandoned. The *1./schwere SS-Panzer-Abteilung 101* destroyed several enemy tanks. When the 3rd Company attacked later on, three *Tigers* were knocked out. The first one lost was *Tiger 311* of *SS-Untersturmführer* Streu, who was killed. Then *Tiger 312* of *SS-Unterscharführer* Richter was knocked out. Richter's arm was torn off, and he had to have the stump tourniqueted with an intercom cable. The *Tiger* of *SS-Unterscharführer* Novy was also lost, with Novy being captured.

Years after the war, this out-of-focus photograph showing Endemann's *Tiger* 221 surfaced in private hands. Since the left track is missing, it may have been hit in the running gear and become immobilized. The crew was probably either killed or taken into captivity. (Jean Restayn)

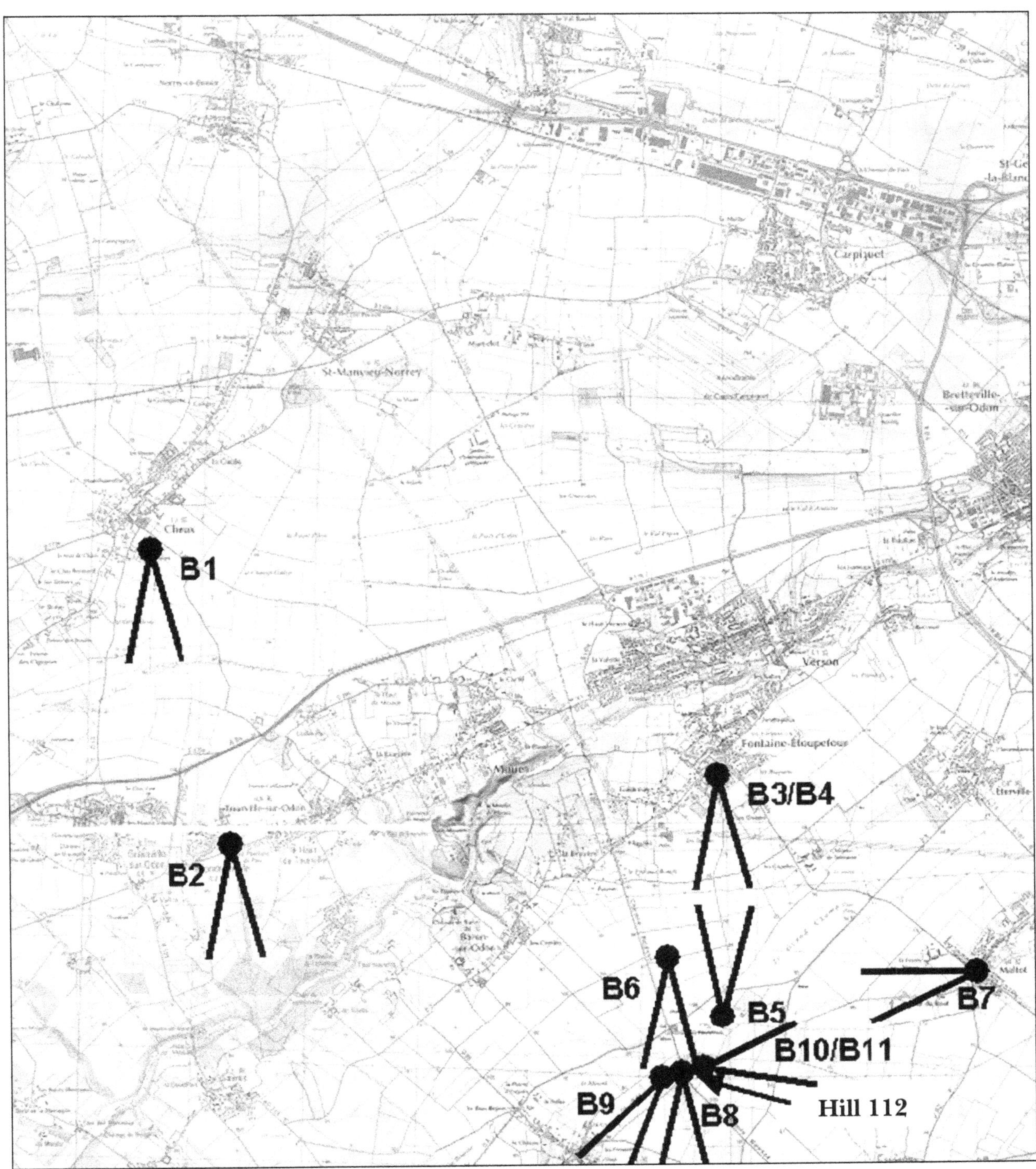

This map marks the vantage points for the various terrain images that deal with the fighting for Hill 112. There are British viewpoints (B1–B4 and B6), the German viewpoint (B5 and B7) and general views from the hill itself (remaining markers).

S

This view from the southern edge of Fontaine-Etoupefour shows that the difficulties for the British were just starting with the crossing of the Odon. The road leading away from the observer heads directly towards the eastern edge of Hill 112 across several kilometers of completely open terrain. This is the reason why the subsequent fighting waged back and forth for several weeks and why the *Tigers* were able to employ their superior range to great effect. About 200 meters farther down the road, there was an almost rectangular fruit orchard off to the left that was covered with low-standing trees and vegetation. It temporarily offered the British some concealment, until the orchard was swept away several days later by artillery.

S

The same road seen from the perspective of the German defenders. The enemy could be attrited from forward positions long before he even approached within range of Hill 112, which was located about 1.5 kilometers behind this vantage point.

S

The view past the fruit orchard to the south to the intersection of D8 and D36. The cross is a memorial to the fighting. Hill 112 is about 1,000 meters beyond and off to the right. The tall stand of trees in the middle of the image marks the crest of the hill today.

View of Hill 112 from the direction of Maltot. To the left is the highest point of the hill. To the right is the previously mentioned fruit orchard. The rectangularly shaped patch of woods on the hill was appropriately referred to as the *Wäldchen der halben Bäume* ("Patch of woods of half trees") after it had been hit numerous times by artillery.

S

This view from Hill 112 to the south clearly demonstrates why the British had to gain control of that high ground. They would have had a clear shot to the Orne (in the middle of the photograph) and then into the open terrain south of Caen. That would have created the decisive breakthrough.

An account of the fighting by the 7th Battalion of the Royal Tank Regiment, which was employed frontally against Hill 112, is contained in Peter Beale's *Tank Tracks*:

> On the right of 9 RTR, 7 RTR were attacking Hill 112 in support of 129 Brigade. They had made substantial progress, but at 0933 hrs a strong enemy counter-attack was made on Hill 112. 7 RTR suffered a number of casualties including their CO, Lt.-Col. Gaisford, who lost an eye, and the 2 i/c Major Bob Fleming who was killed. The right flank of 9 RTR's advance was thus enfiladed, and anti-tank fire was also reported from the high ground dominating Maltot to the west of the River Orne. The impetus of the attack was failing—two Tigers were in Maltot making the advance of the infantry extremely difficult and A Squadron's movement was hampered by a troop of Tigers at the southern slope of Hill 112, firing north-east.
>
> At 1156 hrs A Squadron were still struggling to support the infantry in Maltot who were now confronted with another Tiger. The German infantry were now counter-attacking and only nine tanks of A Squadron were left. Major Douglas Ballantine, OC A Squadron, dismounted in an attempt to make contact with the CO of the 7th Hampshires (Lt.-Col. D.W.G. Ray), but was severely wounded by mortar fire and subsequently died.
>
> By 1200 hrs 2 i/c A Squadron (Capt. Bert Mockford) reported that he had only four tanks capable of fighting, and further reports stated that counter-attacks were being made with tanks and infantry from north-east and south-west of Maltot.
>
> The battalion was disposed as follows:
>
> B Squadron and elements of A in hull down positions on spur south of Chateau de Fontaine with infantry and anti-tank guns dug in.
>
> C Squadron had joined Battalion HQ in forward rally after release by 4th Dorsets. BHQ had been mortared and shelled periodically causing severe casualties among the wounded that had been brought in.
>
> From 1300 to 1600 hrs there was a stalemate, the enemy making no attempts to push their counter-attack any further. A new plan was devised whereby A Squadron 7 RTR (Major Dick Joscelyne) were to put the 5th Battalion Duke of Cornwall's Light Infantry (5 DCLI) on Hill 112 and C Squadron 9 RTR to put 4th Dorsets into Maltot. B Squadron were to give support from the right in the opening phase. 4 Armoured Brigade were waiting to go through.
>
> The advance began at 1640 hrs and despite anti-tank fire from south-west of Maltot C Squadron had put the infantry into the village by 1700 hrs. But ten minutes later C Squadron were being shot at from the rear, for once again enemy tanks had infiltrated under cover of the spur north-east of Hill 112. Eight Tigers were also moving in on the left flank, and the infantry were pulling out of Maltot under pressure.
>
> At 1935 hrs C Squadron was also forced to withdraw under the cover of supporting fire from B Squadron. Mortaring and shelling was almost continuous and at 2030 hrs all tanks rallied at the FUP; later they moved to join A Echelon north-east of Mouen to replenish and collect reinforcements.

✠

Under the cover of darkness, an immediate counterattack was supported at Maltot north of the road to St. Martin. As a result of the heavy enemy fire, it only advanced a few hundred meters and was finally broken off.

Contrary to normal practice, the fighting continued during the night. The Scots succeeded in establishing themselves on Hill 112.

The tide turned at first light on 11 July 1944, however. The hill was taken under attack from two sides, this time from the side facing Esquay as well. Only Eterville could not be taken back. The counterattack to reestablish the old main line of resistance at Hill 112 began at 0515 hours.

SS-Rottenführer Trautmann has provided an impression of the intensity of the fighting:

> At first light on 11 July, we executed our attack towards the north—determined to take the hill this time by storm! We attempted to approach the hill in a concealed fashion through a shallow defile on the side of Hill 112 that faces Aunay. A short-range reconnaissance aircraft, comparable to our *Fieseler Storch*, turned in a wide spiral above us, came back and then turned to the west in a steep curve. [This was] for us a bad omen: these machines were superbly equipped with radio equipment.
>
> Probably no more than ten minutes had gone by when the dance number from Hell increased to a hurricane. High-explosive rounds landed on the turret and the hull; tree bursts plucked off the crowns of trees. Our mechanized infantry [*III./SS-Panzer-Grenadier-Regiment 29*] could no longer raise their heads, and many great comrades remained lying on the slope.
>
> Our *Tigers* knocked out a few Churchills [which were supporting the 5th Duke of Cornwall's Light Infantry] in rapid sequence. You could say that the so-called box woods, a cattle pasture that was ringed by a square hedgerow, was packed to the brim with all sorts of knick-knacks!
>
> When Knecht's tank was being badly threatened from two sides, we went to his aid. We came roaring up at 20 kilometers an hour over ditches and through earthen walls and took up Tommy in our sight picture while still moving. After the third round, which penetrated the jacket of his main gun, the turret remained half out of the hull.
>
> The enemy was bringing in antitank guns all the way over to the left in the hedgerow-ringed cattle pasture. The crews were spreading the gun trails apart in an agitated fashion and were already taking their first casualties as they were doing this. The Anglo-Saxons sure were brave!
>
> In the meantime, we had slowly worked out way up to them and quickly made the positioning of the dark brown guns a wasted effort.
>
> Once again, the enemy fired a thick wall of smoke, which pinpointed our tanks shortly before they reached the high ground. In this milky soup, our *Tiger* received several hits on the rear and the turret. Our tank commander ordered the driver: "Forward, step on it!"
>
> This smoke had to end somewhere—and then we were through it.
>
> "Driver, stop!"
>
> We had a sight in front of us that every *Tiger* [crew] could only wish for. The Tommies were clearing their positions barely 100 meters in front of us. Halftracks and carriers curved back and forth and loaded up personnel and equipment. Our

tank commander gave a brief fire command: "Radio operator: Engage when ready . . . Loader: Load AP . . . Gunner: Engage at will . . . "

Two Churchills, which had been posted directly in front of us in the undergrowth as security, were set ablaze while they were still aiming their main guns at us. We then fired high-explosive rounds and the turret machine gun at the numerous targets being presented. The fog had disappeared in the meantime.

The following radio message came from our company commander, [*SS-Obersturmführer*] Kalss, again and again: "Pull back immediately to the company's location." We really would have liked to have kept on pursuing the bolting enemy!

✠

Three enemy tanks, eight antitank guns and fifteen armored vehicles were destroyed by the *Tigers*. *Tiger 232* of *SS-Unterscharführer* Winter received a hit from an antitank gun. The 1st Company attacked through a defile along the side of Hill 112 facing Avenay; in the process, it exploited the smoke that the English were firing. The *Tigers* knocked out seven enemy tanks and eight antitank guns. The *Tiger* crew of *SS-Oberscharführer* Canesius mistakenly engaged a neighboring tank—that of *SS-Oberscharführer* Knecht—with three rounds. It missed, however, because its main gun was out of adjustment. A *Tiger* of the 3rd Company was hit and set ablaze. The acting commander of the 3rd Company, *SS-Untersturmführer* Klust, was relieved by the battalion commander because he had refused—certainly not without some justification—to attack into terrain where the visibility was restricted by the smoke rounds.

✠

In contrast to the fighting at Hill 112, the fighting for Maltot turned out to be less successful for the Germans. Chester Wilmot, a war correspondent of the BBC, described the fighting:

> By now that wood was enveloped in smoke—not the black smoke of hostile mortars but white smoke laid by our guns as a screen for our infantry who were now being forced to withdraw.
>
> We could see them moving back through the waist-high corn, and out of the smoke behind them came angry flashes as the German tanks fired from Maltot. But even as the infantry were driven back another battalion was moving forward to relieve them, supported by Churchill tanks firing tracer over the heads of the advancing men. They moved right past our hedge and out across the corn. The Germans evidently saw them coming, for away off on our right flank machine-guns opened up and then the nebelwerfers . . .

A straddle of Moaning Minnies sent Wilmot diving for cover, "forcing as much of myself as possible into an old German dugout." The Hampshires were withdrawing with three hundred of their men killed, wounded or missing. But someone had blundered. The Dorsets were already moving forward to help them. They found in Maltot not the Hampshires but the enemy Tiger and Panther tanks:

> Jerry must have been observing every move and allowed us to come right up close, thus cutting us off. Suddenly the whole party was cut down by a burst of fire

from a Spandau . . . No one dared to put his head above the corn, as soon as Jerry observed the slightest movement a burst of fire would be the reply.The high-velocity 88 mm cannon of the [tanks] opened up to the right of them and to the left of them. A blinding flash in the corn, and men were lying killed and wounded before the sound of the gun had reached them. A dull thud, a fountain of earth thrown into the air, and a Churchill tank was in flames. Carriers and anti-tank guns were being torn apart. The few Churchills not sending spirals of smoke into the air ran for the safety of the ridge behind them. What hope had they against the superior guns of the German tanks. Major Whittle kept going with his Bren carrier, "with the corn almost level with the sides, and wishing it were much higher."

This photograph demonstrates why the British attacked frontally. The view from Hill 112 to the southwest towards Esquay shows how the terrain was even steeper and could be dominated by flanking fires.

E

B10

View from Hill 112 to Maltot. The village, slightly elevated in relation to the surrounding terrain, had clear views of Hill 112 from certain vantage points. Consequently, it was the German objective to control the village as much as possible.

B11

A similar view from Hill 112, this time to the east towards Feugerolles. In the left background behind that village, St. Martin can be identified. The village is in a depression, which facilitates lateral movements of forces.

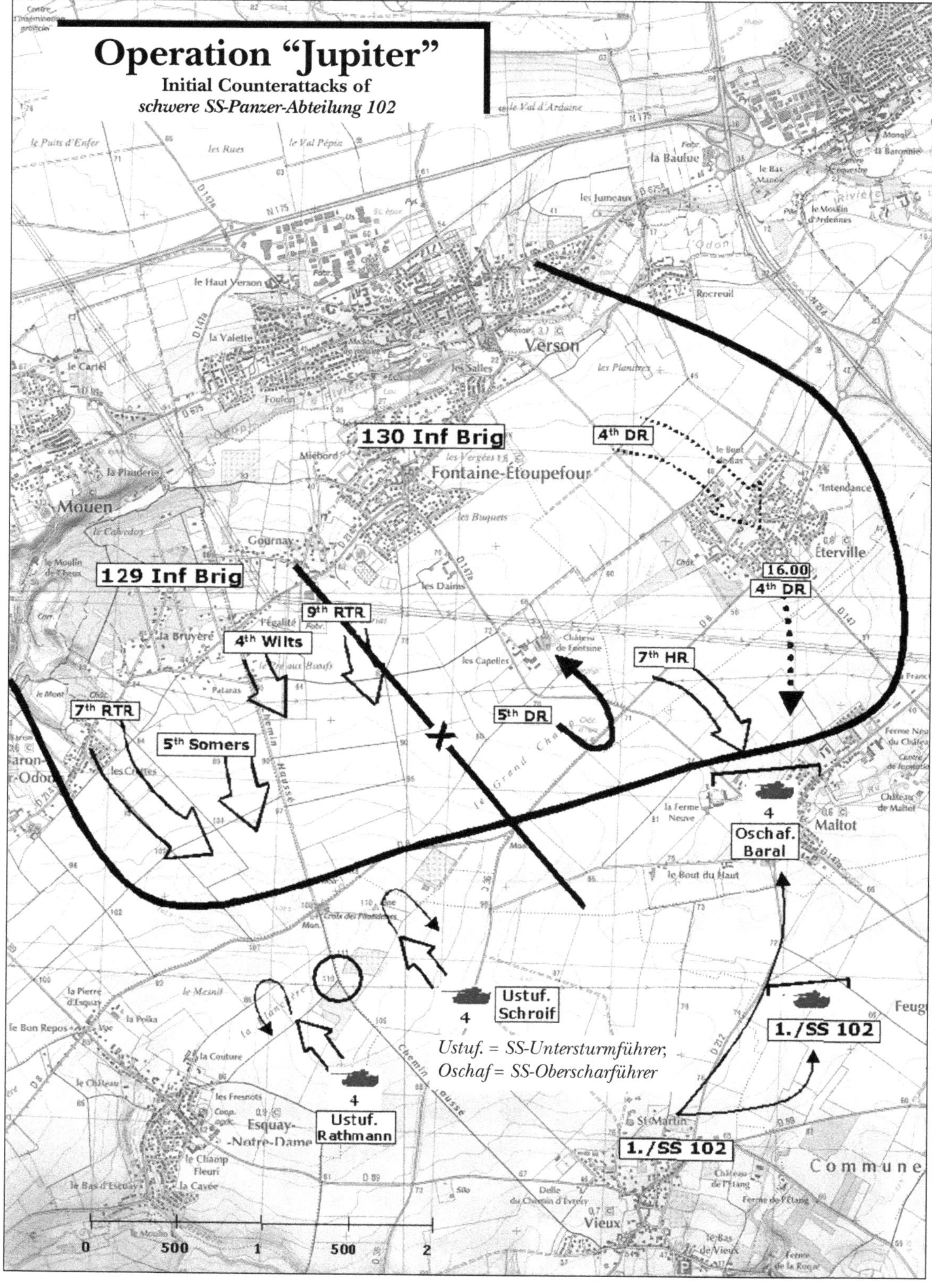

Operation "Jupiter"
Initial Counterattacks of
schwere SS-Panzer-Abteilung 102
130 Inf Brig
129 Inf Brig
4th DR
16.00
4th DR
9th RTR
4th Wilts
7th HR
5th DR
7th RTR
5th Somers
4
Oschaf.
Baral
4
Ustuf.
Schroif
1./SS 102
Ustuf. = SS-Untersturmführer,
Oschaf = SS-Oberscharführer
4
Ustuf.
Rathmann
1./SS 102
0 500 1 500 2
Verson
Fontaine-Etoupefour
Mouen
Éterville
Maltot
Esquay-Notre-Dame
Vieux

The fighting on this day also continued after the onset of night. J. J. How described this in his book, *Hill 112*:

> Waiting and watching at the foot of the German slope was Untersturmfuehrer (Lieutenant) Martin Schroif. He had been there in his Tiger tank since midday. The heavy [tanks] had been withdrawn from the summit to avoid the British artillery fire. He had heard the shell fire rise in a great crescendo and had watched as the hilltop disappeared in great clouds of dust and smoke.
>
> I saw panzer grenadiers coming back down the slope and I then knew that the British must have attacked again and that we would be sent to drive them back. It was almost dark when the order came. On the right I could see the Tigers of No 1 Company already moving on to the slope. My objective was the Kastenwäldchen [Box Woods]: We got to within about three hundred metres of it. I halted the company and opened fire. I pushed forward on the left into a hollow in the ground. We couldn't have been more than a hundred metres away. We fired with machine-guns and sent high explosive into the tree tops. Machine-gun fire rattled on the armour and we could see the muzzle flashes of the anti-tank guns.
>
> The 10th SS Frundsberg Division had not waited. It was important not to allow the British to dig in with anti-tank guns. The panzer grenadiers were attacking with the Tiger tanks and two companies of 9th SS under command [probably two companies of *SS-Panzer-Regiment 9*].
>
> It was confusion that dominated this battle on the top of the hill. At night darkness and fear are natural partners. An exploding shell is a flash of blinding light, a crack of doom, and a shower of sparkling red-hot splinters. Battle is fought in a gigantic display of death-dealing fireworks. Tank crew are blind but for the flashes of light that throw everything into startled view. It is a brave man who will man an anti-tank gun kneeling in a shower of splinters showering down from the tree tops.
>
> Casualties were heavy on both sides. The German infantry could not get forward through the heavy and accurate British artillery fire: the Tiger tanks feared to move closer without infantry protection. The stalemate was broken when it was discovered that the British were not holding the front edge of the wood. The panzer grenadiers took it over. The Tiger tanks moved forward with them.
>
> One of the German tanks got to within fifteen yards of the British command post. Major Roberts and Sergeant Hill tackled it with a PIAT, but the bomb failed to explode. The German tank then moved off. Others, however, continued manoeuvring all over the battalion area and having, as they doubtless believed, cleared the wood, they came up over the crest of the ridge on either side of the orchard and started moving down the northern slopes.
>
> It must have been two of these Tigers that crossed the plateau and moved down the British slope, moving blindly into the trenches of the Wiltshires. They did not open fire and no one thought they could be the enemy until Major Jeans saw the black cross. One Tiger crashed past Private Pipe, upsetting his mug of tea. It roared, a great blob in the darkness, "moving in the direction of the Somersets."

I dreamt I was in a tropical forest and huge trees were crashing down on me.

"Are you alright, sir ? Are you alright ?"

It was the corporal. A Tiger tank had come through the hedge and gone right over me, crushing my compass and binoculars which were laid out by my side. It had halted not far away—a darker patch in the night. I called for a two-inch mortar flare and took up the No 1 position on the gun.

Alas for Captain Perks's chance of knocking it out, the mortar flares had been left behind. The Tiger clanked uncertainly away into the night.

By midnight the battle for the little wood had settled down uncomfortably with the Cornish Light Infantry much reduced in numbers. They were holding one half of the wood and the panzer grenadiers were a hundred yards away along the bottom hedge. An optimistic report that the Kastenwäldchen was in German hands had sent the Tiger tanks back down the hill. Panzer Group West received a report that Hill 112 had been recaptured.

Just before midnight the commander of the 9th SS Hohenstaufen Panzer Grenadier Regiment [either *SS-Panzer-Grenadier-Regiment 19* or *SS-Panzer-Grenadier-Regiment 20*] arrived with the news that the divisional columns were meeting head-on with supply vehicles moving back from the front. In many of the narrow country lanes there was no room to pass. The panzer grenadiers had taken to their feet and were marching the last seven kilometres.

Battle and disorganisation follow each other just as night follows day. As at Maltot, so at the little wood on top of the hill, but with the added disadvantage that enemy bombardment and counter-attack had ushered in darkness to compound the confusion and uncertainty. The Cornishmen had been given no time to sort themselves out: one company was still missing and another was so weak from casualties that it was unable to take over the front edge of the wood as had been arranged. The battalion commander had about three hundred infantrymen; he had the battalion six-pounder anti-tank guns and four seventeen pounders of the Royal Artillery. It was very dark. There had been no chance to examine the lay of the land. The enemy was close by, with German machine-guns hammering the darkness with nervous strings of tracer from the far end of the wood.

All night long the artillery fire from both sides plastered the hill. "We got no sleep," said one of the panzer crewmen who was sitting it out at the foot of the hill. Zemlitz, the runner from 10th SS, said he went to sleep despite the continuous shell fire, he was so exhausted: "One of our mortar sections, firing at the greatest possible elevation into the little wood, gave it everything, but the *Engländer* [Englishmen] had moved in in strength."

The Duke of Cornwall's Light Infantry hung on, wondering what the dawn would bring. About three o'clock in the morning the panzer grenadiers of the 9th SS Hohenstaufen Division arrived and dug in on the German slope. Like the Cornishmen, they had had no sleep for over twenty-four hours.

It was the British who attacked first. With the first streaks of dawn fifteen Sherman tanks came suddenly into view from behind the British crest. They roared over the road, past the Calvary cross, and on along the track of the ancient Roman road to the little wood. The Scots Greys, for it was they, were working on the theory that the faster they went the less likely was the enemy to turn them into "Ronson Lighters."

They were answering the call of Lieutenant-Colonel James for help in turning those German machine-gunners out of the bottom end of the wood. It didn't take them long. The Germans had adopted their usual defence: small forward outposts with the bulk of the troops and the [tanks] held hidden on the reverse slope.

The growing light of dawn revealed a greater danger. Lieutenant-Colonel James had climbed a tall tree. He could see the low ground beyond: "Enemy infantry in large numbers forming up to attack!" was his shouted warning. He remained at his dangerously exposed vantage point to shoot the British artillery on to the target.

Back on the crest overlooking the village of Esquay an observation officer of the 94th Field Artillery was excitedly shouting orders to his battery five miles back at Cheux. The Western slope of 112 was alive with German infantry and [tanks].

The Germans attacked at 0615 hours. By that time the hill had all but disappeared in the smoke and dust of the artillery fire.

Leading the attack from the south was the company of Tiger tanks commanded by Untersturmfuehrer Martin Schroif. In a series of bounds, one lot of [tanks] covering the others, they climbed up the slope in a hail of shellfire. They rolled on past the panzer grenadiers, who looked up with unshaven, dusty sweat-covered faces and waved as the Tigers roared on. They were happy in the knowledge that they were not alone, that the [tanks] would sort it out for them. Schroif was three hundred yards from the Kastenwäldchen, where he had been during the attack the night before. Through the dust and smoke he saw the vague shapes of two Shermans. He fired twice in rapid succession and knocked them both out. He looked at his watch. It was twenty minutes to seven. Shellfire was falling. The British were mixing in more smoke. He pushed on towards the edge of the wood, where he knocked out a third Sherman tank and put several anti-tank guns out of action. Unterscharfuehrer (Corporal) Winter in [*Tiger*] No 232 was hit by an anti-tank gun firing from the northern edge of the plateau.

Tigers were also leading the attack up the hill from the Esquay side, using a sunken lane which gave some cover. A British spotting plane, a Lysander, was now circling in the skies above, sending targets back to the artillery. Within minutes a great barrage of shells had almost blotted out the slope. Trautmann, a wireless operator in one of the Tigers, has described the attack

> . . . shells were exploding on the hull and turret; they were breaking off the branches in the tree tops! Our panzer grenadiers couldn't even raise their heads. Many brave comrades were left dead on the slopes.

This advance from the west brought the German tanks to the large paddock extending beyond the wood. It was here that the remnants of the "lost" company of the Duke of Cornwall's Light Infantry had dug in. Wireless Operator Trautmann continues his account:

> On our left was an enclosure where our opponents were trying to bring an anti-tank gun into action. The crew was frantically pulling down the fence, and it was here that they suffered their first casualties. Brave they were, those Anglo-Saxons! In the meantime we had worked our way closer, and we quickly made the manhandling of that dark-brown gun a superfluous exercise!
>
> As the Tiger tank worked its way past the paddock and the wood beyond, it was fired at and hit several times by anti-tank guns. None of them penetrated. The Cornishmen were learning the dangerous way that they were wasting their time firing a six-pounder anti-tank gun at a Tiger tank. Neither this gun nor the 75 mm gun of a Sherman would penetrate the front armour of a Tiger, even at very close range.

The British were sending supplies across the plateau and bringing back the wounded. To hide this from the enemy they had laid a thick smoke screen. The Tiger tank pushed on cautiously:

> This smoke must come to an end soon—suddenly we were through! Scarcely a hundred yards in front of us the Tommies were getting out. Trucks and carriers were curving this way and that, loading and unloading. Our commander came through on the intercom "Armour-piercing-fire when ready! Hull machine-gun—fire when ready!" Two Shermans were standing on guard directly in front of us. Even as they were traversing their guns we sent them up in flames. All the time our company commander was coming through on the radio: "Pull back immediately! Pull back! Pull back level with the company!" [See above for more accurate translation of the German original. Note also that Trautmann's original account refers to these tanks as Churchills.]
>
> The Scots Greys had lost five of their Shermans. They were hopelessly outnumbered and outgunned by far heavier tanks. Only the Sherman Firefly with the seventeen-pounder gun had any chance at all against a Tiger. They retreated back over the British crest. From hull-down positions they continued to give what support they could.
>
> The Cornwalls were on their own again. The battalion dead lay everywhere. Amongst them was Lieutenant King killed whilst standing on an embankment to direct the artillery fire, hit, it seems, by shrapnel from the barrage he had himself brought down. Little could be done for the wounded. The Bren carriers had been destroyed whilst trying to get them back to safety. Just one of the Tiger tank companies claimed in its war diary to have destroyed eight of them. The same company claimed also the destruction of three anti-tank guns. Destroyed or not, it made little difference to the Cornishmen, who were unable to man them in the withering fire of the enemy [tanks]. Many anti-tank crewmen lay dead or wounded.
>
> The little wood was a conspicuous landmark, perched on top of the hill on the enemy side. It was a convenient size for the artillery to neutralise and steadily blow to pieces: "Their shells burst amongst the trees, throwing splinters downwards and searching out the narrow slits without head cover which was all in the way of defences that the troops had been able to dig for themselves." They watched from these holes in the ground, bleary-eyed from lack

of sleep, nerves twisted to the last turn, as one great Tiger tank after the other prowled round and round, throwing high-explosive into what was left of the trees and machine gunning anything that looked suspicious. It seemed to them that all was lost. It was only a matter of time. They would be overrun.

But the attacking panzer grenadiers, too, were in a bad state. They had been caught in the open by the killing power of the British artillery, "defensive fire such as we East Fronters had never known; the Russians had never [had] as many guns as this." The slopes leading up to the Kastenwäldchen were covered with German dead and wounded. The Tiger tanks might roam at will around the wood; only the panzer grenadiers could take it over. They were decimated, disorganised and demoralised, unable to move. Stalemate. The Germans were pulling back to think again.

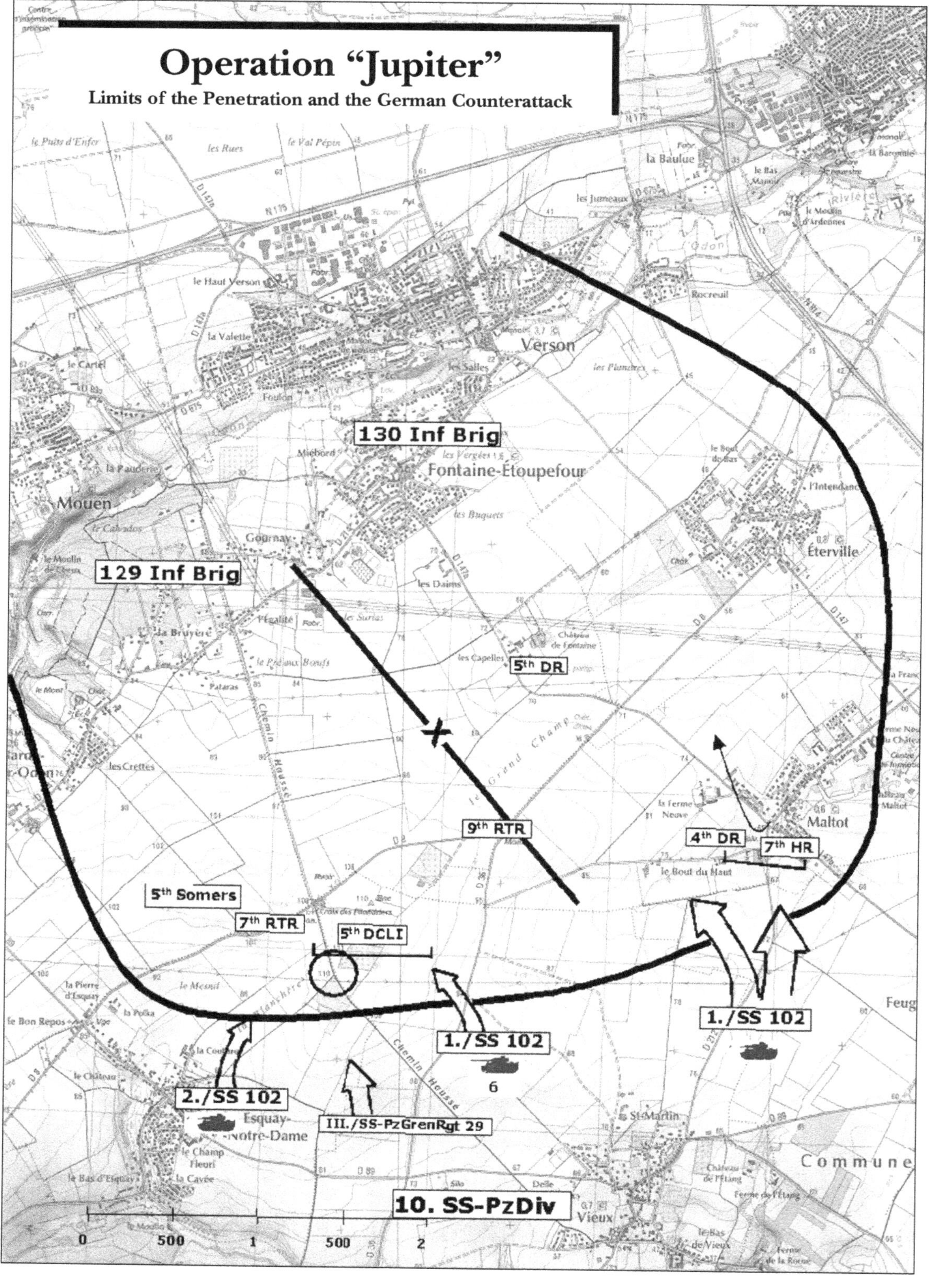
Operation "Jupiter"
Limits of the Penetration and the German Counterattack
130 Inf Brig
129 Inf Brig
5th DR
9th RTR
4th DR
7th HR
5th Somers
7th RTR
5th DCLI
1./SS 102
1./SS 102
6
2./SS 102
III./SS-PzGrenRgt 29
10. SS-PzDiv
Verson
Fontaine-Étoupefour
Mouen
Gournay
Éterville
Maltot
Esquay-Notre-Dame
Vieux
la Baulue
Rocreuil
le Haut Verson
la Valette
les Salles
le Cartel
Foulon
Mièbord
les Buquets
les Daims
la Bruyère
les Capelles
les Crettes
le Grand Champ
la Ferme Neuve
le Bout du Haut
le Mesnil
la Pierre d'Esquay
le Bon Repos
la Polka
le Château
le Champ Fleuri
la Cavée
le Bas d'Esquay
St-Martin
Commune
Feug
0 500 1 500 2

In the days that followed, the fighting raged with differing degrees of intensity for the high ground and the terrain between the Odon and the Orne. At the beginning, this fighting was supported by *Tigers* of *schwere SS-Panzer-Abteilung 101*; later on, this support was provided solely by *schwere SS-Panzer-Abteilung 102*. What remained of *schwere SS-Panzer-Abteilung 101* was moved to the area around Bretteville-sur-Laize (south of Caen) on 13 July 1944, where it was intended for it to assist in stabilizing the situation along the Bourguébus. The tough battles of attrition between the Odon and the Orne southwest of Caen lasted for the *Tigers* of *schwere SS-Panzer-Abteilung 102* until the end of July. The British XII Corps was able to perform its mission, which was to exert permanent pressure in this sector in order to prevent the withdrawal of as many potential German reserves as possible.

✠

Here is a detailed account of the continued operations in this area:

On 12 July 1944, *Tigers 212* and *214* were positioned in order to observe and screen Hill 112. Even before first light, portions of the high ground were again occupied by the British, because the German infantry outposts had to pull back from the hill due to the intense enemy artillery fire.

On the next day, *Tigers 212, 213* and *233* again occupied screening positions.

The 1st Company took Hill 112 again around 0400 hours. On its right was the 2nd Company. *Tiger 321* of the 3rd Company *102* was west of the hill; from the same company, the *Tiger* of *SS-Untersturmführer* Schienhofen was in St. Martin. He was joined in screening there by two *Tigers* of the 2nd Company. In all, there were twelve *Tigers* operational.

On 14 July 1944, two *Tigers* performed screening duties; there were nine operational tanks in all. Due to the threat of air attack, the 2nd Company moved to Amayé.

At the start of 15 July 1944, the situation remained unchanged. During the day, the British pounded the high ground with the heaviest of artillery fire. As a result, only the *Tigers* could remain on it. *Tiger 212* of *SS-Unterscharführer* Kuhlemann had to be sent to the rear after receiving a direct hit by artillery. An enemy attack at 2230 hours was turned back. At this point, only eight *Tigers* were operational.

On 16 July 1944, the 2nd Company bivouacked in a fruit orchard south of St. Martin, while one tank screened on Hill 112. Seven *Tigers* were still operational. Grenadiers from the *10. SS-Panzer-Division "Frundsberg"* dug in on the hill. The "Box Woods" had completely changed its appearance. Trees reduced to barren stumps by artillery fire rose skyward. From this point on, it was referred to as the *Wäldchen der halben Bäume* ("patch of woods of half trees"). The 1st Company was employed northwest of Maltot, where four Churchills were knocked out.

The *Tigers* were employed again on 17 July 1944 to screen.

The situation in the sector of the *2./schwere SS-Panzer-Abteilung 102* was stable on 18 July 1944. While screening, *Tiger 224* of *SS-Unterscharführer* Oberhuber knocked out three enemy tanks and an antitank gun towards evening. Only five *Tigers* were operational.

The 3rd Company was hit by a heavy bombing raid. Five of its seven tanks were hit and were unavailable for an extended period of time. The remaining two tanks were sent to the other two companies.

On 19 July 1944, it was quiet in the sector of the 2nd Company, which was screening. Eight tanks were again operational. English armored ambulances recovered the dead; German soldiers helped them.

Two British antitank guns that were brought forward on 20 July 1944 were knocked out by the screening tanks. At 2000 hours, the 2nd Company was relieved by the 1st Company. It then marched through Amayé and into the woods east of Lieu des Pres, where it received urgently needed rest.

✠

The most exposed and isolated of the British posts were those at the Le Bon Repos crossroads and the Maison Blanche farm five hundred yards farther up the hill. They had been captured a few nights earlier by the Glasgow Highlanders.

> Some men from the Welsh arrived one night and took over. With the light of dawn the Welshmen realised that they were in full view of the enemy who were in Esquay, four hundred yards down the road, and on the slopes on both sides. Any movement brought a sniper's bullet. They were imprisoned in their trenches all through the long summer day. Food in fourteen-man packs they collected at night. They tossed the tins from one trench to another, counted out the cigarettes and sweets, and looked thoughtfully at the sheets of toilet paper also provided, hoping that it would be only in the dark that the urge came to use it. Confined to their narrow trenches throughout the hours of daylight, they passed the time warming up the tins and making frequent brews of compo tea over the sickly fumes of a Tommy Cooker. From time to time there would be a diversion: the snout of a long 88mm gun would appear over the bald hump of the hill and the turret of the Tiger tank that owned it would come slowly into view. A couple of rounds would swoosh past leaving a vacuum that took the breath away and threatened to collapse the lungs.
>
> These Tommies who had pushed well forward into German territory and pinched the outposts were seen by the enemy as a provocation and a nuisance. 10th SS had taken over [*10. SS-Panzer-Division Frundsberg"*]. They would do something about it. One afternoon they attacked with assault groups of panzer grenadiers, six Tiger tanks and supporting artillery fire. The outpost at La Maison Blanche was quickly overrun. Some survivors escaped back over the crest to the safety of the British slope. The battle at Le Bon Repos, however, went on until well into the night. No one came back from there.

✠

The 21st of July 1944 was quiet. The 1st Company screened with some of it elements, the 2nd Company performed maintenance and the 3rd Company attempted to fix the damage caused by the air raid.

On 22 July 1944, the 2nd Company was alerted. It initially moved up to Amayé with eight tanks, where it received the mission to advance to Maltot along the road and to the right of it. Two *Tigers* were lost during the march. Heavy artillery fire started. Four Churchills that attempted to leave the village were knocked out.

SS-Sturmmann Trautmann has provided a first-hand account of this fighting:

> There were things going on in Maltot the entire night. You could make out movements with the binoculars. We were also able to

repeatedly ascertain the sound of tracks during the night.

A few *Tigers* got the mission to clear Maltot. Our tank commander ordered us to move out: "*Panzer marsch!*" We had scarcely left the vegetation when we transitioned to the attack. The humming noise in the headphones and the noise of the engine and the tracks drowned out the inferno outside.

Only dim light penetrated into the radio-operator's station from the [commander's] cupola. He could identify the face of the driver off to the left over the transmission. If the radio operator leaned back, he could see his tank commander up above in the cupola. The hatch was usually open, despite the heavy fire.

The Canadian-occupied village got closer and closer. Soon you were ale to see individual fighting positions between the trees and the bushes of the gardens by the houses. The artillery observer above, who was constantly following us, had reported our approach to his batteries a long time ago. They were then doing their part to ensure we were welcomed properly.

Impacting artillery rounds tossed up the dry earth, covered the buildings and turned over walls. When the clouds of dirt are ripped asunder, you can get a quick glimpse of the church tower, from which a tattered Red Cross flag was hanging from its highest opening.

Boy, an entire salvo of rounds was now coming over us! Our tank commander fidgeted up there impatiently on his seat, eyed with a quick glance our surroundings and issued a fire command to our gunner with his practiced calmness and exactitude: "Off to the left . . . 500 . . . muzzle flash!"

Albert traversed the turret. Four enemy tanks were rolling towards us on the road running perpendicular into us. Long hull; small, compact turret: Churchills. Our tank commander gave directions to only engage the first and then the last of the olive-green giants. Fire when ready!

The first Churchill was turning in place; it had been immobilized! While the radio operator was taking the dismounting crew in his sights, the second tank was already burning. Oil-black clouds of smoke blocked out the sun. The two middle tanks curved wildly about. They saw that they were boxed in on the road and had to go over the embankment. Their fate was quickly sealed: Tank number 3 received two hits in the hull above the running gear. No one climbed out. The final tank was eliminated with two rounds in the rear. Seconds later, fine, white smoke climbed out of the hatches. With a terrible bang, the rear deck hatches weighing hundreds of pounds flew into the air. A stream of flames shot out of the engine compartment; it soon hit the ammunition as well.

Suddenly, there were small, black explosive puffs above the ground in front of us! Immediately following that was a radio message directed to us: "Watch out! AT on the edge of the woods!"

We reacted as quick as lightning: "more to the right . . . more to the right . . . quicker!" Then: "A touch left . . . stop!" The turret traversed with a slight humming noise. Kaboom! The concussion from the main guns snapped our heads back. Another two rounds and then we continued.

The fire slowly abated, but close-air-support aircraft then appeared and plastered us with their rockets.

"Button up!"

We had been running around for three hours. In the meantime, a few *Tigers* had gone around Maltot. We could figure out from the radio traffic that we could advance no further. One *Tiger* had received a few antitank-gun rounds. Two of the crew were wounded. We had to wait until the patch of woods that flanked us was cleared.

The attempts by the grenadiers to eliminate the antitank-gun belt were not crowned with success. The efforts of several *Tigers* in flanking positions to fire into Maltot also did not help. As a result, the *Tigers* had to withdraw in the fading light of day.

The 2nd Platoon eliminated three antitank guns on the northern edge of Feugerolles-sur-Orne. During the night, the forces transitioned to screening operations 600 meters north of Feugerolles at the fork in the road 600 meters south of the church at Maltot. Seven *Tigers* of the 1st Company were employed on Hill 112 and engaged the infantry of the 5th Wiltshire Regiment that were hard north of Maltot. The regiment had retaken the town on this day.

On 23 July 1944, eight *Tigers* of the 2nd Company were in position. In the morning, they turned back a British tank attack; six enemy tanks were knocked out. Two additional British tanks were also knocked out by the 1st Company, which was employed to the left. After German infantry had closed up, the tanks were pulled back to a covered position 200 meters behind the main line of resistance. One *Tiger* continued to screen at the northern exit of Feugerolles. *Tiger 214* of *SS-Unterscharführer* Kuhlemann suffered running gear damage after it was hit by artillery.

On 24 July 1944, eight Churchills attempted an advance on St. Martin from Maltot; all eight were destroyed by the tanks of the 1st Company.

The 2nd Platoon of the 2nd Company supported an attack east of the Orne from positions northeast of Feuguerolles. This support met with limited success, since visibility was limited and the engagement range was too great.

On 25 July 1944, the 2nd Company continued to screen as it had previously done and engaged enemy movements on Hill 67 and on the northern outskirts of St. André-sur-Orne. Three enemy tanks and four antitank guns were eliminated. A large swarm of medium bombers plowed up Hill 112 and the terrain as far as St. Martin. Following them, large numbers of fighter-bombers swooped in. The *Tigers* were peppered with harmless hits. As if a miracle, there were no losses among the screening tanks. The results would have most certainly been different with the more lightly armored *Panzer IV*. The 3rd Company relieved the 1st Company on Hill 112. The latter company then encamped at Cropton.

The 26th of July 1944 saw the 1st Company employed against enemy movements on Hill 67 and on the northern outskirts of St. André-sur-Orne from positions west of Feuguerolles. Again, three enemy tanks and four antitank guns were knocked out. One *Tiger*, that of *SS-Unterscharführer* Oberhuber, was penetrated on the driver's side by a flank shot from an antitank gun. The crew bailed out; the driver was killed and the radio operator lost an arm.

The situation remained unchanged for the 2nd Company. In the morning, it opened fire numerous times against the enemy east of the Orne.

The days that followed were relatively quiet; a portion of the tanks continued to screen.

The operations of this battalion at the end of July 1944 were intentionally covered in more detail in order to demonstrate that there was not a constant stream of large-scale operations. But it was just these numerous skirmishes and pinprick enemy actions that ended up being so grueling on the crews. In addition, there were the constant barrages that were built into the artillery harassment fire plans as well as the obligatory attacks from close-air-support aircraft. The crews were constantly in a state of anxiety; they did not know when large-scale attacks would come. In the time remaining when they were not involved in active operations, they had to work on their tanks, which had also been placed under duress due to the constant wear and tear and battle damage, in order to keep them operational. The numerous bits of artillery shrapnel and automatic weapons fire of the fighter-bombers led to frequent mechanical problems, for example, when air ventilator blades were damaged or coolant leaked out.

On 1 August 1944, *schwere SS-Panzer-Abteilung 102* was pulled from the line and moved into the area around Vire and to the east of it in order to support the *9. SS-Panzer-Division "Hohenstaufen."* We will discuss this operation later. In the meantime, let us take a look at the situation as it developed on the other end of the area of operations in question, the area to the east of Caen.

Every battalion had a reconnaissance platoon that was usually equipped with the *Sd.Kfz. 251*, such as seen here.

A *Tiger* of *schwere SS-Panzer-Abteilung 102* that was knocked out on 10 July 1944. It can be identified by the *Blitzrune* ("lightning rune") on the rear hull. Below: In between operations, the tanks had to be camouflaged carefully so as not to be identified by the enemy aircraft that were constantly in the air.

This sequence of photographs shows the 1st Company of *schwere Panzer-Abteilung 503. Pz.Kpfw. VI Ausf. B* (King Tiger) preparing to rail load at Eisenach. The crews are replacing the regular tracks with "transport" tracks, designed to allow the tanks to pass railroad maximum-width requirements.

The last image shows a tank crew still in a relaxed mode during the rail movement. There is an air guard posted next to the main gun, but the driver has time to read a newspaper. All of that would soon change. It was more than three weeks later before the battalion arrived in Normandy. As the sketch map below demonstrates, this battalion also had to undergo an arduous road march that lasted for days.

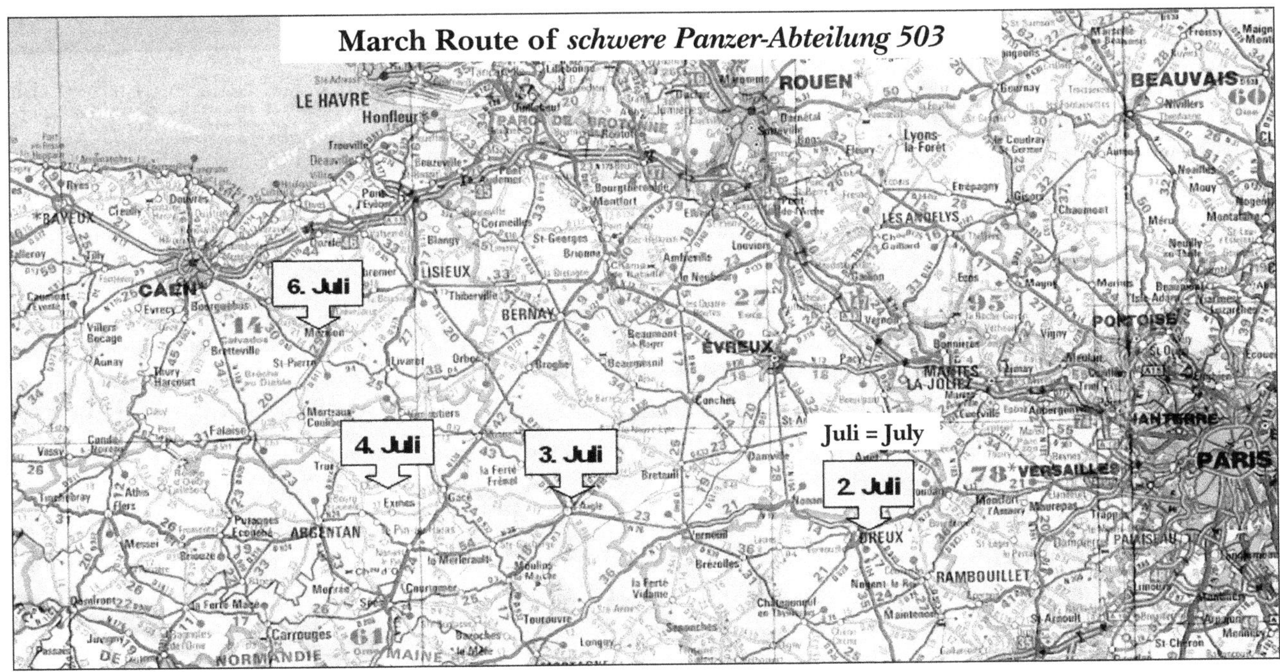

CHAPTER 6

Arrival of the Third Tiger Battalion

On 26 and 27 June 1944, *schwere Panzer-Abteilung 503* was loaded on eight trains and dispatched in the direction of the Invasion Front. As a result of the systematic Allied air attacks on the rail networks, especially in France, the transport trains frequently had to be detoured. They did not reach the designated railheads of Houdan and Dreux, some 70 kilometers west of Paris, until 2 and 3 July.

The battalion's companies moved to their future area of operations east of Caen via Verneuil, L'Aigle, Argentan and Falaise in a series of night marches. Road marches during the day were impossible due to Allied fighter-bomber activity. The battalion moved every night from 2300 to 0300 hours, at which time it took up concealed positions in some woods. Another leg of the march was conducted the following night. During the last nighttime road march, the first vehicle was lost. This was on 3 July and in the 3rd Company. A bridge over a railway cut collapsed under the weight of the tank in the vicinity of the village of Canon (near Mezidon). *Tiger 323* of *Feldwebel* Seidel crashed onto the rail line. In the process, it received such severe damage that it could no longer be repaired, even though it was recovered. Without a shot being fired, the company suffered its first complete loss and its first injured soldiers on the Normandy Front.

Schwere Panzer-Abteilung 503 was allocated to the *LXXXVI. Armee-Korps* and was initially placed under the operational control of the *16. Luftwaffen-Feld-Division*. On the previous day, the *Luftwaffe* field division had taken over the sector of the *21. Panzer-Division*. After the heavy losses that this *Luftwaffe* division took on the following day in the fighting for Caen, its sector was taken back by the *21. Panzer-Division* on 8 July 1944. *Schwere Panzer-Abteilung 503* was then placed under the operational control of *Panzer-Regiment 22*, the division's tank regiment. At this point in time, *Panzer-Regiment 22* had only one battalion, and it was issued with *Panzer IV's*. The regimental commander was *Oberst* von Oppeln-Bronikowski; the commander of the *I./Panzer-Regiment 22* was *Hauptmann* von Gottberg. Together with *schwere Panzer-Abteilung 503*, the tank regiment's sole battalion formed the immediate armored reserve of the division. The *Tiger* battalion was assigned an assembly area east of Troarn; the battalion commander was directed to report to Troarn daily for a meeting in the evening with the regimental commander.

Up to the point of arrival of the battalion in its new area of operations, the situation had developed as follows in the invasion front:

With growing losses, twenty-one divisions of the *Wehrmacht* were defending between the mouth of the Orne and the west coast of the Cotentin Peninsula—a frontage of 140 kilometers. The British had held a 25-square-kilometer bridgehead (approximately 15.5 square miles) east of the Orne since the start of the invasion. A cohesive front line and corresponding well-established positions were not available. As a result of constant local attacks, defensive successes and fixing operations, the forward-most lines were in a constant state of flux. The Allies had not yet been able to achieve a decisive breakthrough. It was clear to everyone, however, that this is exactly what they would attempt to achieve.

On 8 July 1944, the Battle for Caen started. As ordered, the German forces evacuated the city on the night of 9–10 July 1944 and pulled the front back to the east bank of the Orne River. Consequently, the southeast march routes out of the city were in German hands, and they blocked any further Allied advance into the Falaise plain.

The increasing artillery activity in the days that followed, under which *schwere Panzer-Abteilung 503* also had to suffer, and the attempts to expand the Orne bridgehead all pointed to an imminent British attack. Where would it take place? It was considered improbable that the enemy attack would proceed directly from Caen, since it would mean a contested river crossing over the Orne. An attack to the south or southeast from out of the Orne bridgehead appeared more likely.

✠

By order of *Panzergruppe West* on 9 July 1944, the *I./Panzer-Regiment 22* and *schwere Panzer-Abteilung 503* were brought forward into the rear of the main battle area. This was contrary to the recommendations of both of the battalion commanders, the *21. Panzer-Division* and the *LXXXVI. Armee-Korps*. From this point forward, the *Tiger* battalion was located only a few kilometers behind the main line of resistance at the eastern Orne bridgehead.

The headquarters of *schwere Panzer-Abteilung 503* moved to Emiéville. The *1./schwere Panzer-Abteilung 503* was southeast of this village, as were the companies of the *I./Panzer-Regiment 22*. The *2./schwere Panzer-Abteilung 503* encamped northeast of Emiéville, and the *3./schwere Panzer-Abteilung 503* was in a patch of woods on the land belonging to the stud farm at Maneville, some 2.5 kilometers from the battalion command post.

✠

During the second week of July, the battalion commander, *Hauptmann* Fromme, had to be admitted to the military hospital in Paris for approximately ten days as the result of an inflammation of his eye, which had been previously injured in combat. In his absence, *Hauptmann* Scherf assumed acting command of the battalion, with *Leutnant* von Rosen assuming his place in command of the 3rd Company. The companies conducted reconnaissance of the potential future areas of operation so that they would be prepared for all eventualities. One of the tank companies of the battalion was always on rotation as an "alert" company, which meant that it had to be ready to move out at a moment's notice for a twenty-four hour period. For the time being, however, it remained quiet at the front.

✠

On 11 July 1944, the waiting period was over; the battalion would experience its first test in Normandy.

The 3rd Company was alerted around 0530 hours. After a short but intense artillery preparation, British tanks and Canadian infantry had broken through the main line of resistance between Cuverville and Colombelles. They then took the high ground north of the industrial complex of Colombelles. *Luftwaffen-Jäger-Regiment 32*, which had been in position there, had withdrawn to Cuverville. This opened the road to Giberville and the area east of Caen to the enemy.

As a result of the immediate counterattack launched by the 3rd Company from Giberville to the north, the former main line of resistance could be reoccupied without any battalion losses. Eleven Shermans and four antitank guns were destroyed; two Shermans were captured without damage and sent to the German rear. After *Luftwaffen-Jäger-Regiment 32* reoccupied its positions late in the afternoon, the *Tiger* company was pulled out of the line and sent back to the assembly area at Maneville.

Leutnant Freiherr von Rosen has provided the following firsthand account of this operation:

> Be prepared to move out immediately . . . I was personally ordered to the battalion command post. I issued my orders quickly, briefed *Leutnant* Koppe and was taken to the command post on the motorcycle. There I was briefed on the situation: The enemy had succeeded with tank and infantry forces in overrunning the main line of resistance at Colombelles, which was being held there by a battalion from the *16. Luftwaffen-Feld-Division.* The last reports received from up front indicated that the enemy was already some three kilometers northwest of Giberville. A large concentration of armor had been observed. Speed was of the essence. I received the following mission: The 3rd Company was to eliminate the enemy forces that had broken through in an immediate counterattack; restore the former main line of resistance; and hold this position until further orders were received.

At the company's location, the tank engines had already been warmed up; the tank commanders were waiting at the commander's tank for my return from the command post. Briefing the tank commanders went quickly; just thirty minutes after being alerted, the company was moving at high speed towards Giberville. I moved ahead of the company, established contact with the forces on the northern outskirts of the village and, from the roof gable, had good fields of observation into the terrain to be attacked. A few of the enemy tanks could be easily identified in a farmstead that was two kilometers away.

I moved back to the company and informed it of the latest situation. Then: "*Panzer marsch*, prepare to engage!" The first tank (*Leutnant* Koppe) had barely reached the northern outskirts of the village, when it started to receive intense main-gun fire. There was a slight hesitation, then the company spread out.

The 1st Platoon under *Feldwebel* Sachs veered off to the left and the 2nd Platoon (*Leutnant* Koppe) to the right, while I remained on line with the two platoons. The 3rd Platoon (*Leutnant* Rambow) stayed behind me. In the course of executing this maneuver, the tanks received a considerable number of hits. At this distance, they could do little damage to us. I then issued the order by radio to initiate bounding by platoons. This meant one platoon provided cover and fired, while the other platoon advanced.

There was no reaction to my order, however. I radioed it again. Still, nothing stirred. Instead, my tanks were exchanging fire with the enemy. In our case, nothing much could happen because of the great distance; in the case of the enemy, however, the effect of our fires was easy to recognize in the form of thick, black clouds of smoke.

When nothing continued to stir among our ranks, I threatened by radio to traverse my turret to six o'clock and fire to the rear, if everyone did not move out immediately.

While this was happening, enemy tanks were hitting my tank the entire time. Then I saw through the vision slot of my commander's cupola that my tank's antenna had been shot off and no radio messages could be transmitted. At this point, it was clear why my orders had not been executed. I then had my tank bound forward 300 meters and, when I looked around, I saw to my satisfaction that the 1st Platoon following me, while the 2nd and 3rd Platoons continued to fire. And then we conducted the attack without radio traffic; all of the movements were done as if on auto-pilot. One platoon fired and covered; the other one took a bound forward.

There wasn't too much more to be seen of the enemy tanks, because the farmstead, where they had set up, was a single black cloud of smoke.

Then the enemy infantry also withdrew under cover of artificial smoke. When the smoke allowed a little more visibility, I saw a few enemy tanks left. Another Sherman went up in flames with every round fired from our main guns from this extremely short distance to the enemy. The crews even left their intact tanks in panic and terror. We received no more fire, and the last 200 meters were covered in a single bound. We were at the farm and had reached the former main line of resistance. All of this took perhaps thirty minutes.

I set up the company to screen; the terrain offered little cover. We had barely completed these movements, when an aerial artillery observer appeared overhead. Shortly thereafter, we were plastered with a barrage from the artillery that left you stunned.

This lasted about two or three minutes, then it became quiet again. We moved our location from time to time—sometimes 500 meters forward, sometimes 500 meters to the rear—so as to avoid the artillery fire, which covered us again with the next salvo twenty minutes later. We were out there on the serving platter for nearly eight hours before the infantry came up and occupied its old positions.

My tank received a direct hit from the artillery. Thank God, the English used sensitive fuses and, thank God, the turret armor had been reinforced with a second armored plate shortly before we had left Germany. All of us in the tank were knocked about quite a bit. The lights went out, and we were all affected for a few moments.

With regard to the tank itself, a few weld seams had been ripped open, with the result that I had to get into another tank. During one of the longer breaks in the artillery fire, I took a closer look at the enemy tanks. Twelve Shermans were burnt out. Most of them had 75-millimeter main guns; a few of them had the more modern 17-pounder (Sherman II "Firefly"). Four 57-millimeter antitank guns had been destroyed.

I then discovered two completely untouched Shermans between the buildings of the farm. When they had attempted to turn around, they had collided and the crews had then abandoned them. One of the tanks was a command tank, and I found a whole handful of marked-up maps, signals instructions, orders, etc. I then went with them on the shortest route to the battalion command post, which was temporarily located on the rail line at Démouville.

It was there that *Hauptmann* Fromme had arrived in the course of the morning from the hospital in Paris. When I made my report to him, I received the mission of bringing both Shermans back, if possible. I went back up front and arrived just as the infantry arrived and relieved us. *Leutnant* Koppe led the company back to its old encampment at Maneville, where everyone disappeared into the same holes they had occupied previously. I stayed up front with my tank and two drivers of the maintenance section. After we tried for some time, we actually got both Shermans running and freed up again.

We moved the two Shermans, escorted by a *Tiger*, back under the eyes of the English, who were able to see all this from not too great a distance. We considered this a triumph. But we were not allowed to be triumphant for too long. With the exception of a few artillery attacks, the next few days were quiet. There were more and more indicators, however, that pointed to a large-scale attack on the part of the English. After our success on 11 July, we thought we would be able to deal with it—but we really had no idea what lay before us . . .

In the first assembly area occupied in Normandy—in this instance, the 1st Company in the woods near Chateau Cantaloupe—the tanks were still outside artillery range. (*BA*)

The same vantage point, separated by more than sixty-five years. In the woods off to the viewer's left, traces can still be found of tanks that parked there off the trail. (*BA*)

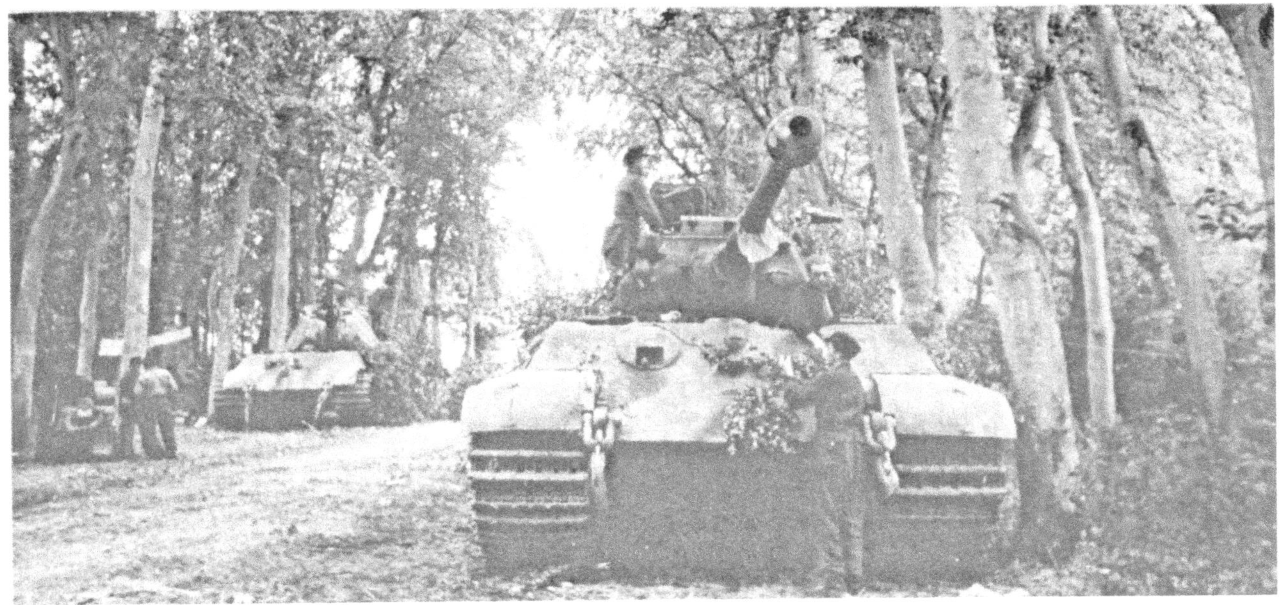

One of two tanks from the 1st Company to park in the woods can be seen in the lower photograph. (*BA*)

Two English prisoners of war are put to use distributing rations in the assembly area. Two days later, they were sent to a prisoner-of-war camp in Germany. (*BA*)

The approach march continued under cover of darkness. In these images, we see the 3rd Company marching through the village of Magny-la-Champagne. (*BA*)

NW

C1

The view from Cuverville towards modern-day Colombelles shows that the *Tigers* had to cross a large stretch of open terrain. The industrial areas had already suffered considerably as a result of the previous fighting.

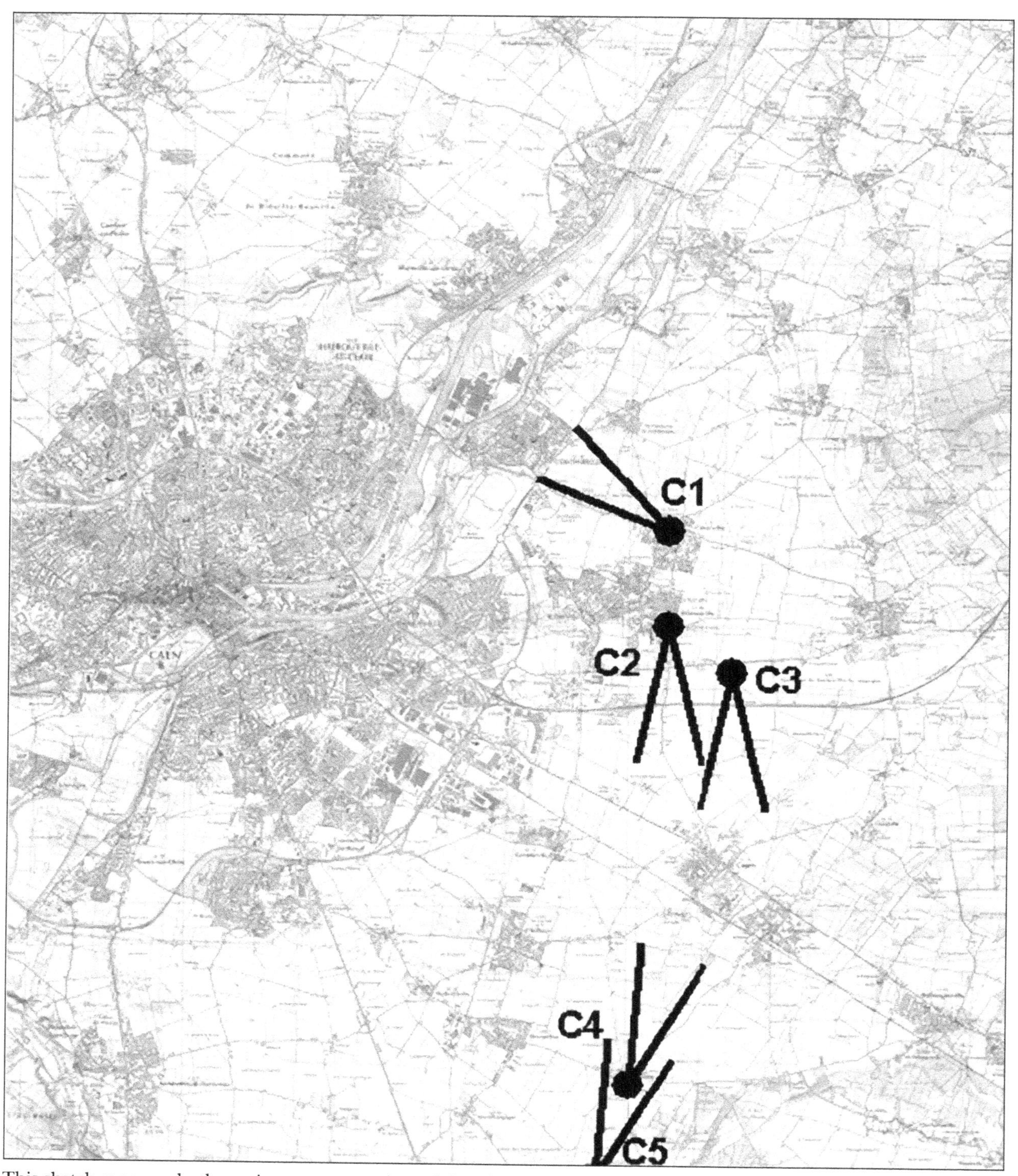

This sketch map marks the various vantage points of the photographs taken to illustrate the attack on Colombelles (C1), the British viewpoint from the line of departure for the attack (C2 and C3) and the German vantage point for the same attack (C4 and C5).

View from Démouville to the south, that is, from the enemy's location coming out of the bridgehead (Banneville is the leading group of buildings). It can be seen how far the attack objective—the ridgeline at Bourguébus—is from the line of departure. In the lower photograph, the view is from the Sannerville–Démouville road in the direction of Cagny, which is easily identifiable by the water tower in the middle of the image. Cagny was halfway to the Bourguébus ridgeline and was to prove to be a bulwark of the German defenses that was difficult to crack.

The British were able to advance past Manneville quickly. At that point, the broken terrain and depressions favored the employment of German flat-trajectory weapons, which could fire at short range. In addition, attacks in the flanks by *schwere Panzer-Abteilung 503*—initially by the 3rd Company and, later, by the 1st Company—caused considerable losses among the British. The view from the German side from Four (above) and Bourguébus (below) shows how the attack area slopes down. Also of note is the railway line that runs across the direction of attack just south of Cagny, which can only be crossed in a few places. Consequently, the defenders were afforded numerous opportunities to deliver flanking fires.

CHAPTER 7

The Hell of Operation "Goodwood"

After *schwere Panzer-Abteilung 503* left a lasting impression on the British on 11 July 1944, the *Tiger* crews were understandably in a good mood. The German tanks had proven superior in a tank-on-tank engagement, and the armor leaders on the other side had proven too cautious.

It proved at cross purposes, however, that the assembly areas of the battalion were located within engagement range of the enemy artillery. This questionable measure was justified by saying that bringing the tanks forward at the start of the attack would scarcely be possible when the expected enemy offensive started with its corresponding preparation through aerial attacks and wide-ranging naval artillery.

A similar discussion at operational level had taken place even before the invasion started, e.g., between *Generalfeldmarschall* Rommel and *General der Panzertruppen* Geyr von Schweppenburg. This discussion resulted in almost all of the German armored formations being held considerably to the rear. But that which is expedient at the operational level does not necessarily hold true at the lower tactical level.

Today we are familiar with the events of 18 July 1944 and how this deployment close to the front was quite certainly an incorrect decision.

In expectation of the enemy offensive east of the Orne, *Generalfeldmarschall* Rommel, the commander-in-chief of *Heeresgruppe B,* visited the Orne area during the afternoon of 15 July 1944. He visited first the *346. Infanterie-Division,* then the *16. Luftwaffen-Feld-Division* and, finally, the *21. Panzer-Division.* He was briefed by the leaders on the situation and the organization of the forces. Details concerning countermeasures for the expected offensive were discussed.

During the discussions at the command post of *Generalmajor* Feuchtinger (*21. Panzer-Division*) at Billy (4.5 kilometers southwest of Argences), the 6th of June and the missed opportunities on that fateful day became the topic of conversation once again. The field marshal complained that the *21. Panzer-Division* had been echeloned too far to the rear. Rommel overlooked the fact—or simply did not want to see—that he could have determined from the map where the elements of the *21. Panzer-Division* were during his visits of 11 and 18 May 1944. Rommel could have effected change quickly through the issuance of clear orders.

Generalmajor Feuchtinger sought to vindicate himself and pointed out an order from *Panzergruppe West,* which he had followed, to explain the positioning of his division. For his part, Feuchtinger complained that elements of his division were attached to the *716. Infanterie-Division* on 6 June 1944. The latter division had moved *Panzer-Jäger-Abteilung 200* against his will from the area north of Caen to the west.

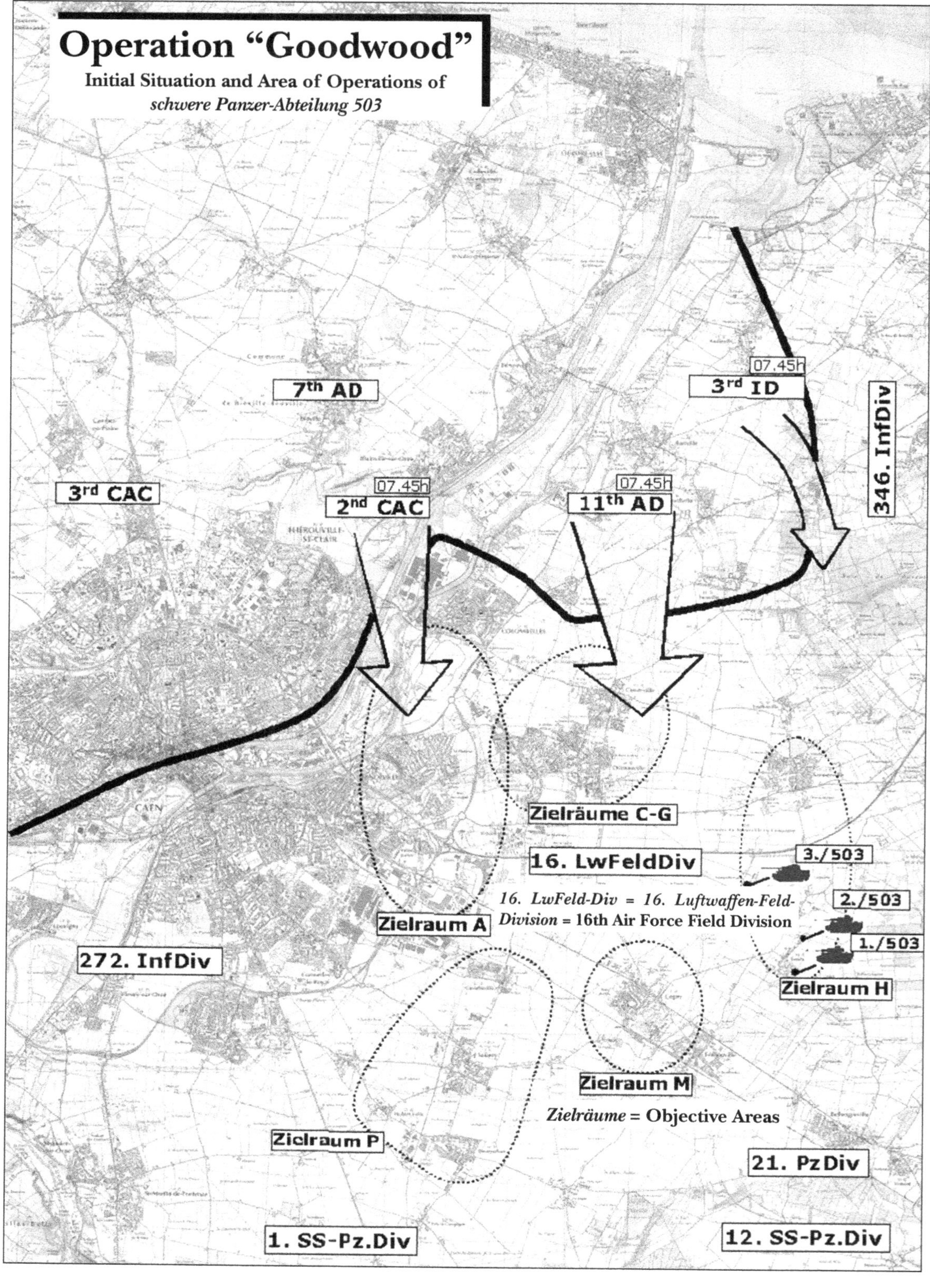
Operation "Goodwood"
Initial Situation and Area of Operations of
schwere Panzer-Abteilung 503
07.45h
3rd ID
346. InfDiv
7th AD
3rd CAC
07.45h
2nd CAC
07.45h
11th AD
Zielräume C-G
16. LwFeldDiv
3./503
16. LwFeld-Div = 16. Luftwaffen-Feld-Division = 16th Air Force Field Division
2./503
1./503
Zielraum A
272. InfDiv
Zielraum H
Zielraum M
Zielräume = Objective Areas
Zielraum P
21. PzDiv
1. SS-Pz.Div
12. SS-Pz.Div

The commander-in-chief of *Heeresgruppe B* then pointedly complained about the personal absence of the divisional commander in those decisive first hours of the invasion. The field marshal was in a position in which he did not have to justify his own absence. By 15 July 1944—the seventh week of the lost battle to stop the invasion—all of this discussion certainly made little sense.

All the same, *Generalfeldmarschall* Rommel depicted the overall strategic situation without pulling any punches in a letter to *Generalfeldmarschall* von Kluge, the commander-in-chief in the West. His letter ended with the words: "Our forces are fighting heroically at every location, however, the unequal struggle is drawing to a close. I must ask you to draw your own conclusions from this situation."

On the afternoon of 17 July 1944, *Generalfeldmarschall* Rommel was badly wounded during his return from a visit with the *I. SS-Panzer-Korps* during a strafing attack at St. Foy-de-Montgomery (*nomen est omen*?). A few hours before the start of the British offensive, he became a casualty. Von Kluge assumed command of *Heeresgruppe B* as well.

On 17 July 1944, the commander-in-chief of *Panzergruppe West*, *General der Panzertruppen* Eberbach, reported to the commander-in-chief West that his armored forces were facing an imminent British attack. Enemy concentrations were being reported east of the Orne, in Caen and in the area between Noyers and Vendes to the west of Caen. The request for more personnel and equipment and the introduction of fresh formations was categorically turned down by *Generalfeldmarschall* von Kluge, who stated that there was absolutely nothing left.

The British forces in question were the newly formed British VIII Corps, which had relieved the British XII Corps in the Odon sector. It probably does not need to be emphasized that the British casualties suffered during Operation "Epsom" had immediately been made good, in contrast to the Germans.

Because the enemy had carefully camouflaged his approach march and kept his tanks in the area north of Caen and west of the Orne until the last moment, *Panzergruppe West* was not certain when and where the attack would take place. Quite to the surprise of the German forces at the front, there were two substantial German air attacks against enemy concentrations on the Orne during this time period.

How did all this shape up from the point of view of the employment of the *Tigers*?

Montgomery had already received a bloody nose several times with his massed attacks west of Caen (Hill 112, among other locations) and also east of it. In spite of oppressive superiority and also acute losses on the German side, the British had not been able to succeed in making the decisive breakout out of the invasion area. It was intended to finally bring this about as the result of a special effort.

Field Marshal Montgomery, seen here with Prime Minister Churchill, wanted to force the decision and finally break out of the bridgehead. For the first time, he committed three entire armored divisions.

To this end, it was intended for three complete armored divisions—an operational first—to bring the exhausted British and Canadian infantry forward. They would move out of the bridgehead on the Orne *en masse.* Another factor of note was the willingness to establish new "standards" with regard to air and ground-based fire preparations. Air support of a hitherto unknown extent was assembled after the target catalog of the strategic air forces of both the British and the Americans was effectively exhausted for the express purpose of supporting Montgomery's field-army group. Never before had such a concentration of bombs been dropped on such a small area. A few numbers should make this clear.

From 0545 to 0630 hours on 18 July 1944, no less than 1,056 British heavy bombers (Lancasters and Halifaxes) bombed target area "A" (eastern edge of Caen), "H" (Sannerville to Emiéville) and "M" (Cagny). From 0700 to 0730 hours, 529 US medium bombers attacked target areas "C" to "G" (the breakthrough area running from Cuverville—Giberville—Démouville—Mandeville). The final attack was formed by 482 American bombers, which attacked target area "P" (Bourguébus—Hubert-Folie—Grentheville). In all, some 7,800 tons of bombs were dropped by 2,077 aircraft. By way of comparison: Dresden was attacked by "only" 1,084 bombers in February 1945, which dropped 3,425 tons of bombs.

In terms of artillery support, there were 720 medium and heavy guns with up to 250,000 shells available for firing. The artillery preparation started at 0630 hours and lasted more than an hour. Not included in these totals are the light artillery and the mortars that were used for direct fire support.

In addition, several hundred fighter-bombers, which were always in the skies during the day anyway, need to be counted as well.

It is important to mention that bombs with fragmentation effect were employed in the actual breakthrough sector, whereas heavy high-explosive bombs were used elsewhere. The British wanted to avoid serious restrictions on armored movement as a result of the formation of large craters. They had already made this discovery to their detriment in a few previous operations.

Finally, thirty-three artillery regiments of all calibers as well as naval artillery were employed.

The devastating effect of such area bombardments of this duration on the forces in position and the tank crews can scarcely be judged by those who were not there. The statements of those effected, such as the one by former *Leutnant Freiherr* von Rosen, the acting company commander of the *3./schwere Panzer-Abteilung 503*, speak for themselves. The same also applies to the pictures of tanks that were hit:

> I was in the position we had dug out under my *Tiger 311* with *Unteroffizier* Werkmeister. Although it was a bit cooler there, it was more comfortable than in the tank. The remaining three members of the crew were sleeping in the tank. On 18 July, I was awakened at about 0600 hours by the intense noise of engines in the air. Still half asleep, I heard the sound of falling bombs. They hit about 200 meters in front of us, but the concussion was so strong that the tank shook. It was immediately clear to me that the attack was aimed at us, but there was no time to think about it. The air was filled with the rushing of the falling bombs, and I instinctively pressed firmly against the ground. Then came the ear-bursting crash

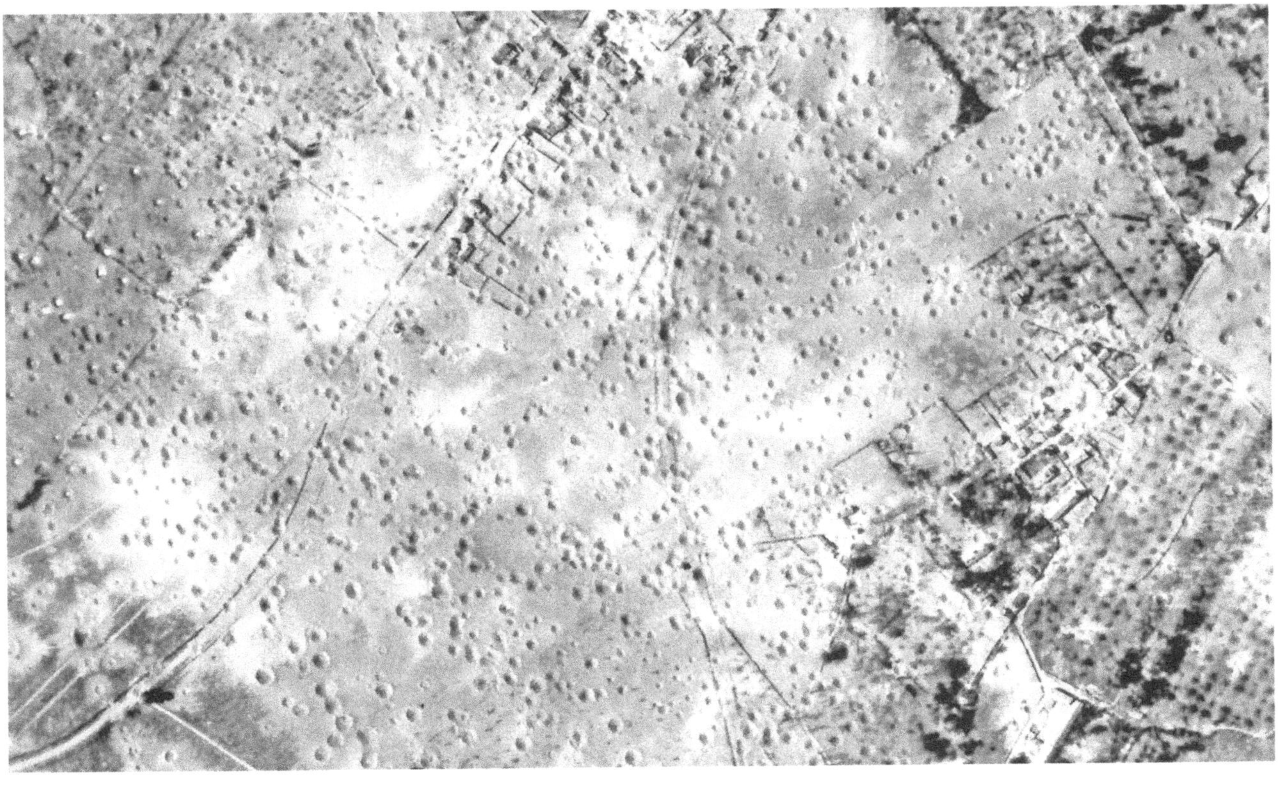

of the detonation. The earth heaved, but I was not yet hit. I was still alive. And then, again, I heard the rush of the falling bombs and again the detonations. I felt completely helpless against that power, there was no escaping, I could not think of anything at all. I have no idea how long that lasted. All conception of time was lost.

Suddenly, *Unteroffizier* Werkmeister and I were thrown into a corner by the concussion. I was completely covered with earth and lay, unconscious, for a while, until the slow return of consciousness and the realization I was still alive. But then the next bombs came and with them, the realization that this was not all a bad dream, but that, at that instant, I truly had no choice but to let that firestorm engulf me again. As I remember, it lasted—with short pauses—a good two and a half hours. It is hardly possible to describe that period of time with words. I only know that I lay under my tank, held my ears and bit the blanket so as not to scream. Finally the attack seemed to come to an end. As I crept out from under the tank . . . what a picture!

Of that once so beautiful park, all that were left were splintered trees that lay every which way, plowed up meadows and gigantic bomb craters that were so numerous that they overlapped each other. It was a gray, hostile moonscape enveloped in an impenetrable dust cloud that made it hard to breathe. Trees were on fire, as were the fields of grain, and one saw the red reflection of the fires in the thick clouds of smoke. I went to the tank beside me, *Unteroffizier* Westerhausen's tank. It had taken a direct hit and tongues of flame played in the wreckage. There was no trace left of the crew. I worked my way through the craters and over giant trees, through a true primeval forest, and then got to *Oberfeldwebel* Sachs's tank. In front of it there was a giant crater. The tank had been tossed by the concussion and lay on its turret, the running gear in the air. We found two of the crew, dead, and no trace of the others. Two excellent men of the company maintenance section had been killed. They, too, had sought refuge under that tank.

I immediately ordered the tanks readied for action. First they had to be shoveled free, since they were covered in earth right up to the turrets. Trees had been toppled onto them, tracks torn off—how were we to ever get the company ready for action? The work had to be broken off frequently, because the naval artillery began to register on us with heavy 42 cm [16 inch] rounds. At that point I also noticed that, 15 meters in front of my tank, there was a 6- or 8-meter-deep crater in which the *Tiger* could have easily fitted. The heavy armor plate on the rear of the tank was severely deformed, as if a shell had struck it. The concussion had torn off the engine's radiator. It is still unclear to me today what could have caused that. In any case, my tank was unserviceable and I had to change tanks yet again.

Our situation became ever more uncomfortable. We could hear tank and machine-gun fire at a short distance. Had the British already gotten as far as our position? It was impossible to establish communications with the battalion. So I set out on foot to try to accomplish that. Leaping from crater to crater, diving for cover at every on-rushing salvo, I reached the route to Emiéville. Fewer bombs had fallen there, and I was able to make better progress. Around a curve in the road, *Tiger "I"* approached me with the commander in it. The carpet bombing had also hit the area of the battalion command post, but the attack had not been as intense there as it had been at the location of the 3rd Company. The battalion commander, *Hauptmann* Scherf, and the officers and soldiers of the battalion staff survived the carpet bombing packed tight together in the narrow winding staircase in the steeple of the building. The building itself was demolished, but the steeple remained standing.

I received orders from the battalion commander to set out with the 3rd Company as rapidly as possible and form a defensive front on the left flank of the attack corridor at the buildings of the stud farm at Mandeville. It might have been 1000 hours, perhaps even later, when we finally had six tanks ready. They were ready for a maintenance facility, but at least they could move and bring their weapons to bear. It was difficult to find a route through the sea of craters without having a tank slip into a gigantic hole. But we succeeded and, after a 1.5 kilometer move along the park wall, we took up position southwest of Mandeville.

But even tank crews that were not directly affected by the bombing attacks left their vehicles demoralized and awaited their capture.

It is nothing short of a miracle that the few remaining operational tanks were able to launch counterattacks a few hours later and that there were devastating British tank losses as a result of it.

The wall to the stud farm mentioned in the text, with the water tower of Cagny in the background. The repaired tanks were supposed to go into position along the viewer's right.

This series of photographs shows how badly hit the 3rd Company of *schwere Panzer-Abteilung 503* was. Four *Tigers*—such as *322* above—were total write-offs. All of the rest were badly damaged to varying degrees. In the best of cases, they were only conditionally operational.

The idyllic Manneville stud farm was badly damaged (current view above). All of the tanks were buried under debris and knocked-over trees and had to be dug out before they could even be worked on. (Wirton)

Tiger 313 of *Oberfeldwebel* Sachs was hit the worst. The fifty-six ton tank was flipped over by the force of the detonations. In the process, the tracks were ripped off, as well as a portion of the actual running gear.

The 2nd Company was not affected as much as the 3rd Company. Both of these images show *Tiger 213,* which was flung into a bomb crater. Since the enemy was approaching, it could not be recovered. (Wirton)

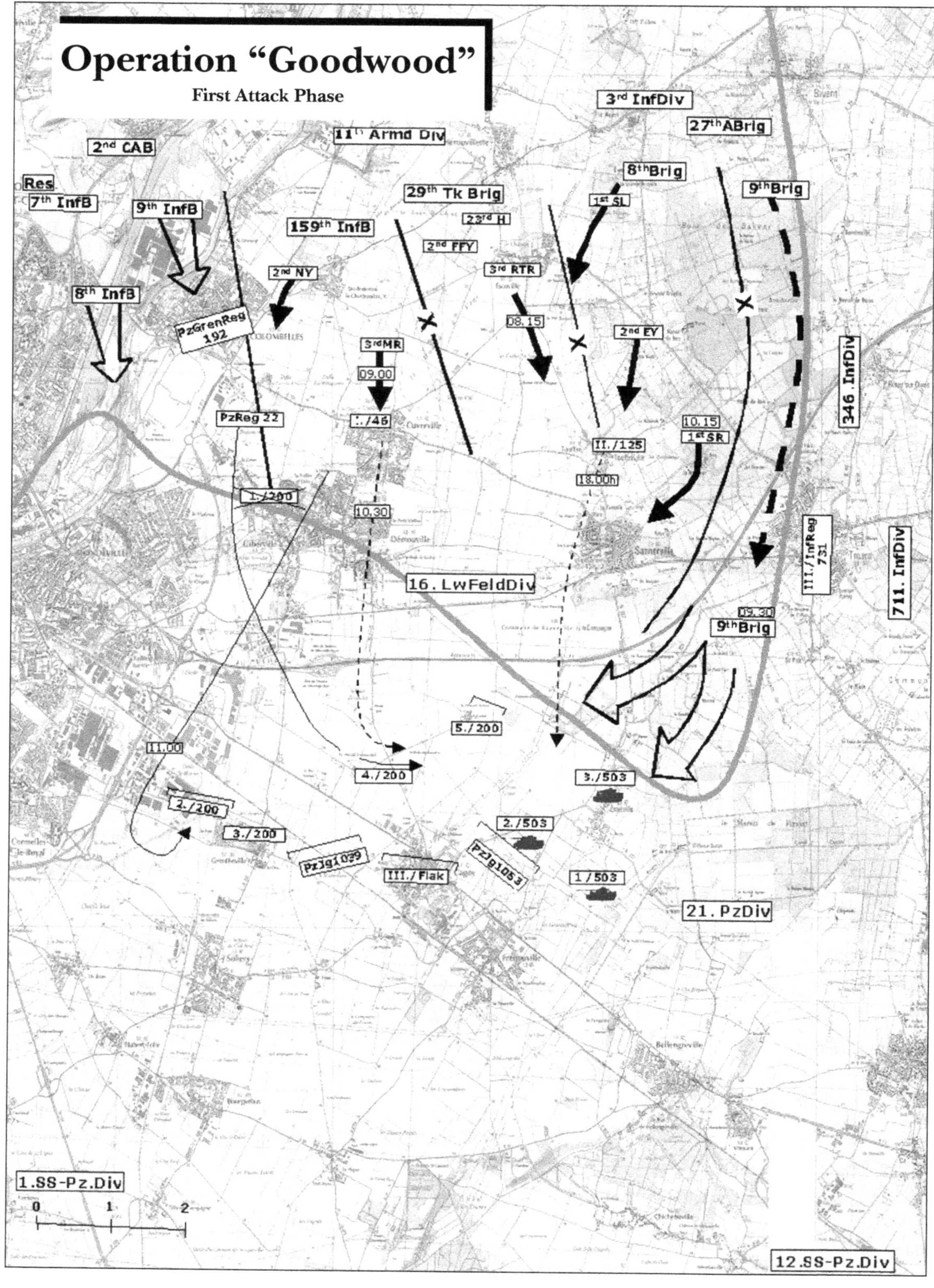

Operation "Goodwood"
First Attack Phase
3rd InfDiv
27thABrig
11th Armd Div
2nd CAB
Res
7th InfB
9th InfB
8thBrig
9thBrig
29th Tk Brig
1st SL
23rd H
159th InfB
2nd FFY
2nd NY
3rd RTR
8th InfB
PzGrenReg 192
08.15
2nd EY
3rdMR
09.00
346. InfDiv
PzReg 22
I./46
10.15
1stSR
II./125
18.00h
I./200
10.30
II./InfReg 731
711. InfDiv
16. LwFeldDiv
09.30
9thBrig
5./200
11.00
4./200
3./503
2./200
2./503
3./200
PzJg1039
III./Flak
PzJg1053
1/503
21. PzDiv
1.SS-Pz.Div
0
1
2
12.SS-Pz.Div

British tanks—Shermans armed with the 75mm main gun—are bunched up. That main gun was essentially ineffective against the *Tiger*.

The British offensive started at 0745 hours. It received direct support from the artillery, which took the German infantry positions under fire. Immediately after the last bombers had turned away, the enemy brought his armor and infantry forces up to the line of departure running from St. Honorine to Escoville. The first armored formations to attack were A and B Squadrons of the 3rd Royal Tank Regiment of the 29th Armoured Brigade of the British 11th Armoured Division. Starting at 0815, they advanced behind a rolling barrage through a line cleared through the mines and into a cloud of smoke and dust. The first thirty-two tanks initially moved in a column through the lane. Once cleared of it, they dispersed and advanced in a broad formation across the open terrain south of Escoville to the south.

Right behind them were the tanks of the 2nd Fife and Forfar Yeomanry. They were followed in turn by the 23rd Hussars. This represented the entire 29th Armoured brigade of the 11th Armoured Division. Soon there were more than 200 tanks that were advancing behind the rolling barrage of the artillery.

From a tactical assembly area east of St. Honorine, the enemy advanced with the 159th Infantry Brigade of the 11th Armoured Division. The infantry was escorted by the tanks of the 2nd Northhamptonshire Yeomanry. This force advanced through the tall grain in the direction of Cuverville. Only individual groups of light infantry of the *I./ Jäger-Regiment 46* offered any resistance. German artillery fired sporadically and without exactness.

The 3rd Battalion of the Monmouthshire Regiment of the 159th Infantry Brigade reached Cuverville around 0900 hours and took it around 1030 hours. As a result of the time involved, it can be seen that the British tanks only advanced slowly. They were primarily employed to support the infantry.

The tanks of the 2nd Northhamptonshire Yeomanry attacked in the open terrain between Colombelles and Cuverville. By doing so, they provided cover to the flank of the forces that were attacking past Cuverville. The *1./Sturmgeschütz-Brigade (Feld) 200* had to take the full force of the bombing at Démouville and was completely destroyed. The brigade's 2nd Battery pulled back in the face of the overwhelming superiority of the attackers and occupied new positions south of the Caen–Troarn rail line by 1100 hours.

Panzer-Regiment 22, which was employed south of the Colombelles–Cuverville road, only had a few, conditionally operational tanks left. Several of these were knocked out by the attacking British.

Starting at 0745 hours, the Canadian 3rd Infantry Division of the Canadian II Corps also attacked. The division's 8th Infantry Brigade attacked in

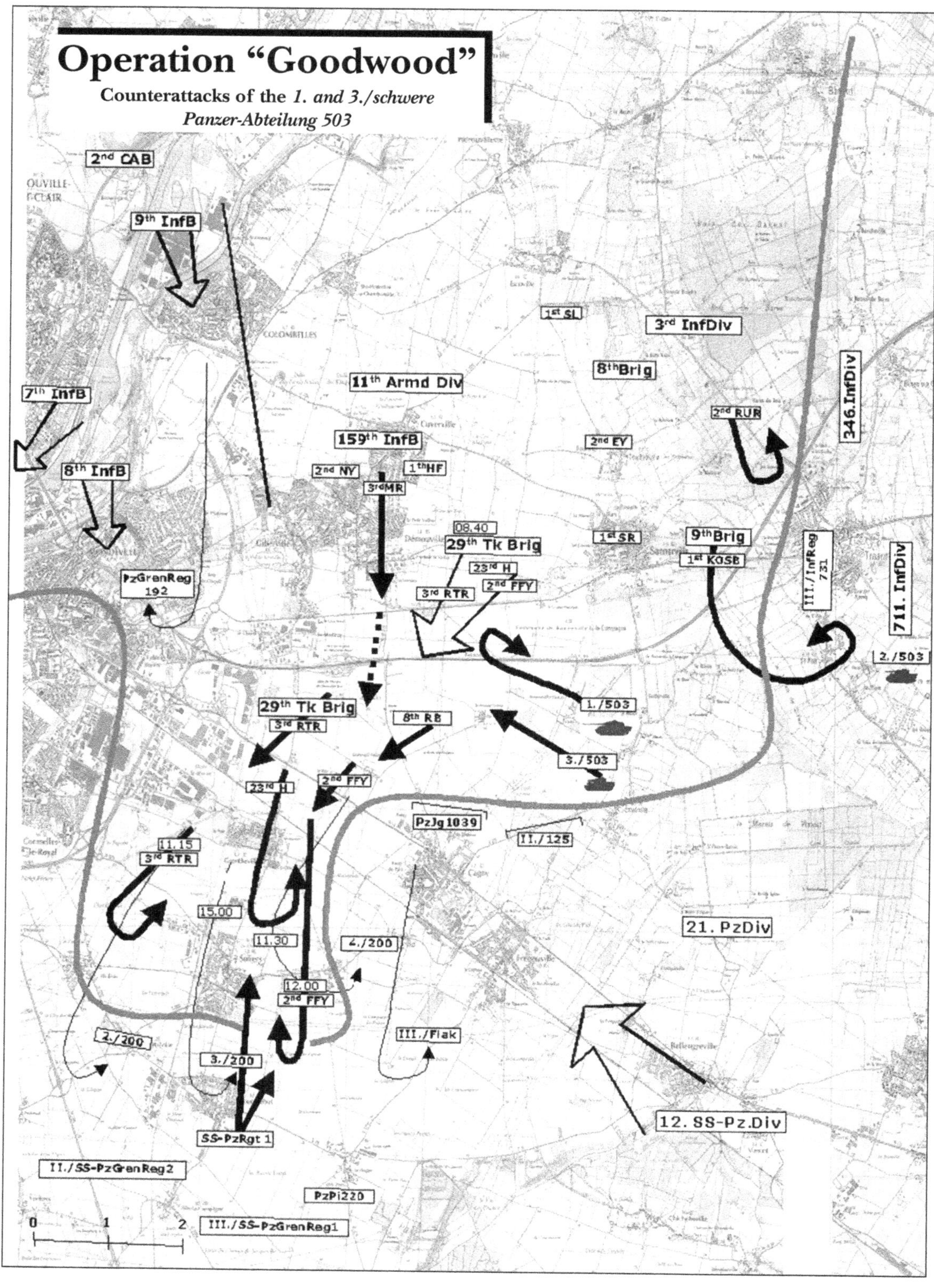
Operation "Goodwood"
Counterattacks of the 1. and 3./schwere Panzer-Abteilung 503
2nd CAB
9th InfB
7th InfB
8th InfB
11th Armd Div
159th InfB
2nd NY
1thHF
3rdMR
1st SL
3rd InfDiv
8thBrig
2nd RUR
2nd EY
346.InfDiv
08.40
29th Tk Brig
23rd H
2nd FFY
3rd RTR
1st SR
9thBrig
1st KOSB
III./InfReg 731
711. InfDiv
2./503
PzGrenReg 192
1./503
29th Tk Brig
3rd RTR
8th RB
3./503
23rd H
2nd FFY
PzJg 1039
II./125
11.15
3rd RTR
15.00
11.30
2./200
12.00
2nd FFY
21. PzDiv
2./200
3./200
III./Flak
12. SS-Pz.Div
SS-PzRgt 1
II./SS-PzGrenReg2
PzPi220
III./SS-PzGrenReg1
0
1
2

the direction of Giberville and Mondeville. It was supported by tanks of the Canadian 2nd Armoured Brigade. Following behind, the 9th Infantry Brigade advanced along the Orne towards the industrial area of Colombelles. Its objective was to advance on Vaucelles so as to take the remaining portions of Caen southeast of the Orne. For the time being, the division's 7th Brigade remained in Caen as a divisional reserve. It was intended for it to cross the Orne in the city later on. Additional objectives were the high ground north of St. André-sur-Orne and the village of Verriéres on the road running from Caen to Falaise. The mission of taking these objectives would fall to the Canadian 2nd Infantry Division during a later phase of the battle plan.

Elements of *Panzer-Grenadier-Regiment 192* of the *21. Panzer-Division* defended against the Canadians at Colombelles. For the time being, the *I./Jäger-Regiment 32* was still holding out at the palace north of Colombelles that was right on the Orne. The carpet bombing did not extend this far, so the fighting positions in the woods and at the palace were still intact. Initially, the Canadians did not

During the advance of the 1st Company of *schwere Panzer-Abteilung 503* in the direction of Démouville, *Tiger 101* was knocked out. As a result of an explosion in the fighting compartment, the main gun was apparently blown off.

make good progress at this location. The steel works at Colombelles had been a target of the bombing and had been largely destroyed. A German forward observer directed artillery missions onto Cuverville from one of the factory chimneys that was still standing. Giberville could no longer be held after the loss of the few *Panzer IV's* of *Panzer-Regiment 22* along the road from Colombelles to Cuverville and the withdrawal of the *2./Sturmgeschütz-Brigade (Feld) 200.* The British 3rd Infantry Division attacked on the east flank, also starting at 0745 hours. It was supported by tanks of the 27th Armoured Brigade. The division's 8th Brigade was the lead element; it was supported by the tanks of the 13th/18th Hussars. The 1st Battalion of the South Lancashire Regiment attacked Le Pré Baron; the 2nd Battalion of the East Yorkshire Regiment attacked Touffréville. The latter village had largely been spared from the wrath of the carpet bombing. The *II./Panzer-Grenadier-Regiment (tgp) 125* had not been hit as hard and offered bitter resistance. The battalion was supported by fire from the assault guns of the *5./Sturmgeschütz-Brigade (Feld) 200* from Le Prieure. It was not until 1100 hours that the Yorkshires penetrated into Touffréville. The situation became increasingly critical for the German grenadiers during the course of the afternoon; around 1800 hours, they had to abandon the village.

The British were concentrating their artillery fires on Sannerville, Banneville and Emiéville. Their objective was Troarn. While the fighting for Touffréville was continuing furiously, the 1st Battalion of the Suffolk Regiment attacked Sannerville starting at 1015 hours. Sannerville had been bombed to bits, and there was no appreciable resistance there. By 1220 hours, the village was considered lost; it took until 1600 hours for Banneville to fall.

While the 8th Brigade was attacking these localities—Touffréville, Sannerville and also Banneville—the 9th Brigade started its advance at 0930 against the bombed-out villages of Mandeville and Emiéville. In the latter case, there was not much left of the village. The English soldiers attacked in some areas while mounted on Shermans of the 27th Armoured Brigade, which was supporting them.

The way to Troarn was blocked by elements of the *346. Infanterie-Division,* together with rapidly brought-up forces of the *711. Infanterie-Division.*

With this, we have an overview of the initial phase of the British attack.

In the meantime, determined tankers of *Panzer-Regiment 22* and *schwere Panzer-Abteilung 503* were working feverishly at Emiéville and Mandeville to try to recover at least a few tanks out of the chaos of the badly bomb-damaged assembly areas. They could hear the sound of approaching enemy tanks in their ears. Fortunately for the *Tiger* battalion, the 1st and 2nd Companies had not been as severely hit as the 3rd Company. Nevertheless, some of the tanks had been damaged and there were also personnel casualties. Within the 2nd Company, *Tiger 213* had been hit by a bomb and flung down an embankment. There was no time left to attempt to recover it.

Towards 1000 hours, the 3rd Company succeeded in getting six tanks moving; four had been destroyed by the bombing (among them, *Tigers 313* and *332*). In the course of the short immediate counterattack into the left flank of the British Guards Armoured Division south of Lirose, which had been occupied by the 2nd Battalion of the King's Own Shropshire Light Infantry since 1000 hours, it was determined that the main guns were out of adjustment. Only about every third round was a hit. Another shock for the tank crews was the fact that two *Tigers* were knocked out by means of clean penetrations. It was later found out that the 8.8-centimeter *Flak* that were in Cagny had engaged them by mistake.

About two hours later, several *Tigers* of the *1./ schwere Panzer-Abteilung 503* conducted an immediate counterattack along the road from Troarn towards Démouville along with tanks that had been dug free from *Panzer-Regiment 22.* In the process, the company commander's tank got stuck in a crater and had to be blown up. Another *Tiger II* was knocked out. At that point, the company turned south. The loss of *Tiger 112* presents an interesting story. The tank's gunner, *Gefreiter* Thaysen, gave this firsthand account after the war:

> As I remember it, the English attack started at 1500 hours. Up until that time we kept ourselves busy wiping away sweat. It was a blistering hot summer day. We could scarcely keep the hatches open because of the on-going artillery fire.
>
> The attack that started at about 1500 hours was supported by a tremendous number of British tanks. The main line of resistance was overrun in a few minutes. Only the 1st Company and a few antitank guns held for a little time. Soon the British were between, in front of and behind us. As a result, neither the English nor we knew who or what was where. In the meantime, both the German and English artillery fired wildly into the midst of it all. And, of course, the British and German infantry were right in there, too.
>
> *Tiger 112*, the tank in which I was the gunner, was engaged with one Englishman while others fired on us. That caused my tank commander (a newcomer, without combat experience), to well, let's say . . . have the tank put in reverse, almost in a panic. We lunged back, right through a hedge, the type you usually found there.
>
> Obviously, the tank commander was a bit out of it, since he had to have seen that another tank was behind the hedge. In any case, there was a jolt, and we were hung up with an Englishman. There was no way that we intended to ram the enemy, all the more so since we ran into him with the rear of the tank, and I was still at twelve o'clock, busy with the Tommy who was firing at us.
>
> We had barely hit the Englishman when, an antitank gun—probably a 75 mm *PaK*—firing at the Englishman hit us instead. It hit us in the left between the track and the running gear. The round penetrated and sliced the seat right out from under my backside. I found myself on the turret floor. At the same time, the round tore open a shell casing and the propellant charge ignited in a jet of flame. There was nothing for us to do but to bail out, and quick. The radio operator, loader and tank commander were the first ones out. The driver, Horst Becher, was able to grab his pistol and, after bailing out, did target practice against the Englishmen who were around the tank. And that was quite a sight, since he still had his headphones on with the ripped-out cords dangling.
>
> On dismounting through the turret hatch, I landed on a member of the English crew who, presumably, was also somewhat out of it. Apparently he thought I was one of his crew. For a moment, we looked at each other in a daze. Then a rush of heroism awoke in both of us. Each grabbed for the place he's normally find his pistol. Heroism failed from a lack of lethal materials. Since our tank had started to burn, both of us started to crawl away from it and, since things were lively all around, we both sought cover

in a hole behind the Tommy's tank. With one of us in the left corner and the other in the right one, we eyed each other and each tried to convince the other by gesticulation that the other was his prisoner. Since it turned out that each of us had opposite opinions about that, both of us shrugged our shoulders, grinned at each other and bolted for our own sides.

In contrast to this is the differing version offered by the opposing Sherman tank commander, Lieutenant Gordon:

My name is Gorman and, at the time of Goodwood, I was a platoon leader in the 21st Irish Guards Armoured Regiment, which was equipped with Shermans. During the afternoon of 18 July, we were fighting in the hedgerow country northeast of Cagny. Two or three groups, each with four or five *Tigers* that were making good use of cover, seemed to be opposing our 5th Guards Armoured Brigade. They would suddenly emerge from their cover, fire, and cost us several losses. We attempted to attack with the company closed up, whereupon the *Tigers* again disappeared into their cover, only to appear again and repeat the whole process anew.

This was my first time in action, and I was excited. I had got across the little stream running into Cagny from the northeast, but the rest of my troop had got stuck. However, I pushed on alone for a bit and found plenty of targets and was beginning to think this war business was not too bad after all; in fact, I was beginning to enjoy myself.

But this didn't last too long. Glancing to my left, I saw to my horror the unmistakable shape of a [*Königstiger*] coming through a hedge less than 200 yards away and directly approaching me.

I ordered my gunner: "Traverse left . . . steady . . . on . . . fire!"

He fired, and I saw to my dismay the 75 mm round hit the front of the *Tiger*, bounce off and go zinging straight up into the air. I ordered the gunner to fire again, but a hollow voice came up from the bowels of the tank, saying: "Gun jammed, sir!"

This was a situation for which I had not been trained, and I did not know what to do. Glancing anxiously at the *Tiger*, I saw with horror that his long gun was slowly traversing around in my direction.

Someone had once told me that when in doubt the thing to do was advance, so I ordered my driver to advance at full speed

and ram the *Tiger.* We lurched forward, gathered speed, and hit him in the middle with a terrific crash, just before he got his main gun trained on me.

Both crews bailed out upon impact and, since the air was full of lead, both crews dove for cover. My wireless operator saw a convenient slit trench and, jumping into it, found it already occupied by the *Tiger's* crew. At this point, both crews were in the trench and eyed each other suspiciously.

I got out of there and crawled, brought up the 17-pounder Sherman of my platoon and succeeded in finishing off the *Tiger.* I then collected my crew and the *Tiger's* crew, and we went back to our lines and I climbed into another tank.

I recount this little story, because it may well be the only example in the late war in which an army unit used the old naval tactic of ramming. [Reverse-translated into English from the German text.]

Gorman probably hoped that his version of what happened would be accepted without too much question. Fortunately, we are not limited to assumptions. A previously unpublished photograph from the Canadian Military Archives disproves Gorman's story. The tracks made by the tank <u>moving in reverse</u> can be clearly seen <u>in front of</u> the *Tiger.* There is also a sharp turn to the left, that is, in the direction of the Sherman. This proves that the *Tiger* rammed the Sherman. The fact that the *Tiger* was in reverse is also demonstrated by the drooping of the track behind the drive sprocket. If the tank had been moving forward, it would have been tight. It is also not true that the German crew was taken prisoner immediately afterwards.

Gorman probably intended his story to cover for his own miserable performance. If the Sherman had

Oberleutnant Oemler led the attack of the 1st Company in *Tiger 101*, but his tank ran into a bomb crater. Since the tank could not be evacuated, it was blown up. (NAC)

only run into the *Tiger*, it could have been put back into operation again. This was not possible, however, since the tank had been hit on the left-hand side of the turret after the *Tiger* had been fired at. A later engagement by a Sherman Firefly is pure fantasy. The two hits of a German antitank gun on both of the tanks are easily seen in the photos. A memorial at the scene attests to Gorman's "heroic deed." The victor always writes the history books . . .

A further advance of the British on Troarn was stopped by the *2./schwere Panzer-Abteilung 503* and the remaining tanks.

The lead element of the 29th Armoured Brigade—the 3rd Royal Tank Regiment—was attacking in the center of the offensive sector without infantry support. It moved quickly over the wide-open plain east of Cuverville and Démouville and reached the Caen–Troarn rail line around 0840 hours. It had moved behind the rolling barrage of the artillery and had encountered no appreciable resistance. The regiment stopped briefly at the rail line. During this time, the artillery pieces were given new gun-laying information, and the tanks of the 2nd Fife and Forfar Yeomanry that were following closed up. For the time being, the tanks of the 23rd Hussars still remained a reserve behind the two battalions. The attackers, who wanted to reach the Caen–Vimont rail line quickly at this point, were entering a zone that had been spared from bombing.

The hour had come for *Sturmgeschütz-Brigade (Feld) 200* and other antitank elements. Three intact batteries were in good positions at Le Prieure, Le Mesnil-Frémentel and Grentheville. In addition, the brigade's 2nd Battery, which had pulled back from its positions north of Giberville, was directed into new positions west of Grentheville. The 8.8-centimeter *Flak* battery of the *III. Flak-Korps* that was positioned in the fruit orchards on the northern edge of Cagny had also survived the bombing fairly well and was ready to fire. The antitank guns of *Panzer-Jäger-Abteilung 1039* and *Panzer-Jäger-Abteilung 1053* were hidden in well-camouflaged positions. Those antitank guns and the assault guns of *Sturmgeschütz-Brigade (Feld) 200* opened fire and knocked out sixteen Shermans in the space of a few minutes as they were starting to cross the rail line.

The assault guns were employed skillfully. They harassed the attackers by quickly changing positions while still maintaining camouflage and effectively engaging from covered positions. In addition, the tanks of the 23rd Hussars that were following were effectively engaged from the vicinity of Emiéville, while they were crossing the first rail line from Caen to Troarn.

As they crossed the second rail line (from Caen to Vimont), the English wound up outside the range of their own artillery. As a result, they had to continue their advance without their accustomed artillery. Despite their heavy losses, they attacked in two armored groups from the area of Grentheville in the directions of Bras–Hubert-Folie and Soliers–Bourguébus–Four.

Because the British were attacking at the time without infantry, they bypassed Grentheville on both sides and were not able to clear the village.

The *3./Sturmgeschütz-Brigade (Feld) 200* and a *Nebelwerfer* element with seventy-two tubes were holding out in Grentheville. Constantly changing positions, the assault guns in Grentheville engaged the enemy to the east and the west and knocked out several enemy tanks.

Around 1130 hours, Le Mesnil-Frémentel was attacked by the motorized infantry of the follow-on 8th Battalion of the Rifles Brigade. This attack was also supported by tanks. Elements of the *I./Panzer-Grenadier-Regiment 125*, which had been demoralized and weakened by the previous bombardment and the several hours of artillery fire, marched into captivity.

The *4./Sturmgeschütz-Brigade (Feld) 200*, which had lost a 10.5-centimeter assault gun as a result of the heavy artillery fire, pulled back from Le Mesnil-Frémentel starting at 1130 hours and took up new positions at Le Poirier. The *2./Sturmgeschütz-Brigade (Feld) 200* also took up new positions; it moved to Hubert-Folie.

The *3./Sturmgeschütz-Brigade (Feld) 200* held out in Grentheville until 1500 hours, before it pulled back to new positions south of Soliers. The *Nebelwerfer* unit in Grentheville was then overrun.

The lead tanks of the 3rd Royal Tank Regiment reached Bra and Hubert-Folie at 1115 hours.

Tanks of the 2nd Fife and Forfar Yeomanry were east of Bourguébus at 1200 hours. It now proved fortunate for *Sturmgeschütz-Brigade (Feld) 200* that it had pulled back to new positions and had avoided its own destruction as a result.

The assault gun brigade then reinforced the rearward defensive sector that was being formed by elements of *Panzer-Pionier-Bataillon 220*, *Panzer-Aufklärungs-Abteilung 21*, *Panzer-Jäger-Abteilung 21* and the *III. Flak-Korps.*

German artillery and rocket launchers joined the fight throughout the day.

By noon, the British attack had lost its impetus. Although they had succeeded in overrunning the forward-most German positions and gaining terrain in the depths of the battlefield, they had still not broken through the German defensive system.

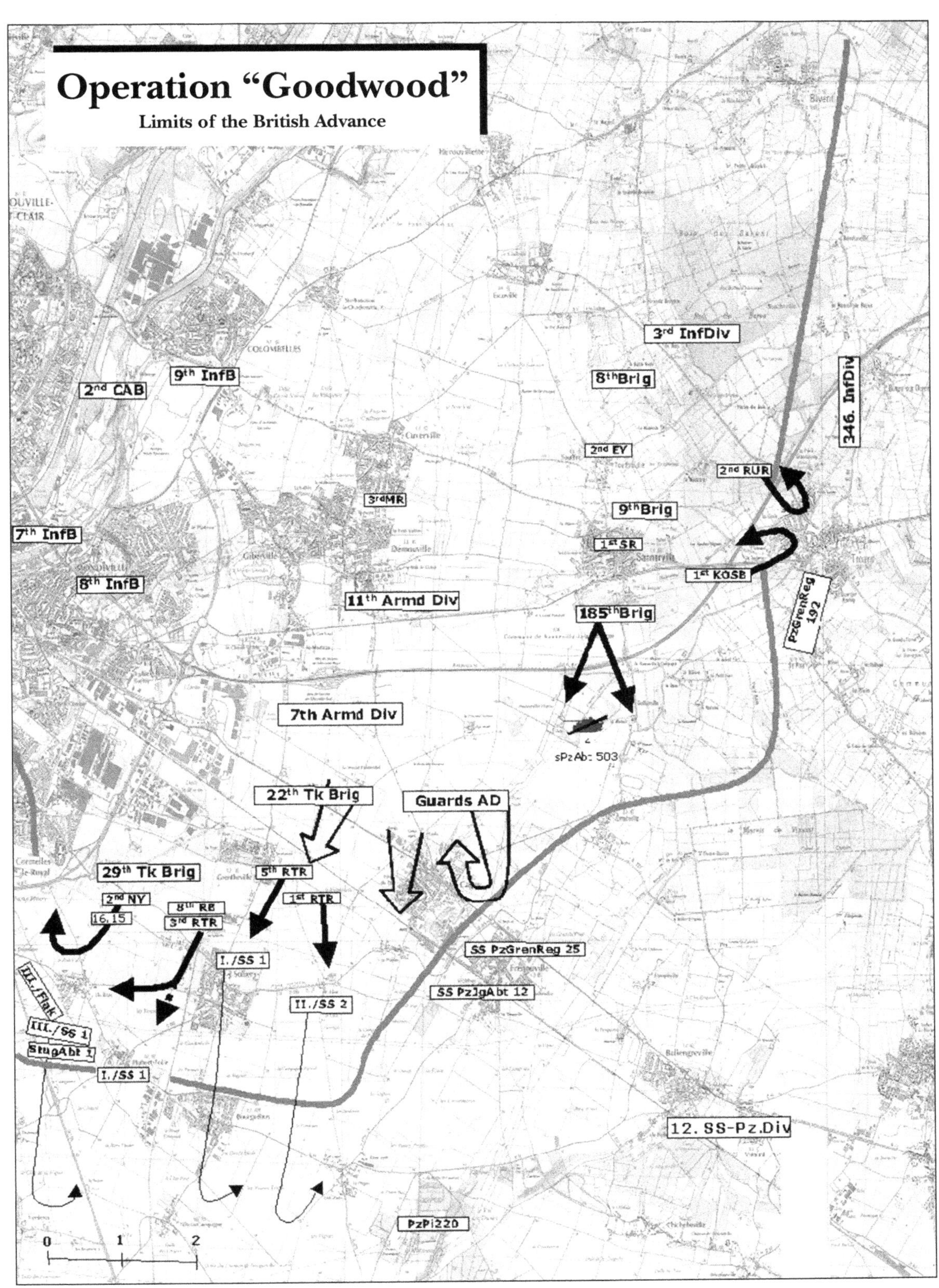
Operation "Goodwood"
Limits of the British Advance
3rd InfDiv
8thBrig
346. InfDiv
2nd EY
2nd RUR
9thBrig
1st SR
1st KOSB
PzGrenReg 192
185thBrig
2nd CAB
9th InfB
3rdMR
7th InfB
8th InfB
11th Armd Div
7th Armd Div
sPzAb: 503
22th Tk Brig
Guards AD
29th Tk Brig
5th RTR
1st RTR
2nd NY
16,15
8th RB
3rd RTR
SS PzGrenReg 25
I./SS 1
II./SS 2
SS PzJgAbt 12
III./Flak
III./SS 1
StugAbt 1
I./SS 1
12. SS-Pz.Div
PzPi220
0
1
2

CHAPTER 8

German Defensive Measures

Panzergruppe West started receiving initial reports around 0830 hours concerning "extremely heavy barrage fire and bombing on the east Orne bridgehead at Colombelles in the sector of the *16. Luftwaffen-Feld-Division.*" In addition, the *LXXXVI. Armee-Korps* reported "approximately 100 enemy tanks from St. Honorine to the south." At 0930 hours, another message followed: "Enemy broken through to just north of Cagny with 40–50 tanks."

The commander-in-chief of *Panzergruppe West*, *General der Panzertruppen* Eberbach, ordered the *I. SS-Panzer-Korps* to immediately employ the *Panther* battalion of the *1. SS-Panzer-Division "Leibstandarte SS Adolf Hitler"* to engage the enemy tanks at Cagny. This division had just been relieved during the period from 13 to 17 July 1944 by the *272. Infanterie-Division* and was the corps' reserve in the area defined by Tilly la Camgagne–Cintheux–Brettville-sur-Laize –Bully–Ifs.

The *Panther* battalion of *SS-Panzer-Regiment 1* reached the area between Bras and Bouguébus around noon and prepared to launch a counterattack. Grenadiers of the *III./SS-Panzer-Grenadier-Regiment 1* and the *II./SS-Panzer-Grenadier-Regiment 2* quickly followed behind. From their elevated positions, the tanks had a good overview of the open attack terrain of the British.

The *Panthers* attacked to the north in small groups and knocked out tanks of the 2nd Fife and Forfar Yeomanry. The *Panthers* also turned back an attack of the 23rd Hussars east of Soliers in conjunction with the 3rd and 5th Batteries of *Sturmgeschütz-Brigade (Feld) 200.*

The *Panthers* pounced from good positions and knocked out numerous enemy tanks. Extremely heavy fighter-bomber attacks on the tanks prevented the continuation of the ordered counterattacks in the direction of Hubert Folie and Frenouville.

In the meantime, the Guards Armored Division had been brought forward with the mission of supporting the attack of the 11th Armoured Division by advancing in the direction of Vimont. The approach of the Guards Armoured Division had been delayed due to the chaos in the Orne bridgehead. Towards 1100 hours, however, the first elements of this division advanced west of Emiéville.

At the same time, the thin defensive line of the *II./Panzer-Grenadier-Regiment 125* running from Cagny to Emiéville was reinforced by two *Pak* of *Panzer-Jäger-Abteilung 1039* and a few tanks.

It was not until around 1600 hours that the 32nd Guards Brigade and the tanks of the 5th Guards Armoured Brigade moved out for their first operation in Normandy by heading in the direction of Cagny. *Oberstleutnant* von Luck ordered the *Flak* in Cagny to be blown up and the village to be abandoned.

The continued attack of the Guards Armoured Division on the road from Caen to Vimont was turned back with a loss of sixty British tanks. Three guns of *Panzer-Jäger-Abteilung 1039* were responsible for twenty-seven enemy tanks all by themselves. By evening, the 11th Armoured Division had lost 126 tanks. The attacking force moved back to the rail line running from Caen to Vimont.

During the afternoon, initial groups of the *12. SS-Panzer-Division "Hitlerjugend"* moved up along the Caen–Vimont rail line as additional reinforcements. They occupied positions at Frénouville. The commander-in-chief of *Panzergruppe West* had urgently requested *Heeresgruppe B* to release this division at 1305 hours. Because this division had been pulled out of the line for battlefield reconstitution and had been earmarked for employment with the *15. Armee*, the *OKW* first had to grant its permission. This took place at 1500 hours.

✠

Although the attack in the area of the enemy's main effort outside of Hubert Folie and between Soliers and Four came to a standstill during the afternoon, intense fighting had developed on the flanks. On the western flank, starting at 1030 hours, the 3rd Battalion of the Monmouthshire Regiment and the 1st Battalion of the Herefordshire Regiment of the 159th Infantry Brigade got held up in Cuverville while under heavy artillery fire. Towards 1200 hours, however, the 3rd Battalion of the Monmouthshire Regiment prepared to attack again, this time with tanks of the 2nd Northhamptonshire Yeomanry. Under a blazing midday sun, the men of Monmouthshire advanced through tall grain in the direction of Démouville.

The 1st Battalion of the Herefordshire Regiment linked up with the attack through the fruit orchards east of Démouville. There it was taken under heavy fire by a German tank force that was coming from Emiéville and attacking in the area south of Lirose. The British advanced into Démouville and had the village firmly in their hands by 1400 hours. They took 250 prisoners there.

Following this, the British forces that had taken Démouville linked up with the advance of the 4th Battalion of the King's Shropshire Light Infantry and moved in the direction of Le Mesnil-Frémentel. At was at Le Mesnil-Frémentel that the British in this sector dug in for the night.

During the night, the 7th Armoured Division arrived in this area. It had also been held up by the chaotic traffic conditions in the narrow bridgehead.

The *I./Jäger-Regiment 32* had initially held up the Canadians along the Orne at the Colombelles *chateau*. The Canadian 9th Brigade suddenly pulled back in its attack sector. An air attack that followed at 1300 hours was the reason. The air assault had no effect, however. Even the defended chateau was not hit. Following this, the entire divisional artillery of the Canadian 3rd Infantry Division suddenly placed barrage fire on the chateau, resulting in fires breaking out in the palace. It had to be abandoned by the Germans at 1515 hours.

After taking the palace, the Canadian attacked in strength along the Orne and through the industrial area of Colombelles. Colombelles proper was lost. The *II./Panzer-Grenadier-Regiment 192*, which was then being attacked in the industrial area, saw itself in an ever-more precarious position over the next few hours. Eventually, it was surrounded. Although the enemy had difficulty in bringing his armor through the sea of bomb craters, it was not possible for the Germans to hold the industrial area. The battalion fought its way through to the south in the direction of Mondeville.

The Canadian 8th Brigade attacked Mondeville. The fighting revolved around individual bomb craters. The Canadians attacked with special vigor around 1800 hours. The German battalion commander decided to fight to the last and sent a corresponding message to the leadership of the *21. Panzer-Division* at 2020 hours.

In the evening, the Canadian 7th Brigade attacked across the Orne against the friendly forces to the left of the *II./Panzer-Grenadier-Regiment 192*, the *272. Infanterie-Division*. French civilians helped the Canadians. Canadian combat engineers quickly erected additional military bridges over the Orne during the night.

Despite the difficult situation, a fleeting opportunity presented itself for the *II./Panzer-Grenadier-Regiment 192* to break out to the southeast. By doing so, it was able to maintain its combat cohesiveness.

After it had taken Touffréville, Sannerville and Banneville, the British 8th Infantry Brigade was held up by the *III./Infanterie-Regiment 731* of the *711. Infanterie-Division* on the eastern side of the battlefield.

The attempt of the British 9th Infantry Brigade to take Troarn miscarried. Under the cover of tanks, the English succeeded in taking a bridge over the Cours de Janville Creek. There was fighting at the brickworks northeast of Sannerville. The 2nd Battalion of the Royal Ulster Riles, which was also supported by tanks, attempted to take Troarn by attacking it from the northwest. Farther to the south, the 1st Battalion of the King's Own Scottish Borderers attempted to bypass the city of Troarn to the south and then attack it from the southeast. Tanks of the East Riding Yeomanry of the 27th Armoured Brigade supported all of those efforts.

At 1800 hours, the 2nd Battalion of the Lincolnshire Regiment also moved out, although its intent was to divert attention from the advance of the Royal Ulster Rifles in the north. The fighting lasted into the night, and all attempts of the English at Troarn were turned back by the grenadiers of *Panzer-Grenadier-Regiment 125* and elements of other units. Troarn remained firmly in German hands on this day.

As 18 July 1944 drew to a close, the front lines in all sectors of Operation "Goodwood" firmed up.

An impressive portrayal of the fighting from the point of view of the British is given in Patrick Delaforce's history of the British 11th Armoured Division:

> The dawn of the big attack! The whole regiment [23rd Hussars] was spread out on a fairly open plain, sloping forward; our objective a high ridge of land in front of us and to the right about five miles away. We had advanced about four miles [behind the 3rd Royal Tank Regiment and ahead of the 2nd Fife and Forfarshire] without much trouble and reached the line of the main railway. So far so good! But now we had no air support and the artillery barrage had ceased. Shells and mortars were still exploding all over the place.
>
> At 0945 3 RTR/8 RB [3rd Royal Tank Regiment / 8th Rifle brigade] had reached the first hurdle of the Caen–Troarn railway line where the very deep ditches slowed down the advance of 3 RTR. Jim Caswell reported that the artillery barrage was now too far ahead. Soon the right flank of my squadron

was threatened by three camouflaged Tigers concealed in a wood to our left on Bourguébus Ridge. Most of our twenty tanks were hit in a matter of minutes. We were on the right of our regiment so I ordered the driver to make a left turn so that we could get into a good position from which to fire back . . . the Germans had by now obviously collected their wits together after the first colossal onslaught and things rapidly became very unpleasant for us. Armour-piercing shells began coming in from all directions and tanks of 3 RTR began brewing up. Then on our left Panthers appeared and the fun really began.

We could see some of the leading tanks on fire and sad little parties began to come back on foot. They were the survivors of the leading crews. All looked smoke grimed and the black-skinned figures of badly burned men staggered along with the help of the more active.

Captain Lemon was now less confident:

> We did not hit the crust of the enemy, the 21st and the 12th SS Panzer divisions—it was just as the leading tanks were level with Hubert-Folie when the fun began. I saw Sherman after Sherman go up in flames and it got to such a pitch that I thought that in another few minutes there would be nothing left of the Regiment!

This was 3rd RTR, the most experienced tank regiment in the British Army.

✠

Major Bill Close, OC of A squadron [OC = officer-in-charge = company commander], wrote:

> [I saw] several anti-tank guns among the trees . . . the gunners frantically swinging their guns round towards us. In the cornfield around us were many multi-barrel mortar positions which were already firing over our heads. They were quickly dealt with in some cases by simply running over them with the tank. But the SP anti-tank guns [of Major Becker's Battery] were a different matter. Opening fire at almost point-blank range they hit three of my tanks out of the nineteen in action, which burst into flames and I could see that the 3 RTR squadron on my left also had several tanks blazing furiously. My orders were to pass on and bypass the village.
>
> So 3 RTR charged through one of the tunnels of the 20-yard tall Caen-Vimont railway embankment to keep moving towards the villages of Bras and Hubert-Folie:
>
> Three Tiger tanks suddenly opened up from some trees on the left. Within minutes most of our tanks were hit. I swung the tank around to a better fighting position. I saw an 88-mm gun pointing right at us—a bright muzzle flash—a missile screamed past just overhead. "Reverse," I shouted, "Reverse." Back we went—but we were hit. The gunner was killed instantly. The wireless operator had collapsed badly wounded to the turret floor.
>
> . . .
>
> There was some firing on our left and we caught up with (Brigadier) Roscoe Harvey in a wooded area facing a little hamlet called Le Mesnil-Frémentel, about 1,000 yards west of Cagny. The area was

being heavily mortared, the flail tanks of the Westminster Dragoons were firing at the hamlet and on the left some 300 yards nearer Cagny were a whole squadron of the Fife and Forfarshire Yeomanry all knocked out and some burning. It wasn't quite so bad as it looked. 3rd RTR had gone on in a south-westerly direction and were now putting a squadron the other side of a high railway embankment which ran from north to south. The Fife and Forfarshire had gone on south leaving Le Mesnil-Frémentel on their right and had now halted because of the decimation of their rear squadron. The 23rd Hussars were well back on the left as some German tanks had come to life in that area.

The General now made a rare mistake. He felt that Cagny must be firmly held since strong fire from there had wrecked the Fife and Forfarshire. So he ordered an 8 RB attack on the village to be cancelled and for the 23rd Hussars to "mask" Cagny without getting knocked out. Theoretically if they kept further west—near Le Mesnil—they would be safer.

So Brigadier Roscoe Harvey ordered 23rd Hussars forward to the Fife's assistance. B squadron's first troop was hit and blazing within seconds:

> The squadron was in full view of the Panthers and completely outranged by their guns; nearly all their Fireflies were knocked out and the 75s were virtually useless at long range. C squadron on B's left was now within 300 yards of Four ahead of them. They took out a Tiger [probably the *Tiger* mentioned above] and a Panther outside Cagny on the left but suddenly without warning the whole squadron was hit by a terrible concentration of fire from Four virtually at point-blank range. Everywhere wounded and burning figures ran or struggled painfully for cover while a remorseless rain of AP riddled the already helpless Shermans.

The 23rd Hussars, who came through the stricken Fife and Forfarshires, who now had only sixteen tanks left, themselves started to take heavy tank losses. They were attacked by Tiger tanks, survivors from the von Luck group from Manneville, now commanded by Lieutenant [*Oberleutnant*] von Rosen. Two of their eight Tigers went up in flames, shot clean through their armour plate in front as they advanced towards Le Prieuré. British tanks were simply unable to pierce the Tigers' frontal armour, so it was the Cagny 88-mm anti-aircraft crews, unfamiliar with tank recognition, who had mistaken Tigers for Shermans. The morale of the other Tiger crews suffered and their counter-attack petered out.

Between Frénouville and Four, south of Cagny, 2nd Fife and Forfarshire were caught by flanking Panther fire and both CO [commanding officer] and 2 i/c [second in command] were hit and wounded. So 23rd Hussars in reserve were sent to help, but despite destroying several Panthers they met the same fate, and twenty Shermans were brewed by 88 mm and Panthers in Four. The fields south of the Caen-Vimont-Paris railway embankment were strewn with knocked-out tanks from 3 RTR, 2nd Fife and Forfarshire and 23rd Hussars. Ambulances and stretcher bearers arrived at dusk to search, find and succor the survivors. It was a disaster area.

At the end of the day, the British 2nd Army had gained ground to the south and taken a few villages after destroying the forward-most portions of the German main line of resistance. This was accomplished through an unusually intense air attack that was followed by an artillery barrage and, finally, a massive armored assault. Even though this had been its objective, it had not reached the localities of Bras, Hubert-Folie, Soliers, Four, Le Poirier and Frénouville, all of which were still in German hands.

During the night of 18–19 July 1944, the *LXXXVI. Armee-Korps* ordered the *21. Panzer-Division* pulled from the line to be repositioned. Its former sector from Frénouville to the church at Emiéville was to be assumed by the *12. SS-Panzer-Division "Hitlerjugend."* After the relief-in-place, the division was to occupy a line running from the church at Emiéville–St. Pair–Troarn.

What remained of the *16. Luftwaffen-Feld-Division*—two battalions of infantry and a *Pak* platoon with three guns—was consolidated with the *21. Panzer-Division* by order of the corps during the night of 18–19 July 1944. As a result, the end strength of the *21. Panzer-Division* was raised by some 1,500 personnel. Excluded from the consolidation order were the officers of the *Luftwaffe* division as well as its signals and transportation elements. These elements were then employed in the rear area; later on, they formed the cadre and nucleus for the newly forming *16. Volks-Grenadier-Division.* A portion of the divisional artillery was transferred to the *711. Infanterie-Division.*

✠

The relief-in-place of the *21. Panzer-Division* was started with the *12. SS-Panzer-Division "Hitlerjugend,"* which was brought forward again, at 0530 hours on 19 July and was completed by noon. *Panzer-Grenadier-Regiment 125* of the *21. Panzer-Division* assumed the sector starting at the church at Emiéville on the left-hand sector of the division. *Panzer-Grenadier-Regiment 192* assumed positions running from St. Pair to Troarn. The friendly forces to the right remained the *346. Infanterie-Division.*

In time, twenty-two additional *Panzer IV's* were recovered from the crater landscape at Emiéville. After these were repaired, the tanks were assembled at St. Pair by 22 July 1944. The *Tigers* of *schwere Panzer-Abteilung 503* that were operational or capable of being repaired were assembled at Le Mesnil de Bures, east of the *Bois de Bavent.*

During the night of 18–19 July 1944, both sides attempted to regroup and reorganize and prepare for the continuation of the fighting the next day.

In the meantime, all of the British 7th Armoured Division had also assembled in the area of Le Mesnil-Frémentel, where it encamped. The badly battered 29th Armoured Brigade assembled at Grentheville. During the night, the British succeeded in recovering a large number of damaged and/or abandoned tanks on the battlefield.

The tank losses suffered by the British 11th Armoured Division and the Guards Armoured Division were largely replaced in the course of the night. The situation was quite different on the German side. As a result of the speedy replacement of lost vehicles, the British were able to field three completely full armored divisions for the continuation of the attack.

✠

During the night, the British infantry was able to close up with the tanks. The majority of the artillery was brought across the Orne. The morning of 19 July 1944 started more quietly—in stark contrast to the previous day—even though there was intense fighting at a few places.

Along the Orne, the Canadians had taken all of Mondeville and Fauburg de Vaucelles after the *II./ Panzer-Grenadier-Regiment 192* had abandoned those two villages and marched off to Troarn.

The *272. Infanterie-Division* was unable to hold Fleury-sur-Orne. As a result, the Canadians had taken the suburbs of the city of Caen. The fighting continued in the new sector for the *21. Panzer-Division* (Emiéville–St. Pair–Troarn).

The 9th Brigade of the British 3rd Infantry Division renewed its attack on Troarn. At 1000 hours, the 1st Battalion of the King's Own Scottish Borderers attacked along the road to the train station. Its attack was supported by tanks, but it was rebuffed. At 1045 hours, an attack followed by the 2nd Battalion of the Royal Ulster Rifles. There was bitter fighting around a church. Five British tanks were knocked out.

A German counterattack at La Croix de Pierre bogged down in the face of strong enemy defensive fire.

During the early-morning hours of 19 July 1944, the British 185th Brigade attacked at Manneville and Cuillerville and penetrated into the abandoned villages. The British were able to take in the handiwork of their bombs in the patches of woods at Manneville and Cuillerville. They found four destroyed *Tigers* from *schwere Panzer-Abteilung 503* as well as a number of other destroyed major items of equipment: twelve *Panzer IV's*, three *Panzer III's*, seven *SPW's* with 2-centimeter *Flak* and 4 *PaK*.

During the afternoon of 19 July 1944, the English moved out to land another punch in the center of the attack zone. After an intensive barrage on the villages of Bras and Hubert-Folie from the artillery that had been brought forward the previous night across the Orne, the tanks of the 2nd Battalion of the Northhamptonshire Yeomanry attacked Bras from the north starting at 1615 hours.

At the same time, the 3rd Royal Tank Regiment moved out with twenty-five tanks in the direction of Hubert-Folie, which was being defended by the *I./SS-Panzer-Grenadier-Regiment 1*. When the enemy tanks got to the point that they had reached the previous day, they were once again brought to a standstill in the face of concentrated defensive fire.

When the English attempted to bypass Bras to the west, the enemy tanks ran in the engagement area of an 8.8-centimeter *Flak* battery of the *III. Flak-Korps* and the assault guns of *SS-Sturmgeschütz-Abteilung 1*. The enemy armored forces had ventured too far forward and lost half of their vehicles. What remained pulled back in the direction of Cormelles.

In the meantime, the 3rd Royal Tank Regiment, which had originally been attacking Hubert-Folie again, was sent against the village of Bras from the northeast in a change to the attack plan. This time, the English succeeded in penetrating into Bras. In accomplishing this, they were supported by the motorized infantry of the 8th Battalion of the Rifles Brigade and also helped by the thick clouds of smoke that had been caused by the barrage fire that had preceded the attack.

After succeeding in knocking out nine enemy tanks, the defending grenadiers of the *III./SS-Panzer-Grenadier-Regiment 1* and the supporting assault guns of *SS-Sturmgeschütz-Abteilung 1* pulled back to a new line some two kilometers south of Bras.

That same afternoon, the British 7th Armoured Division moved out to attack at 1700 hours, following heavy barrage fire on the objective area. The 5th Battalion Royal Tank Regiment of the 22nd Armoured Brigade attacked Soliers with some 70 tanks. The combat outposts of the *I./SS-Panzer-Grenadier-Regiment 1*, who were screening in the village, pulled back in accordance with their orders to a line some two-three kilometers farther to the rear. Soliers was lost to the enemy.

Another attack, this one by the 1st Battalion Royal Tank Regiment, was launched against Four. This led to the withdrawal of the combat outposts of the

II./SS-Panzer-Grenadier-Regiment 2 to their rearward positions. By 1500 hours, Four had already been abandoned, with the exception of a few screening elements.

The fighting was bitter south of Four. A new German line was established north of Bourguébus and La Hogue. For the time being, Bourguébus continued to be held. The attempt by the "Desert Rats" to continue to advance on both sides of Bourguébus was turned back at the new defensive positions of the *1. SS- Panzer-Division "Leibstandarte SS Adolf Hitler."*

Then, at 1700 hours, the Guards Armoured Division attacked Le Poiriere and Frénouville. The attack was turned back from Frénouville thanks to the reinforced *SS-Panzer-Grenadier-Regiment 25* (*Kampfgruppe Waldmüller*), which was supported by *SS-Panzer-Jäger-Abteilung 12.* Le Poiriere, however, was lost.

While poor weather prevented appreciable enemy air activity during the first part of the day, it cleared up in the afternoon. Enemy aircraft appeared in great number and participated in the fighting against ground targets.

After another heavy artillery barrage, tanks of the 2nd Fife and Forfar Yeomanry attacked Hubert-Folie again, with support from a company each from the 8th Battalion of the Rifles Brigade and the 4th Battalion of the King's Own Shropshire Infantry. Even though a few *Tigers* of *schwere SS-Panzer-Abteilung 101* and several 8.8-centimeter *Flak* joined in the fighting, it was no longer possible to hold Hubert-Folie.

For the barrage "spectacle" on Bras and Hubert-Folie, the English fired some 100,000 shells. Although the British 11th Armoured Division had gained some ground, it still had not succeeded in achieving a decisive breakthrough.

During the afternoon of 19 July 1944, *Panzer-Grenadier-Regiment 125* moved out of Emiéville and attacked in the direction of Cuillerville with two companies and support from six tanks from *Panzer-Regiment 22.* The attack bogged down in the heavy defensive fire of the British. Because further bombing attacks were feared during the night, all of the forward positions along the main line of resistance were only occupied by weak outposts. To the rear, the Germans worked feverishly in improving defensive positions. In Bourguébus there was only a single *Tiger* screening.

✠

From the British perspective, the events of 19 July 1944 looked like this:

> Because of the heavy tank losses, General O'Connor now assigned the 11th Armoured Division the limited objectives of taking Bras, some 4 miles south-west of the overnight harbour, and Hubert-Folie, some 3 miles west-south-west. 7th Armoured were to take Soliers and Bourguébus, and the Guards Armoured was pitted against Cagny to the west and Four to the south. . . .
>
> During the day the division achieved its two objectives, again at a heavy cost. Another sixty-five tanks were written off. The German command had reacted quickly to the massive threat posed by Goodwood.

7th Armoured took Four and the Guards Le Poirier, but Goodwood was now contained.

✠

During the night of 19–20 July 1944, the British attacked the new positions of the *21. Panzer-Division* in the area of St. Pair and Troarn. The attack was preceded by a two-hour artillery preparation. *Panzer-Grenadier-Regiment 192* was able to fend this attack off.

On the morning of 20 July 1944, the 5th Battalion Royal Tank Regiment attacked again. It was able to take Bourguébus, which was only lightly defended, with its B Squadron. In the process, the single *Tiger* screening there—turret number *231*—was knocked out. In addition, two abandoned *Panthers* were also captured in the village.

Only combat outposts of the *12. SS-Panzer-Division "Hitlerjugend"* were positioned in Frénouville. A new line had been established just north of La Hogue during the night. The attacking 32nd Guards Brigade of the Guards Armoured Division could not be kept out of Frénouville, however, it was stopped from a further advance on Vimont.

Towards 1630 hours, the Canadian 2nd Infantry Division broke through as far as St. André-sur-Orne and St. Martin de Fontenay. It had attacked via Hills 72 and 61 south of Ifs with infantry and tanks after a heavy barrage-fire preparation. Heavy fighting took place into the night along the streets and roads. Both localities remained contested as a result. The Canadians took responsibility for Bras and Hubert-Folie.

On the afternoon of 20 July, the weather turned and there were severe storms and cloudbursts. This began three days of rain. The loamy ground on the plain east of the Orne turned into a morass. The fronts began to solidify, and the men of both sides suffered in their foxholes, which filled up with water.

Still feeling the impact of the tough defense offered by the Germans, the losses suffered and the onset of bad weather, General Montgomery called off Operation "Goodwood." The commander of *Panzer-Regiment 22, Oberst* von Luck, commented as follows after the war:

> The British failure to capture the Bourguébus ridge was because the British tank advance was too slow and no British infantry was advancing in close contact with tanks to break any kind of resistance. Also a strong British night attack south-east on the 18th could have probably opened the way for further advance on the 19th.

He admitted to one stroke of luck in that the great Allied air bombing had not reached the two anti-tank/anti-aircraft battalions on Bourguébus ridge.

> If German troops trained on the Russian front had been entrusted with the attacking role in Goodwood, the attack would have been made very early in the morning with one infantry division in front assisted by armoured assault guns to break through the first resistance followed at once by armored divisions to break through.

General "Pip" Roberts would have agreed. General O'Connor would have disagreed.

The Army commander, General Miles Dempsey, told Chester Wilmot after "Goodwood" had finished:

> The attack we put in on 18 July was not a very good operation of war tactically, but strategically it was a great success, even though we did get a bloody nose. I didn't mind about that, I was prepared to lose a couple of hundred tanks. So long as I didn't lose men. We could afford the tanks because they had begun to pile up in the bridgehead [500 or more Shermans lying idle]. Our

> tanks losses were severe but our casualties in men were very light. If I had tried to achieve the same result with a conventional infantry attack I hate to think what the casualties would have been.

✠

The course of Operation "Goodwood" was intentionally described in such detail so as to demonstrate the main burden of the defensive fighting was not necessarily borne by the tanks. As a result of the heavy bombing attacks, they would not have had the chance anyway.

The end result of Operation "Goodwood" is well known. The British were only able to gain approximately twelve kilometers of ground. Of the 877 tanks employed, 437 were knocked out or destroyed. Even now, it is attempted again and again to try to make this and other bad decisions on the part of General Montgomery look good by arguing that the main purpose of the offensive was to tie up as many German forces as possible so that the operations of the Americans could be successfully executed. This does a disservice to the bravery of the German infantry and the few tanks employed there.

What was problematical for the German side, however, was the fact that armored forces that they had hoped to be able to pull out of the line—the *1. SS-Panzer-Division "Leibstandarte SS Adolf Hitler"* or the *12. SS-Panzer-Division "Hitlerjugend"*—had to be recommitted into the fighting. As a result, any hopes of being able to launch a major counteroffensive in the near term were finally buried after Operation "Goodwood."

✠

It should be emphasized that *schwere SS-Panzer-Abteilung 101* assisted considerably in defending against the British. The armored elements of the enemy's attack force that had advanced the furthest were engaged and destroyed from positions on high ground near Bourguébus as well as by means of local counterattacks. These were done in conjunction with armored elements of the *1. SS-Panzer-Division "Leibstandarte SS Adolf Hitler."*

Schwere SS-Panzer-Abteilung 101 and its *Tigers* participated in the following engagements:

During the first counterattack of 18 July 1944, several enemy tanks were eliminated west of Hubert-Folie and north of La Guinguette. One *Tiger* was knocked out by a Firefly of the 5th Battalion Royal Tank Regiment south of Soliers. (It was dispatched by a round through a haystack.)

On 19 July 1944, there were scattered operations undertaken by the operational tanks. The 3rd Company was employed at Chicheboville. The commander of the company, *SS-Obersturmführer* Raasch, was knocked out in *Tiger 305* by friendly fire (antitank guns) and killed.

On 20 July 1944, one *Tiger* of the 2nd Company was knocked out by forces of the City of London Yeomanry at Bras. *Tiger 231* was knocked out at Bourguébus. The 3rd Company was employed at the *Ferme Beauvoire.*

On 24 July 1944, six *Tigers* of the 3rd Company under the command of *SS-Hauptsturmführer* Heurich were in position in a patch of woods at Garcelles-Secqueville.

It must also be said, however, that the enemy did manage to get out of the confinement of the Orne bridgehead and that the losses sustained on the German side could not be replaced.

✠

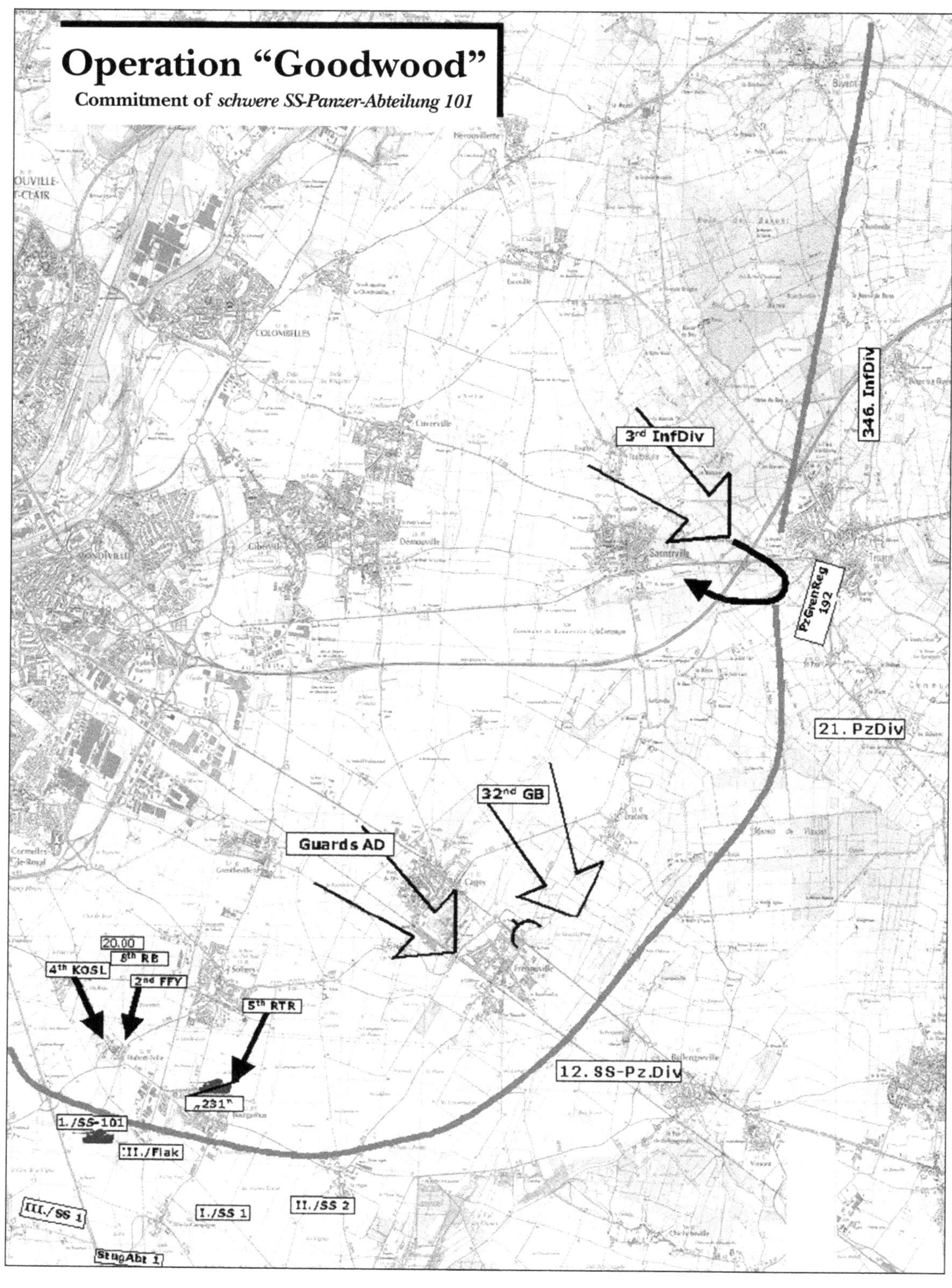
Operation "Goodwood"
Commitment of schwere SS-Panzer-Abteilung 101
346. InfDiv
3rd InfDiv
PzGrenReg 192
21. PzDiv
32nd GB
Guards AD
20.00
8th RB
4th KOSL
2nd FFY
5th RTR
12. SS-Pz.Div
„231"
1./SS-101
II./Flak
III./SS 1
I./SS 1
II./SS 2
StugAbt 1

Until the last week of July, senior German commanders were counting on a continuation of the offensive by the English and the Canadians in the area south or east of Caen as soon as the bad-weather period ended.

For these reasons, *Generalfeldmarschall* von Kluge, who had also assumed command of *Heeresgruppe B* on 19 July 1944 after Rommel had been wounded, reinforced the defensive forces in this area. His first step was to pull the *2. Panzer-Division* (*Generalleutnant* von Lüttwitz) out of the line south of Caumont and replace it with the *326. Infanterie-Division* (*Generalleutnant* von Dabrich-Waechter), which had been brought forward by the *15. Armee.*

The *2. Panzer-Division,* which had set up for the defense for six weeks behind dense minefields, was assembled in the woods around Bretteville-sur-Laison, Fresney, Les Moutiers and Barbery, all to the south of Caen and east of the Orne.

Generalfeldmarschall von Kluge then requested the *116. Panzer-Division* (*Generalleutnant Graf* von Schwerin) be brought forward into Normandy from the area around Amiens east of the Seine. It had previously been on stand-by there at the disposal of the *15. Armee.* It was intended for this armored division to be moved into the St. Lô area to reinforce the *7. Armee,* which was being hard pressed by the Americans.

When the *116. Panzer-Division* was brought forward, it was initially halted east of the Orne by *Generalfeldmarschall* von Kluge. He was toying with the idea of relieving the badly battered *21. Panzer-Division* with it. It was then intended to earmark the headquarters of the *XLVII. Panzer-Korps* (*General der*

Tiger 231, knocked out at Bourguébus on 20 July 1944. (Jean Restayn)

Panzertruppen Freiherr von Funck) with the command and control of these two armored divisions.

Up to this point, there had been five German armored divisions fighting in the Caen area. With the addition of the *2. Panzer-Division* and the *116. Panzer-Division*, there was a total of seven armored divisions, plus all of the heavy tank battalions. Of the armored divisions, six were positioned east of the Orne in anticipation of the continuation of the enemy offensive there.

The bulk of the German armored formations were therefore within the command area of *Panzergruppe West*.

The *7. Armee*, which was defending in the American sector, had considerably weaker armored forces at its disposal: the *2. SS-Panzer-Division "Das Reich,"* the *Panzer-Lehr-Division* and the *17. SS-Panzer-Grenadier-Division "Götz von Berlichingen."*

General Montgomery had thus attained a portion of what he had stated was his intention: to fix the majority of the German armored divisions at Caen by the forces of his British 2nd Army, thus making it easier in the west for the Americans with their U.S. 1st Army (General Bradley) to break out into the open into the depths of France. At the same time, the pressure he was exerting in the area around Caen continued to offer the threat of a breakout towards Paris.

The Battle of Normandy Nears Its Decisive Phase

In the first seven weeks of the Battle for Normandy, the Germans had brought up an additional twenty divisions on top of the seven divisions that were already in the area on the day of the invasion. As a result of the almost complete Allied air superiority and the resulting continuous air attacks on the logistics lines of communications, hardly any of the additional divisions that were introduced arrived at full strength and were operational as an integral formation.

As they arrived, they were committed into the fight—as battalions or regiments.

Of the 127,247 personnel that had been reported as killed, wounded or missing within *Heeresgruppe B* by 27 July 1944, only 14,594 men had been replaced. Of the 225 tanks that had been completely lost during the first few weeks of fighting, a total of 17 new tanks had been issued up to that point to replace them. Tank losses up to 23 July 1944: 406 total losses in *Panzer IV's*, *Panzer V's*, and *Panzer VI's*, with 353 other tanks under repair. During the same time period 75 assault guns were written off and 117 were being repaired. The equipment losses of the enemy during the same period were 2,395 tanks and 402 aircraft.

While all this was transpiring, the Allies were bringing in thirty-six divisions by sea without any interruption. The superiority of the enemy increased daily. Any materiel losses could be replaced by the depots that were already located in the bridgehead. By the last third of July, the Allied bridgehead was ready to burst at the seams. More than 2,000,000 soldiers were facing one another in Normandy.

On 21 July 1944, one day after the attempt on Hitler's life and still with impressions of the "Goodwood" offensive on his mind, *Generalfeldmarschall* von Kluge passed on *Generalfeldmarschall* Rommel's last estimate of the situation to Hitler:

> . . . under these circumstances it must be anticipated that the enemy will succeed in the not-to-distant future—especially in the sector of the *7. Armee*—to break through and advance into the depths of France. The consequences are enormous. Our forces are fighting heroically everywhere, however, the unequal struggle is coming to a close.
>
> I must ask you to draw the appropriate conclusions from this situation.

THE CANADIAN FAILURE

An intense attack started at 0330 hours on 25 July 1944 in the sector of the Canadian II Corps (General G. G. Simonds) on both sides of the Caen–Falaise road seemed to confirm the evaluation of the senior German headquarters that the Allied main effort would continue to be in the Caen sector. This was Operation "Spring," which was launched together with elements of the British 7th Armoured Division and the Guards Armoured Division.

There was intense fighting for the localities of Tilly-la-Champagne, Verrières, St. Martin-de-Fontenay, St. André-sur-Orne, May-sur-Orne and Fontenay-le-Marmion.

In bitter defensive fighting and counterattacks, the *272. Infanterie-Division*, the *1. SS-Panzer-Division "Leibstandarte SS Adolf Hitler,"* elements of the *9. SS-Panzer-Division "Hohenstaufen"* and an armored *Kampfgruppe* of the *2. Panzer-Division* turned back the Canadians, in what would be their most casualty-intensive fighting of the Normandy campaign.

The Canadian 3rd Infantry Division attempted to bite into granite when it attacked the *1. SS-Panzer-Division "Leibstandarte SS Adolf Hitler"* at Tilly-la-Champagne, and it suffered heavy casualties. *Tigers* from *schwere SS-Panzer-Abteilung 101* supported the defensive fighting from good positions at locations such as Garcelles-Secqueville. Even the initial success enjoyed on the left in the sector of the *272. Infanterie-Division* was overturned by determined immediate counterattacks.

It was to be in the American sector that the major decision concerning the breakout from Normandy was reached.

OPERATION "COBRA"

After difficult fighting that was also casualty-intensive for the Americans, St. Lô was taken during the evening of 18 July 1944. As a result, the Americans were poised to break out along the St. Lô–Périers road. They had obtained the jump-off positions needed to launch Operation "Cobra," the breakout into the open terrain of France by the U.S. 1st Army.

Originally, this attack had been planned for 20 July 1944, that is, two days after the start of the British-Canadian Operation "Goodwood," thus allowing the Germans no respite. Once again, it was intended for an operation to commence with the full impact of all available combat aircraft at one location. The Allied air forces needed two days after the horrific carpet bombing of 18 July 1944 east of the Orne to prepare for another aerial onslaught of this magnitude. But the bad weather conditions on 20 July 1944 postponed this intention in addition to ultimately leading to the breaking off of Operation "Goodwood" east of the Orne.

This delay appeared to benefit the Germans, because it afforded them the opportunity to mass armored forces at Caen. By doing so, however, they went to the wrong place.

The *Panzer-Lehr-Division* under *Generalleutnant* Bayerlein had been fighting in the area west of St. Lô ever since 11 July 1944, where it had engaged the Americans in casualty-intensive fighting on both sides in the broken *bocage* country.

In order to make good the casualties that resulted from the constant artillery fire, the *5. Fallschirm-Jäger-Division* of *Generalmajor* Wilke, which was still in the process of being formed, was brought forward from the Bretagne region.

The *Panzer-Lehr-Division* and the *5. Fallschirm-Jäger-Division* defended in a line running from St. Lô through Périers to Lessay. Both divisions were

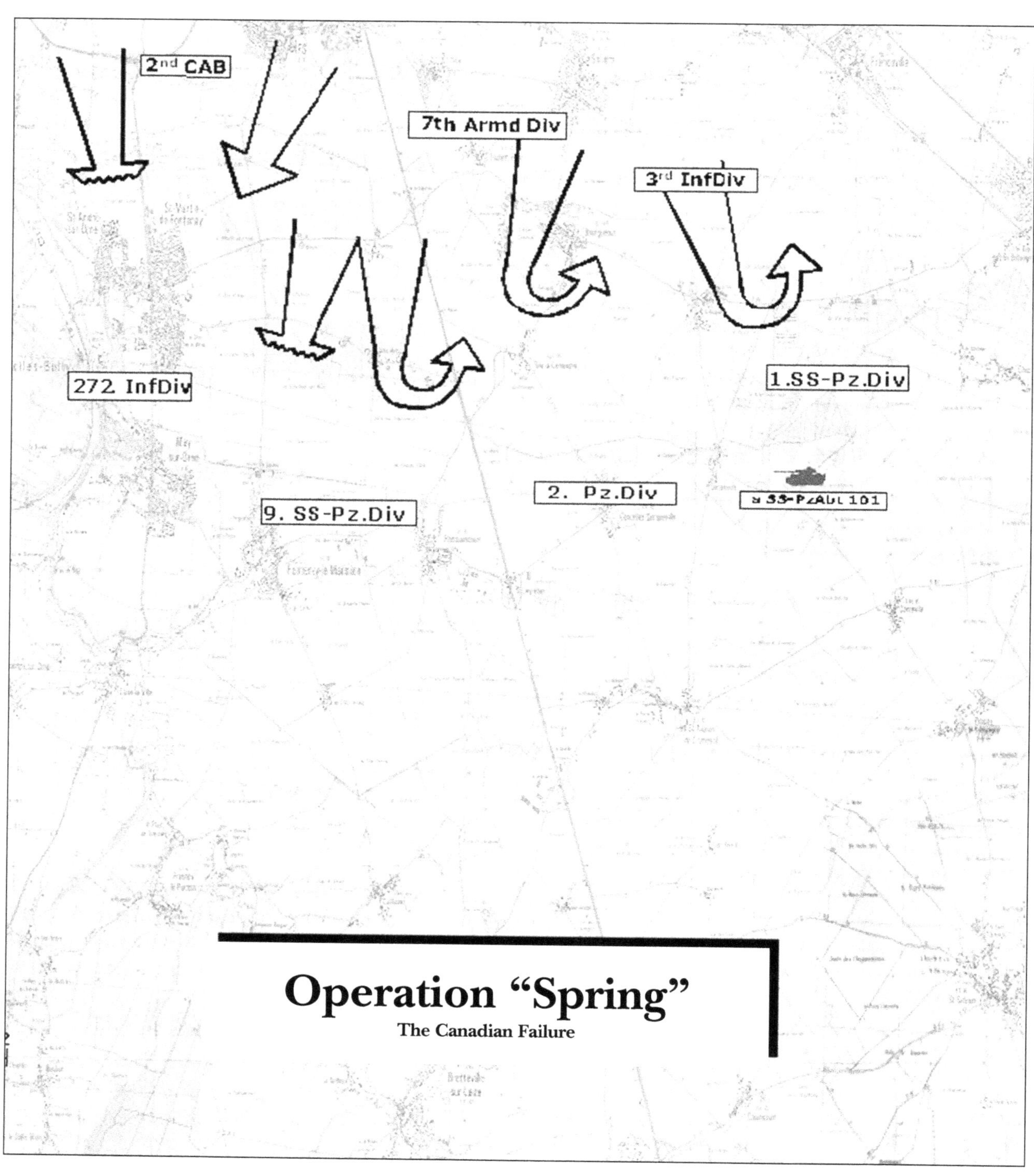

Operation "Spring"

The Canadian Failure

under the command of the *LXXXIV. Armee-Korps* (*Generalleutnant* von Choltitz).

The Americans had placed two armored divisions and four infantry divisions against the *Panzer-Lehr-Division*. This was a massing of some 140,000 men and 500 tanks. To that number were added some 1,000 artillery pieces.

The Americans hit at 0940 hours on 25 July 1944. The Allied air forces attacked with 2,264 bombers dropping some 6,000 tons of bombs. For the first time, there were some 300 tons of napalm as well. It was dropped in the area of Hebecrevon, south of the Périers–St. Lô road. Once again, it was another carpet bombing, the likes of which were feared by all German combatants in Normandy. It virtually destroyed the *Panzer-Lehr-Division*.

The divisions of the U.S. VII Corps moved out at 1100 hours behind the barrage fire of American artillery. They broke through the lines from Périers to St. Lô against what amounted to a delaying action. On the morning of 27 July 1944, they advanced across a line defined by Marigny and St. Gilles with the intent of breaking through to the south.

The commander of the *Panzer-Lehr-Division* sent the following bitter message to *Heeresgruppe B* and the commander-in-chief West at 2215 hours on 27 July 1944:

> 1. After 49 days of the hardest fighting imaginable, the *Panzer-Lehr-Division* has been eliminated today.
>
> 2. Broken through on all sides, the enemy is now continuing to roll from St. Gilles to the south.
>
> All requests for assistance in terms of forces have remained unheard up to this point, because one did not want to believe how serious the situation is.

Because the *7. Armee* was not in a position to prevent the expected breakthrough of the Americans with its own forces, *Generalfeldmarschall* von Kluge ordered the immediate movement of the headquarters of the *XLVII. Panzer-Korps*—including the *2. Panzer-Division* and the *116. Panzer-Division*—out of the area around Caen and into the area west of St. Lô.

At the same time, the U.S. VIII Corps attacked in the western half of the Cotentin Peninsula to the south from a line running from Lessay to Périers. The corps reached Coutances. By the afternoon of 28 July 1944, it broke though the weakly held lines of the *242. Infanterie-Division* and the *91. Luftlande-Division* that were defending there.

The left wing of the *7. Armee* had been smashed.

The U.S. 4th Armored Division reached Avranches during the evening of 30 July 1944. Advancing further, it established a bridgehead over the Selune at Pountaubault. The door to the Bretagne was then open for General Patton, who was ready to advance into the open French terrain with his U.S. 3rd Army.

In the meantime, the British had also been preparing their next blow.

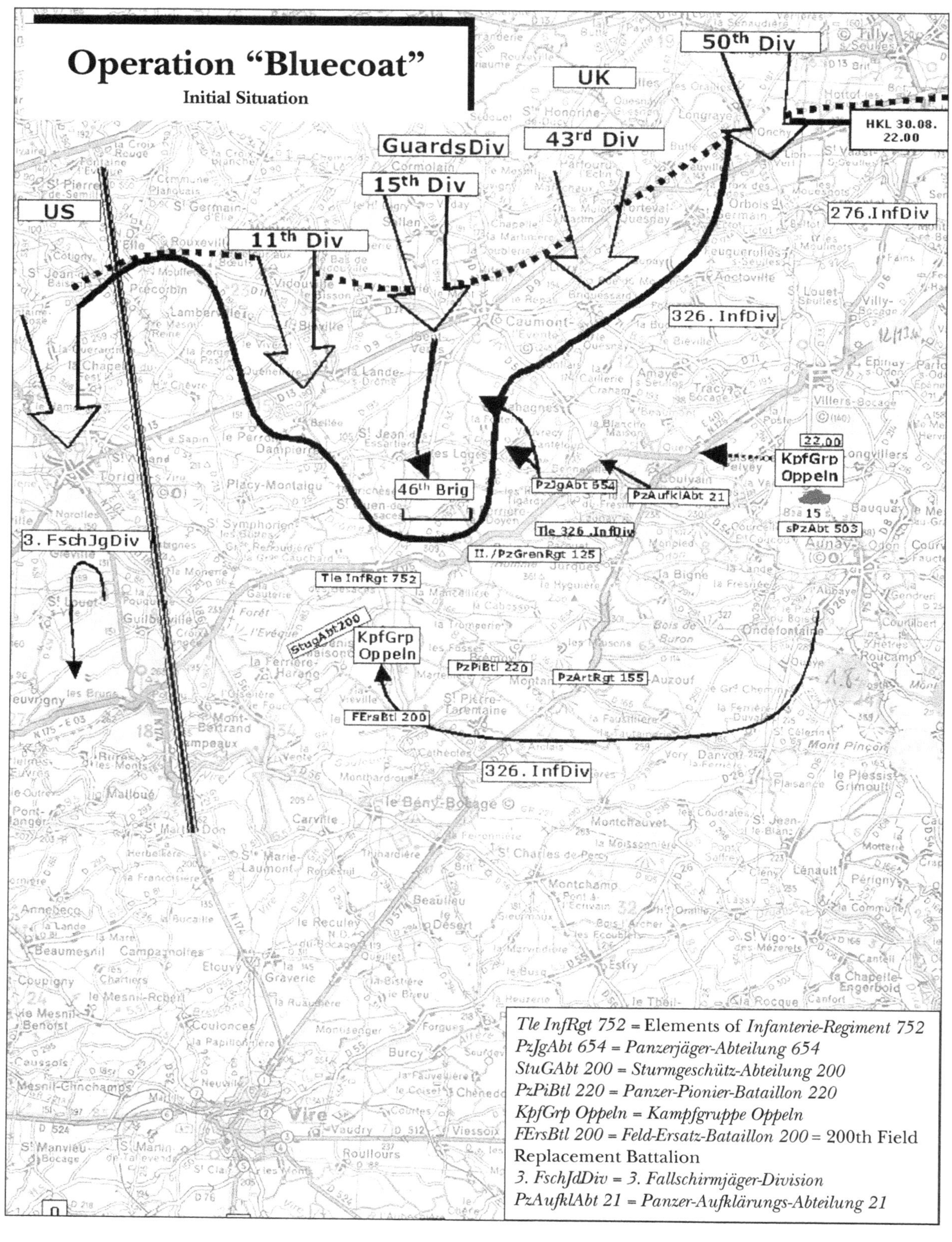
Operation "Bluecoat"
Initial Situation
UK
US
50th Div
HKL 30.08. 22.00
43rd Div
GuardsDiv
15th Div
11th Div
276.InfDiv
326.InfDiv
46th Brig
PzJgAbt 654
PzAufklAbt 21
22.00
KpfGrp Oppeln
15
sPzAbt 503
Tle 326.InfDiv
II./PzGrenRgt 125
Tle InfRgt 752
3. FschJgDiv
StugAbt 200
KpfGrp Oppeln
PzPiBtl 220
PzArtRgt 155
FErsBtl 200
326.InfDiv
Tle InfRgt 752 = Elements of Infanterie-Regiment 752
PzJgAbt 654 = Panzerjäger-Abteilung 654
StuGAbt 200 = Sturmgeschütz-Abteilung 200
PzPiBtl 220 = Panzer-Pionier-Bataillon 220
KpfGrp Oppeln = Kampfgruppe Oppeln
FErsBtl 200 = Feld-Ersatz-Bataillon 200 = 200th Field Replacement Battalion
3. FschJdDiv = 3. Fallschirmjäger-Division
PzAufklAbt 21 = Panzer-Aufklärungs-Abteilung 21

CHAPTER 9

Operation "Bluecoat"

In the area of Caen on the eastern flank of the wavering Normandy front, heavy traffic was suddenly observed on the roads heading towards the west. This was in addition to continued large areas of concentration among the enemy. The English, who were apparently withdrawing their tanks from the high ground at Bourguébus, were taking pains to mask their movements through smoke.

✠

General Montgomery had not been happy with the way the outcome to Operation "Goodwood" was treated among the Allied staffs and in the press in Great Britain and the United States. He felt that his intentions had been interpreted incorrectly. His strategy would be a topic of debate well into the post-war period. He stated the following in his memoirs after the war:

> But my primary strategic objective was and remained to concentrate large armored forces on the eastern flank southeast of Caen, somewhere in the area of Bourbuérgus, so as to fix German armored forces there. It was intended, as a result, to facilitate the breakout of the Americans in the west.
>
> We did not advance against the more highly elevated terrain until armored forces of the 2nd Army started Operation "Goodwood" on 18 July 1944. However, as soon as the armored advance did not make any headway—partly due to the heavy rainfall that turned the area into a sea of mud and partly due to the determined resistance of the enemy—I called off the operation. [Reverse-translated from the German text of the original English.]

Certainly also a viewpoint of things designed to divert attention away from mediocre leadership qualities.

✠

General Montgomery's deliberations after the conclusion of Operation "Goodwood" were simple and his corresponding decisions logical: If almost all of the German armored divisions were assembled in the area around Caen in front of his sector—as was readily apparent—and, by extension, they represented almost all of the German armored forces available on the entire battlefield, then he was compelled to attack at a point where there were no more armored formations at all.

These conclusions were reinforced by the failure of the attack of the Canadian II Corps on 25 July 1944 on both sides of the Caen-to-Falaise road in "Operation "Spring". In the face of the bitter resistance offered by the *1. SS-Panzer-Division "Leibstandarte SS Adolf Hitler,"* the *272. Infanterie-Division* and battle groups from the *9. SS-Panzer-Division "Hohenstaufen"* and the *2. Panzer-Division,* the operation had failed miserably.

On the morning of 26 July, there were four *Tigers* of *schwere SS-Panzer-Abteilung 101* employed in the attack zone of Operation "Spring." These *Tigers* supported a counterattack of the *1. SS-Panzer-Division "Leibstandarte SS Adolf Hitler"* against the Canadian Royal Regiment, which was attacking at Verrièrres. They engaged a company of the 1st Royal Tank Regiment.

✠

The area in the sector of Montgomery's 2nd Army where there were almost no more German tanks was on the other end of the battlefield on the western flank. It was the area south of Caumont and Villers-Bocage, where the *2. Panzer-Division* had just been pulled out of the line. General Montgomery wanted to have the attack launched there in order to support the anticipated breakout of the U.S. 1st Army west of St. Lô in the western part of the Normandy front.

General Montgomery wanted to create another hot spot in front of the sector of the British 2nd Army so as to continue to fix German forces there. Otherwise, they would most certainly be committed into the area of operations of the *7. Armee*, which was being threatened by the Americans.

On 27 July 1944, General Montgomery issued his orders, and the British started considerable repositioning in order to move the focal point of their activities from around Caen to the area south of Caumont. Operation "Bluecoat" was being prepared.

The staff of the Canadian 1st Army (Lieutenant General Crerar) had already been flown into Normandy from England. On 23 July 1944, it assumed command over the Canadian II Corps and the British I Corps, thus giving it command over the eastern flank of the Normandy front on both sides of the Orne.

The first division pulled out of the Orne area—once again moving from east to west—was the British 11th Armoured Division. It was followed by the 7th Armoured Division and then the Guards Armoured Division.

General Dempsey shifted the front of his 2nd Army to the west as far as the area around Caumont. He linked up with the American sector there. The battered British armored divisions had been able to quickly make good their losses from the full equipment depots.

✠

For Operation "Bluecoat," the following forces were assembled:

- Right (west) flank: British VIII Corps (Lieutenant General N. O. Connor):
  - 15th (Scottish) Division
  - British 11th Armoured Division
  - Guards Armoured Division and the
  - 6th Guards Armoured Brigade
- Left (east) flank: British XXX Corps (Lieutenant General G. C. Bucknall):
  - 43rd (Wessex) Division
  - 50th Northhumbrian Division
  - 7th Armoured Division
  - 8th Armoured Brigade

The attack objective: The taking of the high ground from Bény to Bocage and the city of Vire. The two corps were to exert pressure, fix the German forces and prevent them from using the dominant Mont Pincon as a defensive bulwark.

General Montgomery's exhortation to his 2nd Army: "Step on the gas to Vire" General Dempsey had assembled in the area around Caumont no less than three infantry divisions, three armored divisions and two armored brigades, with a total of more than 1,000 tanks. These forces were approaching the sectors of the *276. Infanterie-Division* and the *326. Infanterie-Division.*

✠

The *276. Infanterie-Division* of *Generalleutnant* Badinski had arrived from southern France on 19 June 1944 and relieved the *Panzer-Lehr-Division.* This division was facing three British divisions and an armored brigade, all of which had already experienced their baptism of fire.

The *326. Infanterie-Division* of *Generalleutnant* Drabisch-Waechter, which had heretofore enjoyed a quiet time at the *Pas de Calais* in the sector of the *15. Armee,* had just recently arrived in Normandy. This division, the left-wing division of *Panzergruppe West,* saw itself also facing three divisions, of which two were armored, and an armored brigade.

There were no German armored formations in this area, except for a few damaged tanks still left from the recently relieved *2. Panzer-Division.* The only antitank force available to the corps was *schwere Panzerjäger-Abteilung 654*—equipped with the *Jagdpanther* tank destroyer—which was in direct support of the corps.

Command and control of these two infantry divisions fell to the headquarters of the *LXXIV. Armee-Korps* (*General der Infanterie* Straube), which had just arrived from the Bretagne on 27 July 1944.

The friendly forces to the left—on the right wing of the sector of the *7. Armee* of *SS-Obergruppenführer* Hausser—was the headquarters of the *II. Fallschirm-Korps* of *General der Fallschirmtruppe* Meindl.

When an observer looks from the high ground at Caumont to the south, then three groups of hills assume a dominating position over the otherwise broken *bocage* country: Hill 365, Mont Pincon and, farther to the west, Hills 361 and 309.

Hill 361 was the first day's objective for the 43rd Wessex Division, which had already been engaged in difficult fighting at Hill 112 (west of Caen) at the end of June. The objective of the 15th (Scottish) Division was Hill 309.

Due to the surprisingly rapid progress of the American attack in the area west of St. Lô (Operation "Cobra"), the start of Operation "Bluecoat" was moved forward two days from its original start date of 2 August 1944. This was done even though not all of the British forces had closed on their assembly areas.

✠

The 30th of July 1944 started with a gray, muggy morning. In the interest of keeping their intentions secret, the British forewent their normal practice of having a long-lasting artillery preparation that had been preceded by an aerial bombardment.

For this reason, identified targets were not bombed and placed under considerable artillery fire until the attack started. Heavy bombers of the British Bomber Command carpet-bombed the positions of the *276. Infanterie-Division* four times. Medium bombers of the U.S. 9th Tactical Air Force carpet bombed the area of the *326. Infanterie-Division* three times. Low-lying, thick clouds interfered with the bombing runs, so that a portion of the 1,000 bombers could not identify their targets and had to return to base with their bomb loads. The carpet bombing was timed to coincide with the start of the armored attack or shortly afterwards.

The British 50th Northhumbrian Division attacked behind a rolling barrage at 0600 hours.

Moving along the Caen–Caumont road and supported by a brigade of tanks, the division moved against the positions of the *276. Infanterie-Division.* For the most part, however, it was initially repulsed. The right wing of the *326. Infanterie-Division* was also able to hold out initially against the attack at St. Germain d'Ectot. The *326. Infanterie-Division* had to pull back in its center, however. Towards noon, forces of the 43rd Wessex Division broke through at Briquessard and reached Cahagnes by evening. They were not able to take their day's objective of Hill 361.

The 15th (Scottish) Division broke through at Sept-Vents, advanced in the direction of St. Jean-des-Essartiers and then reached Loges. Towards 1900 hours, Churchills of the 6th Guards Armoured Brigade reached the dominant terrain of Hill 309. Infantry of the 46th Brigade quickly followed. The Scots dug in on Hill 309. They dragged their antitank guns up the hill by hand. Counterattacks launched by local reserves of the *326. Infanterie-Division* remained without effect.

Although two *Jagdpanther* of *schwere Panzerjäger-Abteilung 654* were able to knock out a few tanks of the 6th Guards Armoured Brigade with their effective 8.8-centimeter main guns at Loges and on Hill 226 around 1800 hours in an immediate counterattack, they were unable to turn back the attackers.

Individual groups of the *326. Infanterie-Division* were still holding out east of Hill 309 in La Ferriére-au-Doyen and in the *Bois du Homme* (Hill 361).

Farther to the west, tanks of the British 11th Armoured Division approached Dampierre while advancing along the Caumont–Torigni road. They had had to breach German minefields, which initially had caused them some difficulties. They took the village of Dampierre in the evening.

Some of the infantry of the *326. Infanterie-Division,* who had been overwhelmed by the carpet bombing attacks, fled to the rear in panic. The command post of the *326. Infanterie-Division* had been destroyed in aerial attacks and two regimental command posts had been overrun by tanks.

During the night of 30–31 July 1944, the enemy prepared to continue his offensive in a patch of woods north of St. Martin-des-Besaces. At 0400 hours on the morning of 31 July 1944, infantrymen of the 4th Battalion of the King's Own Shropshire Light Infantry of the 11th Armoured Division reached the road west of St. Martin-des-Besaces. A few tanks of the *2. Panzer-Division* that had remained behind knocked out some armored cars and kept the enemy from immediately penetrating into the village. The only other German "tanks" in the area were dummy tanks that had been set up to deceive the enemy.

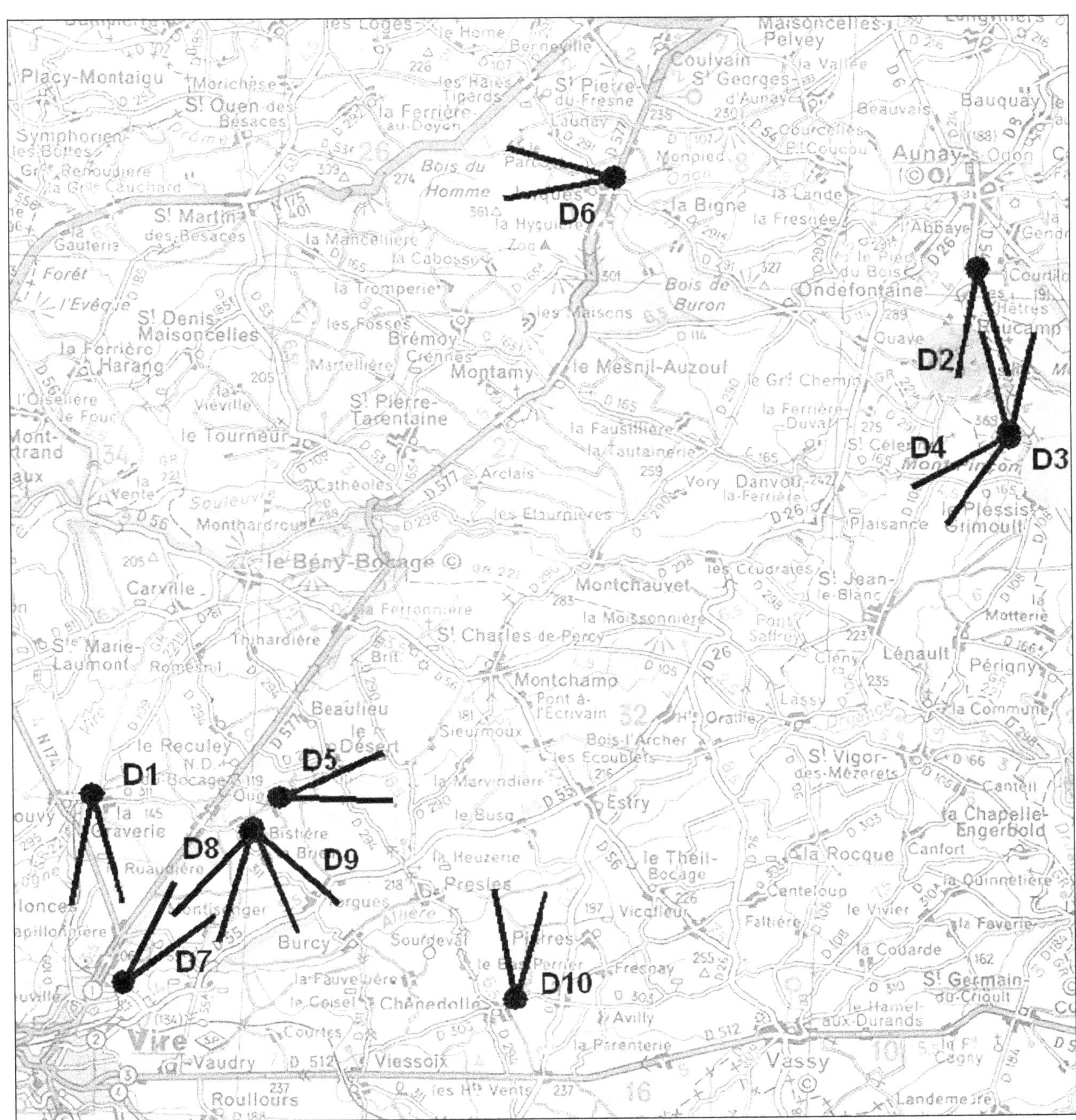

This sketch map shows the location of the vantage points in the photographs that follow for the area of operations of *schwere Panzer-Abteilung 503* at Mont Pinçon and to the north, as well as the operations of *schwere SS-Panzer-Abteilung 101* at Vire.

Above: British view to the south in the direction of Vire, which is located approximately in the middle of the picture behind the cut in the ridgeline. For the British, the attack meant an assault of several kilometers over largely open terrain. The Americans, for their part, had already passed Vire on the viewer's right behind the hill mass. Below: British vantage point to the south from the heights of Mont Pinçon.

Above: The view from Mont Pinçon towards the British lines. The advantages to the defenders are quite obvious.
Below: The view to the southwest. The open terrain favors maneuver warfare. For the Germans, it offered little opportunity to effectively hold up the enemy. The objective of Operation "Bluecoat" was to take that terrain, creating the prerequisites for the final breakthrough.

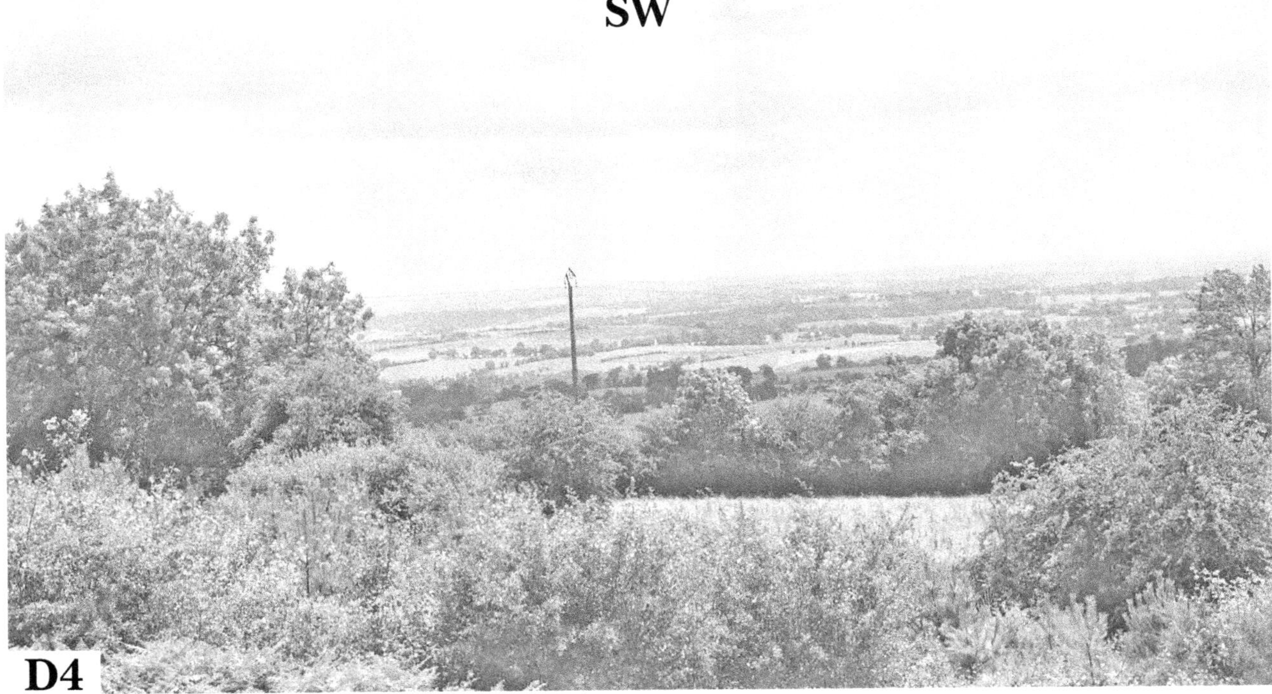

THE EMPLOYMENT OF THE *21. PANZER-DIVISION*

The initial reports of the *LXXIV. Armee-Korps* concerning the start of a new enemy offensive in the area around Caumont arrived at *Panzergruppe West* around 0800 hours on 30 July 1944.

The extent of the enemy attacks could not be determined yet by *Panzergruppe West* at that early hour. After the arrival of additional adverse reports, however, the headquarters was already considering the employment of an armored group from the *21. Panzer-Division* around 1000 hours. But *General der Panzertruppen* Eberbach did not order the *I. SS-Panzer-Korps,* to which the *21. Panzer-Division* had been attached since 27 July 1944, to immediately dispatch an armored force from this division to the *LXXIV. Armee-Korps.*

After hours of uncertainty regarding developments at the sector being attacked south of Caumont, *Kampfgruppe von Oppeln* left its bivouac area in the Forêt de Cinglais at 1715 hours. It was still light when it started its march to the west and in the direction of Coulvain.

The commander of the *Kampfgruppe, Oberst* von Oppeln-Bronikowski, had been awarded the Oak Leaves to the Knight's Cross on the previous day (29 July 1944) as the 536th member of the German Armed Forces to receive this high award. It had been presented for his achievements as commander of *Panzer-Regiment 22,* which had been in action in the invasion front since the very beginning.

Kampfgruppe von Oppeln consisted of the *I./Panzer-Regiment 22* (with approximately 40 *Panzer IV's*) and elements of *schwere Panzer-Abteilung 503* (15 *Tigers*), the *I./Panzer-Grenadier-Regiment 192,* the *1./Panzer-Pionier-Bataillon 220* and the *III./Panzer-Artillerie-Regiment 155.*

At the end of July 1944, several rail shipments arrived, whereby *Panzergruppe West* received thirty-four *Panzer IV's* and twenty-four *Panthers* as replacements for all of its forces. Of these, *Panzer-Regiment 22* received a grand total of twelve new *Panzer IV's.*

The approach march of *Kampfgruppe von Oppeln* took some time, occurring as it did during daylight conditions and therefore under the constant threat of aerial observation and attack from the enemy air

Tiger 131 on the move. It was one of two *Tiger I's* of the 1st Company, which was otherwise issued *Tiger II's.*

forces. In addition, the road march through the small localities with their narrow streets and across bridges with marginal load capacity for the heavy tanks caused numerous halts.

The first elements of *Kampfgruppe von Oppeln* did not reach the area around Coulvain until around 2200 hours on this 30 July 1944. It took nearly five hours for a march distance of thirty-five kilometers. The commanding general of the *LXXIV. Armee-Korps*, *General der Infanterie* Straube, waited impatiently for the arrival of the *Kampfgruppe*.

He intended to pass the *Kampfgruppe* through the gap between Hill 309 and the *Bois du Homme* and push it into the line running from La Ferrière-au-Doyen to Dampierre. This intent was passed on to *Panzergruppe West* at 0010 hours on 31 July 1944. It in no way corresponded to reality and demonstrated how little the headquarters of the corps understood of the actual situation. By this time, Hill 309 was firmly in the hands of the 15th (Scottish) Division.

Nevertheless, *Kampfgruppe von Oppeln* received the order from the *LXXIV. Armee-Korps* to attack north of the Bois de Homme and to the west in the early morning hours of 31 July 1944. The *Kampfgruppe* was to roll up the enemy and establish a new main line of resistance running from about 1.5 kilometers north of the Bois du Homme road to St. Martin-des-Besaces.

At 1930 hours of 30 July 1944, the Operations Officer of the *21. Panzer-Division* was informed telephonically by the chief-of-staff of *Panzergruppe West* to be prepared for the rest of the division to have to be attached to the *LXXXIV. Armee-Korps* that evening. At 2200 hours, the divisional commander was personally instructed by the commander-in-chief of *Panzergruppe West* to join *Kampfgruppe von Oppeln* as soon as possible.

The commander of the *326. Infanterie-Division*, *Generalleutnant* Drabsich-Waechter, briefed the commander of the *21. Panzer-Division*, *Generalmajor* Feuchtinger, more thoroughly on the actual situation at the infantry division's command post at 0500 hours on 31 July 1944. In the course of this, it was found out by *Generalleutnant* Feuchtinger that the assumption of the corps that the *326. Infanterie-Division* still held the road on both sides of St. Martin-des-Besaces and the Bois du Homme was incorrect. This had not been the case since noon on 30 July

A dummy *Tiger* in the sector of the *21. Panzer-Division.* A fighter-bomber occasionally fell for the deception and attacked the *"Tiger."*

View of La Bistière in the direction of the terrain south of Bény Bocage, affording a look into the British attack zone from the west. *Schwere Panzer-Abteilung 503*, which was reinforcing the *21. Panzer-Division*, was one of the formations that fought on the high ground along the horizon. The *II. SS-Panzer-Korps* was committed along the viewer's right. Initially, the British were under extremely heavy pressure.

1944. There were only small groups from *Infanterie-Regiment 752*, which had been employed on the left of, at and south of St. Martin-des-Besaces. The situation in the Bois du Homme was unclear.

In fact, the estimate of the situation by the leadership of the *326. Infanterie-Division* was also not completely correct. The 4th Battalion of the King's Own Shropshire Light Infantry did not reach the road west of St. Martin-des-Besaces until 0400 hours on 31 July 1944. In the meantime, *Kampfgruppe von Oppeln* had established positions southeast of St. Martin-des-Besaces on the road running from there to the Bois du Homme.

It was difficult for the newly arrived German forces to get oriented in their new area of operations. A detailed overview of the actual situation was missing. Under these circumstances, it was initially impossible to even consider an attack during the morning hours, especially since it was paramount at the moment to also screen against the anticipated new enemy attacks.

The leadership of the *21. Panzer-Division* was therefore in agreement with the measures taken thus far by *Oberst* von Oppeln-Bronikowski. It also had to make other decisions itself, since it was already under considerable fire.

✠

The elements of the division that began to arrive were positioned as follows:

- *Panzer-Aufklärungs-Abteilung 21*: In the area north of the Bois du Homme as far as Benneville
- *II./Panzer-Grenadier-Regiment 125*: In the Bois du Homme
- *II./Panzer-Grenadier-Regiment 192*: Attached to *Kampfgruppe von Oppeln*, south of St. Martin-des-Besaces

- *Panzer-Pionier-Bataillon 220*: At the disposal of the division, west of Brémoy
- *Feld-Ersatz-Bataillon 200*: Division reserve, south of St. Martin-des-Besaces
- *Panzer-Artillerie-Regiment 155*: Behind *Panzer-Grenadier-Regiment 125* and *Kampfgruppe von Oppeln.*

Sturmgeschütz-Brigade (Feld) 200, which was not brought up from the area around Troarn until the afternoon of 31 July 1944, screened south of St. Martin-des-Besaces and southeast of the *Forêt l'Evêque.* It was intended for the rest of *Panzer-Grenadier-Regiment 125,* which was still in its approach march, to be funneled into the area of le Bény-Bocage.

The great concern of the *LXXIV. Armee-Korps* was understandable. The left flank of the corps had been shattered and was open. There was no more contact with the friendly forces to the left, the *3. Fallschirm-Jäger-Division* of the *I. Fallschirm-Korps* of the *7. Armee.*

The Forêt l'Evêque, the boundary of *Panzergruppe West* to the *7. Armee,* was completely unsecured, and the situation was also uncertain, which would later prove to have fateful consequences. The danger existed that the enemy could penetrate though this gap to the south.

On the night of 30–31 July 1944, the enemy was also quite busy. He was preparing for the continuation of the fight.

Early in the morning of 31 July, just after sunrise, the 43rd Wessex Division attacked again at Cahagnes. As a result of the immediate counterattack of elements of *Panzer-Aufklärungs-Abteilung 21,* the fighting proved intense and costly; in some cases, it was close-quarter fighting. Prior to the enemy renewing his attack later, Cahagnes was bombed once again. He then succeeded around 1730 hours in penetrating into the heap of rubble that was once this village. Late in the evening, the enemy reached St. Pierre-du-Fresne. As a result, he was at the foot of the Bois du Homme.

Considerably more dangerous was a development farther to the west. Reconnaissance elements of the 2nd Battalion of the Household Cavalry, which reported directly to the British VIII Corps, were reconnoitering on the road on both sides of St. Martin-des-Besaces.

The 11th Armoured Division then advanced in two attack wedges. Tanks of the 3rd Royal Tank Regiment moved out at 0800 hours along with the 8th Battalion of the Rifles Brigade from the patch of woods north of St. Martin-des-Besaces. Half an hour later, tanks of the 2nd Fife and Forfars Yeomanry and infantry of the 4th Battalion of the King's Own Shropshire Infantry attacked St. Martin-des-Besaces from the west. All of these formations were well known to the men of the *21. Panzer-Division* from their fighting during Operation "Goodwood."

St. Martin-des-Besaces was lost around 1100 hours. The remaining elements of the *326. Infanterie-Division* pulled back to the positions of *Kampfgruppe von Oppeln* southeast of St. Martin-des-Besaces.

At 1630 hours that afternoon, the Guards Armoured Division, which had previously been held in reserve, was ordered to advance on le Tourneur through St. Martin-des-Besaces. It had been in position in the area around Caumont. Forces from this division then suddenly appeared in the evening south of St. Martin-des-Besaces and in front of Hills 192 and 238.

Heavy fighting ensued, in which elements of the *326. Infanterie-Division, Sturmgeschütz-Brigade (Feld) 200* and *Feld-Ersatz-Bataillon 200* were involved. Hill 192 and the village of Le Val changed hands several times.

Even more threatening, however, was the way the second attack wedge of the 11th Armoured Division developed farther to the west. It was there that other elements of the 2nd Battalion of the Household Cavalry found an important gap while reconnoitering. They advanced rapidly across the narrow paths in the woods of the completely unsecured Forêt l'Evêque and through La Ferrière-Harang. West of Le Bény-Bocage, they took an intact and unguarded bridge over the Souleuvre.

The English were encountering resistance from neither the *326. Infanterie-Division* of *Panzergruppe West* nor the *3. Fallschirm-Jäger-Division* of the *7. Armee.* The enemy had hit the boundary between these two field armies, and he reported his surprising success via radio at 1030 hours.

✠

The leadership of the British VIII Corps recognized the opportunity being offered and reacted quickly.

Initially, six Cromwell's of the 2nd Battalion of the Northhamptonshire Yeomanry moved through the Forêt l'Evêque towards the captured bridge. East of La Ferrière-Harang, they engaged the assault guns of *Sturmgeschütze-Brigade (Feld) 200* that were just then arriving.

Following soon thereafter were the tanks of the 23rd Hussars and the combat-experienced 3rd Battalion of the Monmouthshire Regiment. Starting at 2000 hours, they secured the bridge. The aforementioned assault guns also encountered and engaged tanks of the 23rd Hussars.

In the meantime, the 1st Battalion of the Herefordshire Regiment established contact with the Americans. That evening, this battalion and tanks of the Fife and Forfar Yeomanry screened the western flank of the British 2nd Army west of the road at Pont Aunay.

The British had succeeded in making a breakthrough and the left flank of *Panzergruppe West* was hanging in the air.

The armored car company of *Panzer-Aufklärungs-Abteilung 21,* which was reconnoitering in this area, took some prisoners southwest of the Forêt l'Evêque. After they were interrogated by the intelligence officer of the *21. Panzer-Division,* the enemy situation became somewhat clearer.

The *I./Panzer-Grenadier-Regiment 125* was being hurried into sector from the area of operations of the *1./SS-Panzer-Division "Leibstandarte SS Adolf Hitler"* south of Caen. It was being positioned to cover the left flank at Le Bény-Bocage. The battalion suffered casualties during the afternoon as a result of heavy attacks from the air.

By then, the 3rd Battalion of the Monmouthshire Regiment was already combing the woods near Le Bény-Bocage. A counterattack against these elements by the *I./Panzer-Grenadier-Regiment 125* that evening proved unsuccessful.

In order to avoid an encirclement, the commanding general of the *II. Fallschirm-Jäger-Korps* (*General der Fallschirmtruppe* Meindl) ordered his *3. Fallschirm-Jäger-Division* to pull back to the south bank of the Vire during the night of 31 July–1 August 1944. *Fallschirmjäger* of the division, who had previously screened on Hill 205 west of Le Bény-Bocage, pulled back. That evening, tanks of the 23rd Hussars were on Hill 205.

At this point, the *21. Panzer-Division* was faced by the 11th Armoured Division, the Guards Armoured Division, the 15th (Scottish) Division and, north of Jurques, elements of the 43rd Wessex Division. These developments were followed with great concern by the divisional leadership at the command post at St. Pierre-Tarentaine. The enemy was attacking in great force and was once again proving his great superiority in artillery and air resources, which he was employing to good effect.

In contrast, the trench strength of the German mechanized infantry battalions was barely more than 200 men, despite the receipt of replacements and additional manpower from the shattered *16. Luftwaffen-Feld-Division.* Facing the few tanks of *Panzer-Regiment 22* were a considerably greater number of enemy tanks. It was only thanks to the fact that the *bocage* country was not good terrain for tanks that the English did not simply move on through and achieve an even greater breakthrough.

Despite the terrible situation, the *21. Panzer-Division* and what remained of the *326. Infanterie-Division* succeeded by themselves in temporarily holding up the enemy during the course of 31 July 1944, especially in the area south of St. Martin-des-Besaces. The *21. Panzer-Division* conducted two immediate counterattacks by infantry against Hill 309 to wrest it from the Coldstream Guards. These did not succeed.

At the conclusion of its approach march, *Kampfgruppe von Oppeln* had forty-one operational *Panzer IV's*, eight *Tigers* and twelve *Jagdpanthers* of *schwere Panzerjäger-Abteilung 654.* Five *Tigers* were left along the way due to minor mechanical problems. The *Kampfgruppe* then received orders to support the third attempt to take back Hill 309.

Right at the start of the effort, roughly one third of the *Panzer IV's* were rendered non-operational by massed Typhoon fighter-bomber attacks from the 83rd Tactical Group. The remaining tanks attempted to take Hill 192, further to the south, that evening. Hill 192 was along the avenue of approach of the Guards Armoured Division towards St. Martin-des-Besaces.

The fact that the British 11th Armoured Division had made a dangerous breakthrough along the boundary between *Panzergruppe West* and the *7. Armee* could not be ascertained by the German side just yet.

The commander-in-chief of *Panzergruppe West* and the commanding general of the *LXXIV. Armee-Korps* had pinned their hopes on a counterattack of the *21. Panzer-Division* from its tactical assembly area southeast of St. Martin-des-Besaces to the west in order to eliminate the threat from this area and reestablish contact with the *7. Armee.*

The forces of the *21. Panzer-Division* were barely sufficient, however, to seal off the breakthrough area around St. Martin-des-Besaces. The enemy controlled the high ground to either side. At the moment, it was imperative for the Germans to establish a new main line of resistance where they were. The possibility of conducting a counterattack, as had been ordered by the corps, was something that needed to be considered only afterwards.

✠

Because the counterattack from the *Bois de Homme* towards Hill 309 had not yet taken place, the commanding general of the *LXXIV. Armee-Korps, General der Infanterie* Straube, leveled serious accusations against the leadership of the *21. Panzer-Division* on the evening of 31 July 1944.

General der Infanterie Straube ordered the attack again, this time for the morning of 1 August 1944—despite all the objections of the armored division. The *21. Panzer-Division* pointed out that the necessary concentration of forces by the division for the counterattack would necessitate its pulling those same forces out of their recently established defensive positions south of St. Martin-des-Besaces. This, in turn, would give the enemy another opportunity to break through to the south. This objection by the division was ignored by the corps. The fateful danger that would be presented to the corps' continued open left flank by the withdrawal of forces was likewise not noted. Finally, the division stated that the forces of the *21. Panzer-Division* were inadequate for conducting such an attack. This objection was also discounted at the heated meeting held at the corps command post around midnight on 1 August 1944.

General der Infanterie Straube insisted on continuing the ordered attack based on a differing estimate of the situation. In fact, he also doubted a reported advance of enemy armored forces that was already taking place west of Le Bény-Bocage. He told the commander of the *21. Panzer-Division* that any further contrary discussion from him would result in his being court-martialed.

The senior commands became aware of the fact during the evening of 31 July 1944 that the Americans had reached Avranches. A glance at the map would have given an indication that the collapse of the front in Normandy had started.

THE COUNTERATTACK OF THE *21. PANZER-DIVISION* IN THE BOIS DU HOMME

Although he was convinced that he was right and worried about the expected losses, *Generalmajor* Feuchtinger decided to execute the attack that had been ordered by the commander-in-chief of *Panzergruppe West* and passed on by the *LXXIV. Armee-Korps* so as to spare the division the trauma of also receiving new leadership. The division issued the necessary orders.

During the initial morning hours of 1 August 1944, the grenadiers of *Panzer-Grenadier-Regiment 192*—each battalion with a fighting strength of barely more than 150–200 men—left their just completed positions in the area southeast of St. Martin-des-Besaces. They assembled for the attack at La Ferrières-au-Doyen and established contact with the *II./Panzer-Grenadier-Regiment 125*, which was screening in the Bois du Homme.

Approximately twelve to fourteen *Panzer IV's* of *Panzer-Regiment 22* and eight *Tigers* of *schwere Panzer-Abteilung 503* moved to a tactical assembly area in the wooded area, a terrain less than ideal for armor.

The unrealistic expectations of the commander-in-chief West with regard to the success of an attack on the Bois du Homme are amply illustrated here: A view from the German vantage point towards the woods, which start in the background.

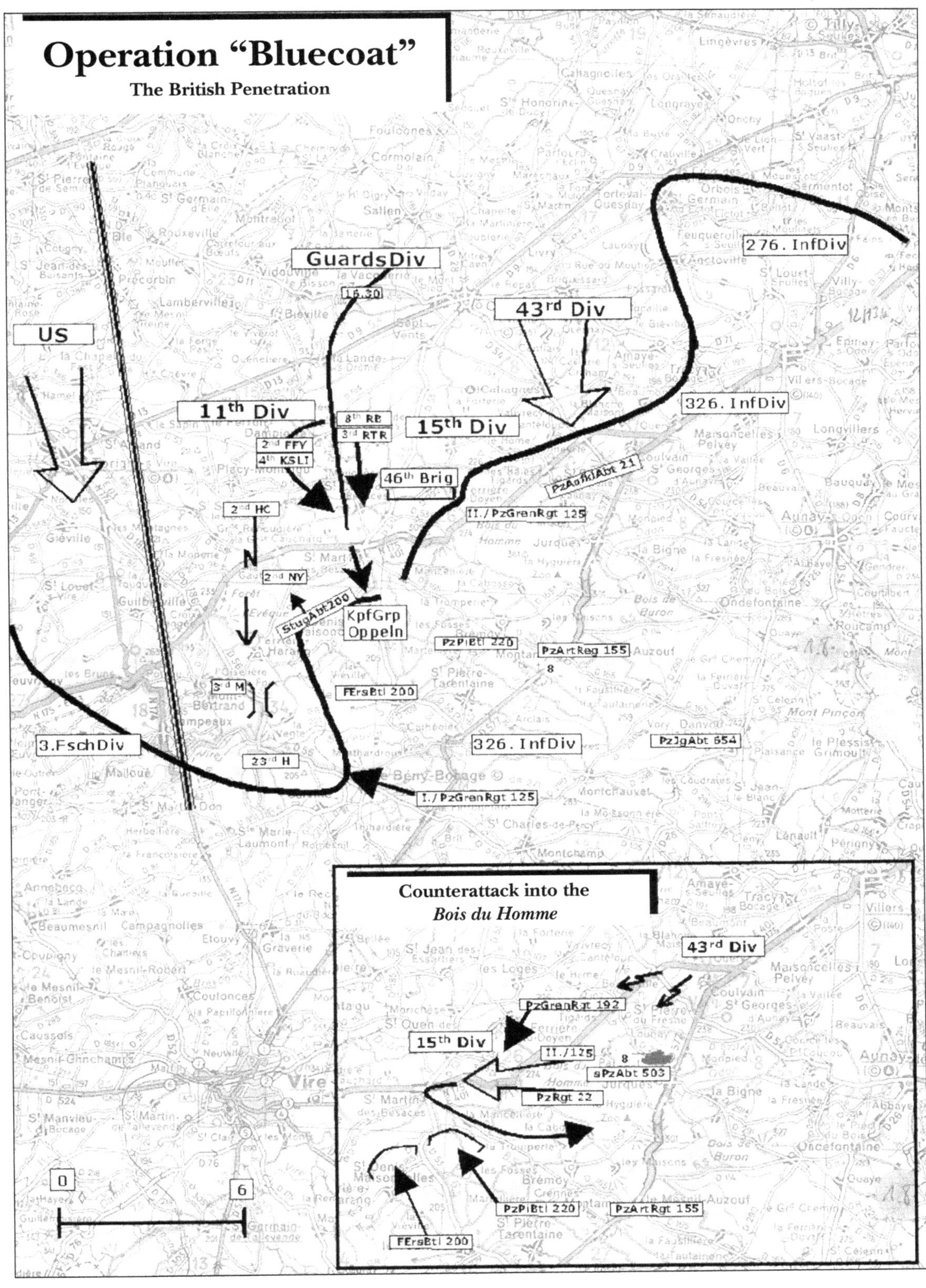

Operation "Bluecoat"
The British Penetration
US
GuardsDiv
16.30
43rd Div
276. InfDiv
11th Div
8th RB
3rd RTR
15th Div
326. InfDiv
2nd FFY
4th KSLI
46th Brig
PzAufklAbt 21
II./PzGrenRgt 125
2nd HC
2nd NY
StugAbt200
KpfGrp Oppeln
PzPiBtl 220
PzArtReg 155
3rd M
FErsBtl 200
3.FschDiv
23rd H
326. InfDiv
PzJgAbt 654
I./PzGrenRgt 125
0
6
Counterattack into the Bois du Homme
43rd Div
PzGrenRgt 192
15th Div
II./125
sPzAbt 503
PzRgt 22
PzPiBtl 220
PzArtRgt 155
FErsBtl 200

It was intended for all of the battalions of *Panzer-Artillerie-Regiment 155* to support the attack. It was anticipated that there would be no support from the *Luftwaffe* or separate artillery formations. *Oberst* Rauch led the attack group.

Feld-Ersatz-Bataillon 200 and *Panzer-Pionier-Bataillon 220,* each with approximately 200 men, then assumed the now very thinly held positions in the area south of St. Martin-des-Besaces. Approximately 70 men of the *326. Infanterie-Division* were consolidated with the two battalions.

A few *Panzer IV's* from *Panzer-Regiment 22* were positioned as "corset stays" among them. Heavy casualties were already being received in the Bois du Homme, even before the attack could begin, as the result of clashes with assault groups of the 43rd Wessex Division, which were reconnoitering in the woods from the direction of St. Pierre-du-Fresne.

As a result, the positioning of *Kampfgruppe Rauch* was identified by the enemy. The Scots of the 15th (Scottish) Division could also clearly hear from Hill 309 the sounds of tanks in the woods below them and received ample warning.

At 0530 hours on 1 August 1944, a thirty-minute artillery preparation from *Panzer-Artillerie-Regiment 155* pounded Hill 309. At 0640 hours, *Kampfgruppe Rauch* moved out from La Ferrière-au-Doyen to the south and from concealed positions in the northeast portion of the *Bois du Homme* to the west. At the cost of high casualties, the *Kampfgruppe* was able to penetrate through the Bois du Homme against heavy enemy resistance coming from Hill 309, which had been armed to the teeth with numerous defensive weapons. Late in the morning, it almost reached Hill 309.

The attack was then carried out from there farther to the west and north of the road to St. Martin-des-Besaces. Every meter of ground was contested in the face of extremely heavy enemy defensive measures, which were effectively supported from the air.

Seven squadrons of Typhoons from the Royal Air Force's 83rd Tactical Group joined in the fighting. Their main target was the tanks, which they engaged with rockets. Heavy smoke, both natural and artificial, reduced visibility.

As a result of the effectiveness of the heavy enemy artillery fire, predominately from the northern edge of Hill 309, the grenadiers bogged down and were no longer able to follow the tanks. The attack stagnated around noon. Additional forces to sustain the attack were not available.

In his book about the Coldstream Guards, *Second to None,* Julian Paget presents the following account of the failed attack:

> . . . at dawn on 1 August infantry and King Tiger tanks from 21st Panzer Division counter-attacked from [La Ferrières-au-Doyen]. General von Kluge had wasted no time in moving armour from Caen.
>
> The Panzergrenadiers suffered heavily, but the Churchills made little impression on the Tigers. RAF Typhoons and lack of automotive power, however, hindered the German tanks. Lieutenant Christopher Schofield and his troop bore the brunt of the defence. He called down medium artillery onto the Tigers, forcing their withdrawal around 1600 hours, when they were caught from a flank by the rest of Major Jocelyn Hambro's No 1 Squadron, who inflicted 200 casualties. Artillery broke up a later attack, but Hill 309—"Coldstream Hill"—was firmly in British hands and Coldstream Churchills supported an attack on La Mancelliere, a mile south.

Around noon, the division received orders from the corps to call off the already failed attack in the Bois du Homme and on Hill 309. The corps finally admitted that the attack could not lead to success, and it needed forces to stabilize the situation on the left wing of the corps.

At the same time, the enemy increased his pressure south and west of St. Martin-des-Besaces by attacks of the Guards Armoured Division as well as continued operations of the 11th Armoured Division in the deep left flank of the *21. Panzer-Division.*

Hills 192 and 238, northeast of St Denis-Maisoncelles, were lost. In the effort to retake Hill 192 from the 1st Battalion of the Coldstream Guards, *Tiger 112* was hit on the gun mantlet and later developed running-gear problems. In expectation of another counterattack, the British infantry pulled back from the hill. The situation became critical, because the flank guard provided by *schwere Panzerjäger-Abteilung 654* came under pressure from the 4/7th Royal Dragoon Guards and one of its *Jagdpanthers* was lost.

The Dragoon Guards were supporting the advance of the 43rd Wessex Division on La Bigne. A second *Jagdpanther* was hit when two *Tigers* showed up by chance. Encouraged by their success, the crews of A Squadron continued to advance. They scaled a steep slope to the top of the hill, where they saw the two *Tigers.* The two *Tigers* had had bad luck and had bottomed out; they had been abandoned by their crews. The British tankers set both tanks ablaze, and the crews were soon rounded up.

The division command post at St. Pierre-Tarentaine was attacked by surprise from the west about 1500 hours by British tanks. The command staff had to pull back, losing valuable vehicles in the process.

Towards evening, the British approached Le Tourneur. During the first few hours of 2 August 1944, they took another intact bridge over the Souleuvre without a fight. On the left wing of the division, the 11th Armoured Division could not be stopped either. After a fight, the *I./Panzer-Grenadier-Regiment 125* had to abandon Le Bény-Bocage on the morning of 1 August 1944. A few armored vehicles were lost in the village.

Forces of the 11th Armoured Division occupied Hill 266 east of Le Bény-Bocage and blocked the

This photograph and the two on the next page show one of the two *Tigers* abandoned at La Bigne. This tank is *Tiger 123.* (Bovington Tank Museum)

important road from Vire to Caen (the current D577) at La Feronnières. Another important bridge over the Souleuvre fell into the enemy's hands at Cathéolles. There were no more forces available to the division to defend in its center sector and on its threatened left wing.

What the leadership of the *21. Panzer-Division* had feared had happened.

✠

The English were already reconnoitering in the direction of Vire without interference and could have taken the city in a *coup de main* given the right circumstances. After discussions among the Allies, however, the city of Vire was no longer an objective for the British 2nd Army. Instead, the taking of the city was relegated to the U.S. V Corps. The new attack objectives for the British 2nd Army were:

- XXX Corps: Advance to the Orne
- VIII Corps: Advance in the direction of Condé-sur-Noireau and Flers.

✠

After receiving orders from the corps to pull back at 1600 hours, *Kampfgruppe Rauch* withdrew. It took additional heavy casualties from the enemy's heavy artillery fire and his forces, which were pursuing from Hill 309. When extremely heavy artillery rounds started impacting in the wooded terrain, several nervous tank drivers bottomed out their tanks—so much so that they could no longer free themselves or be recovered. Several *Panzer IV's* of *Panzer-Regiment 22* were knocked out or lost through rocket attack.

Crews that tried to recover their tanks or blow them up were taken prisoner. The same fate awaited many of the grenadiers, who were certainly happy to have escaped the hell of the fighting in Normandy. Many armored vehicles and equipment were lost. More than 200 soldiers of the *21. Panzer-Division* were killed or lay wounded south of La Ferrière and in the *Bois du Homme.* The division suffered a 30 percent loss rate among the forces it had employed in the attack.

The Bois du Homme became hell for *Kampfgruppe Rauch.* The operation conducted on 1 August 1944 in the woods was, in the final analysis, senseless. It was conducted with insufficient forces against an extremely strong enemy who was prepared to defend. The few German tanks that had been available were weakened further by the losses suffered in the operation. The *326. Infanterie-Division* also suffered heavy losses.

✠

The following was noted in the daily logs of *Panzergruppe West* on 1 August 1944:

> 1930 hours: The attack of the *21. Panzer-Division* did not succeed, because the enlisted personnel provided from the *16. Luftwaffen-Feld-Division* did not live up to the demands placed on them.

A wildly imaginative account on the part of the senior command.

✠

Forces from the 43rd Wessex Divisions pursued and attempted to reach Hill 361 in the process. As they did this, they captured two field medical treatment facilities and numerous wounded and medical personnel were captured. Under terrible weather conditions and a downpour, the English reached the hill during the night of 1–2 August 1944, where they dug in. With forty men for every

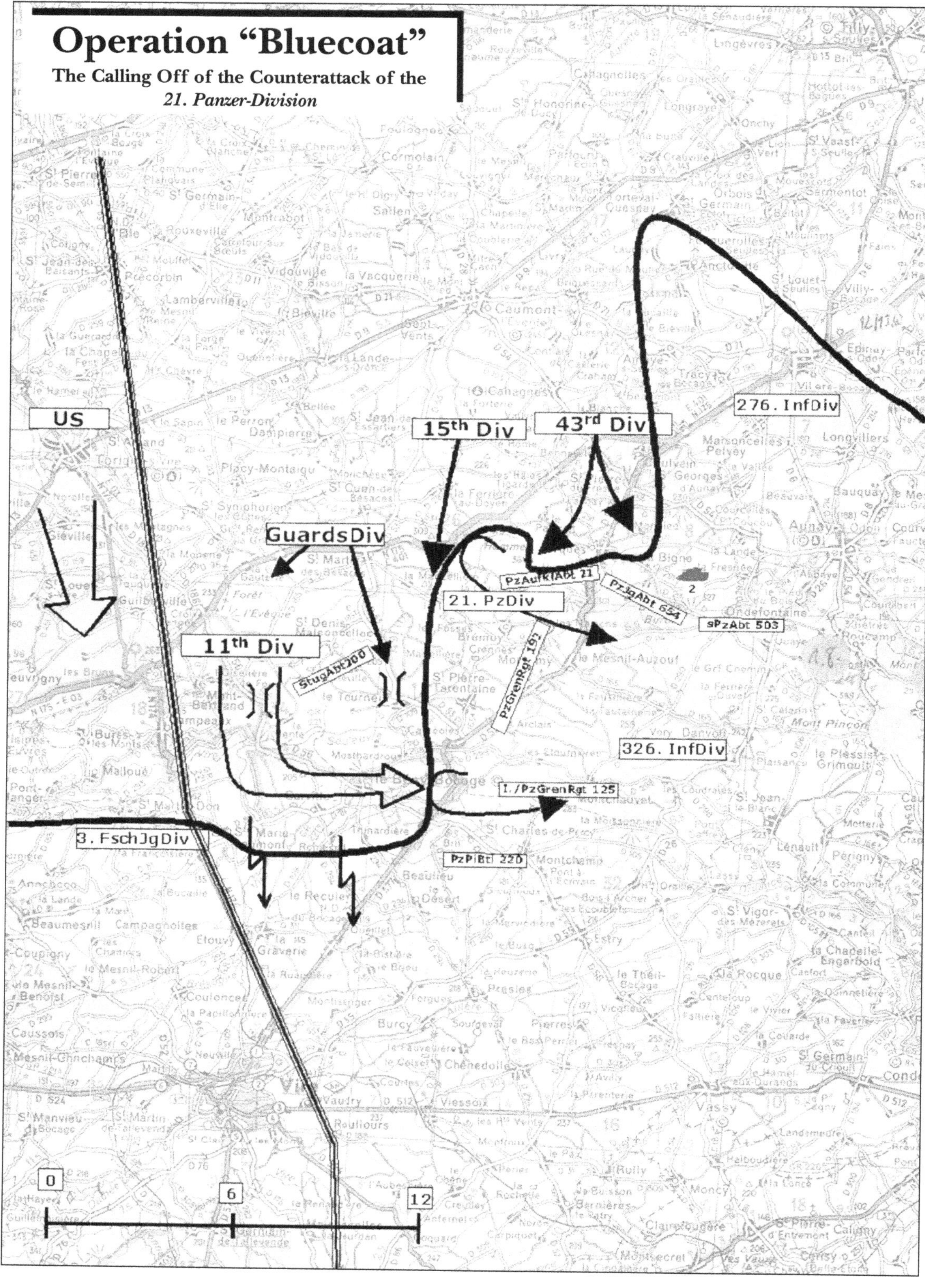
Operation "Bluecoat"
The Calling Off of the Counterattack of the
21. Panzer-Division
US
15th Div
43rd Div
276. InfDiv
GuardsDiv
PzAufklAbt 21
PzJgAbt 654
21. PzDiv
sPzAbt 503
11th Div
StugAbt 200
PzGrenRgt 192
326. InfDiv
I./PzGrenRgt 125
3. FschJgDiv
PzPiBtl 220
0
6
12

gun, they hauled antitank guns up to the top and placed them into position.

They advanced into the pile of rubble that once was Jurques during the first hours of the morning and then headed in the direction of La Bugne. The 15th (Scottish) Division also pursued. The Scots took Galet and la Mancelliére, southeast of St. Martin-des-Besaces.

✠

Due to the failure of the attack in the Bois du Homme and then the especially threatening development in the area around Le Bény-Bocage, the situation for the *21. Panzer-Division* was becoming extremely difficult. It was practically fighting by itself in this sector.

The corps had ordered the division to give up the terrain it had recaptured. It was then to fight a delaying action and establish a new main line of resistance in the area defined by St. Pierre-Tarentaine–north of Le Mesnil-Auzouf–La Bigne, with a strong flank guard oriented towards La Terrerie.

The division's command made efforts to establish a new main line of resistance running through Hills 301 and 321 and east of Brémoy with *Panzer-Grenadier-Regiment 192.* Combat outposts were to be placed in Brémoy, west of Montamy and in St. Pierre-Tarentaine. *Panzer-Aufklärungs-Abteilung 21* attempted to establish a thin screening line south of Jurques.

Covering the left wing were the *I./Panzer-Grenadier-Regiment 125* and *Panzer-Pionier-Bataillon 220.* They were positioned on both sides of La Terriere but not in it.

✠

Despite the good success enjoyed so far, the commanding general of the British XXX Corps, Lieutenant General B. C. Horrocks, was not satisfied with the way the attack had progressed and ordered a breakthrough to Jurques and Ondefontaine.

To the surprise of both friend and foe alike, a German fighter-bomber attack occurred in the middle of the night. Despite this attack, La Bigne was encircled towards midnight by the 43rd Wessex Division. This was done despite a strong German defense that was supported by high-angle fire and several *Jagdpanthers.* The English suffered heavy losses. A British tank was destroyed from a distance of nearly two kilometers by a *Tiger,* whose round struck the rear of the vehicle. This fighting has been recounted in an impressive manner in a book already mentioned, *By Tank into Normandy*:

> On August 2 the squadrons went their own way and our own route became more intense and dangerous. We started at dawn, with my tank about fourth from the front. The infantry of the 7th Hampshires were with us, walking alongside the tank and covering our flank. Then we arrived at a T junction, which was mined, along with the fields around it. The column halted to allow the sappers to come up and clear the mines, when suddenly a Tiger tank emerged from cover and moved to the high ground overlooking the road. It opened fire at about 2,000 yards and hit a tank further back in the column. With both ends of the road now blocked, we were bottled up and the Tiger was out of our range.
>
> I shouted: "Gunner, traverse right. Steady . . . on . . . Tiger. Smoke. 1,750 yards. Fire when ready." Our shot landed just in front of the Tiger and the smoke soon obscured it from view. We fired again, this

time just to the left of the tank, aiming to keep plenty of smoke between us and it. Other tank commanders did the same, while the air officer accompanying us called up four Typhoon fighter-bombers off the cab-rank to fire their rockets at the Tiger. We fired some red smoke to identify the target, and then the planes came in, very low and with a tremendous roar. The second plane scored a direct hit and, when the smoke cleared, we could see the Tiger lying on its side minus its turret and with no sign of any survivors. It was an awesome display of firepower and demonstrated only too clearly how important control of the skies was to our ultimate success.

...

We continued on through the afternoon of August 2, heading towards Jurcques [Jurques]. There was increasingly stiff opposition, with several more Tigers being spotted.

...

Sporadic fighting had gone on in the area all through the night and losses were mounting. A Squadron was held up near St Pierre-du-Fresne by a Jagdpanther with an 88-millimetre gun but eventually broke through. Sergeant George Dring, that inveterate destroyer of tanks, stalked a Tiger on foot and then directed his own tank in to kill it.

THE *II. SS-PANZER-KORPS* IS BROUGHT UP

The commander-in-chief of *Panzergruppe West*, *General der Panzertruppen* Eberbach, recognized that despite the continuing danger in the sector of the *I. SS-Panzer-Korps* on the right wing of his field army (south of Caen and east of the Orne), the decisively critical sector was now apparently on his left wing in the sector of the *LXXIV. Armee-Korps.*

This estimate of the situation was shared by the commander-in-chief West, *Generalfeldmarschall* von Kluge.

Based on this development, *General der Panzertruppen* Eberbach made his decisions and, starting at 1500 hours on 1 August 1944, ordered the headquarters of the *II. SS-Panzer-Korps* to move immediately from the area around Caen to the left wing of the field army. *SS-Gruppenführer* Bittrich's corps consisted of the *9. SS-Panzer-Division "Hohenstaufen,"* the *10. SS-Panzer-Division "Frundsberg," schwere SS-Panzer-Abteilung 102* and *Werfer-Brigade 8.*

The forces to either side of the *10. SS-Panzer-Division "Frundsberg,"* the *271. Infanterie-Division* and the *277. Infanterie-Division*, had to broaden their frontages to cover the sector of the departing *SS* division.

The mission of the *II. SS-Panzer-Korps* was as follows: Bring the enemy attack at Coulvain to a halt and close the gap between the *II. Fallschirm-Jäger-Korps* (*7. Armee*) and the *LXXIV. Armee-Korps* (*Panzergruppe West*) by counterattacking at Hill 205 (west of Le Bény-Bocage).

The *10. SS-Panzer-Division "Frundsberg"* received the mission to eliminate the enemy threat in the Coulvain–Jurques area by counterattacking. It was earmarked to be the righthand neighbor of the *21. Panzer-Division.*

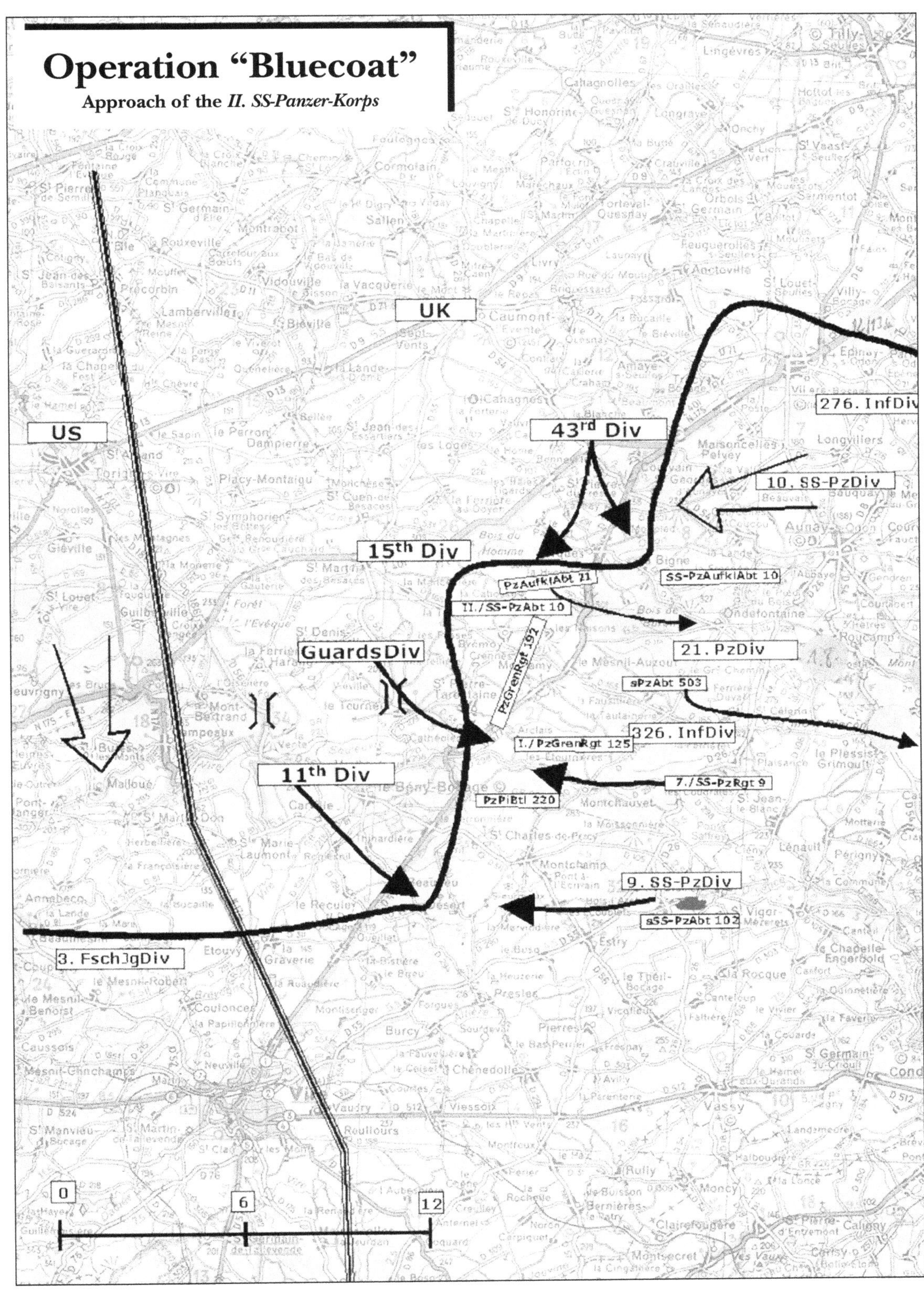
Operation "Bluecoat"
Approach of the II. SS-Panzer-Korps
UK
US
43rd Div
276. InfDiv
10. SS-PzDiv
15th Div
PzAufklAbt 21
SS-PzAufklAbt 10
II./SS-PzAbt 10
21. PzDiv
GuardsDiv
PzGrenRgt 192
sPzAbt 503
326. InfDiv
I./PzGrenRgt 125
11th Div
7./SS-PzRgt 9
PzPiBtl 220
9. SS-PzDiv
sSS-PzAbt 102
3. FschJgDiv
0
6
12

The mission for the *9. SS-Panzer-Division "Hohenstaufen"* was to close the gap between the left flank of *Panzergruppe West* and the *7. Armee.* It was to be supported by *schwere SS-Panzer-Abteilung 102* and take up position to the left of the *21. Panzer-Division.*

The *21. Panzer-Division*—or, to be more precise, what was left of it—was attached to the *II. SS-Panzer-Korps.* The headquarters of the *LXXIV. Armee-Korps* was left with the command of the *326. Infanterie-Division* and the *276. Infanterie-Division.*

The first elements of the approaching *10. SS-Panzer-Division "Frundsberg"*—*SS-Panzer-Aufklärungs-Abteilung 10*—reached La Bigne around 2200 hours.

To the great relief of the leadership of the *21. Panzer-Division,* the grenadiers of *Panzer-Grenadier-Regiment 192* and the reconnaissance soldiers of *Panzer-Aufklärungs-Abteilung 21,* tanks of the *II./ SS-Panzer-Regiment 10* arrived into the area south of Jurques and in the Bois du Homme early in the morning of 2 August 1944. They took over securing Hill 301. *Panzer-Grenadier-Regiment 192* secured Hill 321, and a portion of *Panzer-Aufklärungs-Abteilung 21* could be pulled out of the line.

The first elements of the *9. SS-Panzer-Division "Hohenstaufen"* also arrived during the morning of 2 August 1944 in the lefthand sector of the *21. Panzer-Division.* These forces included *SS-Panzer-Aufklärungs-Abteilung 9, SS-Panzer-Regiment 9* (with thirty-one *Panthers,* seventeen *Panzer IV's* and twenty-eight assault guns) and an *SPW* battalion. The main body of the division followed in the course of the day.

The boundary between the *9. SS-Panzer-Division "Hohenstaufen"* and the *21. Panzer-Division* was the Souleuvre River, whereby the latter division was also given the mission of securing the high ground north of the river and south of Cathéolles.

The arrival of two, visibly strong *Waffen-SS* divisions on both wings of the *21. Panzer-Division* was received with a sigh of relief. By the evening of 2 August 1944, the *21. Panzer-Division* and the largely destroyed *326. Infanterie-Division* were no longer basically alone in their fight in a critical situation on the left wing of *Panzergruppe West.* Despite this, the *21. Panzer-Division* was still engaged in active combat operations.

On the morning of 2 August 1944, the division was being attacked again, this time on the left flank in the sector of *Panzer-Grenadier-Regiment 125.* The Guards Armoured Division attacked starting from the area of le Tourneur at 0900 hours and attempted to advance on Monchauvet via Cathéolles with additional forces brought up from le Tourneur. An enemy attack on Arclais and Hill 200 was turned back by *Panzer-Grenadier-Regiment 125* and elements of *Panzer-Pionier-Bataillon 220.*

In the heavy fighting and close-quarters combat that ensured, the grenadiers of the *21. Panzer-Division* saw that they were no longer fending for themselves. The newly inserted friendly forces on the left, the *9. SS-Panzer-Division "Hohenstaufen,"* effectively supported them by employing its *7./SS-Panzer-Regiment 9.*

The British Guards Armoured Division attacked with infantry elements on the morning of 3 August 1944 against the positions on the left wing of the *21. Panzer-Division* at Arclais. This attack was supported by tanks. Once again, the British were turned back. Additional assaults by the 15th (Scottish) Division were also repulsed at St. Pierre-Tarentaine, Montamy and Brémoy.

Late in the afternoon of the same 3 August 1944, the English repeated their armored attack north of Arclais with reinforced forces. The grenadiers of *Panzer-Grenadier-Regiment 125,* who had been worn down by the very strong artillery fires, had to pull back. The enemy was able to advance as far as Les

Haies, even though several tanks were knocked out. This meant that Montchauvet was directly threatened.

During the night of 2–3 August 1944, elements of the 43rd Wessex Division conducted an attack just in front of Hill 321 on the right wing of the *21. Panzer-Division.* This attack and another attempt to bypass the hill were barely turned back by *Panzer-Grenadier-Regiment 192.* Heavy enemy artillery fire was placed on the adjoining German forces on Hill 301.

Although the *10. SS-Panzer-Division "Frundsberg"* was able to turn back heavy attacks on Hill 301, it was unable to completely prevent the enemy from infiltrating into the broad expanse of woods nearby and in the vicinity of hill.

Panzer-Grenadier-Regiment 192 started to falter. By midday on 3 August 1944, Hill 321 was lost. The English reached the road to Jurques and advanced as far as La Bigne. It was apparent that one of their objectives was Le Mesnil-Auzouf.

The friendly forces on the right, the *10. SS-Panzer-Division "Frundsberg,"* was then facing the 7th Armoured Division of the British XXX Corps in a line running Saulques–Pitot–St. Georges-d'Aunay. The British division was being employed for the first time. There was bitter fighting for Hill 188. An attack by the British armored division coming from La Bigne and advancing through the Bois du Buron in the direction of Ondefontaine was turned back.

The *10. SS-Panzer-Division "Frundsberg"* then launched a counterattack from the areas of Ondefontaine and Aunay-sur-Orne in the direction of La Bigne and St. Georges-d'Aunay. As a result of the seesaw, bitter fighting, it appears that the English temporarily gave up their plans for an attack in the direction of Aunay-sur-Odon

Because of his lack of success, the commander of the 7th Armoured Division, Major General G. W. E. J. Erskine, was relieved of command on 3 August 1944 and replaced by Major General G. L. V. Verney.

A vivid portrayal of this British failure can be found in the history of the 11th Armoured Division:

> Four Panthers and a Tiger had attacked the Grand Bonfait position.
>
> On the very far right flank 2nd Northants Yeomanry were patrolling vigorously. One squadron passed through Montisanger and reached the Paris-Granville railway line; another headed towards Etouvy and the third towards Vire via N 177 which appeared to be empty of Germans and Americans.
>
> But by early afternoon Tiger tanks supported by infantry caught and savagely mauled the regiment around La Bistiére, north of Vire, and at La Papilloniére road junction, 2 miles away from Vire.

The following passage appears in *The Charge of the Bull* by Jean Brisset:

> However, after 1400 hours everything changed for the worse. "B" Squadron, returning from Vire, reported that Tiger tanks, accompanied by infantry, were advancing in their direction. Immediately, the F.O.O. [forward observer officer] with them gave the enemy positions to the gunners but at the last moment the guns were ordered to wait because Typhoons were on their way to attack the enemy. An air O.P. [observer pilot] went up to direct them but was promptly shot down by the enemy so that the Typhoons never found their target.
>
> Because of this the enemy tanks were able to get in among the Northamptonshire tanks without a single shot having been fired at them. It was now too late to order the British artillery to intervene because the

damage would have been inflicted on both sides. A tank battle started but the Tigers, their sides protected by the slope and thickness of their armour, had no fear of the 75mm's and immediately took the initiative. Three British tanks were destroyed and the others were hit while retreating to form a new defensive square a little to the north of the highway. While they battened down they were mauled by other Tigers situated on the high ground to the west of Burcy. These same tanks also threatened to cut off the squadron that had reached the Paris—Granville railway line near La Lande. That squadron was ordered to retreat. At the same time another enemy detachment attacked Headquarters Squadron in position at La Bistiere. Soon the three squadrons began to lose one tank after another without being able to do anything to the Tigers. When night fell, it was the turn of the panzergrenadiers to infiltrate into the positions held by the Northamptonshires and they found new victims with their panzerfausts. At daybreak, 31 men did not answer the roll call and many tanks had been destroyed.

That evening the 2nd Warwicks of 3rd British Division were brought into action and behind a barrage and smoke screen retook Presles, thus allowing ambulances to collect the wounded and dead of 8 RB [Rifle Brigade] and 23rd Hussars. It had been a long hot day all along the divisional front line with 4 KSLI [King's Own Shropshire Light Infantry] stoutly holding their corner, but 3 RTR [Royal Tank Regiment] and 2nd Northants Yeomanry suffering heavy losses of tanks and men.

Problematic for the entire strategic position from the German side was that the German measures lagged behind those of the Allies or that the superiority of the Allies was too great. The impression had been successfully created that the British offensive efforts continued to remain east of the Orne. Although the Germans detected British troop movements, they were not in a position to divine the overall intent of the Allies.

Although the left (eastern) shoulder of Operation "Bluecoat" was able to be held as a result of the employment of the *21. Panzer-Division* (reinforced by *schwere Panzer-Abteilung 503*), the attackers a bit farther to the west were able to advance in the beginning against considerably less resistance. The enemy could not be stopped in his advance south towards Vire.

Towards the end, there was a sort of completion on the part of the British to outflank the enemy. Unfortunately for the Germans, the *9. SS-Panzer-Division "Hohenstaufen"* and *schwere SS-Panzer-Abteilung 102* were not dispatched to the area until nearly two days after the start of Operation "Bluecoat." Consequently, they arrived too late. On top of everything else, the American 9th Infantry Division had already broken through farther to the east at La Ferrière Harong.

EMPLOYMENT OF THE *9. SS-PANZER-DIVISION "HOHENSTAUFEN"*

Schwere SS-Panzer-Abteilung 102, which had passed its baptism by fire at Hill 112, received orders in the course of the afternoon of 1 August 1944 to move into its new area of operations. It reached Roucamps and bivouacked there after having moved through La Caine–Hamars–Campandre at night.

Although this sounds simple enough, it was quite a different thing for the actual tank crews. Due to the danger from aircraft, which were also active at night—especially the artillery aerial observers—the armored vehicles always moved without lights, always accompanied by huge clouds of dust. In addition, there was the constant artillery harassment fire along the roads and at road intersections, coupled with the lively vehicular traffic—both coming and going—and, in some cases, the difficult, turning road network. At most, only the radio operators and gunners could sleep for periods at a time.

Once at the new location, the armored vehicles had to be refueled as soon as possible, since the tanks had probably used up almost all of their fuel supplies. Just for moving the tracked vehicles of *schwere SS-Panzer-Abteilung 102* from one side of the front to the other in the sector of *Panzergruppe West*, more than 20,000 liters of fuel were consumed. This corresponded to twelve fuel trucks full of gas.

This, in turn, meant that the transportation battalion of the corps had to be brought into support the division. The refueling was done manually in complete darkness. The crews had to haul fuel canisters to their vehicles, sometimes more than several hundred meters. Up to thirty 20-liter (5-gallon) cans of fuel were needed, which then had to be handed up to a waiting crew member on the back deck of the tank. Once emptied, the canisters had to be hauled back to the impatiently waiting logistics personnel. Depending on their location, the crews sometimes also had to try to do all this without making any noise. Occasionally, main-gun and machine-gun ammunition were also stockpiled up front. All this led to the crews being completely exhausted before they even started operations.

Another problem for the formations was the fact that the leaders were not familiar with the situation and the terrain in the new area of operations.

With an effective date of 2 August 1944, *schwere SS-Panzer-Abteilung 102* was attached to the *9. SS-Panzer-Division "Hohenstaufen."* In contrast to *schwere Panzer-Abteilung 503*, which had been attached to the *21. Panzer-Division* and fought as part of the division's tank regiment, *schwere SS-Panzer-Abteilung 102* formed a separate *Kampfgruppe. Kampfgruppe Weiß*—named after the commander of the *Tiger* battalion, *SS-Sturmbannführer* Weiß—consisted of the *Tiger* battalion and the attached *SS-Panzer-Aufklärungs-Abteilung 9*.

The remaining armored elements of the division—thirty-one *Panthers*, seventeen *Panzer IV's* and twenty-eight assault guns—formed *gepanzerte Gruppe Meyer*. It was initially intended to employ both *Kampfgruppen* separately from one another, especially since the area that had to be covered was so large.

The initial mission of *Kampfgruppe Weiß* was to reestablish contact with the *3. Fallschirmjäger-Division* north of Vire and, above all, secure the city. Vire was of great importance, because almost all of the supplies and logistics for the *7. Armee* were routed through this city, which was already being heavily shelled.

The battalion's 2nd Company initially received the mission to move to St. Jean, turn west once there and then screen the large loop in the road three kilometers to the northwest. It was intended for the 1st Company to go into position one kilometer south of its sister company's location.

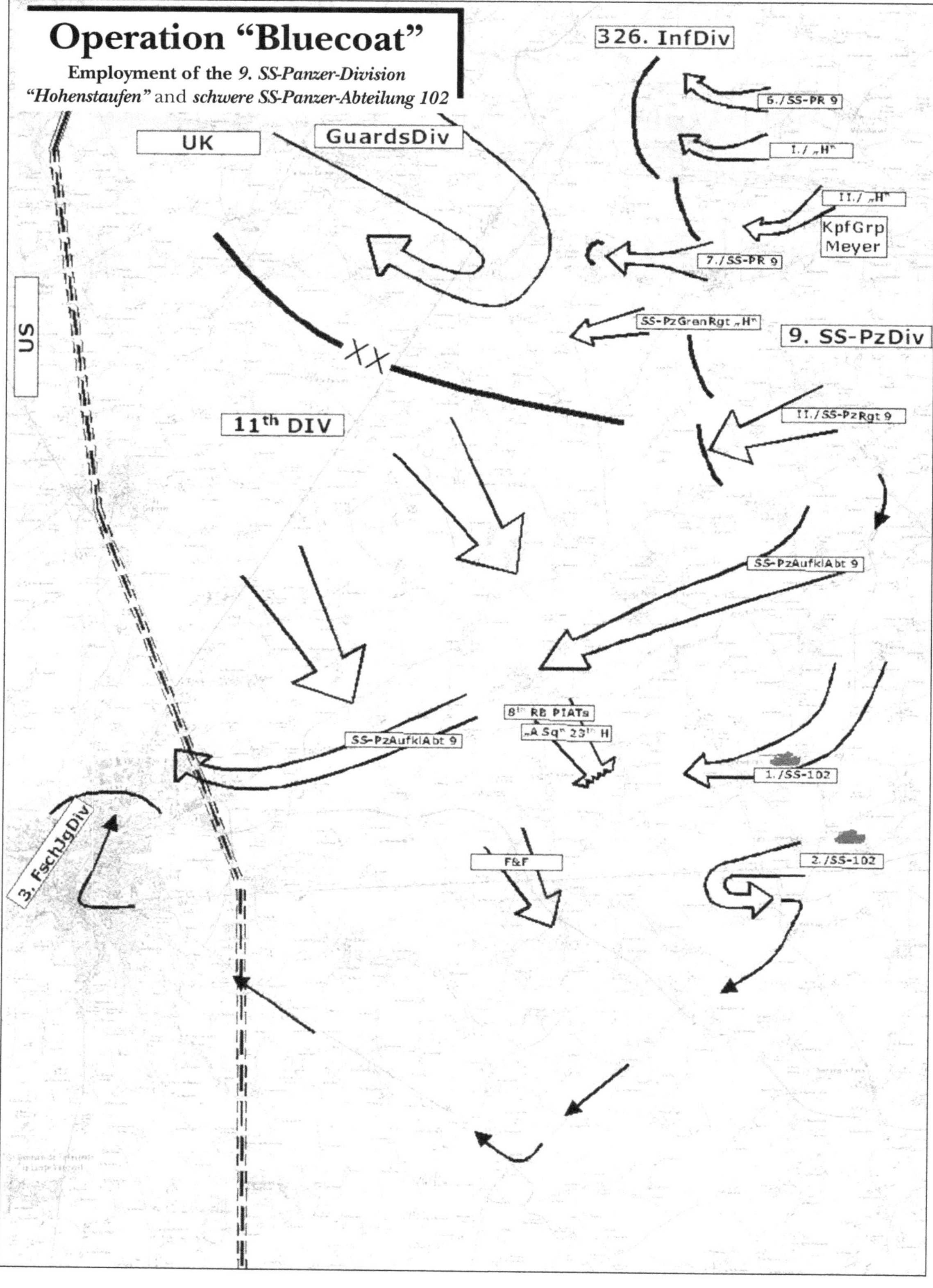
Operation "Bluecoat"
Employment of the 9. SS-Panzer-Division "Hohenstaufen" and schwere SS-Panzer-Abteilung 102
326. InfDiv
UK
GuardsDiv
US
9. SS-PzDiv
KpfGrp Meyer
7./SS-PR 9
SS-PzGrenRgt „H"
II./SS-PzRgt 9
11th DIV
SS-PzAufklAbt 9
SS-PzAufklAbt 9
8th RB PIATs
„A Sq" 23rd H
1./SS-102
2./SS-102
F&F
3. FschJgDiv

By the morning of 2 August 1944, *Kampfgruppe Meyer* was already in the crisis area. It was screening along a line running Arclais–woods two kilometers west of Montchauvet–Montchamp–fork in the road southwest of Le Grand Bonfait. The commanding general intended to close the gap between Le Beny and Bocage with two flanking attacks from the west and the east. To this end, *schwere SS-Panzer-Abteilung 102* was to be moved up through Estry, Chenedollè, Viessoix and Vire to the main road running from Vire to Villers-Bocage. From there, the battalion was to move along the road to the northeast.

But at Chenedollé, the *1./schwere SS-Panzer-Abteilung 102* was already engaged with enemy tanks that had moved forward. It was clear to *SS-Sturmbannführer* Weiß that it was imperative to move as rapidly as possible to the area outside the northern outskirts of Vire and block there. He therefore had his 1st Company continue to conduct a reconnaissance-in-force in this direction. The company had to engage several enemy tanks. It then continued to move along the Vassy to Vire road in the direction of the latter city.

The lead platoon lost a tank at Le Hauts to an antitank gun. The battalion's 2nd Company established positions to screen along the Tinchebray–Vire road. Towards evening, contact was established in Vire with forces of the *3. Fallschirmjäger-Division.* For the time being, the immediate danger to Vire had been averted.

✠

SS-Rottenführer Trautmann has provided a vivid description of the establishment of contact with the *Fallschirmjäger* and the initial fighting in Vire and to the north. The account is written in the third person for the most part, so it is important for the reader to remember that Trautmann was the gunner of the company commander, *SS-Untersturmführer* Martin Schroif:

> Our arrival gave our comrades new hope, especially since all of them were without heavy weapons. It was obvious to us that we had to do something immediately after the initial enemy reconnaissance efforts. Vire—the large roadway transportation hub—had to be set up for defense as quickly as possible, especially concentrating on the roads leading out of town. One *Tiger*, or even several, at all these points, with *Fallschirmjäger* providing close-in security. Outposts between the individual strongpoints!
>
> A few *Fallschirmjäger* accompanied the tanks, acting as guides to lead the *Tigers* through the shot-up streets to their respective strongpoints. The reconnaissance patrol had barely returned to the tank company when we were told: Orders are being issued! After a brief operations order, the tanks were already rolling out; the *Fallschirmjäger* were mounted on them.
>
> Loritz's platoon occupied positions at the train station in the northern suburbs; the other tanks were divided up among the various roads leading out of town. The company headquarters was located on the northern slope, where everything could be observed. A half hour later, all of the *Tigers* reported that they had occupied their assigned positions.
>
> That night, the motorcycle messengers reported that the objective had been reached; in the morning, the messengers returned with new orders for 2 August. They stated: The company will attack at 1000 hours with the *"Frundsberg"* reconnaissance battalion. Its objective is the northern exits

The view from the edge of Vire towards La Bistière shows that the advance of *Kampfgruppe Weiß* was anything but a "walk in the park," since it had to approach across relatively open terrain.

of La Bistière. The 1st Company moves out from Estry. It will link up with the 2nd Company there [La Bistière], so as to encircle the enemy armored units that have broken through to the south.

The company was resupplied in the morning. It assembled shortly before 1000 hours in the northern suburb of the city. Short meeting to issue orders. To the astonishment of all, the reconnaissance battalion consisted of the commander and about 20 lightly armed infantrymen. A rifle company and an antiaircraft machine gun from the *Fallschirmjäger* also joined up.

Right at 1000 hours, Schroif raised his arm and gave the signal to start engines. The column then moved out, with Loritz's platoon in the lead. Things proceeded rapidly at least as far as the fork in the road north of Vire. The tanks moved slightly staggered; that way, at least two of them had fields of fire to the front. The infantry proceeded to the left and right among the hedgerows, thus preventing any surprises from the flanks.

The commander of the reconnaissance battalion had told us that friendly patrols were out to our front. We had scarcely reached the fork in the road, when we were able to identify a tank and several men in the vegetation along the road about 500 meters in front of us. It could not be determined with certainty whether it was the enemy.

Suddenly, however, a small armored car moved up behind the tank and then took off to the north. Because it could only be seen for a few seconds, it could not be knocked out. A fire command was issued immediately: Engage at will!

While the first rounds hit the tank, there was a howling above us in the air. The infantry jumped under cover. Our area was within enemy artillery range.

Schroif issued orders: Continue to march!

Although the tank that had been engaged in front of us had received several hits, it did not fly into the air. Closely behind it and along the side roads were four Cromwells, all of which were knocked out. We then stopped for a short period, until the infantry had closed up.

The terrain in front of us sloped downwards, only to climb again later on. The last three tanks provided cover; the main body rolled rapidly down the hill and then up the other side. The remaining tanks then followed with infantry on board.

Our attack objective, a small village, could be identified about 600–700 meters ahead. The infantry proceeded to the left and the right through the fields; the *Tigers* then moved out. Soon, the first buildings were reached.

Then it got crazy! Close to the road, protected from observation by buildings and high hedges, were enemy tanks: Shermans! But the two lead tanks, Loritz and Streng, worked in an exemplary fashion together. They knocked out one tank after the other.

Those of us in the remaining tanks also had our hands full. We were getting a lot of fire, especially from the high ground to the left, which was filled with row after row of hedges. It looked like we were dealing with tanks, nothing but tanks! We notified each other by radio whenever we were hit, so the others could get out of the enemy's fields of fire.

We received a lot of hits, especially in the running gear. Schroif gave orders again and again to fire into this or that vegetation. We slowly found our targets: In one place, a shot of flames rose to the sky, then at another place. The enemy fire became weaker. The road started to climb. When we were next to the last building, the middle of the column was heavily engaged again, while the lead elements continued to advance.

The rounds landed between and among us like dazzling bolts of lightning. There was another hit in the running gear. The company commander had all the main guns fire off to the left! Once again . . . massed fire . . . group of vegetation off to the left. Two tanks flew into the air again! It was an engagement at pointblank range: 50–100 meters.

Schroif continued to receive hits from the building he was in front of, until several high-explosive rounds also put an end to this enemy defensive effort. The advance was then continued. The road climbed; the attack objective was reached.

It was then imperative to find a good defensive position in the terrain. The lead elements had reached the hill, when new fire from the left flank was received. We were hit; the radio quit working. Did something bad happen? What was going on with the radio operator? The driver?

By physically grabbing the gunner and yelling at him, he was told to fire in the direction that the fire was coming from. The first round had barely left the barrel, when the *Tigers* to the rear also joined in. They knew what was going on immediately and supported us with heavy fire. The lead platoon continued to move briskly down the slope and climb again on the far side. Now, at the most important moment, the radio had stopped working. What was to be done? Schroif signaled Harlander to come up to him; Harlander had to pass on orders to the company:

Stop immediately . . . objectives reached! Jupiter 1: Take position on line with me oriented north! Jupiter 2: Screen to the right and left at the road intersection 100 meters to the rear.

The *Tigers* rolled into their assigned positions. Rosowski was in the process of turning when he received six damaging hits from about 30 meters away. They took deep chunks out of his turret. The seventh round was Rosowski's. It went into the hedge from where he had taken the hits. A long tongue of flame shot skyward and a loud bang signaled the effectiveness of this round: The enemy tank flew into the air!

A short while later, an aerial observer flew over our positions. The 2-centimeter antiaircraft automatic cannon took him in its sights, but he disappeared with a dive and was gone. Soon artillery fire was falling in our area.

Around 1500 hours, the commander of the reconnaissance battalion went back to Vire with an *SPW* and the antiaircraft machine gun to report to the battalion [*schwere SS-Panzer-Abteilung 102*] that the attack objective had been reached and that 22 enemy tanks had been knocked out without any friendly complete losses. There had only been battle damage in our company. Unfortunately, radio communications did not exist, because the distance was too great.

The area that had been reached was then combed by smaller groups, usually two tanks and a few infantry. In the process, different pockets of resistance that still existed were eliminated. Several additional trucks were knocked out by evening. Two armored cars were captured and a motorcycle messenger was captured.

At this point, we were blocking the approach route of the English Guards Armoured Division. We took a liaison officer, an English captain, prisoner, along with his armored car. The radio set in his vehicle was very loud and we could monitor all of the enemy radio traffic. The vehicle was immediately sent to the corps for exploitation!

The sounds of heavy fighting could be heard off to the right flank. It was [*SS-Obersturmführer*] Kalss, who was working his way forward to us, supported by rocket launchers. For a period of time, he could only be heard weakly in the radio.

Schroif then sent a patrol off to the right, which was supposed to reconnoiter for enemy positions, the terrain and the approach of Kalss. One tank was sent with the patrol, but it was only able to follow for a short distance, since the terrain was too poor for tank movement. After an hour and a half, the patrol came back with heavy casualties: It had run into an ambush in the broken terrain!

Unfortunately, we could no longer spare anyone to work their way towards Kalss. Besides, we were being increasingly pressured from the north. Assault detachments had to be turned back along the road, especially after night fell.

During the night of 2–3 August 1944, we received supplies. Rations also came in the early morning hours.

About 1000 hours, Kuhlmann's tank arrived from the maintenance facility. It immediately received a mission: Enemy tanks were again trying to get past us to the left of the road! Skillfully brought forward by a few infantrymen, Kuhlmann was guided into a good firing position. In a short period of time, he knocked out three tanks. The same good fortune befell us a little farther to the rear to the right of the road. Five enemy tanks were in a defile. Three were definitely knocked out there, and the others caught fire and burned up as well!

Towards evening, the enemy tried to get our tanks again with assault detachments. He was approaching from the north on both sides of the road! The *Tigers* were just waiting for the best moment. Trees in front of us were blown up and then fell across one another on the road. The assault detachment scattered and our machine guns and high-explosive rounds landed among the soldiers.

Despite our efforts, however, the enemy approached closer and closer, because the terrain offered excellent concealment. The few infantry we had with us could not provide close-in security for the entire semicircle of *Tigers*. As a result, the tanks worked in pairs, firing occasionally to clear the area around them.

Nerves were at the breaking point. Everyone was listening into the darkness for the slightest sound. By doing so, we were successful in keeping the enemy at bay.

At about 2330 hours, Schroif sent a tank to the fork in the road south of us. Its mission was to observe retrograde movements from there, screen to the northwest and, above all, hold up any pursuing enemy so as to allow a withdrawal.

When the order to pull back arrived at 2300 hours, the vehicles with the worst battle damage to their running gear were the first ones sent back with mounted infantry. Bringing up the rear were the vehicles that were still intact.

The withdrawal proceeded in an orderly fashion. Vire was reached around 2400 hours. Large formations were concentrating there. While we held out for two days far to the front, they had established a new front here.

The company set up three kilometers south of Vire on the road and got opportunity to work on repairing its considerable battle damage. Two work sections from the maintenance company were also assigned for this.

Hard days of fighting were behind us, and we had been successful! The company had achieved a respectable success without any losses of its own: 28 enemy tanks had been knocked out and additional ones damaged; 14 trucks had been destroyed; two armored cars had been captured, along with prisoners; and two motorcycle messengers had been taken prisoner and their vehicles captured.

The first enemy contact north of Vire has been portrayed by the British as follows:

> Suddenly in the middle of the afternoon some German Tiger tanks and infantry appeared mysteriously from the outskirts of Vire and advanced slowly and ponderously up the road behind B squadron towards RHQ [regimental headquarters]. There was little our Cromwells could do to stop them, and due to some confusion between the gunners and rocket-firing aircraft they got within striking distance of RHQ, who

SW

Two views from the British standpoint. Above: From La Bistière towards Vire. Below: From the La Bistière–Vire road to the southeast towards the high ground north of Chênedollé. These views illustrate why the Germans were able to successfully hold up the British for several days.

SE

> withdrew losing lives and soft vehicles. As the night turned foggy, enemy infantry proceeded to stalk our tanks on foot with bazookas and a number were lost and crews captured.

In the meantime, there had been heavy fighting for Montchauvet. The British came to recognise that the headlong advance they had enjoyed was over for the time being. The enemy advance was temporarily stopped at Presles. On the other hand, German counterattacks did not make much progress. As a result, *Kampfgruppe Meyer* was reinforced with the *II./SS-Panzer-Grenadier-Regiment 19.*

The fact that the British attack momentum was, in the final analysis, limited by the German resistance is vividly portrayed in the following account that is taken from *Operation Bluecoat* by Ian Daglish:

> By nightfall, the fighting units of 11th Armoured Division were established in good defensive positions. Yet the position of 11th Armoured was far from secure. During the afternoon it had become clear to "Pip" Roberts, in his tactical headquarters at le Reculey, that the advance had progressed far enough. The "horns" of the Black Bull division were its tank regiments. These had plunged deep into enemy territory, and had paid a price. Of the division's 145 Sherman tanks ready for action at the end of 1 August, thirty-one were reported lost at the end of the day; six of these the vital, 17-pounder armed Fireflies. And the Black Bull's left flank was a concern. Fresh in Roberts' mind was the recent memory of GOODWOOD, where the delayed arrival of the Guards Armoured Division had led to his division's left flank becoming dangerously exposed. Then, he had pushed on and taken heavy losses. Now, Roberts worried about the fluid situation of his rear areas. He frankly dreaded the thought of German armour rampaging among the transport columns that were the life blood of his fighting units.
>
> Yet another legacy of GOODWOOD influenced "Pip" Roberts. Barely a week previously, on 24 July, an 11th Armoured Division conference had been held to review lessons learned from the GOODWOOD battle. One of the first of these was that the final objective should have been a topographical feature. That was to say, an advance should come to a halt on ground that lent itself to being held: *"finishing on a tactical feature on which either hull down or covered positions could be occupied."* As things stood at the end of 2 August, the two principal battle groups of the division were established on substantial ridgelines, offering both visibility over the enemy and the relative shelter of the reverse slope. And as the final consideration, in its present positions the entire force of 11th Armoured Division was still within the protective umbrella of VIII Corps' artillery. Roberts determined that there would be no further advance.
>
> Late in the afternoon, O'Connor visited Roberts at Le Reculey and, as luck would have it, the general's arrival was heralded by a German artillery strike. Nothing could have been more convincing in support of Roberts' argument. 11th Armoured Division would hold its ground. What is more, O'Connor promised infantry reinforcements in the shape of 185 Brigade from 3rd (Infantry) Division. By 22.30 hours, the division's

armoured regiments were receiving the order to hold the ground they were on.

The closing of the gap at Vire by *Kampfgruppe Weiß* is also described by Daglish:

> While 11th Armoured Division was putting on the brakes, Kampfgruppe Weiss was pushing forward hard. *SS*-Sturmbannführer Hans Weiss's own unit of Tiger tanks had experienced a nightmare journey even to reach the battle area. Setting off after nightfall from their ambush positions on the southern slopes of Hill 112, they drove their 60-ton monsters through the hours of darkness along winding country roads already jammed with west-bound traffic. With the dawn came the added burden of constant watchfulness for signs of an imminent air raid. Their plan was to route southwards from Estry to join the main highway for a straight run west into Vire.
>
> Passing through Estry, it seems that Obersturmführer Kalss' leading 1st Company decided in mid-afternoon to try a short cut, taking a right turn off the main southbound road to head towards Chenedolle. Shortly after, Kalss reported that he had run into a British armoured spearhead, and had destroyed a number of British tanks. His claim was no exaggeration: it was these Tiger tanks "that had crushed the 23/Hussars' A Squadron. But Weiss's travel arrangements had not allowed for an encounter with enemy armour so far south. Like other German commanders that day, he and his subordinates had to update their plans in light of developments. We can safely assume that the tank engaged by the 8/RB PIATs in Chenedolle was likewise a Tiger of SS Pz.Abt. 102 as the column probed to find a clear route to Vire. Weiss was not looking for a fight so far from his objective. But he could not ignore the threat when his was the only available force in the area. Recognising that a major British armoured breakthrough must have taken place, and with no other force immediately to hand, Weiss ordered his 1st Company, under Kalss, to take up defensive positions around Chenedolle. This left his 2nd Company led by Untersturmführer Schroif to complete the battalion's primary mission.
>
> Bullets rattled against the turret of my tank and great sheets of fire and smoke billowed up where the rockets had hit the ground. Time and again they screamed down on us. Then the attack stopped as abruptly as it had started.
>
> The "tiffies" did little physical damage to the tanks. Though the sixty-pound rockets packed an awesome punch, they were extremely inaccurate and direct hits on tanks were rare. But the air attack was not in vain. As a direct consequence, Streng relates, "Schroif decided to make a detour. We turned back and moved further south." KG Weiss had been persuaded that the direct highway to Vire was not an option. Instead, Schroif's company turned back to the Hauts Vents crossroads and detoured south on the Tinchebray road before turning north again for Vire. Time was lost. The company of heavy tanks did not arrive in Vire until 20.35 hours (21.35 Allied time), and reached the northern suburbs only just in time to see last of the Northants Yeomanry's Cromwells driving off. The extra distance had cost more

than time. A night and a day of grinding forward had worn out the heavy vehicles as well as their crews. Streng again:

> The Panzers of Reisske and Münster broke down and had to be left at the roadside. We were pushing the engines hard. That and the warm summer evening [were] causing them to overheat.

The second major element of *Kampfgruppe* Weiss was *Hohenstaufen's* reconnaissance battalion. This unit resembled neither the Cromwell-equipped Welsh Guards nor the Household Cavalry with its light armoured cars. *SS-Panzer-Aufklärungs-Abteilung 9* was a mixed force of well armed and fast armoured vehicles and infantry. Its five companies included two SPW companies ("Panzerspähwagen"), the first equipped with light, fast armoured cars and the second with turreted half-tracks.[1] Two *SPW* companies ("Schützenpanzerwagen") were composed of soldiers mounted in small, armoured half-track personnel carriers. A fifth heavy weapons company mounted in medium half-tracks included support guns, antitank guns, and engineers. While specialising in reconnaissance, for which speed was more important than firepower, this battalion could also muster the resilience to hold the line and even the brute force to conduct armoured assaults. Led by the charismatic *Hauptsturmführer* Viktor-Eberhard Gräbner, the unit had successfully made the transition from the open Russian steppe to the Normandy bocage.

1 Editor's Note: These were *Sd.Kfz. 250/9* light armored half-tracks, armed with a *2-cm KwK 38* automatic cannon.

Gräbner's [formation] was the most mobile element of *Kampfgruppe Weiss.* About 16.00 hours on 2 August, Gräbner's headquarters was at Estry. But long before, advance parties from the battalion had been infiltrating the roads from Estry towards Vire. It was not Gräbner's style to take the same roundabout route as the heavy Tiger tanks, and through the day elements of *SS-Panzer-Aufklärungs-Abteilung 9* ranged the country lanes across the path of the advancing British. As we have seen, vehicles of the 2nd Company [armored-car company] had already fallen to the guns of the advancing 23/Hussars and 2/Fife and Forfar Yeomanry. As the day wore on, men and half-tracks of the 3rd Company (SPW) penetrated the British rear areas around Presles and Burcy, as evidenced by the fate of Steel Brownlie's A Squadron. Using speed and cover, small groups of reconnaissance vehicles penetrated as far as the outskirts of Vire, and by 19.00 hours were able to confirm that the town of Vire, though devastated, was still free of the enemy. Entering the town, they made contact with antiaircraft troops of *3. Fallschirmjäger-Division.* The gap blown between two German field armies when Dickie's bridge fell to the British had begun to close.

✠

By the end of the day, the greatest danger was temporarily over for the German field-army boundary positions. Thanks to the British hesitation outside of Vire, it was possible to once more stave off a collapse of the front.

✠

On 3 August 1944, *Kampfgruppe Weiß* attacked. It was the mission of the 2nd Company to attack north along the Vire–Caen road along with the *3./SS-Panzer-Aufklärungs-Abteilung 9*. It was then to block the road just north of La Bistiére.

The firsthand account of *SS-Unterscharführer* Streng conveys a memorable impression of this day as well as the extreme psychological pressures the crews were subjected to:

> At 0730 hours, the commander of the armored reconnaissance battalion of the *9. SS-Panzer-Division* [*"Hohenstaufen"*] personally issued his orders:
>
> The *Tiger* company would advance together with the 3rd Company [of *SS-Panzer-Aufklärungs-Abteilung 9*] along the Vire–Caen road to the north and block the road just north of La Bistiére. Move-out was most likely at 1100 hours, since the grenadier company had to be brought up and the *Tigers* needed to be topped off.
>
> When you are about to go into combat, you don't talk about death. You smoke a cigarette and talk about food, about the weather, about superficial things and occurrences and smile about them.
>
> You act like a soldier, even here in a fleeting assembly area on the northern part of the city, a few minutes before a risky attack from which some will certainly not return.
>
> To the minute, at 1100 hours, Loritz headed north as the lead platoon leader on the right-hand side of the road. My *234* and I went to the left of the road. A squad of dismounted grenadiers covered to the outside of each of us.
>
> The main body of the *Tigers* followed behind us—seven in all—slightly staggered. Behind them was a company of mounted *Panzergrenadiere*. Bringing up the rear were the self-propelled guns of the light *Flak* unit, which were providing the antiaircraft defense for the massed power of our attack column.
>
> We were all in a good mood and convinced that our attack would succeed. We were finally moving forward.
>
> The *SS* grenadiers were marching in column behind one another, their machine guns under their arms and their squad leaders to the front. They had smiles on their faces as they walked along in the roadside ditch; our combat vehicles were moving at a walking pace.
>
> An oppressive, flickering heat from the scorching August sun lay over the countryside; above us was a cloudless, dark-blue summer sky. Nervously alert, the driver sat behind his wheel, the gunner behind his optics and the radio operator at his bow machine gun, operating the receiver and transmitter.
>
> In a somewhat sloppy manner, the loader laid the antitank and high-explosive rounds within reach on the turret floor. From the turret hatches, the tank commanders towered out, denim sleeves rolled up, observing the terrain ahead of them with their binoculars.
>
> After crossing the fork in the road, whose passage was blocked by the skeletons of burned-out cars, the lead elements of the attack encountered the enemy three kilometers north of Vire. The *Kampfgruppe* hesitated. It was still uncertain whether German tanks of a counterattack that was

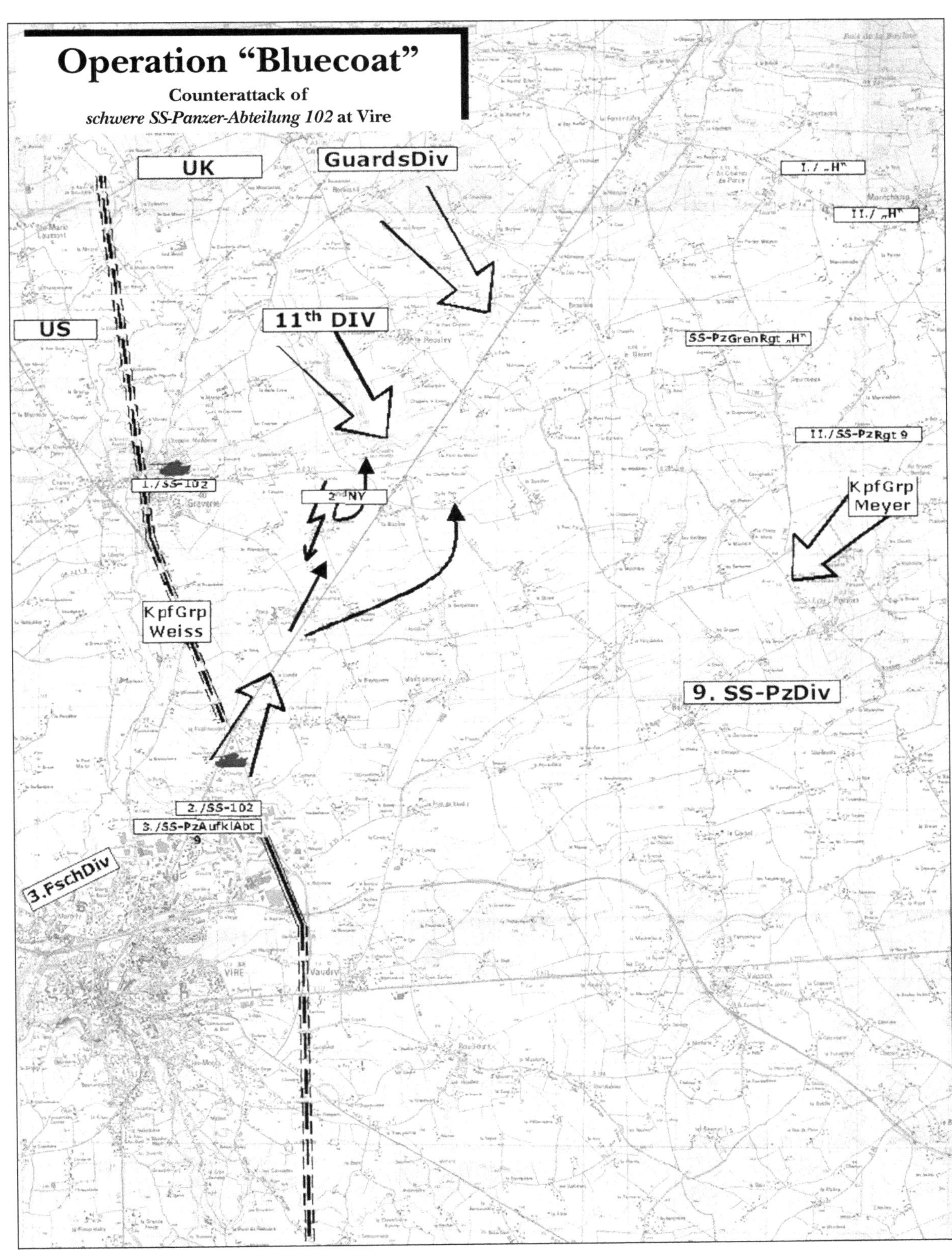
Operation "Bluecoat"
Counterattack of
schwere SS-Panzer-Abteilung 102 at Vire
UK
GuardsDiv
I./„H"
II./„H"
US
11th DIV
SS-PzGrenRgt „H"
II./SS-PzRgt 9
1./SS-102
2nd NY
KpfGrp
Meyer
KpfGrp
Weiss
9. SS-PzDiv
2./SS-102
3./SS-PzAufklAbt
9
3.FschDiv
VIRE
Vaudry

taking place at the same time as that of our 1st Company had advanced this far. We were forbidden to fire. We radioed our observations back and forth as to whether we should or should not engage. Anxious minutes passed. Schroif continued to hesitate. Suddenly, an English armored car raced up in front of the Cromwell tank, which was at the high point of the slowly rising road that was in the middle of fir trees to either side.

Brown figures climbed up on the tank and looked over at us. Because English armored cars were also being used by German forces at the moment, we were still uncertain.

By then, perhaps eight minutes had passed. On the other side, the brown figures jumped into the four-wheeled armored car and disappeared as fast as lightning behind the high ground. Without awaiting further orders, Loritz and I issued fire commands. The sounds of two thunderous reports from the 8.8-centimeter main guns came at the same time. A flash followed by gray-blue smoke came from the muzzle brakes in front of the vehicles. There were flashes on the far side when the rounds hit the running gear and the upper part of the hull. With clashing and clanging, the loader put the second round into the chamber. The fighting compartment was filled with acrid, blue fumes from the discharge. The ventilator in the turret roof sucked the exhaust fumes into the open.

The next fire command was issued calmly through the intercom system: "Second round . . . aim higher . . . fire." The second round flashed just below the main gun on the upper hull. Hazy white clouds escaped momentarily from the Cromwell. When Loritz fired his second round, the belly-shot enemy tank disappeared completely in clouds of smoke.

I had a start and ducked. My shoulders brushed against the narrow, round opening of the hatch. It was pulsating . . . whistling . . . rushing above me. And then impact followed impact into the earth and rocked it. It bellowed and thundered all around us. Shrapnel from the artillery shells landing nearby howled through the air, and pieces of the ground fell back to earth with a dull thud.

Even though the concussion of the exploding shells barely disturbed us inside the tank, thick swaths of powder smoke enveloped our attacking column and blew across our heads like a warm breath. The heavens had descended with smoke and thunder. A torrent of ricocheting rounds on the road. Leaves and branches twirled to the earth from the crowns of the trees.

The engines grew louder. *Panzer marsch!*

The lead tank elements slowly up the road.

Shortly after crossing the first rise and passing the knocked-out enemy tank, the grenadiers who had hurried on ahead of us pointed out a threat along a path in the woods through their energetic waving. Loritz eliminated this threat from a few meters away. As a result of his antitank rounds striking home, the second Cromwell was knocked out. It was in the path leading off to the right.

Impeded from advancing through the broken and dense terrain, we asked the grenadiers to deploy to both sides of the tanks to protect us against hunter/killer teams. Dismounted squads then secured our flanks in the densely vegetated and wooded terrain. They moved up to 30 meters in front of our lead elements. At this point, we had to pay extremely close attention. I constantly searched the attack area, my neck stretched out and eyes glues to the binoculars. My head was only a little bit out of the hatch above the vision slots. Bending forward and backward, I twisted around on the leather pad of my seat to search the air space above me for enemy aircraft. The tanks of our company rattled and howled as dark, dense objects behind me; they were dispersed at equal intervals to both sides of the road. And, once again, I observe to the front, between the always-suspicious hedges and cuts in the woods, which an experienced opponent knows how to use so well and so successfully for both the offense and the defense.

Often blinded and fooled by the sleight-of-hand offered by the various colors, my eyes sought a brief respite in the shadowy, humidly hot interior of the fighting compartment.

The needle on the tachometer trembled around 1,500 RPM's; the thermostat was in the red zone due to the snail's pace we were moving and had already climbed to 90° [194° Fahrenheit]. Fog-like, warm-smelling oil and gasoline vapors penetrated through the slits in the firewall separating the engine from the fighting compartment.

The rising and falling scratchy sounds in the intercom and radios buzzed monotonously.

A glance at my watch. We had been moving for more than an hour. Large vehicular columns came into view in front of us; they were 3,000 meters away and only slightly visible behind the gullies. We immediately took them under fire with high-explosive rounds. The German rounds burst with easily identifiable clouds formed from the explosives among the columns. The vehicles turned off into the next available path in wild panic and raced away from the area. By the 5th and 6th rounds, the road looked as though it had been swept clean, and only individual motorcycle messengers flitted along.

An enemy reconnaissance aircraft flew parallel along our line of advance at low altitude. I could easily make out the colorful rings on the wings. The Englishman was actually flying quite unabashedly low. He turned over the road in a steep spiral and flew placidly to the east of us along our tank column. He was not engaged by our *Flak*. He seemed to hover about at 200 meters. I swung myself behind the antiaircraft machine gun. Took a quick aim and squeezed the trigger. Damn! The stupid belt jammed! Only a few individual tracers rattled skyward.

In the meantime, this blowfly disappeared behind the hills on the far side of us, flattened out and started to land. Over there they probably had a clear picture of our intentions, strength and direction of march; we would probably not have to wait long for a reaction.

I had the tank pick up speed and was following right behind Loritz and off to the side so as to be able to protect him in the event of any unpleasant surprises.

Unnecessary talking during an attack is taboo inside of a fighting vehicle. Observations are exchanged in shorthand. You can almost hear someone swallowing or clearing his throat through the throat mikes and the headphones.

A mountain slope lying about seven kilometers to the north was then placed under heavy rocket-launcher fire in support of our 1st Company. The entire slope was covered in black, yellow and white clouds of smoke for several minutes.

Loritz and I were at the entrance to the village of La Bistiére by then. A further move to the northern edge of the locality was ordered by radio as well as the taking and securing of the hill beyond it.

Nothing was stirring among the thick shrubs and along the village street. The windowpanes rattled slightly and the walls shook somewhat from the weight of our tanks.

Suddenly, a Frenchman jumped out of his house door to the lead tank. He was yelling something confusing to the tank commander, who was bending over towards him. He gesticulated with his arms and pointed off to the left. Something wasn't quite right here!

For reasons unknown, Loritz took hardly any time to listen to the civilian; certainly, there was danger in the air.

Only a few meters separated us from the street crossing in the middle of the village. The friendly infantry had not yet closed up. I stayed where I was, waiting to see what would happen.

✠

Loritz stepped on it and moved out. Ten more meters—suddenly, a blinding flash of lightning, a crash, black smoke and vapors. Hit in the left-hand running gear in the middle of the street. At this moment, I expected a lance of flame that would have to shoot out of the vehicle. But the vehicle appeared to be unshaken and moved across the street into the protection of the building facades. I was shaking, but not because the earth was moving. I was trembling from the inside out.

I was sorely tempted to approach and destroy the enemy tank on his left flank, taking my tank through the gardens and the walls, crushing everything without hesitation in front of me. Unobserved and still behind the building, Loritz swung his turret to the left. He had his tank move out and pressed forward onto the other side of the street. Suddenly, a long lance of flame shot out from his main gun; the windowpanes shattered from the concussion of the report of the gun and tiles fell from the roofs. The tank disappeared in a black cloud of gunpowder smoke.

Then it was my turn to get across the road. Driver . . . Fourth gear . . . Step on it! The engine roared and the tracks rattled and clanked over the asphalt. As quick as lightning, I looked to the left and to the right. The English tank, 30 meters off to the side in a fruit orchard next to a trail, burst asunder with a huge flash and with a thunderous racket. A massive mushroom cloud of smoke and flame formed for a few seconds above the trees and arched upwards towards the blue sky. Burning flames engulfed the glowing sides of the tank in a sea of fire.

Any remaining resistance in La Bistiére was quickly broken.

The leading elements of the armored attack force were just north of La Bistiére and at the objective just after 1300 hours.

Loritz and I were just about to continue the attack into the next village, when we were urgently ordered back by radio by Schroif to the ridgeline.

I took an excellent pair of binoculars from the light English tank that was behind the high ground and had been abandoned by its crew. But we needed to be careful. After quickly conversing with Loritz, we moved back into position on both sides of the ridgeline on the northern edge of La Bistiére.The grenadier company was then guided into position along the ridgeline that ran all the way around the village. It dug in behind hedges and bushes in a thin line.

For the second time, an artillery or reconnaissance aircraft flew over the attack area. It then set down a short while later at the location of the English battery north of the cemetery and the church adjoining it on the road to the left.

Moments later, I took the terrain behind it under high-explosive main-gun fire. Everything over there panicked and fled in wild disarray.

The enemy defense became increasingly stronger and more perceptible. Enemy tanks moved into position behind the concealment of the vegetation and the hedgerows. An English infantry attack gained momentum as it come out of its attack positions from the gullies. By leaps and bounds, the khaki-brown attack groups hastened through the gullies, jumped over ditches and hedges and got closer and closer.

At this point, German machine-gun fire rattled in from the left and let its bursts of fire hail down upon the advancing troops. Infantry rounds smacked against the walls and the branches, chirped with a singing sound over my head and then ricocheted off to the crowns of the trees.

And then there was impact after impact into the earth. It groaned and rumbled. Salvoes of hand grenades burst off to the left of my firing position; I could not follow their paths through the thick vegetation and hedges.

On the other side of the road, in Loritz's area, the storming English infantry intended to approach close to the tank using the concealment offered by the folds in the ground and the hedgerows. This was done until the brown rows of attackers finally faltered under the brute force of the automatic weapons and turned around and fled to the rear.

German artillery then joined the fighting. The shells rushed eerily overhead. With a long, drawn-out *huuuiiii* they raced through the air with a hissing and a swishing sound.

Shell after shell exploded on the edges of the surrounding high ground; they tossed earth, wooden timbers, rocks and trees around like chaff through a thrashing machine. Looking like a broad flag, the smoke wound its way into the clear August sky.

From the other side, the English batteries joined in with increased intensity and displays of firepower.

The branches of the trees split apart in the fruit orchards; the crowns of the trees were tilted. It seemed you could hear them moaning as they broke and fell to earth. A torrent of bursting rounds. It hissed . . . buzzed . . . whistled. The dirt splattered.

Those were the claw marks of a raging predatory animal.

Thick, gray masses of smoke covered the village and the surrounding high ground.

Our grenadiers, who had dug in as a sort of living bulwark around the village, suffered heavy losses in dead and badly wounded.

According to radio traffic from Loritz, our tanks was to be repositioned to the left to reinforce the defensive sector there, because the enemy was continuously feeling his way forward and attacking in front of the German lines.

While pulling back to the road, the trees and the bushes were pushed to the side under the force of our broad tracks. The tracks churned up a deep impression in the soft, brown earth. While I was still in the process of moving onto the road surface from the vegetable garden and through its fence and the roadside ditch, I received a terrific hit from a main gun on the side of the hull that was facing the street. Its crashing impact knocked the crew out of its seats and tossed the loose interior fixtures around.

Pale, with fluttering eyes, Mahler turned around towards me; for a few seconds, there was deathly silence in the interior of the tank. At any moment, the second round would have to come knocking on the steel walls, and then it would only be by chance that it didn't penetrate into the engine or fighting compartments and cause the entire steel monster to burst apart with a huge flash.

I yelled shrilly down below: "Driver, back up . . . move out . . . move out!"

The engine roared as it received an unrestricted amount of gas. Ott turned the steering wheel sharply to the right in order to get the front of the tank around. For a few anxious moments, nothing happened. The tank did not move. The report came from a voice cracking with excitement: "The vehicle won't turn." A paralyzing fear could be seen on the faces. Something had to work. Suddenly, the tank moved. It rolled back along its length and then rolled forward again. It bottomed out diagonally in the roadside ditch.

With flying hands in a desperate situation, I tore the smoke candles out of their mounts on the left side of the turret wall. I took off the safety cap and pulled. I then jerked out of the hatch with my upper body and threw the charge in front of the right side of the tank.

Not unlike a powerful jackhammer on hardened steel, the second main-gun round slammed into the steel plates of the tank from somewhere off to the left along the road. The crew was stirred up again. Why didn't it happen this time?

From the outside, thick, milky white smoke crossed over the tank in a concentrated form. For a few moments, it penetrated through all of the slots and slits of the hatches.

The second and third smoke candle flew out of the tank. Everything disappeared into a white wall of smoke—all of the street and the adjoining ridgeline. Pressing our sleeves to our mouths, we breathed in the bitter, foul-tasting stuff, gulping and coughing.

I sent an emergency report three times on the radio to everyone and asked for immediate help: "*Panzer Streng* . . . north edge of the road . . . immobilized by fire . . . recover immediately!"

I stayed at my station with nerves of iron. You just wanted to get out and run away—run away from this tank condemned to death.

The fourth and fifth smoke candles flew in front of the tank. You thought you were going to suffocate and throw up.

Over there, in the enemy's firing position, they certainly must have thought they had eliminated a German tank. At least there were no more rounds knocking on the armored plate.

I ordered the gunner, Mahler, to go to the company commander in order to bring up help immediately, so as to at least pull the tank into the dead zone of the road.

We had known for some time that the right-hand track of the tank had been thrown. It had been torn apart by the hit and was lying diagonally across the street.

Anxious minutes passed impatiently, while we could do nothing. Wasn't any help going to arrive? Finally, finally, Rodinger's tank in the lead, followed by Münster. Rodinger advanced slowly along the road and into a defensive position in front of our tank. Münster stopped off to the side of the road. Everyone jumped out quickly, grabbed tow cables and shackles from their mounts and hooked up the two vehicles.

The cables slowly drew taut, and the tank gave a jerk. Engine roaring, the tow tank pulled our tank out of the ditch and onto the street. Ott was braking on both sides so as to keep the vehicle along its path in conjunction with the tow.

Thank God! At least, it was out of the direct-fire area of the enemy guns at this point.

Rodinger started to engage in a firefight against the enemy guns from the high point in the road.

A heavy German artillery barrage fell once again with astounding impacts on the high ground off to the left of the road. Like the echo of uncountable church bells ringing mightily, the sound of the artillery fire bellowed through the smoke, whimpering and stinking all the way from the crown of the steel-blue sky into some of the German positions. You wanted to hide.

Due to the concussion from a round, my hat twirled through the air and was whipped into a garden area off to the side.

Both the firing of main guns and the arrival of shells lit up the village. The yellow-colored pearl lassoes of both German and English machine-gun fire grabbed for their targets through the crowns of the trees and the vegetation.

The sounds of hell reverberated around us in the bitter infantry, tank and artillery fighting.

All of a sudden, the sound of one threatening main gun round after another being fired could be heard. It came from the group of bushes and hedges off to the right of the road behind the buildings and was aimed at German tanks covering from the rearward road intersection. It was barely 30 meters away.

As a result, the towed and towing tanks that were coming back down the road were in deadly danger. A paralyzing fear overcame everyone; where was this invisible enemy coming from? Once again, another cracking round followed into the middle of the village. Seven round, gaping holes—as thick as a man's arm—in the turret of [*SS-Hauptscharführer*] Rosovsky's tank unmistakably demonstrated the effectiveness of the hits. Three men of the crew tumbled to the ground from the fighting compartment. They were severely wounded from the power of the solid-shot rounds. The remaining two crewmembers had already been killed by the first round.

I jumped over the garden fences in quick bounds and hurried—a hollow charge in my hands—through the walls and the gardens, which covered me, towards what was assumed to be the enemy tank's location in the group of hedges.

Enemy fighter squadrons circled above La Bistiére; an enemy air attack would bring complete confusion and chaos into our ranks.

Before I could even get to him, the English tank broke out of the vegetation with exemplary bravery and headed towards the middle of the village with clanking tracks. Hammering tracer rounds rattled from the front of the tank against the assembled German tanks. Had this tank commander flipped out? Or was he only acting because he did not know our strength?

Piller's tank recognized the danger. He was on the field path leading off to the right and was oriented east, hidden by some vegetation. He traversed his turret to the left and fired an antitank round at a distance of 8 meters into the black body of the vehicle that was racing towards him. What followed next took only a matter of terrible seconds.

A powerful flash tore the hatches off and lifted the entire turret; a gigantic flaming mushroom strove towards the August sky in a series of explosions. The English tank commander was tossed as a burning, black bundle out of the tank, until death brought him relief from his inhumane wounds and suffering hours later.

And, once again, round after round impacted into the earth. Unending explosions tore apart whatever fell into their reach with animal-like tearing claws. The air had become impenetrable. The sky had sunk lower with smoke and haze. The sun only penetrated weakly through a thick veil.

Tracer rounds strayed across and down the road. They sparked and rang out when they encountered hard resistance; they diverted into the air or smacked into lettuce and beet beds. Multi-colored signal lights formed pearls of red, green and white as they fell into the village.

Friendly artillery from firing positions behind Vire slung their loads of iron in powerful barrages. A thundering, spraying curtain of iron placed itself protectively in front of the German grenadiers. The fighting raged back and forth.

Despite the raging attacks, the village of La Bistiére remained in the hands of the *Kampfgruppe*.

The perforated tank *233* was recovered under the cover of the buildings, and my immobilized tank was assigned to it for towing.

Due to the uncertainty of the fighting raging back and forth, Schroif ordered the immediate continued evacuation in the direction of Vire at 1700 hours.

Those wounded lying outside the southern edge of the village were recovered from the roadside ditches, given field dressings and then placed on the hulls of the tanks. They were later transferred to

German ambulances that approached us for their onward transportation.

The damaged vehicles crawled along on the road back to Vire at a snail's pace.

That same evening, based on an order from Schroif received over the radio, both tanks had to hold open the important [La Bistiére to Vire] road for friendly logistics personnel. This was 1.5 kilometers north of the road intersection at Vire and on the high ground that the road crossed, right next to the first enemy tank that had been knocked out.

Messengers and logistics vehicles rolled back and forth on captured motorcycles and armored cars.

We were able to generously treat ourselves to chocolate, crackers, butter, cigarettes—even clean underwear—from what was left on the enemy tanks that had been knocked out along the advance route.

After darkness had fallen, the company commander radioed and stated that the screening duty was considered as ended as of 2200 hours and the vehicles were released to go to the rear command post of [*SS-*] *Panzer-Aufklärungs-Abteilung 9.*

The start of the fighting three kilometers north of Vire—the encounter of the lead platoon of *SS-Untersturmführer* Loritz with the 2nd Northhamptonshire Yeomanry—has been described from the British perspective as follows:

> SS-Sturmbannführer Weiss now had his Tiger Battalion assembled in Vire, together with the greater part of *(SS)* Hauptsturmführer Gräbner's reconnaissance battalion. The first priority was to reach la Bistière, the designated rendezvous with *Kampfgruppe* Meyer. Shortly after midday (13.00 hours, British time) a mixed column set off on its five kilometre advance. Nine Tiger tanks led the way, astride the main road, followed by a Zug (platoon) of Gräbner's infantry, their small reconnaissance half-tracks dwarfed by the heavy tanks, and a pair of self-propelled anti-aircraft guns.
>
> The 2/Northamptonshire Yeomanry had been dogged by misfortune ever since their first actions of the Normandy campaign, and today their troubles were to reach a climax. By sheer bad luck, B Squadron was probing the northern outskirts of Vire as the German column emerged. The Tiger tanks scattered B Squadron's forward Cromwells, which bravely gave battle but as their War Diary related, "their 75mm guns are no match for the Tiger." In a further stroke of bad luck, artillery support was withheld to enable a spotting aircraft to direct rocket-armed Typhoons onto the German formation. But the spotting aircraft was shot down and the FOOs were unable to direct the fighter-bombers.
>
> Reaching the road junction at la Papillonnière, the German infantry dismounted to accompany the leading tanks as they attempted to deploy off the main road towards their objective, the high ground around la Bistière at Points 145 and 119 [modern 144 and 127]. Three B Squadron Cromwells were destroyed around la Papillonnière. The outclassed Cromwells slowly withdrew towards la Bistière, where the regiment's headquarters was trying to improvise a roadblock.

Then, to their horror, a further Tiger tank appeared behind them on the rising ground 500 metres to the east of the road and proceeded to pick off a further three B Squadron tanks as they fell back.

Reaching la Bistière, the survivors of B Squadron had new hope. Here if anywhere, the Tiger tank might be at a disadvantage, ambush at close range giving even the Cromwell tank's 75mm gun a chance of disabling a Tiger. But hope was short-lived. "Though the Tigers were engaged at short range, shells from our guns seemed to have little effect." The leading Tiger was hit at close range as it roared over an open cross-roads but escaped damage and, as soon as it could traverse its heavy turret, dispatched the ambusher in a ball of flame. One Tiger, SS-Unterscharführer Streng's, was indeed immobilized north of la Bistière, though repeated antitank hits succeeded only in giving the crew a fright and damaging a track so that the tank had to be towed to safety.

KG Weiss had stirred a hornets' nest. Instead of uniting with Meindl's paratroops from the west, and still hoping to see *KG Meyer* approaching from the east, they found only enemies around la Bistière. Attempts to move off the main highway achieved little as the country lanes proved simply too narrow for the huge tanks, yet unsupported infantry fell into ambushes. The close terrain saved the Cromwells of C Squadron lined up along the Etouvy—la Bistière road. C Squadron remained on the ridge through the day, covering the retreat of the Northants' headquarters from la Bistière. Restricted to the main highway, the heavy Tiger tanks took up defensive positions around la Bistière, two of them pressing forward as far as the slopes above Point 119, and stopping literally back-to-back, guarding the approaches. In fact, they had unwittingly stopped within half a mile of "Pin" Roberts' 11th Armoured Division tactical headquarters at le Reculey.

✠

Several British attacks were turned back afterwards; six additional enemy tanks and an armored car were knocked out. Hill 119 was taken. Several British attacks there were also repulsed; seven British tanks were knocked out.

During the night, the company screened along Hill 119 and on the road around it. The 1st Company was three kilometers north of Vire at la Graviere and maintained contact with the *3. Fallschirmjäger-Division*. Two more German tanks were lost on this day at that location.

The attacks of the *9. SS-Panzer-Division "Hohenstaufen"* that took placed further to the west at Burcy and in the area of Montchamp were crowned with little success due to a lack of forces. Only *Kampfgruppe Meyer* was successful in dislodging the enemy after tough fighting. This was at Presles. As a result, the British forces at Chenedollé and Burcy were threatened with being cut off.

That night and the following day were characterized by bitter fighting that raged back and forth. The village of Presles had been lost to the enemy again, but it was retaken. Further to the north, Montchamp was also taken from the enemy again.

To a certain extent, *Kampfgruppe Weiß* formed the western portion of the encircling forces around the piled-up British, however, the latter considered themselves to be anything but in a serious crisis situation due to their large numerical superiority.

The *9. SS-Panzer-Division "Hohenstaufen"* was too weak by a long shot, even though it had been reinforced in the meantime by *Kampfgruppe Olboeter* of the *12. SS-Panzer-Division "Hitlerjugend."* The number of armored fighting vehicles on 4 August sank to eighteen *Panthers*, seven *Panzer IV's* and nine assault guns. Of the thirty-four *Tigers* left, only half were operational.

When considering the overall situation, the reader must take into account that the encirclement of the *7. Armee* was starting to take shape after the breakthrough of the Americans at Avranches. In the final analysis, the British really only had to wait.

✠

The 4th of August 1944 was characterized by continuous artillery barrages and enemy attacks. Towards 2000 hours, the enemy exerted strong pressure on La Bistière, and he succeeded in forcing back the German grenadiers. The German artillery fire landed too short and caused friendly casualties. Thanks to the tanks, the enemy attack could be stopped one more time.

Because the *7. Armee* had to swing back during the night of 4–5 August 1944, the *II. SS-Panzer-Korps* also had to react. It took *Kampfgruppe Weiß*, which was employed on the left, back to the northern edge of Vire.

Kampfgruppe Weiß had screened north of La Biestière as well as at la Gravière on this day and had eliminated six enemy tanks in the process. At 2230 hours, the grenadiers pulled back in accordance with orders. The tanks followed ten minutes later and linked up with them 300 meters south of la Biestière. The northern outskirts of Vire were reached at 2320 hours. The *Tigers* were resupplied around midnight and then marched further to the rear.

Despite thick fog, overtired crews, and frequent detours around bomb craters, the tanks reached Pierres at 0420 hours and took up rest positions under a tree-lined road. On the way there, Rodinger's tank fell out due to transmission problems and had to be towed. The crews were not able to rest in their new assembly area, however, as they were ordered to move to Chenedollé.

At Chenedollé, the tankers were briefed by *SS-Hauptsturmführer* Gräbner, who had already reached this area with his *SS-Panzer-Aufklärungs-Abteilung 9.* Manning the front at Chenedollé was *Heeres-Pionier-Bataillon 600.* The three operational *Tigers* of the 1st Platoon of the 2nd Company were directed to support the *1./Heeres-Pionier-Bataillon 600.* The remaining battalion elements established an assembly area along the Tynchebray to Vire road and were in pressing need of maintenance. That same evening, *Tiger 212*, which was employed up front, received a direct hit by an artillery shell and had to be pulled out of the line. During retrograde movements at night, another one of the tanks burned out due to its engine overheating.

Paradoxically, the exposed position of the enemy then created a dangerous situation for *Panzergruppe West.* During the next two days, the previous limit of advance could only be held with difficulty. On 5 August 1944, *Kampfgruppe Meyer* also joined in the fighting at Chenedollé with some success.

In order to defend against anxiously anticipated new English armor attacks, the *Tigers* of *schwere SS-Panzer-Abteilung 102* were brought forward to the northern outskirts of Chenedollé around 0615 hours.

On 5 August 1944, the *9. SS-Panzer-Division "Hohenstaufen"* had to limit itself primarily to defensive operations. On this day, the division—not counting the elements attached to it—had only eleven *Panzer V's,* eight *Panzer IV's* and eight assault guns at its disposal. One of the division's mechanized infantry regiments, which was employed on the right, had its hands full fending off the continuous threat to its right flank. The German tanks attempted to keep the English infantry and armored forces, which were getting continuously stronger, in check. Burcy, Presles, Sourdevalle and the commanding heights of Hills 224 and 242 were taken back by them and firmly held.

By evening, the English penetration "boil" around Sourdevalle had expanded to the villages of Viessoix and Chenedollé. An attack at 1730 hours by *SS-Panzer-Aufklärungs-Abteilung 9* from the area of Chenedollé to the west soon had to be called off as a result of massive artillery fire and aimed fire from tanks. The same was true of an attack by *SS-Panzer-Pionier-Bataillon 9* from the area north of Viessoix on Pavée, even though supported by tanks.

It was then intended for the *10. SS-Panzer-Division "Frundsberg,"* which was closing up, to attack on 6 August 1944.

Tiger crew of an *SS* unit in Normandy wearing the 1944-pattern camouflage uniform.

OPERATIONS OF THE *10. SS-PANZER-DIVISION "FRUNDSBERG"*

On 6 August 1944, parts of the *1./schwere SS-Panzer-Abteilung 102* were employed west of Chenedollé and conducted a counterattack on Le Bas Perrier in the morning with elements of the *10. SS-Panzer-Division "Frundsberg"* that had arrived in the meantime. Four enemy tanks were knocked out. The British infantry—the 1st Norfolks—were also mistakenly attacked by U.S. Army Air Force Thunderbolts. Some of them left their positions in panic and suffered heavy losses. The German infantry did not exploit this situation, however, and was later stopped by enemy artillery.

Here is a British description of the fighting:

> At Le Bas Perrier 23rd Hussars and 2nd Warwicks were soon attacked by Tiger tanks which had infiltrated into the woods during the night.
>
> The Norfolks . . . were getting out of their trenches. They were slaughtered . . . I wondered why the German infantry had not put in an appearance to take advantage of the havoc caused by the Tiger tanks.

✠

Although the British gave up Hill 242 just north of Chenedollé, they put up a fight again for Hill 224 behind it. After heavy fighting, the assault detachments of the *10. SS-Panzer-Division "Frundsberg,"* which were attacking from three sides, took this hill and also Sourdevalle. At this point, however, the offensive power of these elements was exhausted. Heavy artillery barrages and fighter-bomber attacks nailed down the grenadiers of the division. There were not enough forces to close the gap in the front between Burcy and Presles.

Two *Tigers* of the *2./schwere SS-Panzer-Abteilung 102* that had been repaired relieved two tanks that had been badly damaged by artillery fire at the northern outskirts of Chenedollé.

The 7th of August 1944 was intended to bring about a positive turn for the Germans. Early in the morning, the *XLVII. Panzer-Korps* under *General der Panzertruppen Freiherr* von Funck moved out with its four skeleton armored divisions against the overpowering U.S. 3rd Army—a hopeless undertaking from the very outset.

In the area of operations of the *II. SS-Panzer-Korps* on this day, the British succeeded in taking Vire. As a result, the pressure mounted outside of Chenedollé. Although it had barely arrived, the *10. SS-Panzer-Division "Frundsberg"* was pulled out of the line again and ordered further south. It was to be prepared to also be committed in *Operation "Lüttich."* Several *Tigers* of the 1st Company had occupied good elevated firing positions outside of Chenedollé and prevented every attempt by the enemy to advance to the south.

Tiger 134 of *SS-Unterscharführer* Fey knocked out all of C Squadron of the 23rd Hussars in the space of thirty minutes, as if they were on a gunnery range. They had carelessly attempted to move out from the farm buildings at Houssemagne. *Tigers* farther off to the left also scored one "kill" after the other. Of course, none of this changed the fact that the German forces that had been weakened by the withdrawal of the *10. SS-Panzer-Division "Frundsberg"* had to gradually pull back.

The still-standing order to counterattack had to be rescinded by the corps in the face of the unfortunate facts. The number of operational tanks available to both companies sank to ten. The division still had twenty-three tanks; *Kampfgruppe Olboeter* all of seven.

✠

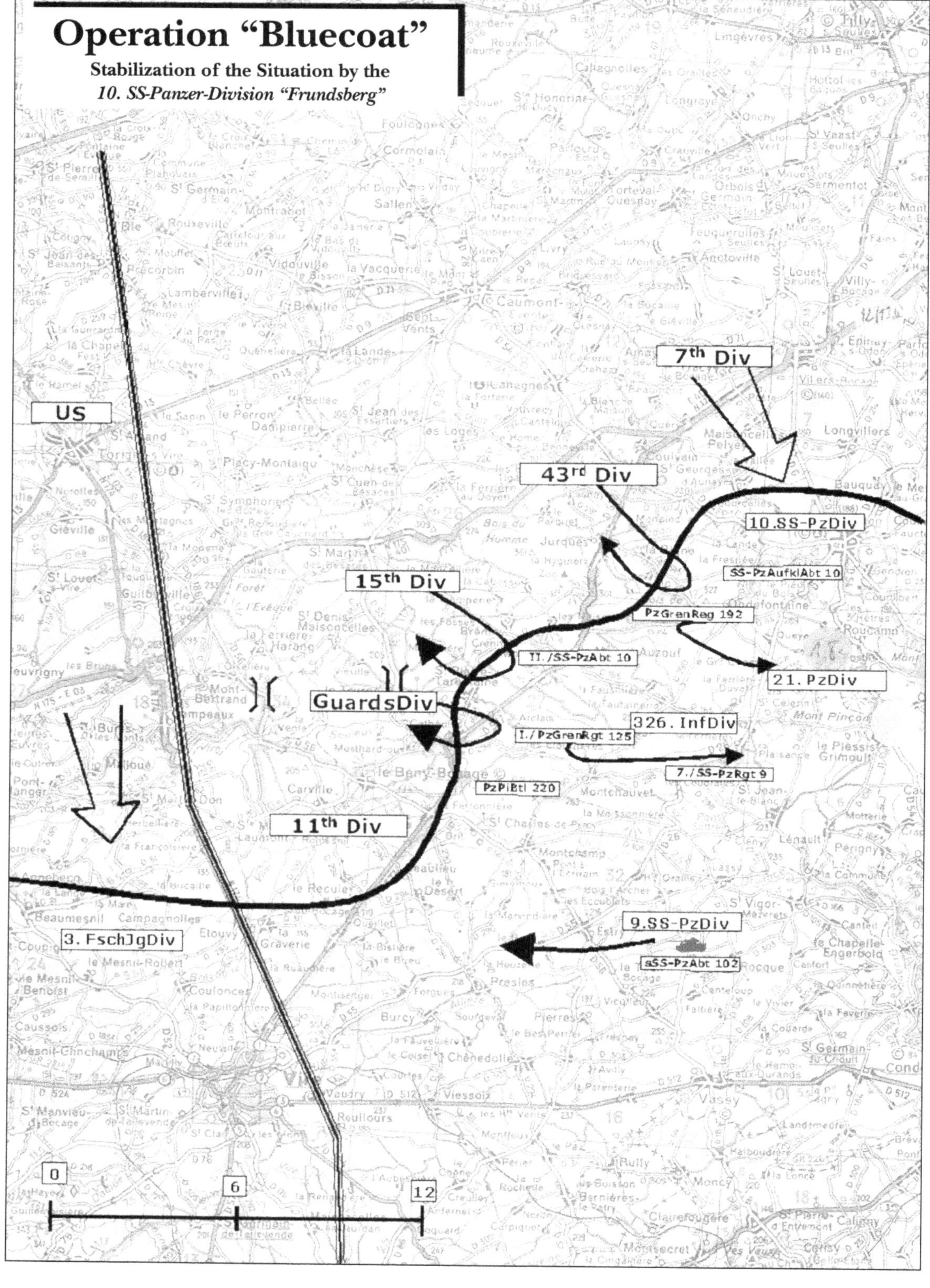
Operation "Bluecoat"
Stabilization of the Situation by the
10. SS-Panzer-Division "Frundsberg"
7th Div
43rd Div
10.SS-PzDiv
SS-PzAufklAbt 10
15th Div
PzGrenReg 192
II./SS-PzAbt 10
21. PzDiv
GuardsDiv
326. InfDiv
I./PzGrenRgt 125
7./SS-PzRgt 9
PzPiBtl 220
11th Div
US
9.SS-PzDiv
sSS-PzAbt 102
3. FschJgDiv
0
6
12

The memorable engagement of *SS-Unterscharführer* Fey is presented in his own words (Fey writes about himself as the tank commander in the third person):

> A few grenadiers to the left of us sounded out the alarm for tanks, and soon we were also able to take in the situation from our *Tiger*. The Shermans were advancing from out of a patch of woods across a slight rise. We identified 10 . . . 15 . . . 20 enemy tanks, with armored cars, halftracks filled with infantry, fully tracked weapons carriers and personnel carriers among them. The entire slope had come alive! The distance was about 1,200 meters. There was no firing as of yet.
>
> Everything looked like a textbook armored attack, with everything that belonged to such an affair. The grenadiers looked at us. You could sense a certain nervousness among them and their company commander. An *Oberleutnant* climbed up to us on the tank: We needed to be opening fire! But that had to be decided by our commander.
>
> The radio operator was told to send a message to everyone: "Fifteen enemy tanks attacking with infantry from the left flank . . . we will open fire at 600 meters!"
>
> An order then arrived via radio from the commander, *SS-Sturmbannführer* Weiß: "*Ruderboot* [rudder boat] to *Ofenrohr 3* [Stovepipe 3]—those were our code names for our *Tigers*—pull back immediately!"
>
> That was just what we needed at the moment!
>
> Our tank commander gave the order to the radio operator not to acknowledge the order and to turn off the receiver immediately. From this point on, we would only transmit!
>
> The enemy tanks had formed up and were advancing in an inverted wedge towards us. The distance to them was still about 800 meters. The loader had long since positioned his antitank rounds. The driver was informed that when he was ordered he would immediately let the tank roll back a few meters on its left track while simultaneously braking the right track. That way, we could get our *Tiger* into a good defensive position in a few seconds. Our counterparts across the way also wanted to get in their shot at us. Our flank, which we were offering them up to this point, was a little too sensitive for that!
>
> Then we were at the point of no return: 600 meters.
>
> We maneuvered our *Tiger* into the desired direction of fire. The gunner had already had his first victim in his sights for some time as a result of the fire command! It was the tank that was furthest forward—right in the middle of the mass of attacking tanks—probably the leader of the group. The second and third targets had also already been established: First the neighbor to the right, then the one to the left! The next targets after that were the Shermans all the way over on the right and the left. They could be dangerous to us if they swung around into our flanks. Even a *Tiger* was vulnerable within the 400-meter line!
>
> Then the order that triggered everything: "AT . . . 600 . . . Fire when ready."
>
> The first round went over the target. But this only paralyzed us for a moment.
>
> "Sight picture at 400 . . . fire when ready!"

The round hit pay dirt! A second round after that—Target!

Next target: "Tank to the left . . . fire when ready!"

This target was also permitted two rounds.

In a short period of time, four Shermans were in flames on the slope. The initial confusion among the enemy was gone by then. He halted and opened fire. We received hit after hit on the turret and on the front slope; nuts and bolts were tossed about in the fighting compartment. The grenadier *Oberleutnant,* who had previously been in the fighting compartment, left our tank in a mad rush and evacuated the positions with his people. There wasn't going to be any more attacks started by him here today.

The radio operator sent continuous reports on the course of the fighting; in between, he had ample opportunity to use his machine gun.

The battalion commander radioed again: "Pull back to friendly lines!"

At this point, we were counting six burning and smoking Shermans. There must have been boundless confusion among their ranks! Their infantry had dismounted and were jumping around seeking cover. Vehicles crashed into one another in their efforts to turn around. That was how the seventh and eight tanks were dispatched. While they were driving into one another while attempting to maneuver, our 8.8 tracked them and provided a quick end. They were burning out right next to one another.

Did minutes pass—or were they hours? We did not know. Our loader, a mountain of a man and an ethnic German from the Volga region of Russia, sank to his knees. As the one closest to the breech, he had sucked down too many fumes and had passed out. And rounds continued to crack against

N

This photograph shows the good firing position of Fey's tank as it was positioned looking towards the Houssemagne farmsteads in the middle of the image in the valley floor.

our tank. The loss of the loader caused an impasse in our tank. The gunner manned the turret machine gun, while the radio operator had already turned his fourth barrel into a glowing mass of steel.

By this time, all of the Shermans had found the range of our *Tiger*. We had to see about getting out of the line of fire. Otherwise, they would eventually find a hole in our defenses.

"Driver, back up . . . Halt!"

It was booming around us once again; the *Tiger* gave a jump backwards. That was a new caliber; it was an antitank gun! Gunpowder vapors poured through the hatches; the hit had come from the left. It was imperative to do something, because the second round had already landed between the driver and radio-operator stations and had rendered the bow machine gun inoperable.

The driver had taken the loader's station after he had passed out. At this point, there was no one driving. The left track had been shot off. As a result, the *Tiger* was immobilized. We could identify the antitank gun by its muzzle flash. It was way off to the left, next to some bushes. The turret was traversed to the 9 o'clock position. Albert was quickly and precisely guided in to the target. An HE round was loaded into the barrel—and then: "Fire when ready!" This enemy cost us three rounds; at that point, pieces tossed high into the air and explosions convinced us that it was over for this well-positioned antitank gun.

The armored engagements continued. We were neither hungry nor thirsty; the fighting had our complete attention. Dripping with sweat and with inflamed eyes, we gasped for breath in the sulfuric stink. After every round was fired from the main gun, a gray-blue cloud escaped from the breechblock closing mechanism. The ventilator attempted in vain to live up to its name. Paul was still lying cross-eyed on the turret floor between Hermann's legs.

There were still some Shermans opposing us. We certainly did not have it easy! While we aimed at the antitank guns, the Shermans took up a sight picture on us. And if we brought the Shermans into our crosshairs, then there was heavy fire from the antitank guns! It was sheer torment to have to deal with two different opponents at the same time. Thus far, 12 burning vehicles were testimony to our fighting.

At this point the battalion commander radioed in after having received our report concerning our *Tiger* having become immobilized: "Blow up the tank and fight your way back!"

But we weren't about to do that. As long as we had a main-gun round and some machine-gun ammunition, we were not going to give up this fight and our tank. Once again, we wrapped ourselves in silence and "forgot" to acknowledge the message.

The radio message from the company headquarters section leader brought out broad laughter despite the shitty situation: "*Ofenrohr 3*, please don't forget to confirm your 'kills'!"

We answered right away: "It would be an honor to receive the headquarters section leader in our tank for the purpose of confirming the 'kills'!"

After that, the headquarters section leader kept absolutely silent.

By this point, both machine guns were no longer operational; the main-gun rounds were running out. Fourteen Shermans had left this temporal sphere and ended their march on Berlin a bit prematurely during the noon hour on a wonderfully beautiful August day northwest of Vire.

All of this had lasted only 30 minutes!

But then the fight continued. We could no longer see any Shermans that were moving or firing at us. But there had been 15 Shermans identified, hadn't there?

A depression in front of us that was filled with trees and vegetation demanded our increased attention. Round after round of high-explosive ammunition was fired, and each one seemed to find a target. Abandoned halftracks and all types of supply vehicles went up in flames. Carriers moving at high speed—some of them outfitted with antitank weapons—shared their fate.

The entire slope was covered with dark-blue smoke that mercifully enclosed the completed drama. From time to time, a tank burst asunder with a thunderous explosion accompanied by a ball of flame that was as high as a house. The smoke from the burning vehicles, which covered the entire area of the fight, allowed a few of the opposing soldiers to escape from the inferno with their lives.

Because we did not know how long we would have to hold out in our tank—all the ammunition had been shot up with the exception of a few rounds—we wanted to stock up and enlarge our stocks in the pause in the fighting that had occurred. The tank commander slid down from the tank quickly and then crawled and ran in order to get out of the enemy's sight. Harassing fire had started. The enemy was slowly raging in on our position after he had realized that his attack in this sector had failed.

Completely exhausted, the tank commander reached a *Tiger* of our company and made himself visible in front of the driver's and radio operator's hatches, both of which were closed due to the continuous artillery fire. After a while, one of the hatches opened, and the tank commander was able to convey his wish for a few antitank rounds—all in vain!

For some inexplicable reason, we were unable to get anything, and the hatches remained closed, whereby every further entreaty echoed away unheard! On to the next *Tiger*—another few hundred meters of crawling, creeping and jumping! The route taken had not been in vain: The tank commander crept back in the direction of his tank with an antitank round in his arm.

The artillery fire increased continuously in intensity. On top of everything else, we were positioned in the open in the middle of a meadow and received our first artillery hits on the turret and the hull. From one of the last radio messages of this day, we discovered that we were to be recovered by three *Tigers* of Schwab's platoon. But it was still a long time until it became dark. For good measure, our radio set then went out as a result of the continuous fire! Fighter-bombers circled above us, dove down and strafed our wonderful *Tiger* with everything they had. It was standing here—immobilized—and looked like it was on a serving platter. Their bombs were getting damned close! Was this to be our end?

But before the next pair approached, we had the idea of how to save ourselves: Smoke candles were placed on the rear deck and the front part of the tank and we pretended to be a burnt-out, destroyed vehicle. We had enough of these smoke candles on board and were able to escape unscathed over time.

Suddenly, however, we became wide-awake and were torn out of our semi-conscious condition: We heard the trusted sound of tracks clanking. But these sounds were not coming from behind us and from our own comrades. On the contrary, they were off to the right of us, where the depression emptied into vegetation and groups of bushes.

We trained our main gun on the group of bushes. It traversed slowly, almost imperceptibly, and was fully depressed. We still had two antitank rounds; one of them was in the breech. Our nerves were stretched to the breaking point: Was there only one tank or were there two? There was only 100 meters between the depression and us.

The driver and the radio operator were perched to jump from their open hatches. Paul, who had since recovered, held the second and last round in his arm. If these two missed and we were out of ammunition, then there was only one thing left to do: Dismount as quickly as you could!

The sound of the tracks and the rumbling came ever nearer. Seconds became an eternity! Perhaps the other one did not know that a German tank was here and ready to fire? Our other *Tigers* had been pulled back for some time now, and we were the ones who had been here in the hot spot the entire afternoon. But the time was over for such thoughts!

The bushes parted in front of us. A smooth, long barrel without a muzzle brake became visible—undoubtedly a Sherman. Then the rounded edges of the turret and the hull appeared.

"Fire!"

Our first round ricocheted. The tracer climbed steeply towards the heavens! It was odd how you noticed such small things in such an explosive atmosphere!

"Drop some . . . fire!"

And we all yelled, because the tracer of our antitank round disappeared right underneath the barrel, that is, right where the turret joined the hull. With a jolt, the tank remained where it was, as if it had been hit by an iron fist. A column of smoke, fine at first, but ever increasing in intensity climbed vertically skyward. The 15th tank of the day. Together with the tank from the same sector from last evening, it was exactly 16—an entire tank company. This did not count the personnel carriers, the halftracks, the small weapons carriers and the other vehicles that were impossible to count. But would we be able to hold up the enemy despite all our successes?!

All of a sudden, it was quiet. We no longer said a word. All of a sudden, we were unspeakably tired and just wanted to wait for the *Tigers* that were supposed to recover us.

With gratitude, we noticed that a protective wall of fire was suddenly placed in the evening hours on the depression and on the adjoining slope with an unbelievable howl and hissing by rocket launchers. It had to snuff out all life there.

The smoke had barely cleared from the last salvo of the *Nebelwerfer*, when the three *Tigers* of Schwab's platoon appeared and recovered us in accordance with a deliberate plan. Two *Tigers* were hooked up to the front;

one *Tiger* provided cover. And that's how we rolled out of there and into the night, our tracks being dragged behind us.

After a short stop at the company command post, where our company commander, *[SS-Untersturmführer]* Kalss congratulated us on our success. We reached Vassy the next morning. But what did out *Tiger* look like? Holes you could stick your head into! The drive sprocket with the final drive and the differential had been shot clean through. The round was still sticking in the hull! The Maintenance Company would be busy for a few days patching things together and welding!

✠

The "boil" in the front at Chenedollé was abandoned during the night of 7–8 August 1944. Every opportunity to shorten the front needed to be used. The 8th of August saw heavy defensive fighting once again, before a deceptive calm settled in. The time was used to improve defensive positions. Unfortunately, *schwere SS-Panzer-Abteilung 102* was detached from the *9. SS-Panzer-Division "Hohenstaufen"* on 9 August 1944. Another lengthy movement across the front—back to the Falaise area of operations—was shaping up. Parallels to the allegory of the tortoise and the hare cannot be avoided . . .

The counterattacks of the *9. SS-Panzer-Division "Hohenstaufen"* and the numerous tank "kills" of *schwere SS-Panzer-Abteilung 102* did not result in stopping the offensive operations of the British 11th Armoured Division and the Guards Armoured Division, but it certainly slowed them down.

With the introduction of the 3rd Infantry Division west of the 11th Armoured Division, the enemy had considerably increased his forces in the sector. As a result, the pressure increased not only against the *9. SS-Panzer-Division "Hohenstaufen"* but also against the burnt-out *21. Panzer-Division.*

In addition, *Operation "Lüttich,"* the German armored counterattack against the American forces, was increasingly ending in a fiasco. It was possible to check the British attacks to a certain extent until 11 August 1944, but the large-scale withdrawals started in this sector as well on 12 August.

SS-Unterscharführer Fey (viewer's left in the photograph) poses with other tank commanders of his company.

THE FINAL FIGHTING OF *SCHWERE PANZER-ABTEILUNG 503*

In order to complete the picture, the final fighting of the reduced *schwere Panzer-Abteilung 503* with the *21. Panzer-Division* should not remain unmentioned.

On 2 August 1944, these tank elements succeeded in holding their own against the Guards Armoured Division. In addition to other casualties during this fighting, the British lost one tank and one infantry carrier.

On 3 August 1944, the *Tigers* were employed on the left flank of the *10. SS-Panzer-Division "Frundsberg"* at Bremoy and Saint-Pierre-Tarentaine. Because the combat strength of the *21. Panzer-Division* had been reduced to about 200 *Panzergrenadiere*, the division commander, *Generalmajor* Feuchtinger, requested that his division be pulled out of the line.

During the course of 4 August 1944, the division conducted a fighting withdrawal and pulled back slowly. The *Tigers* supported *Panzer-Grenadier-Regiment 192* on the left flank of the division. The division then received the order to disengage from the enemy and stand by for orders from *Panzergruppe West*.

Two days too late—around midnight on 6 August 1944—*Panzergruppe West* ordered the front of the *LXXIV. Armee-Korps* to be reinforced with *schwere Panzer-Abteilung 503*, *schwere Panzerjäger-Abteilung 654* and a company of *Sturmpanzer-Abteilung 17*. This was in anticipation of an imminent large-scale enemy attack.

In the end, the *Tiger* battalion was overwhelmed with its new mission to support the *276. Infanterie-Division*. It was intended for the infantry division to unconditionally hold Mont Pincon, since it dominated the terrain for nearly twenty kilometers in the area between the Vire and Odon Rivers.

The front line of the *276. Infanterie-Division* ran from La Lande across the *Mont Pincon* to the southwest of Aunay-sur-Odon, where it formed a boundary with the *277. Infanterie-Division*. It ran north from Quesnée as far as Hill 246, where it formed a boundary with the *326. Infanterie-Division*. *Grenadier-Regiment 986* of the division had dug in along Mont Pincon. The majority of the divisional artillery adjoined the line of high ground and thus dominated all approach routes. *Grenadier-Regiment 987* was positioned on the left, including Hill 252.

Despite this, the positions of the division were somewhat undermanned. In addition, the division did not have its third infantry regiment. *Grenadier-Regiment 988* had been attached to the *326. Infanterie-Division*.

The area around the Druance River had been mined; the crossing as far as La Varanière had been blown up.

Up until 5 August, it remained relatively calm. Then, reconnaissance forces of the 43rd Wessex Division reached Hill 282 near La Roguerie. This had been assisted by the fact that there had been a crisis situation in the sector of the *326. Infanterie-Division* at Saint-Jean-le-Blanc, which had then been stabilized somewhat with the assistance of the *21. Panzer-Division*.

✠

During the morning hours of 6 August 1944, an enemy penetration in the area of St. Jean was cleaned up in conjunction with *Kampfgruppe Schnez* (*schwere Panzerjäger-Abteilung 654*). *Kampfgruppe Schnez* was employed from the north against St. Jean, while the *Tigers*, together with a few assault guns, were sent in from the south. The former main line of resistance was reestablished.

During the afternoon of the next day, both grenadier regiments of the *276. Infanterie-Division* were hit by heavy attacks of the 43rd Wessex Division that were supported by tanks. The British succeeded in forcing the grenadiers of *Grenadier-Regiment 987* from Hill 246. The remaining *Panzer IV's* and the few *Tigers* moved out for an immediate counterattack. To the great joy of *General der Infanterie* Straube, the commanding general of the *LXXIV. Armee-Korps*, the English were ejected from the hill.

The British moved out again and suffered heavy losses. The tide turned, however, when British combat engineers succeeded in clearing the mines on the bridge at La Varinière under extremely heavy fire. This enabled the tanks of the 13/14th Hussars to cross. The main body of the German grenadiers left their positions in an orderly fashion, after they had only succeeded in slowing down the English attack. They destroyed eight enemy tanks. With the assistance of twenty Shermans that remained behind, the British succeeded in forcing the last German rearguards from the hill after more than two hours of intense fighting.

Making things difficult for the defenders was the employment of smoke along the high ground and the start of twilight, which made directed fire by the German artillery no longer possible.

The grenadiers occupied a temporary main line of resistance that ran from Plessis–Grimoult–Crépigny–Hill 246. In the sector of the *277. Infanterie-Division* on the western flank, however, the British 7th Armoured Division had already broken through. The Germans cobbled together all available forces from their rear-area-services personnel in order to solve this crisis situation.

The few operational *Tigers*—eleven according to the report of 6 August 1944—assembled at Plessis-Grimoult during the night in order to block the "Desert Rats." In a surprise thrust from the west, the 5th Battalion of the Duke of Cornwall's Light Infantry penetrated into Plessis-Grimoult and advanced along the main street towards the center of the village. Two *Tigers* from *schwere Panzer-Abteilung 503* were spotted that were in the process of rearming from a truck. The operation was being screened by a *SPW.*

The British took this group under fire with several 2-inch mortars, causing the grenadiers to flee and abandon their *SPW.* Suddenly, one of the mortar rounds hit the ammunition truck, which blew apart with a mighty explosion. The explosion was so powerful that the *Tiger II* next to it had its turret dislodged, and it caught on fire.

The other *Tiger* crew had mounted up in time and was able to pull back. The advance of the British into Plessis-Grimoult happened so quickly that the 5th Duke of Cornwall's Light Infantry suffered only one dead, five wounded and one missing soldier. The *276. Infanterie-Division* lost 44 soldiers, and 125 surrendered to the British.

On 8 August 1944, the *Tiger* of *Hauptmann* Fromme was ordered in the direction of Saint-Pierre-la-Vielle. The strong, continuous enemy artillery fire forced the crew to remain inside the tank.

At the start of 9 August 1944, the British continued their attack and headed in the direction of Crépigny. During the afternoon, the *Tigers* and several assault guns moved out to conduct a counterattack between Le Tremblay and Crépigny. They were supported by grenadiers. After one and a half hours of heavy fighting, the British advance was brought to a standstill. However, a second enemy column succeeded in advancing on Saint-Pierre-la-Vielle. This resulted in the remaining German forces being caught in a vise. On top of everything else, the tanks, which were restricted in their movement, were effectively attacked two times from the air by Thunderbolts. In all, six *Tigers* had to be abandoned. The Germans succeeded in knocking out ten enemy tanks.

On 10 August 1944, the British crossed the Orne somewhat south of Thury-Harcourt. *Generalleutnant* Badinski decided to commit his armored reserve there in order to support the hard-fighting *277. Infanterie-Division.* He likewise employed *Panzer-Artillerie-Regiment 155.*

On 11 August 1944, *Hauptmann* Wiegand screened with the last two operational *Tigers* on the southeastern portion of Saint-Pierre-la-Vieille. Around 1130 hours, the English attacked east past the town with thirty tanks and a large force of accompanying infantry. *Hauptmann* Wiegand, the commander of the battalion's Headquarters Company, was in the process of moving out against the enemy with his two *Tigers*, when his tank was attacked by several fighter-bombers and was immobilized.

Despite still being engaged by the aircraft, *Hauptmann* Wiegand shifted to the other tank as the first three Shermans came over a rise. He immediately set two of the Shermans ablaze; later on, a third tank was knocked out. He forced the British to temporarily break off their attack.

Several minutes later, this *Tiger* was also hit by fighter-bombers. Immobilized, it continued the firefight for a short period of time. The British lost another three tanks. The grenadiers of the *277. Infanterie-Division* continued the unequal struggle the following day without tank support. In the end, however, they had to abandon the town.

On 13 August 1944, the last two *Tigers* of the battalion were attached to *schwere Panzerjäger-Abteilung 654* at Proussy. During the night, the enemy pushed his way forward to Hill 261, two kilometers northeast of Proussy, and occupied it with tanks and infantry. The *Jagdpanthers* and *Tigers* that were in position were blinded by artillery smoke. Both of the *Tigers* were lost.

That signaled the end of the fighting in Normandy for *schwere Panzer-Abteilung 503*.

German antiaircraft weaponry engaged in a hopeless struggle against the swarms of Allied aircraft. A quad 20mm *Flak* of the antiaircraft platoon of *schwere Panzer-Abteilung 503* is seen in action.

A *Tiger II*, which was completely destroyed in Plessis le-Grimoult by the explosion of an ammunition truck next to it, is examined by British soldiers after the fighting. The lower photograph shows the same spot today, primarily recognizable by the church bell tower, which now has a clear view to it.

The same tank as seen from the side. Noteworthy is the fact that this *Tiger II* was one of the few with the one-piece gun mantlet. The bottom photograph shows the same location today.

The view from the rear shows the dislodgement of the turret. The silhouette of a "1" and a "3" can be seen around the escape hatch on the rear of the turret. The middle digit cannot be identified. Since *113* was a *Tiger I* and *Tiger 123* had already been lost on 31 July, this tank is most likely *Tiger 133*.

Photographs taken later on show that the tow cable found a new home. At some point later, the turret slid completely off the tank's hull, revealing the turret race and the interior of the fighting compartment. (IWM)

CHAPTER 10

Operation "Totalize" and Wittmann's Last Engagement

In the meantime, the Canadians had recovered from their setback during Operation "Spring" on 25 and 26 July 1944 in the area of operations north of Falaise. They then made efforts on their part to also bring about the decisive breakthrough.

At the same time, German plans that were completely divorced from reality were in motion to pull out the mechanized forces of *Panzergruppe West* that were southeast of Caen to use them for a counterattack—*Operation "Lüttich"*—against the Americans in the area around Avranches.

Orders to this effect were issued to the *9. SS-Panzer-Division "Hohenstaufen"* on 1 August 1944. The same orders were issued to the *1. SS-Panzer-Division "Leibstandarte SS Adolf Hitler"* on 3 August 1944. However, the intended relief-in-place by the *89. Infanterie-Division* did not start until the night of 4–5 August 1944.

In the end, the *1. SS-Panzer-Division "Leibstandarte SS Adolf Hitler"* arrived too late for the start of *Operation "Lüttich"* on 6 August 1944. In addition, it was no longer available for the heavy defensive fighting that was developing in its former area of operations.

The *12. SS-Panzer-Division "Hitlerjugend"* and *schwere SS-Panzer-Abteilung 101* were left to face the new British offensive. These armored forces had been relieved by the *272. Infanterie-Division* during 5 August 1944 and had already assembled east of the N 158 in the Laison Valley as an operational reserve. The orders to depart for the Condé-sur-Noireau area were supposed to be issued during the evening of 7 August 1944; it would never get to that, however.

The British and the Canadians had completed their preparations for Operation "Totalize" by this point. Supported by flanking attacks from the Orne bridgehead at Grimbosq, the main effort was to take place on both sides of the N 158. The British 51st Infantry Division was to be employed east of the road and supported by the 33rd Armoured Brigade. The Canadian 2nd Infantry Division was to be employed to the east of the road, where it would be supported by the Canadian 2nd Armoured Brigade.

In contrast to the previously conducted offensives, the start of the attack by the main forces on both sides of the Caen–Falaise road was to start in the evening.

✠

In order to maintain at least a small element of surprise, there was to be no artillery preparation prior to the start of the attack. The start of the attack was to be signaled by the RAF's Bomber Command. In all, some 1,020 aircraft dropped a total of 3,462 tons of bombs, primarily on the built-up areas and the terrain along the flanks of the attack. A half hour later, at 2330 hours, the tanks columns crossed the line of departure. The artillery—360 tubes for

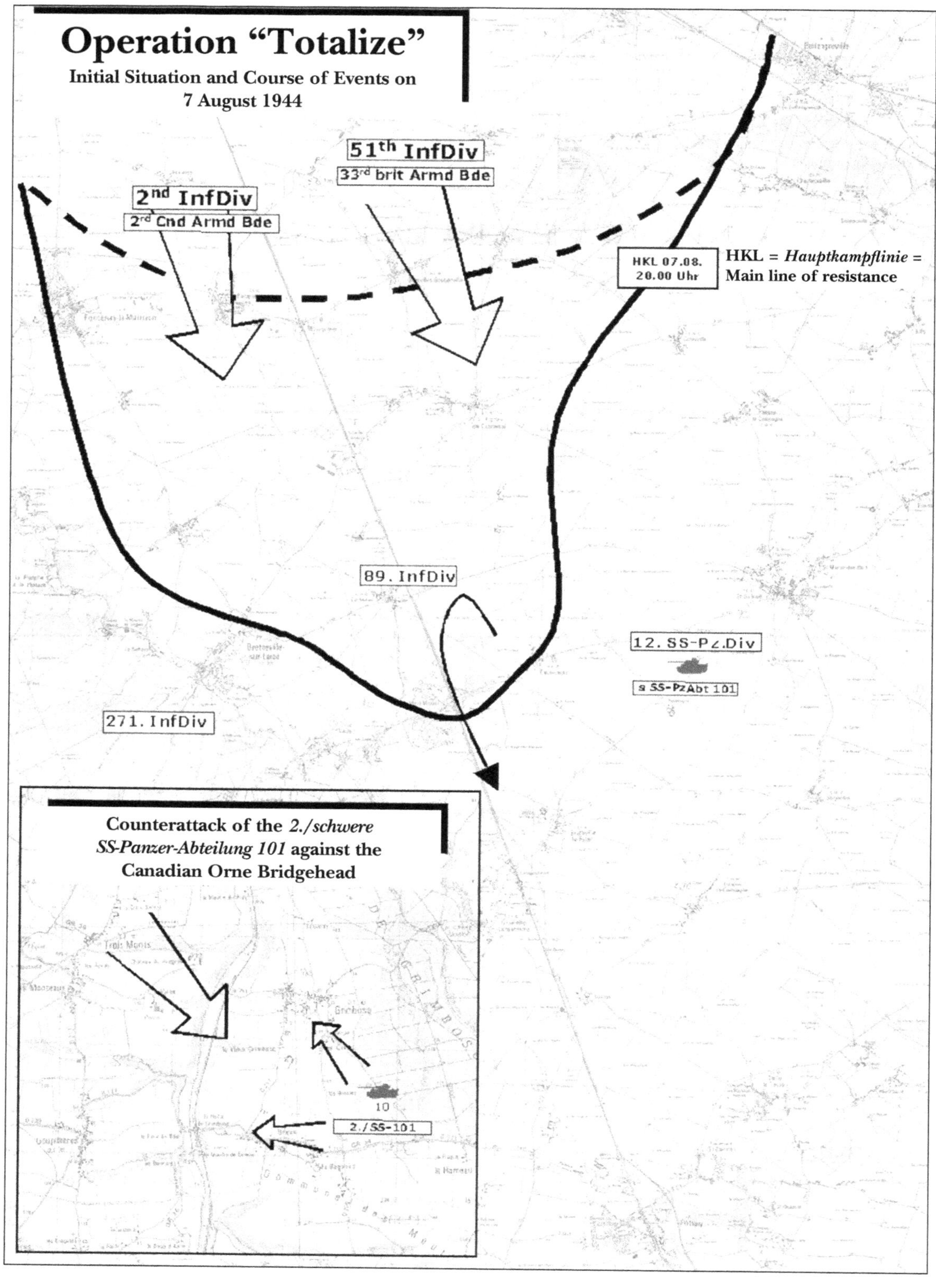
Operation "Totalize"
Initial Situation and Course of Events on 7 August 1944
51th InfDiv
33rd brit Armd Bde
2nd InfDiv
2rd Cnd Armd Bde
HKL 07.08. 20.00 Uhr
HKL = Hauptkampflinie = Main line of resistance
89. InfDiv
12. SS-Pz.Div
s SS-PzAbt 101
271. InfDiv
Counterattack of the 2./schwere SS-Panzer-Abteilung 101 against the Canadian Orne Bridgehead
Trois Monts
Grimbosq
10
2./SS-101

View towards the attack objective of *Tigergruppe Wittmann*, the unobtrusive hills just south and southwest of St. Aignan-du-Cramesnil. The large building on the viewer's left in the top photograph is part of a commercial district south of the village.

The lower photograph demonstrates the British vantage point. On this open terrain stretching more than four kilometers, the *Tiger* commanders thought that the superior range of their main guns would be to their advantage. The wood line seen to the left in the photograph made it impossible to identify the four Shermans positioned on the flanks there.

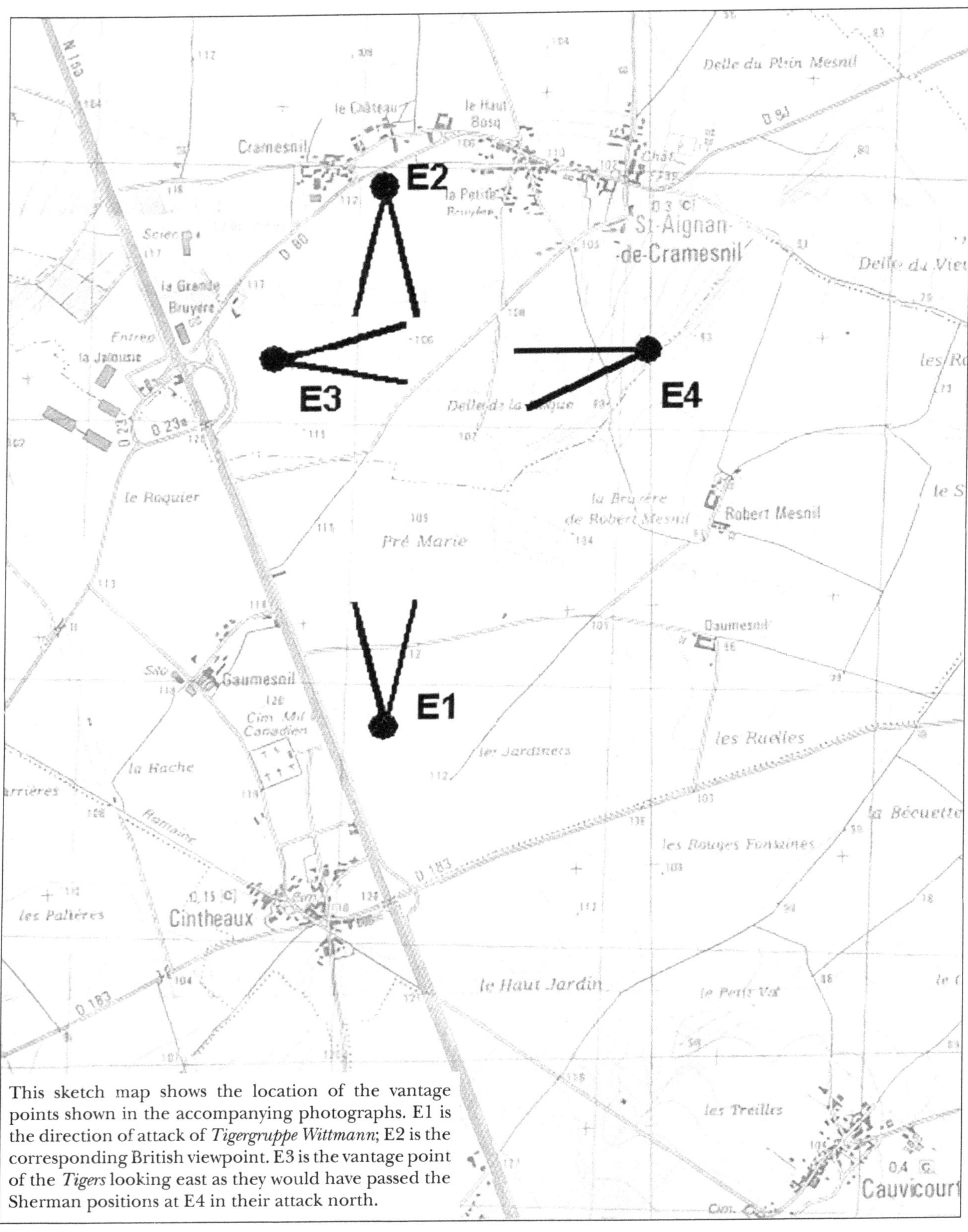

This sketch map shows the location of the vantage points shown in the accompanying photographs. E1 is the direction of attack of *Tigergruppe Wittmann*; E2 is the corresponding British viewpoint. E3 is the vantage point of the *Tigers* looking east as they would have passed the Sherman positions at E4 in their attack north.

the rolling barrage and an additional 360 tubes for counterbattery fire on German positions—opened fire at 2345 hours.

In order to direct the movements of the attack groups at night, the British were imaginative. It was attempted to create artificial moonlight with the assistance of searchlights. Forty-millimeter Bofors automatic cannon fired tracers in each of the respective attack axes; with regard to Hill 122, which formed the boundary between the two attack divisions, it was marked by the artillery with green illumination rounds. Despite all this, nearly all of the attack columns quickly got off track, because the darkness was intensified by the smoke of the artillery impacts.

The British attack was facilitated in its first phase by close support provided by combat engineers and mine-clearing tanks—"Flails"—of the 79th Armoured Division, which had been specially trained for such missions. In the sector of the *89. Infanterie-Division,* hundreds of infantrymen left their positions in panic.

After the *1. SS-Panzer-Division "Leibstandarte SS Adolf Hitler"* had been withdrawn, the Germans could only put up the decimated armored forces of the *12. SS-Panzer-Division "Hitlerjugend"* (and *schwere SS-Panzer-Abteilung 101*) to face this massive attack. Within the latter division, the tank strength was forty-eight (including nine *Panthers*). There were also nineteen operational *Tigers* out of an end strength of twenty-five. Once again, the 8.8-centimeter *Flak* of the *III. Flak-Korps* would play a large role.

Thanks to the use of liaison officers, who were positioned with the divisions in the front lines, the commander of the *12. SS-Panzer-Division "Hitlerjugend," SS-Oberführer* Meyer, received early warning of the start of the attack by the British. He immediately employed *Kampfgruppe Waldmüller* with approximately twenty tanks (including eight to ten *Tigers*). It was to establish a blocking position on the N 158 at Cintheaux.

Meyer went up front, personally stopped forces of the *89. Infanterie-Division* that were flooding back and ordered them to dig in and prepare to defend.

By the evening of 7 August 1944, the British had advanced over the D 183 (Bretteville-sur-Laize–St. Sylvain road) and had taken the group of buildings on the N 158 at Haut Mesnil.

Ten *Tigers* of *schwere SS-Panzer-Abteilung 101* were employed on the right (west) wing of the British offensive against the forces that were moving out of the Orne bridgehead there. For a short period of time, Grimbosq and Brieux were taken; however, when it was attempted to relieve the *Tigers* in Grimbosq with tanks from *SS-Panzer-Regiment 12,* the enemy exploited the situation and penetrated back into the village. An attack on the bridgehead the following morning bogged down in heavy artillery fire. The *Tiger* of *SS-Obersturmführer* Wendorff was hit, but it could be recovered. Wendorff shifted to the last operational vehicle.

The second phase of Operation "Totalize" started the next day at morning twilight. The objective of the attackers was to eliminate the German forces that had occupied the second set of defensive lines and break through to the operational objective of Falaise. These goals were to be supported again by massive aerial attacks, this time by the U.S. 8th Army Air Force. Of the 678 aircraft employed, only 492 found their objective areas. In all, 1,488 tons of bombs were dropped. Two bomber squadrons—each composed of twelve aircraft—bombed friendly forces.

Hardest hit was the Polish armored division in the area of Cormelles as well as the Canadian 3rd Infantry Division. More than 300 soldiers were killed or wounded and many vehicles were destroyed. It had been intended to use both formations in the second phase of Operation "Totalize" and help bring about the final success.

The *12. SS-Panzer-Division "Hitlerjugend"* also suffered heavy casualties as a result of the bomb runs. On 11 August 1944, it was intended to finally take this division out of the line and replace it with the *85. Infanterie-Division.* The *89. Infanterie-Division,* which had only recently arrived at the front, had already sunk to 50 percent of its authorized strength.

A German counterattack was launched on 8 August 1944 into the advance towards Vielle Langannerie by the Canadians and the Poles along the N 158. Its objective was to retake the high ground south of St. Aignan.

Kampfgruppe Waldmüller—the *II./SS-Panzer-Regiment 12* with thirty-nine tanks, the *1./SS-Panzer-Jäger-Abteilung 12* with ten *Jagdpanzer IV's* and ten *Tigers* of *schwere SS-Panzer-Abteilung 101*—was assembled at Bretteville-le-Rabet. During the road march there, one of the *Tigers* collided with the tank ahead of it, that of *SS-Hauptsturmführer* Heurich, with the result that both tanks were unavailable for the attack.

SS-Hauptsturmführer Wittmann (in a headquarters tank, *Tiger 007*) and six other *Tigers* took the lead in moving on Cintheaux. The six other tank commanders were *SS-Untersturmführer* Dollinger, *SS-Untersturmführer* Ihrion, *SS-Hauptscharführer* Höflinger, *SS-Hauptscharführer* Kisters, *SS-Oberscharführer* von Westernhagen (the brother of the battalion commander) and *SS-Hauptsturmführer* Heurich. The *Tigers* headed north along the N 158 towards La Jalousie. There were dense columns of enemy tanks north of the road to Bretteville-sur-Laize as well as south of Garcelles and on the wood line to the southeast of the latter town.

For the German leaders, it was more than a bit surprising that the enemy was standing idly by and not moving out for the attack.

The commander of the *12. SS-Panzer-Division "Hitlerjugend"* decided to take the village of Cintheaux as soon as possible and attack into the masses of

E

The view the *Tiger* commanders would have had as they passed the woods to the east and along the viewer's right. The Shermans were approximately 400 meters farther to the rear in the stand of trees to the left. As a result, they were identified too late.

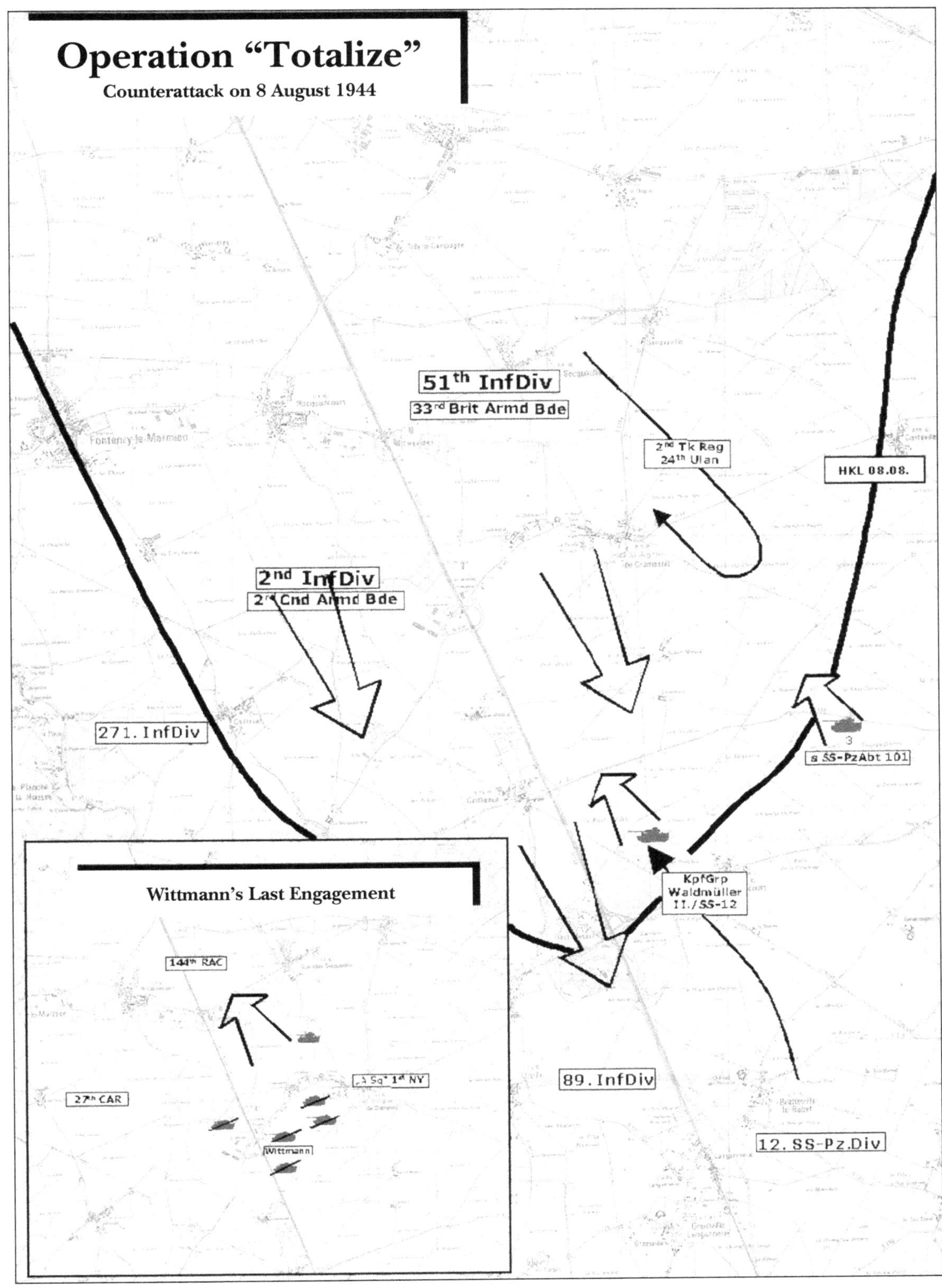
Operation "Totalize"
Counterattack on 8 August 1944
51th InfDiv
33rd Brit Armd Bde
Fontenay le Marmion
2nd Tk Reg
24th Ulan
HKL 08.08.
2nd InfDiv
2nd Cnd Armd Bde
271. InfDiv
s SS-PzAbt 101
KpfGrp
Waldmüller
II./SS-12
89. InfDiv
12. SS-Pz.Div
Wittmann's Last Engagement
144th RAC
27th CAR
Wittmann

This view from the firing positions of the Shermans past the righthand edge of the patch of woods shows how the *Tigers* would have passed right in front of the main guns of the Canadian tanks, exposing their vulnerable flanks.

enemy armor. The woods southeast of Garcelles was ordered as an intermediate objective. Several Canadian Shermans were knocked out there.

Shortly beyond Gaumesnil, the 3rd Platoon of A Squadron of the 1st Northhamptonshire Yeomanry opened fire from the right flank on the moving *Tigers*. The sole Sherman Firefly set three *Tigers* ablaze; the other Shermans knocked out two additional *Tigers*. There were few survivors. *SS-Hauptsturmführer* Wittmann and his crew were killed. A *Tiger* from the 2nd Company that was falling back about 1,500 meters north of this location was abandoned.

In the meantime, three other *Tigers* let forces of the Polish Armored Division approach east of St.-Aignan and were able to knock out seven vehicles. In all, the Poles took heavy losses—the 2nd Royal Tank Regiment lost twenty-six tanks and the 24th Ulan Regiment lost fourteen tanks—and did not have enough confidence to continue the attack.

Without doubt, 8 August 1944 represented a black day for *schwere SS-Panzer-Abteilung 101*, even without the loss of Wittmann. When looking at where this fighting took place, it can be seen how treacherous the terrain is. Moving out over an open stretch of terrain on both sides of the N 158, the *Tigers* could be certain that they would be able to use the superior range of their weapons to full advantage. It was because of this that the crews advanced somewhat carelessly and did not notice in time that a curtain of woods started just to the right of Haut Mesnil, behind which—set farther back—there was a line of high ground. The Shermans had just moved into position on this high ground that was covered in vegetation.

Although they could only see the attacking *Tigers* much later due to the wood line, they were themselves not to be seen. From this hidden position, the Firefly, with it 17-pounder (7.62-centimeter) main gun, which was also dangerous to the *Tiger*, could take its time aiming and engage one *Tiger* after the other. The formation of *Tigers* had made the mistake of not having the outermost tank on the right move with its turret in the three o'clock position. In addition, the *Tigers* were being constantly shelled with artillery. When the first *Tiger* was burning, it took a moment before the enemy could be identified. The other crews desperately attempted to traverse their turrets in the observed direction. This took too long.

In the documentation concerning the 27th Canadian Armoured Regiment in his book, *A Fine Night for Tanks*, author Ken Tout presents a detailed account of what happened:

> The events of 8 August 1944 have been clouded in some mystery and debate, but appear to have been fairly simple. Early an that day [*SS-Hauptsturmführer*] Franz Heurich had taken a group of Tigers down the main road without orders. Hearing this, Wittmann was concerned because it was Heurich's first day in action. Wittmann quickly called for his Volkswagen and, with his good friend, Capt Dr Rabe, drove to Cintheaux where the Tigers were well hidden for fear of air attack by Typhoons and other ground support aircraft. German sources suggest, with some surprise, that RAF ground support was not called on, possibly because of the raid by USAAF heavy bombers which had been planned.
>
> Wittmann met and conferred with [*SS-Sturmbannführer*] Waldmüller, who was finishing his briefing for the counter-attack, and "Panzer" Meyer. Meyer had already studied the serried ranks of Allied tanks visible in the distance (the follow-up forces of Totalize). The instinctive reaction of the three experienced tank commanders was to hit before being hit, and the Garcelles wood and chateau were indicated as an appropriate target from which a German group could then dominate a wide panorama of open slopes packed tight with Allied armour in almost as perilous a situation as the vehicles at Villers Bocage. The decision may have been a desperate throw of the dice in the knowledge of the scarcity of their own resources. As Keegan has commented, "[the tank] companies were now so weak that half-repaired tanks had to be driven out of the battalion workshops only a mile behind the lines. Ominously too, some of the Tigers had to drop out of the action for want of fuel, which was not coming up the line of supply."
>
> Wittmann himself had to take a Tiger (No. 007) other than his usual mount. Although Meyer had left liaison officers in Saint-Aignan and other villages it is debatable whether the three commanders at Cintheaux were fully aware of what awaited Wittmann's troop, or whether the bait of the massed hundreds of static tanks was too much temptation, blurring their logic. What, in fact, awaited was 27 CAR [Canadian Armoured regiment], on Wittmann's left, 144 RAC [Royal Armour Corps Regiment] ahead, and 1st Northamptonshire Yeomanry on the right, all fairly well hidden. These three regiments counted at that moment with about thirty-four Firefly tanks in total, all likely to be within range of Wittmann's route.
>
> It was "A" Squadron 27 CAR with the Royal Regiment of Canada which observed the first movement of enemy counter-attack

along the main road at about 08.00 hours. A number of German tanks, Panthers and Mark IVs, with infantry, ran into the Canadians, and the tank fire destroyed a number of the lighter carriers belonging to the anti-tank platoon and the machine-gunners of the Toronto Scottish. The Canadian Firefly tanks (as with the British, one 17-pdr Firefly with three 75 mm Shermans formed a troop) gave a good account of themselves. Two Panthers and two Mark IVs were knocked out and the enemy withdrew.

Subsequently, Radley-Walters moved his squadron further up towards Gaumesnil. This action no doubt caused the Germans to be wary of their left flank when sending a troop of Tigers down the road. A strong and tenacious Canadian presence on the west side of the road meant that the Tigers approached cautiously, seeking whatever cover they could find on the east side of the road. Their approach did indeed stimulate "A" Squadron of 27 CAR to open fire while "A" Squadron of 1st Northamptonshire Yeomanry was hidden to the east of the Tiger's route. The Tiger commanders, concentrating on the western danger, therefore had their backs to the eastern danger. The complementary actions of the two "A" Squadrons were not prearranged in a master plan but were the logical outcome of the innovative idea of the Night March. This placed the two "A" Squadrons in primarily defensive positions which, to an extent, reduced the overwhelming advantages of power and armour enjoyed by Tigers and Panthers. The reverse of Goodwood was now happening in miniature. But for "Rad" Radley-Walters, as for Tom Boardman at the time, "to us it was just another German tank attack and it wasn't until after the war that I heard about this German ace Wittmann."

"Hullo, William 3 Charlie. Figures three nasties range twelve hundred alongside road. Look like Tigers. 3 Charlie, over." The very slightly raised voice of "A" Squadron's Sgt Gordon ushered in the time of fatal gambles among the orchards. Three Tigers! Only a few weeks earlier one lone Tiger had knocked out twenty tanks of another Yeomanry regiment. The Totalizator would surely set odds of 15 to 3 in this instance. The voice of Capt Tom Boardman, now well known from his Night March conversations, ordered Gordon to hold fire while a plan was quickly concocted.

Three of the 53-ton Tiger tanks, the most feared weapon in Normandy, were moving slowly parallel and near to the main road from Caen to Falaise. Their guns were traversed left to cover the far side of the road. Gordon's troop, commanded by Lt James, was therefore lurking in the orchards on the right of the Tigers. The German tank commanders appeared to feel that they were sheltered on their left by the trees beside the main road and by the road itself which was slightly raised at that point. None of the three Tigers appeared to be watching out to the right. Arriving close to Lt James, Capt Boardman ordered the three 75 mm Shermans, plus his own, to "pepper" the turrets of the Tigers. The 75 mm shot would have little effect on the Tiger armour but would make the commanders close down and restrict themselves to periscope view.

The remnants of Wittmann's *Tiger 007* lying next to road leading to the north. The dot in the middle of the horizon above the lefthand side of the turret is the *Tiger* that had advanced the farthest.

The same viewpoint today.

Even with *Tiger 007*, *Tiger 314* was also hit and knocked out. This photograph was taken several months after the fighting.

Tiger 214 was knocked out at the Bois de Quesnay. This photograph shows Polish soldiers exploring the wreck. (IWM)

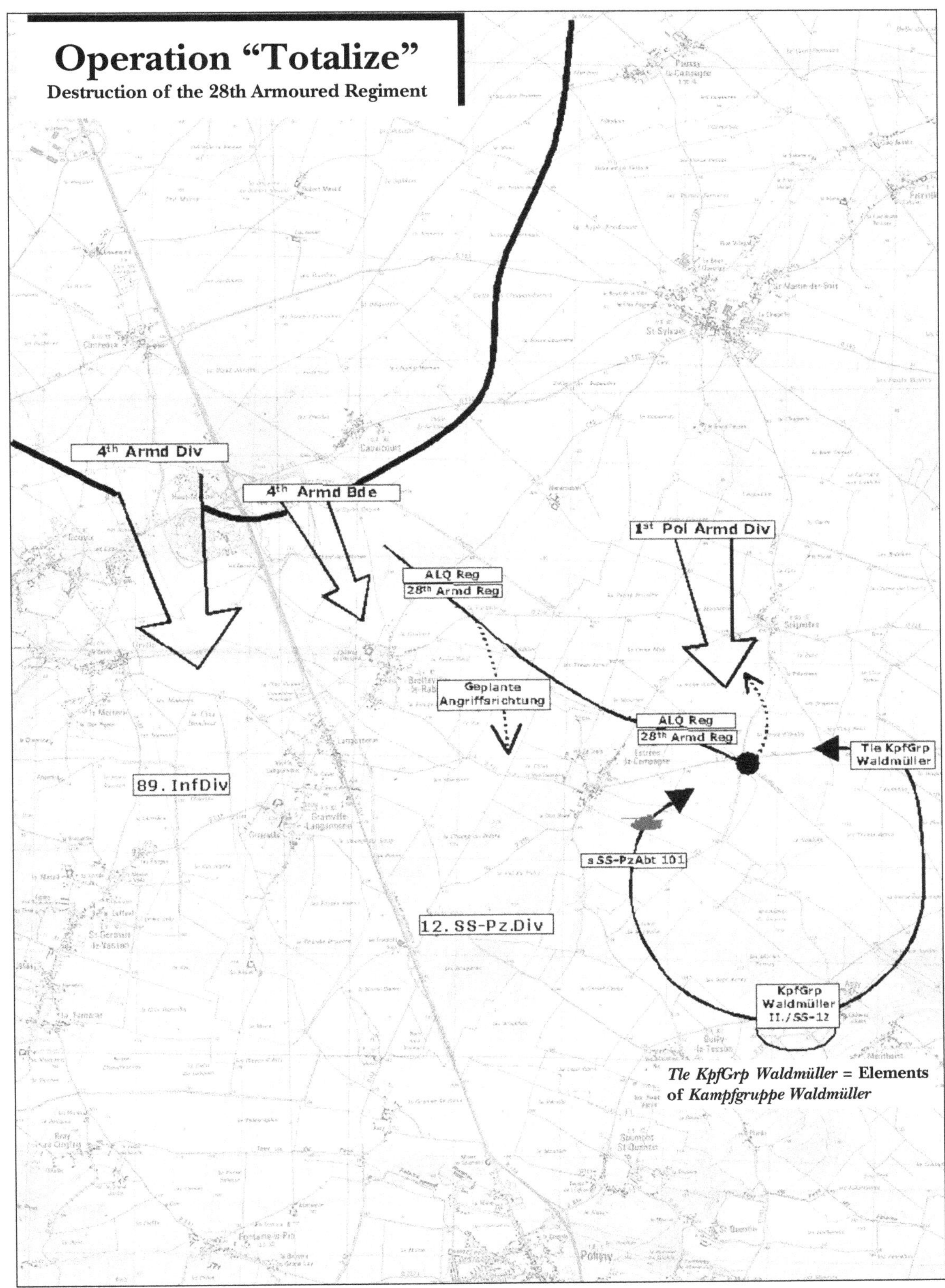
Operation "Totalize"
Destruction of the 28th Armoured Regiment
4th Armd Div
4th Armd Bde
1st Pol Armd Div
ALQ Reg
28th Armd Reg
Geplante Angriffsrichtung
ALQ Reg
28th Armd Reg
Tle KpfGrp Waldmüller
89. InfDiv
sSS-PzAbt 101
12. SS-Pz.Div
KpfGrp Waldmüller II./SS-12
St Sylvain
Poussy la Campagne
St Martin-des-Bois
Cauvicourt
Estrées la Campagne
Bretteville le Rabet
Langannerie
Grainville Langannerie
Gouvix
Cintheaux
St Germain le Vasson
Bray
Bailly le Tesson
Fontaine le Pin
Potigny
St Quentin
Soumont St Quentin
Tle KpfGrp Waldmüller = Elements of Kampfgruppe Waldmüller

Gordon's Firefly would then shoot at the rearmost Tiger.

In 3 Charlie Firefly, Joe Ekins, the shoe clicker from Bedfordshire, lined up his sights and, as the Tigers prowled to within about 800 yd, Boardman gave the order to fire. At 12.40 hours Ekin's boot trod on the trigger button and the immense flash of the Firefly wrapped itself around the turret. Gordon and Ekins blinked deliberately and then opened their eyes to see the shot strike the enemy turret. Ekins fired again. The Tiger started to burn. Immediately the other two Tigers alerted began feverishly to traverse their 88 mm guns towards the Yeomanry. One Tiger fired and Gordon ordered his tank to reverse so that he could find other cover from which to resume firing. A third Tiger shot glanced on the turret hatch of the Firefly, doing no material damage but smashing the heavy steel plate against Gordon's head. Gordon staggered out of the tank and was wounded by a random mortar bomb.

Lt James ran to Gordon's tank, guided the driver into a new firing position under the apple trees and gave the fire order. 12.47 hours—one shot from Ekins and the Tiger's turret exploded. The 75 mm Shermans appeared to have done some kind of damage to the third Tiger, possibly smashing the commander's periscope, for the tank seemed to be circling as though looking for escape from the open field in which it found itself. 12.52 hours—and two more shots from Ekins. The third Tiger started to burn. In Ekins' own words "this all happened in about 12 minutes. All I was thinking was 'get them before they get us.' I fired twice [at the third Tiger]. He started burning. We reversed into cover. We reloaded and sorted ourselves out and sat back waiting."

The enemy succeeded in advancing to Haut Mesnil in the course of the day. The enemy's intent for the following day, 9 August 1944, was to advance at first light and move past Bretteville-le-Rabet on both sides. In the meantime, however, the German resistance had stiffened. There was bitter fighting at Bretteville-le-Rabet.

The commander of the 4th Armoured Brigade, Brigadier General E. L. Booth, then ordered the 28th Armoured Regiment—the British Columbia Regiment—to advance east past Bretteville-le-Rabet in close cooperation with the Algonquin Infantry Regiment. Its objective was to take Hill 195, a dominant terrain feature. By doing so, the Canadians would be in a position to cut off the Germans and hinder a withdrawal to the south over the N 158.

But the combat-inexperienced Canadians made a fatal mistake. Instead of turning right at Estrées-la-Campage (and heading south), they continued straight, thinking they were still going in the right direction. In the process, they submitted incorrect location reports by radio. Some of the tanks lost contact and became completely lost.

The regimental commander reported at 0841 hours that he had been attacked by German tanks, that he had already suffered ten losses of his own and that he desperately needed artillery support. As a result of the incorrect location repots, this was not possible. When the brigade command post sent an additional request for information at 0907 hours, it did not receive an answer. What had happened?

The German side had realized what was going on and had reacted rapidly. *Kampfgruppe Wünsche*, reinforced by seven *Tigers*, was alerted. It assembled in a patch of woods along Laison Creek near Assy, where it was protected from being observed from the south by Hill 140. It was then employed against the Canadians, who were one kilometer east of Estrées-la-Campage. They were taken in a pincers movement, with the *Tigers* coming from the southwest and *Panthers* and *Panzer IV's* coming from the east. The unequal struggle raged for several hours.

Hopes were raised when the Polish Armored Division, which had been committed in this area in the meantime, formed up. These Polish forces had no idea that friendly forces were in front of them, however, and likewise opened fire on the bagged Canadians.

When the Canadians tried to identify themselves with yellow smoke, the German tank commanders noticed the Polish tanks that had advanced forward. The Germans turned them back while also knocking out several of their number. The fighting would have probably ended sooner, had Typhoon fighter-bombers not permanently also joined in the *mêlée.* Only a few Canadian tanks were able to get out. By late afternoon, the 28th Armoured Regiment had lost forty-four Shermans, two Stuarts and one Crusader. One hundred twelve soldiers were killed, including the battalion commander. Thirty-four Canadians were taken prisoner. German losses were slight; there was not a single *Tiger* among them. Thanks to the onset of darkness, what remained of the regiment was able to make it to Polish lines.

EMPLOYMENT OF *SCHWERE SS-PANZER-ABTEILUNG 102* AGAINST THE CANADIAN ORNE BRIDGEHEADS

The 4th Armoured Division was given the mission the following day of finally taking the area around Hill 206 west of Pontigny. It was intended for the Polish Armored Division to take Hill 140. It was possible to take Hill 195—the original objective of the decimated British Columbia Regiment—under the cover of darkness and without too much fanfare. The 22nd Armoured Regiment was then ordered forward so that it could advance on Hill 206 to the south. In the face of the *PaK* barricade that had been established by the *III. Flak-Korps,* this was not possible. In the meantime, the Poles had been able to take Hill 140, but not without heavy losses (once again). The *Tigers* of the *3./schwere SS-Panzer-Abteilung 101* were able to knock out thirty-eight armored vehicles all by themselves.

✠

The bulk of the *2./schwere SS-Panzer-Abteilung 102* was sent from the area east of Vassy via Condé-sur-Noireau to *Kampfgruppe Wünsche* on 9 August 1944, when a breakthrough towards Falaise was threatening as part of Operation "Totalize."

After the vehicles were resupplied, they continued on to the northern outskirts of Bons-Tassily just to the west of the N 158. There they received the order to march to Martainville via Ussy. After the company had started to bivouac in the woods northwest of Tournebu, it was attached to the *271. Infanterie-Division* as its divisional reserve. It then bivouacked in the *Bois Halbout* after a roundabout journey of more than sixty kilometers.

The remaining thirteen operational tanks of *schwere SS-Panzer-Abteilung 102* were also moved on the same morning. Starting at 0700 hours, they left the area around Vire for the *12. SS-Panzer-Division*

"Hitlerjugend," where they were able to arrive in time and participate in the fighting northeast of Hill 140 (see above).

Two *Tigers* of the *2./schwere SS-Panzer-Abteilung 102* were involved in combat as part of the *271. Infanterie-Division* for the first time on 10 August 1944. They fought on the division's left wing. About a dozen enemy tanks and a few armored cars had advanced as far as a depression at Espins, Le Monsul and areas to the west of the latter village. German infantry—some without weapons—was streaming back. Thanks to the presence of the *Tigers*, the infantry got its courage back. *SS-Untersturmführer* Loritz knocked out four enemy tanks.

On 11 August 1944, six tanks of the company were employed around the Bois Halbout. Two of them conducted an immediate counterattack on an enemy tank assembly area southwest of Le Moncel; four enemy tanks were knocked out. During the night, the *Tigers* pulled back to the Bois Halbout.

A report was received at 0700 hours that twenty-six enemy tanks were advancing to the south east of Barbery. The company then screened the roads to Espins and Fresney-le-Vieux with one *Tiger* each, while six tanks advanced along the road through Cingal towards Barbery. They took the high ground north of Cingal and then turned east. There was a report of five enemy tanks that had broken through that were accompanied by infantry. In all, seven tanks and one armored car were destroyed; afterwards, the *Tigers* secured the positions they had won. Towards noon, two hours of heavy artillery fire preceded an enemy attack.

SS-Unterscharführer Günther knocked out three enemy tanks and then had to pull back in the face of overwhelming force towards Tournebu. The five *Tigers* under the command of *SS-Untersturmführer* Loritz that were northeast of Tournebu were immediately ordered back to the Bois Halbout. *Tiger 232* was penetrated by direct hits from two antitank guns. *SS-Unterscharführer* Moldenhauer and his gunner were killed immediately. The badly wounded radio operator jumped out of the tank and was captured. The driver kept his wits about him, pulled out of the column at high speed and returned to the assembly area, where the badly wounded loader could later be recovered.

The village, which had been occupied by the enemy in the meantime, had to be traversed. Loritz and his tanks tore through the town, all weapons firing, and entered the Bois Halbout. Several enemy armored vehicles were destroyed. The trampled-on British fled into the side streets or sought cover in the ruins. Several Germans who had been taken prisoner took advantage of the confusion and were able to flee.

Two *Tigers* screened southeast of Tournebu, while the remaining ones resupplied around 1700 hours on the road 200 meters southeast of Clair-Tizon. Six damaged *Tigers* were dispatched to the Maintenance Company. Differing orders were received, but march orders finally arrived for the company to move to Chateaux de la Motte and to screen north from there.

During the morning of 13 August 1944, the company bivouacked in the woods 500 meters southeast of Tournebu with three operational *Tigers*. It screened to the north from there. When the Essex Infantry Regiment of the Canadian 2nd Infantry Division formed up to attack from the direction of Barbery, the *Tigers* were able to bring it to a standstill.

The mission that had been received in the meantime—to clear the creek-bed area of the Laize in the vicinity of Clair-Tizon and to the north—did not happen, because friendly infantry did not show up. In its place, there was a short advance along the road from Clair-Tizon to the north with forces of the *271. Infanterie-Division.* This was directed against the Canadian Regiment de Maisonneuve, which was attempting to expand its bridgehead over the Laize. Following this, the forces withdrew to ten meters south of Clair-Tizon.

In the meantime, the Canadians had gone over to the offensive again on the N 158. As a result, the danger grew that *schwere SS-Panzer-Abteilung 102* would be cut off.

The operational objectives of Operation "Totalize" could not be achieved, despite a very promising beginning. The attack bogged down along the N 158, and the woods south of Quesnay could not be taken. Farther to the east, only a few patrols were able to get to the Laison River. Once again, the breakthrough to Falaise had not been achieved.

The majority of the German armor moved into the area south of Quesnay as reserves. There were skirmishes for two entire days north of the Laize at le Bu-sur-Rouvres that involved several *Tigers* of the *2./schwere SS-Panzer-Abteilung 102.* The company knocked out seven enemy tanks on 12 August 1944 at this location. In the course of a night attack on the same day, an enemy tank company was surprised while it was refueling and completely destroyed. After this, the company moved to a fruit orchard in the vicinity of Assy and awaited further orders.

The oppressive air superiority caused amazingly few losses among the *Tigers*, but it crippled logistical traffic for most of the day. An ammunition truck of the battalion can be seen above (recognizable by the formation insignia on the vehicle's rear). Whenever possible, the crews used the concealment afforded by the thick woods.

It was even advisable for the crews of antiaircraft weaponry to carefully camouflage themselves. The smaller-caliber weapons were ineffective against high-flying bombers anyway.

CHAPTER 11

Operation "Tractable" and the Breakthrough to Falaise

The quiet 13th of August was used by the British to get ready for their next blow. The objective of Operation "Tractable" was to advance deeply east of Pontigny with the Canadian 3rd and 4th Infantry Divisions, rapidly establish bridgeheads over the Laison and take Hills 184 and 170 on the right (Canadian 3rd Infantry Division) and Epanca and Perrières on the left/east (Canadian 4th Infantry Division). If possible, Versainville was also to be taken.

✠

Towards noon, the artillery marked the target area for seventy-three medium bombers. Once again, the Canadians were imaginative, in that they had gigantic walls of artificial smoke fired by artillery along their flanks. However, this tended to hinder the attackers, and the German antitank and antiaircraft forces had already registered their targets anyway, resulting in the enemy suffering heavy casualties.

Despite this, the Laison was reached in several places and crossed, not least because many German infantry forces did not resist and allowed themselves to be taken prisoner.

Farther to the east, the *2./schwere SS-Panzer-Abteilung 102* road-marched into the sector of the *89. Infanterie-Division* at Maizières. The lead tank of *SS-Obersturmführer* Wendorff was suddenly confronted by two Shermans. He was able to knock out one of them, but the other one set his tank alight. The tank commander and the loader were killed; the radio operator, who was pinned inside, shot himself to avoid being burned alive.

✠

This engagement has been described by Wendorff's gunner, *SS-Rottenführer* Walter Lau:

> After we had celebrated the promotion of Franz Elmer to *SS-Unterscharführer* the previous evening, we had to go back to the front again in the direction of Soulangy. It was the tanks of *SS-Obersturmführer* Wendorff, *SS-Untersturmführer* Hantusch, *SS-Untersturmführer* Henniges, *SS-Oberscharführer* Brandt, *SS-Oberscharführer* Lötzsch and *SS-Unterscharführer* Sowa—all from the 2nd Company.
>
> It was late in the evening. We took up screening positions in a fruit orchard southwest of Assy. There was one man in each of the turrets as a guard. It was a quiet neck of the woods.
>
> During the morning of 14 August, a liaison officer from the Army arrived, probably from the *85. Infanterie-Division*. I

These photographs show Wendorf's destroyed tank. The closed radio operator's hatch shows that the trapped soldier was unable to dismount from the burning tank. The markings on the front slope indicate that it was a tank from the 1st Company, which had already been moved to receive the *Tiger II*. (IWM)

listened inside the turret as he explained the way to a sector that was 8-10 kilometers away, where a penetration was expected.

This fact and our carelessness proved fateful for us. This [what the liaison officer had said] meant that we could take another forty winks, or so we thought. I took my belt off, placed it on the main gun and got as comfortable as I could in the gunner's seat. It was, after all, almost 10 kilometers to go; then we would receive new instructions and a ready position—it was not until then that the war would continue. At least that's what I thought.

It was between 0600 and 0700 hours. We were moving along the narrow road from Assy to Maizieres. Because of the fighter-bombers, we were moving at large intervals, so that the last *Tigers* probably did not see our demise. After moving for about 20 minutes, Wendorff suddenly called out:

"Man . . . two Shermans . . . Lau, fire!"

Then again:

"Fire, what are you waiting for . . . fire!"

A few things had to happen before that could be done—feet on the pedals, main gun released, turret traversed to 2 o'clock. And then I saw the Sherman in the optics. It was only 30 meters away from us on a bend in the road. The first round got him. I had the impression the burst of fire was hitting us right in the fighting compartment. It was my 16th "kill" with Wendorff since the middle of July 1944.

Wendorff was yelling again: "Next to it . . . on the other side of the road . . . another one!"

I continued to traverse by hand and saw the next one. In the next moment, it happened—a truly ear-deafening hit, dead silence and the smell of fire. At some point, I came back to my senses. It was if I were paralyzed. I was in shock and could scarcely breathe, hear or see. My first movement was upwards, where you could pull yourself up into the commander's cupola by grips above the gunner's seat. While doing that, I had to catch my breath. Wendorff was sitting there, but he did not move. I did not feel any blood-soaked clothes; I could not see his face. I thought: There must be something wrong with my eyes.

Then I heard from the radio operator, Fred Zimmermann. He was screaming; I could barely understand him. Franz Elmer, our driver, did not report. The loader lay dead in the fighting compartment. Zimmermann said that he was penned in and his feet were not working. It was burning in the engine compartment and he wanted to put an end to it all with his pistol.

I also felt the burning smoke that took away your breath and biting pain—burns. I was able to hear the final pistol shot of Fred Zimmermann—that also took my breath away. Probably due to the smoke, I started to feel quite good and peaceful. I sank with my head against the black rubber eye guard of the optics. This was the end—or so I thought. I did not wake up until 3 September 1944, when I was at British Hospital No. 99. The driver, Franz Elmer, had bailed out and probably gotten help . . .

SS-Oberscharführer Brandt assumed command and attacked the Canadian 1st Hussars, who were attempting to cross the Laison at Rouvres. The Laison proved itself to be an armor obstacle, even though it was only about two meters wide and less than one meter deep. The Canadians employed fascines that they carried on their tanks. Despite this, several tanks bottomed out. In all, some nineteen tanks were knocked out by the *Tigers*. Despite this, the *Tigers* had to pull back to avoid being outflanked—the river line had been crossed at several places by the enemy.

The *85. Infanterie-Division* in the center sector also suffered losses. In the first assault of the Canadians, there were some 1,010 prisoners. The *12. SS-Panzer-Division "Hitlerjugend,"* which was being held in readiness behind the infantry division, had only fifteen operational tanks.

Starting at 1400 hours, heavy bombers were employed once again. This time it was 669 aircraft dropping 3,723 tons of bombs. Once again, friendly Allied forces were hit at several locations, with approximately 400 friendly soldiers being killed or wounded.

Once again, the Canadians did not succeed in forcing a rapid breakthrough to Falaise.

On 15 August 1944, Brandt's vehicle and another *Tiger* were in position on Hill 160 east of the Caen–Falaise road. The enemy walked right over the accompanying infantry and encircled the tank company's headquarters section. The two *Tigers* knocked out twelve enemy tanks and then broke out. Brandt towed the second tank out.

Six *Tigers* of the *3./schwere SS-Panzer-Abteilung 102* under *SS-Hauptsturmführer* Heurich were in position southeast of Hill 160, where they knocked out several enemy tanks.

By the morning of 16 August 1944, the enemy reached the following line: Soulangy–Epancy–Perrières–Sassy–Ernes (including all locations). Forces from the Polish Armored Division had broken through as far as Jort. The breakthrough had started.

The operations along the Laison were the last coordinated offensive actions of *schwere SS-Panzer-Abteilung 102*. A gigantic pocket began to be formed southeast of Falaise. This was, of course, the result of the unsuccessful *Operation "Lüttich"* in the area of Mortain and the subsequent rapid advance of the Americans.

The abandoned *Tiger 304*.

View of the open terrain approaching Falaise, which enabled the Allied forces practically unimpeded opportunity for maneuver and gave the defender little opportunity to establish blocking positions.

Two images of *Tiger 211*, which was abandoned south of Potigny on 14 August 1944.

Schwere Panzer-Kompanie 316, which was never really ready for deployment, trained at the Bruck an der Leitra Training Area during its activation.

INTERMEZZO IN CHATEAUDUN

At this point, we will briefly discuss the fate of the five *Tiger II's* of *schwere Panzer-Kompanie (FkL) 316.*

In April 1944, the company had five *Tiger II's* and three old *Tiger I's.* It was conducting training in Bruck an der Leitha (Austria). The *Tiger II's* were among the very first models of this tank produced, and they were continuously subject to mechanical failure. On 9 May 1944, the company was moved by rail to Verdun.

Because the *Tiger II's* were not considered suitable for employment at the front, there were deliberations made whether to send them back to Germany or to destroy them. After a series of wanderings on rail transport in July, the *Tigers* finally wound up in the French region of Eure-et-Loire.

The five *Tiger II's* arrived at Chateaudun on 13 August 1944. They were integrated into the defensive positions of the city for use against the advancing Americans. *Tiger 10* was located in the northwest along the *RN 1555*; *Tiger 13* in the west along the *RN 827*, *Tiger 12* at the crossroads of *RN 10* and *RN 824*; and *Tigers 02* and *11* screened towards the north across the Loire at the *Place Le Mail.* The leader of the group was *Leutnant* Schneider.

On 15 August 1944, a reconnaissance patrol of the U.S. 3rd Armored Cavalry encountered *Tiger 12* as it approached from Montigny-le-Ganellon. Three U.S. vehicle crews were taken prisoner by the infantry covering the tank. A jeep and an M8 armored car were halted through turret machine-gun fire. Later on, the tank pulled back to the Rue de Varize.

On 16 August 1944, *Tiger 13* was taken under artillery fire. *Tiger 12* turned back an enemy advance by means of several rounds from its main gun. *Tiger 10* left its position towards evening and closed up with *Tigers 02* and *11* at Le Mail.

During the night of 16–17 August 1944, both *Tigers 12* and *13* were abandoned by their crews. *Tiger 12* was set on fire. Around 0300 hours, the remaining three *Tigers* moved to *Boulevard Kellermann. Tiger 11* broke down there and was left behind. The other two *Tigers* headed east along the *RN 155.* Varize was reached the following night. *Tiger 10* also broke down there and was taken in tow by *Tiger 02.*

Around 2000 hours on 18 August 1944, *Tiger 10* was blown up. *Tiger 02* continued to move in the direction of Janville. Outside of Toury, it drifted to the left due to steering problems, knocked over a tree along the road and stopped. The crew abandoned it.

What happened to the three *Tiger I's* is not certain. They were not at Chateaudun. One was located at Semousy (between Avesnes-sur-Elpe and Beaumont in Belgium).

Tiger 10 moves through Chateaudun prior to the fighting.

Tiger 12, abandoned at the intersection. (RN10/RN824)

In the above photograph, *Tiger 11* is seen in its position along the Loire. It was to the right of *Tiger 02* during the fighting.

Not much was left of *Tiger 10*, since it was blown up by its crew.

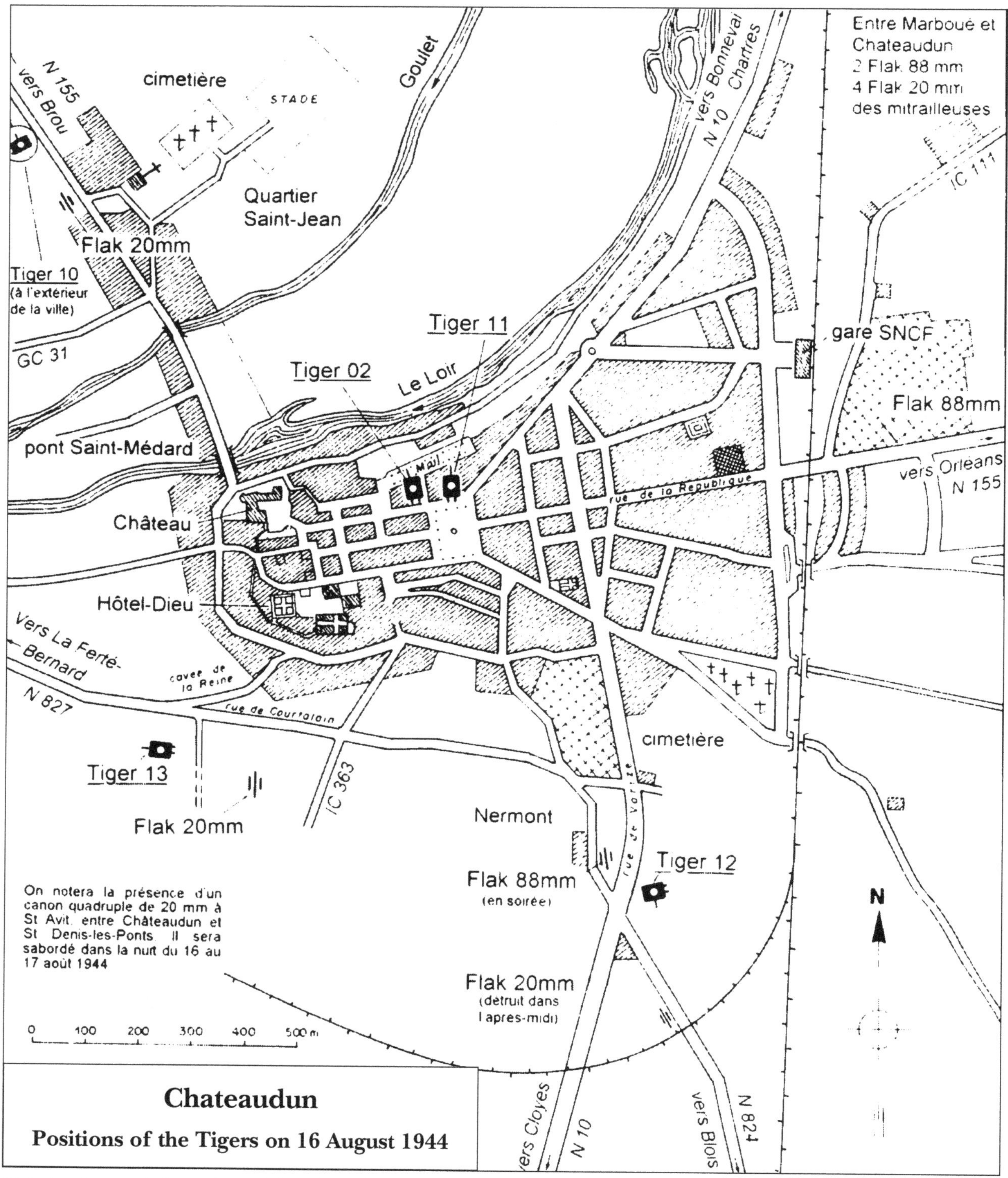

This sketch map is from the article by Eric Santin in Issue 157/158 of the French periodical, *39-45*, published by Edition Heimdal. Santin correctly researched the actions of the five *Tigers* of *schwere Panzer-Kompanie 316* in the village.

This series shows *Tiger 02,* which was abandoned at Toury.

THE FRONT COLLAPSES

In the course of Operation "Tractable" and subsequent operations, the German front increasingly dissolved. What was left of the German armored formations fought their way—sometimes as individual tanks—towards the Seine.

Even if the Allies did not succeed early on in closing the pocket that was forming in the area around Falaise—thanks to the miscalculations of Montgomery and Bradley—it was the sole objective of the German formations in the coming weeks to get over the Seine in one piece.

On 16 August 1944, *Generalfeldmarschall* von Kluge was able to achieve what Jodl called "a certain amount of freedom of action" after repeated conversations with the *OKW*, which continued to make completely unrealistic assumptions. Von Kluge ordered a withdrawal to the following line: Morteaux–Trun–Gacé–Laigle. Even this decision was completely divorced from reality. From the German perspective, a new defensive line should have been established along the Seine, if even there. To have done that would have required a timely withdrawal of powerful combat forces, however.

As a result, completely burned-out remnants reached the Seine with their increasingly depleted inventories of heavy weapons. The next day, *Generalfeldmarschall* von Kluge was relieved by *Generalfeldmarschall* Model. On the trip back to Germany, *Generalfeldmarschall* von Kluge committed suicide.

It was not until 18 August 1944 that the Allies made serious efforts to close the pocket. By then, nearly 50 percent of the almost encircled forces had been able to escape. It was only the devastating aerial attacks that were causing the high losses in materiel and personnel up to that point. On 18 August 1944, there were 3,057 sorties flown; on the next day, the number decreased to 2,535. These figures do not include fighter-bomber sorties. Aerial attacks on the Seine crossing points (e.g., at Rouen) also led to similar success. It was not until around noon on 21 August 1944 that the pocket was closed.

Previously demanding respect—like this *Tiger* of *schwere SS-Panzer-Abteilung 101*—even the proud *Tigers* were fleeing after the collapse of the front.

WITHDRAWAL TO THE SEINE

Only a few tanks even reached the Seine. A large portion of them were lost in the pocket that was being formed around Falaise or as the result of aerial attacks. The greatest number was lost, however, to mechanical problems or a lack of fuel. All the bridges along the Seine had been blown up and there was virtually no ferrying capability of this lift capacity. Only a few tanks were ferried across, often only to be lost during the continued withdrawal in the direction of Belgium. The individual fates of the three *Tiger* battalions provide insight into the occasionally adventurous odysseys of the withdrawing German armored formations.

Let us start with *schwere SS-Panzer-Abteilung 101.*

On 16 August 1944, a towed and damaged tank of the 3rd Company—engine damaged on 9 August 1944 at Cintheaux—could not be crossed over the Seine at Rouen and had to be set on fire by its crew.

The remaining *Tigers* assembled at L'Abbaye on 17 August 1944. The battalion's *Flak* platoon was destroyed on the road from Vimoutiers to Orbec after downing a Spitfire.

One *Tiger* remained behind at Livarot on 18 August 1944 due to track damage.

Two *Tigers* supported the breakout of the *3. Fallschirmjäger-Division* from the Falaise Pocket on 19 August 1944; two additional tanks linked up with *Kampfgruppe Olboeter* and cleared a path through the enemy by fire, during which eight enemy tanks were knocked out.

Three *Tigers* stopped the attack of the 1/7th Queens at Livarot.

On 20 August 1944, several *Tigers* were employed south of Lisieux with elements of the *12. SS-Panzer-Division "Hitlerjugend."*

Two *Tigers* of the 2nd Company were employed west of Vernon on 23 August 1944.

One *Tiger* was knocked out by an M10 "Achilles" of the Norfolk Yeomanry eight kilometers north of Montfort-sur-Risle on 24 August 1944.

Several *Tigers* of the 3rd Company reached the Seine, where they were abandoned. Two of those—*Tigers 321* and *332*—had to be blown up as a result of transmission or engine problems. The company commander of the 3rd Company was captured by the Americans while conducting reconnaissance. *Tiger 324* was abandoned in Rouen.

Several *Tigers* crossed the Seine at Rouen and Elbeuf. They pulled back to Songeons, where they had billeted prior to the start of the invasion. They later had to be abandoned.

On 27 August 1944, *Kampfgruppe [Oberst] Schrader* of the *49. Infanterie-Division* conducted a counterattack along the Gisors to Vernonnet road. Three *Tigers* were in support. The lead tank, *Tiger 222*, was penetrated three times by a 6-pounder when it rounded a curve. The antitank gun was firing newly introduced sub-caliber sabot rounds from virtually pointblank range. The *Tiger* caught on fire, but the crew was able to bail out. A short while later, the second *Tiger* pulled forward, eliminated the antitank gun and its entire crew and then blew apart "D" Company of the 1st Worcestershire Regiment. The remaining English fled in a panic. Because the German infantry did not follow, however, the *Tiger* pulled back and later had to be abandoned.

On 28 August 1944, a counterattack was conducted against the bridgehead at Vernon with two *Tigers* from the 2nd Company (Brandt). Two enemy antitank guns, four carriers and one scout car were destroyed. On 29 August 1944, both of the *Tigers* covered the withdrawal of friendly forces and decimated an enemy infantry battalion. Another *Tiger*, which had belonged to *Kampfgruppe Schrader*, was knocked out south of Tilly. On 30 August 1944, the two *Tigers* turned back enemy attacks in the Gisors and Beauvais areas, one in the morning and one in the evening. Due to a lack of fuel, both *Tigers* had to be blown up.

During a maintenance halt, one *Tiger* of the 3rd Company was caught by surprise outside of St. Martin by a U.S. Sherman and set alight.

One *Tiger* with old running gear was left behind at Marle.

Another *Tiger* was abandoned at the Bois Bourdon (north of Maubeuge).

The withdrawing *Tiger* crews attempted to get their vehicles back to the Seine, either individually or in tow. They hoped to be able to escape by getting over to the other side. On the page on the right, a vehicle from the former 1st Company attempts to tow a badly damaged comrade form the 2nd Company. It gives up the effort in Livarot and leaves it behind.

Several *Tigers* from *schwere SS-Panzer-Abteilung 101*—on the left, *Tiger 321* and, on the right, *Tiger 332*—also reached Elbeuf on the Seine, where they had to be abandoned for the lack of crossing capacity. (*BA*)

Tiger 223 in an open field; the exact location cannot be verified.

German vehicles, including a *Tiger* and *Panther*, await a ferry across the Seine—usually in vain.

Two *Tigers* that were left behind in Rouen, surrounded by other abandoned German vehicles and equipment.

Tiger 221, employed with *Kampfgruppe Schrader* at Vernonnet, was knocked out by an antitank gun. (Grubb) Below: This was the *Tiger* that was left behind at the Bois Bourdon. (de Meyer)

This *Tiger* from the former 1st Company was left behind in Marles. The civilians appear to be wearing "Free French" armbands that identified "Resistance Fighters."

This *Tiger* was abandoned at Genval in Belgium and was rendered combat ineffective by blowing up the main gun. The tank belonged to *schwere SS-Panzer-Abteilung 101.* This can be determined by the fact that the mounting points for the tow cable brackets are flat and not cut into the vehicles as on later models. Only that battalion had that particular version of the *Tiger.* (de Meyer)

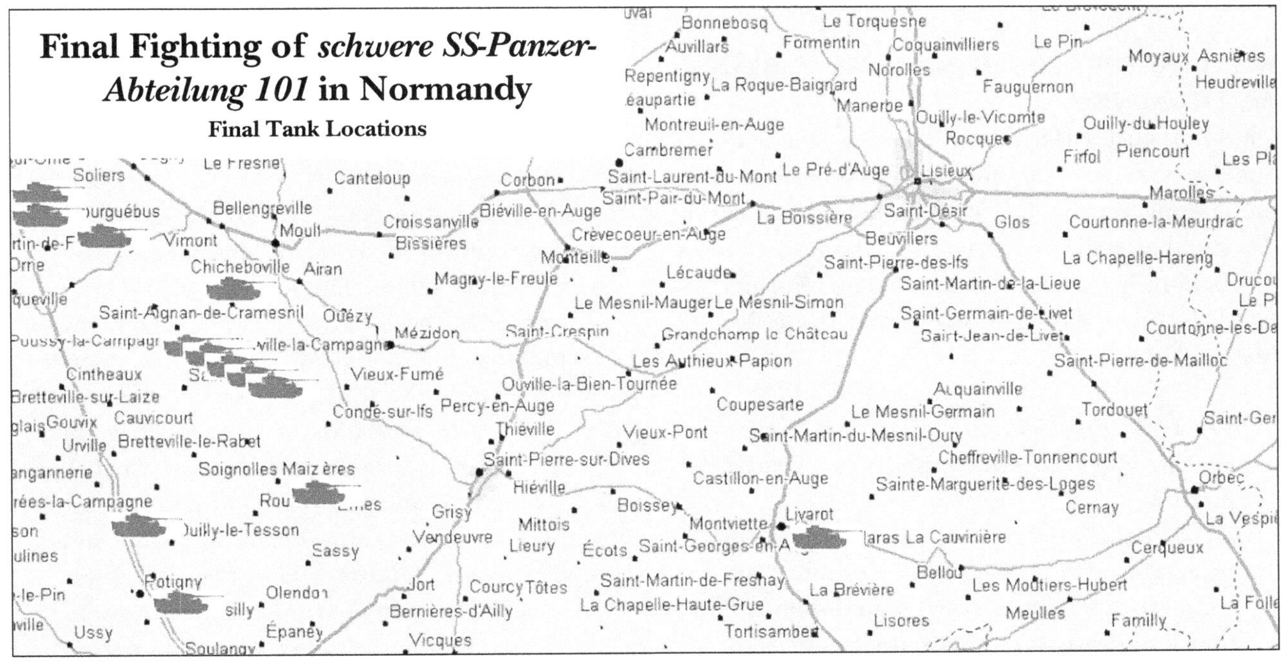

Final Fighting of *schwere SS-Panzer-Abteilung 101* in Normandy

Final Tank Locations

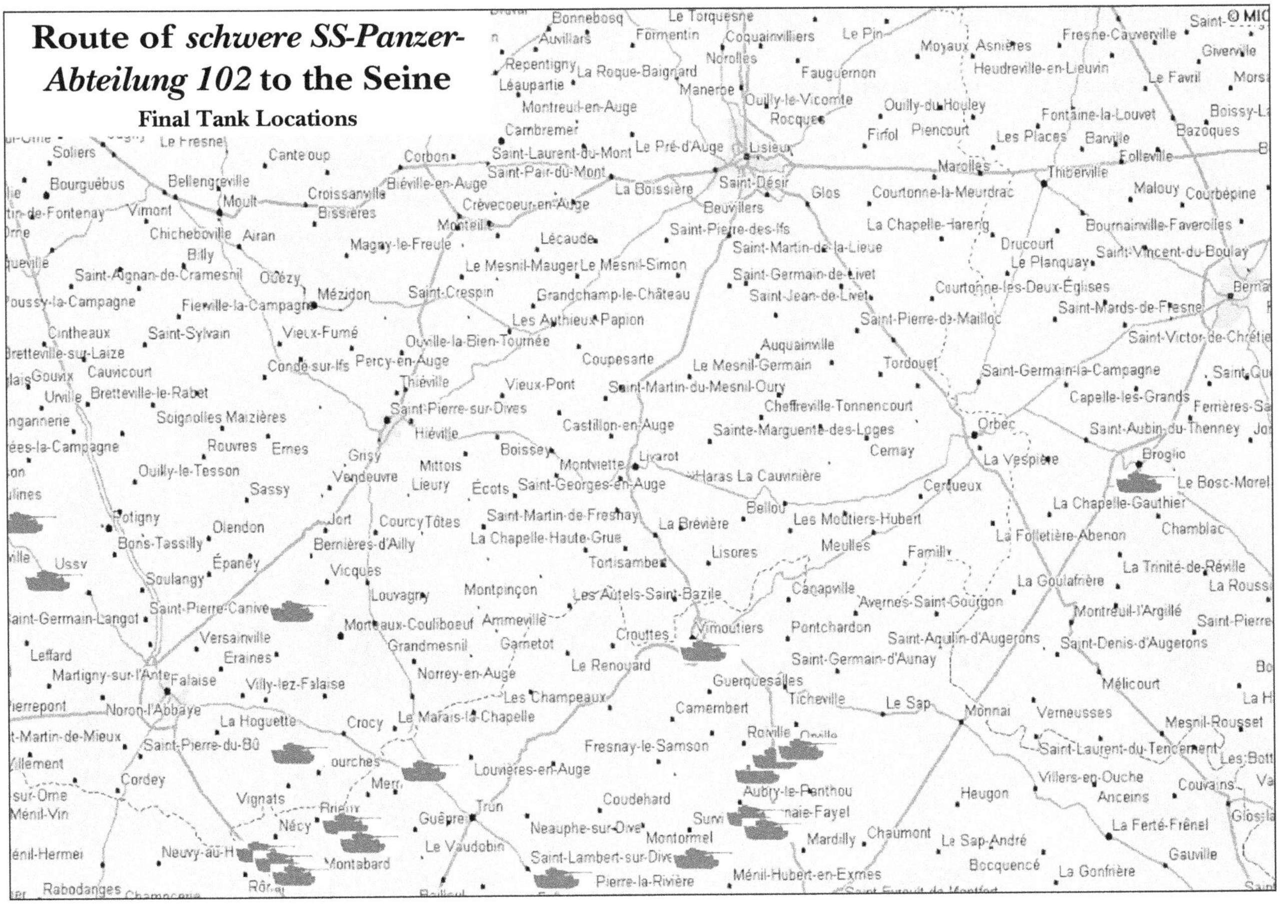

Route of *schwere SS-Panzer-Abteilung 102* to the Seine

Final Tank Locations

WHAT HAPPENED TO *SCHWERE SS-PANZER-ABTEILUNG 102*?

On 14 August 1944, the battalion still had thirty-one *Tigers* on its books, although most of them were undergoing repair. The operational tanks on this day numbered thirteen. The battalion was strewn throughout the greater area of Falaise. Former *SS-Unterscharführer* Streng has provided the following firsthand account:

> On 14 August 1944, the order to pull back to the northeastern outskirts of Falaise arrived.
>
> The *Tigers* moved in a southerly direction in the pale gray of morning. We were surprised by a heavy fighter-bomber attack while we were still on the feeder road of the western bypass into the main road to Falaise: Rockets slammed into the road and the field; trees burst apart; branches, rocks and clumps of dirt twirled around the fighting vehicles, which were fortunately able to flee into a patch of nearby deciduous woods.
>
> We received a new combat mission in the Falaise area. We were given the mission of defending against armored attacks in the area of Tournebous.
>
> Short after 0600 hours there was heavy fog, reinforced by artificial smoke, across the entire sector. The few friendly infantry were soon bypassed and, suddenly, enemy infantry was in front of the company command post, which had shrunk to three *Tigers*. The attack waves bogged down in the fire of our tanks, whereby the English brought up antitank guns and tanks under the concealment afforded by the bushes and the hedges. Münster's tank [*Tiger 212*] was attacked by hand-held antitank weapons and was soon hit in the turret, whereby a part of the crew became casualties.
>
> Schroif and Loritz each set an enemy tank on fire. Shortly thereafter, Loritz's tank [*Tiger 331*] was hit and destroyed from short range. The first round landed in the turret and must have killed the entire crew or at least have badly wounded them, because

The *Tiger* in which the crew of *SS-Untersturmführer* Loritz was killed on 14 August 1944.

none of the hatches were opening. Seconds went by. A second hit, this time in the engine compartment. The gasoline caught on fire!

Engulfed in a sea of flames, the *Tiger* burned out accompanied by numerous explosions with its entire crew on board. Both rage and sorrow accompanied this message of bad news for the company—it had lost one of its best!

A German immediate counterattack launched from the rear only got as far as the tanks with weak forces and bogged down there, because the English defensive fire was overpowering. In order to provide immediate support to the fighting elements, Oberhuber's tank—*Tiger 222*—which had just been released from the Maintenance Company, was ordered to the front via radio.

Five *Panthers* that were employed to the right were also pulled out during the afternoon. It was at this point that the enemy began to attack this area with heavy bomber formations. Coming from the east, masses of bombers dropped their rows and carpets of bombs on the German defensive lines and sowed death and destruction with brutal force along the German front . . .

At this point, we pulled back to the rear with grenadiers who had mounted up. It was right at 1800 hours that we were ordered with our tank to Hill 184 north of Soulangy, where we were employed. Friendly infantry came running back from the front in battalion strength at this location. They were followed by 12 Shermans. At last light we set three of them alight in quick succession, at which point the German infantry started to dig in on the hill.

One *Tiger* screened along the main road between Soulangy and St. Pierre. Late in the afternoon, it freed a shrunken grenadier company from the *12. SS-Panzer-Division "Hitlerjugend"* by means of an immediate counterattack. The company was about to be taken in a pincers by six advancing Shermans. All six of the enemy tanks were knocked out. A short time later, an enemy halftrack column was also eliminated. Because the tank's engine had problems, however, it had to be towed after the onset of darkness by the company commander's tank, which was in position on the western outskirts of St. Pierre.

✠

On 15 August 1944, *Tiger 134* turned back an enemy infantry attack on Versainville; there was a firefight against enemy tanks, of which four were knocked out. At this point, the tank was completely surrounded by Canadian infantry and was being approached by tank hunter/killer teams. It pulled back to Versainville, where it covered the withdrawal of the German forces to Eraines. Two more Shermans were knocked out. Following this, *Tiger 134* also pulled back to Eraines, where the tanks of the battalion commander and Schinhofen were already in position.

The rest of the 1st Company and two remaining operational *Tigers* from the 2nd Company were in position on the northern outskirts of Potigny. An enemy tank was knocked out there. Starting at 1430 hours, the enemy fired smoke rounds throughout the sector. Following a heavy artillery preparation, he broke through the German defensive lines on the right flank.

The German tanks then oriented towards the northwest and conducted a firefight, inasmuch as the visibility allowed it. Towards 1900 hours, Oberhuber's *Tiger* was lost as the result of several hits. At the onset of darkness, the German infantry pulled back further to the south in order to avoid being outflanked. Schroif went to the battalion command post in Versainville and received new orders there.

Around 0300 hours on 16 August 1944, the *Tigers* moved to Vignats; the crossroads 1,500 meters south of Aubigny were blocked by *Tiger 001* and *Tiger 241.* They defended against an attack by the Canadian South Saskatchewan Regiment that was supported by "B" Squadron of the 27th Armoured Regiment. Although two enemy tanks were knocked out, the Canadians advanced past the *Tigers.* As a result, the *Tigers* pulled back to the dominant hill at Villy and Fresné-la-Mère.

Following this, these two *Tigers* were employed in Falaise to support *Kampfgruppe (SS-Obersturmbannführer) Krause* of the *12. SS-Panzer-Division "Hitlerjugend."* They were involved in the street fighting at Eglise St. Gervais and then pulled back to the southern edge of the city at the onset of darkness.

Any type of further coordinated action was ended by the battalion on this day. The commander issued orders to all personnel to try to fight their way through the enemy on their own in the general direction of Vimoutiers.

The two *Tigers* pulled back to Villy by 0230 hours on 17 August 1944 and were resupplied one last time. Orders arrived to cover the northern outskirts of Villy along with three assault guns. A reconnaissance effort by the Canadian Algonquin Battalion was turned back. So was a tank attack around 1630 hours by the Canadian 4th Armoured Brigade from the area north of Damblainville. Liebeskind's *Tiger* was knocked out. Around 1800 hours, an enemy supply column was destroyed.

At 0200 hours on 18 August 1944, *Tiger 241* received orders to pull back to the Chateaux two kilometers south of Fresne-le-Mere and then screen north from there. The 1st Company was to be on the right. When the enemy penetrated into La Hogouettes at noon, the tanks were ordered to move to the railway/road crossing west of Abbaye. *Tiger 124* was towed along towards the northwest outskirts of Abbaye. The tanks defended against an enemy attack around 1700 hours. After darkness had fallen, *Tiger 124* was ordered to be blown up and the remaining tanks ordered to the battalion command post 500 meters east of Vignats. What was left of the battalion was supposed to support the attacks aimed at breaking out of the pocket on 20 and 21 August 1944.

On 19 August 1944, the 2nd Company received the mission of advancing via Vignats to Necy with two drums of fuel in order to link up with the 1st Company, which had run out of fuel. After they were refueled, three *Tigers* withdrew to the northeast. There was enemy contact with forces of the 2nd Monmouthshire Regiment west of Brieux.

In the book, *The Battle of the Falaise Gap,* this engagement is described in detail:

> At about 0600 hours, they could hear the sounds of tanks to the north. Some thought it was Churchills, but the unmistakable rattling [of a Churchill] could not be heard. A few minutes later, three . . . *Tigers* came into view. They were immediately engaged with all available weapons, machine guns and submachine guns, but they moved undamaged through "D" Company and reached the crossing, where "C" Company and the battalion staff were located. The road was blocked by the halftrack of the forward observer.
>
> The lead *Tiger* rammed it and pushed it through the wall of a barn until it had enough room to move past it. Then it attacked the battalion commander's carrier, which had been hastily abandoned . . . in the meantime.
>
> When the path was clear, it moved on to "B" Company. An industrious radio operator had warned the company. One soon heard three loud booms. The battalion staff believed that the *Tigers* had opened fire with their 8.8-centimeter main guns, but the company commander of "B" Company reported a few minutes later that he was sorry to report that one of them had escaped. That was an understatement.
>
> The lead tank had missed the trigger mechanism of the "Hawkins grenades" [antipersonnel mines] that had been placed on the road in the vicinity of the company command post, but the second *Tiger* [that of *SS-Untersturmführer* Schroif] ignited two of them and ran off the side of the road.
>
> The third tank [that of *SS-Unterscharführer* Glagow], which was also moving at high speed like the other two, ran into the tank ahead of him, which had been hit by a PIAT [the British bazooka] in the meantime. The muzzle of his main gun jammed underneath the stowage box of the tank ahead of it. The PIAT round had not penetrated the armor, [however] both crews dismounted as quickly as they could. Those who were not killed were taken prisoner. [Reverse-translated into English from the German text.]

✠

The tank in front, commanded by the commander of the 1st Company (*SS-Obersturmführer* Kalss), was able to break through. Schroif and his loader were able to make their way on foot through to the German lines, even though lightly wounded.

✠

Recently promoted, *SS-Obersturmbannführer* Weiß, the battalion commander, had a worse time of it. His liaison officer, *SS-Untersturmführer* Scholz-Klink, had been captured only recently during a trip to the front. On 19 August 1944, Weiß's small battle staff headed for Vimoutiers in order to assemble the last *Tigers* and lead them within the framework of a *II. SS-Panzer-Korps* counterattack. Weiß was wounded at Trun; one of the wounds to his head was bleeding profusely.

The battalion surgeon, *Dr.* Grünwalder, gave him a shot and intended to have him taken to a clearing facility on a medical *SPW.* Before they could depart, however, an artillery barrage commenced. *Dr.* Grünwalder's arm was torn off and his abdominal wall ripped open. The *SPW* driver applied immediate first aid and then took off. On the way, Dr.

Grünwalder died. His remains were transferred to a clearing facility. The driver, the commander and other soldiers who had joined them attempted to breakthrough. In the process, *SS-Obersturmbannführer* Weiß was shot through the lungs and had a bullet lodged in his pelvis. Unable to move, he was taken prisoner by the English.

✠

Tigers 214 and *222* were employed on the road from Trun to Vimoutiers; one enemy tank was knocked out. There were several air attacks. To the surprise of all, however, dozens of Messerschmitts also attacked ground targets.

One *Tiger* was destroyed by infantry with hand-held antitank weapons during the attack of the South Alberta Regiment against Saint-Lambert-sur-Dive.

While safeguarding the headquarters of the *12. SS-Panzer-Division "Hitlerjugend"* at Necy, three *Tigers* were lost.

On 20 August 1944, several *Tigers* conducted an immediate counterattack from Vimoutiers to Trun. There was enemy contact at Champosoult, and several enemy tanks were knocked out. One *Tiger*, that of Reißke, was abandoned at Vimoutiers, presumably from a blown piston due to a lack of oil, although the tank had frequently been with the maintenance personnel due to dubious mechanical problems. It is still there to this day as a battlefield memorial.

The 21st of August saw several *Tigers* in action at Coudehard and Champosoult. After an engagement with U.S. tanks, Lenz's *Tiger* received a hit in the engine compartment and had to be towed by Kalss's tank. Both tanks then moved to the area west of Aubry-le-Panthous. In the end, they were blown up there due to a lack of fuel. Two towed tanks of the 3rd Company got as far as Le Sap. Two *Tigers*—Rosowsky's tank with a shot-up turret with Streng's tank in tow—were able to get fuel from a column from the *9. SS-Panzer-Division "Hohenstaufen."* They continued to move in the direction of Broglie. The two tanks got to the village of Broglie early in the afternoon of 22 August 1944. The Maintenance Company had moved in the meantime, however.

Other tanks made it through to Rouen. One tank of the 3rd Company was left behind at the edge of Mandeville. It became immobilized after having knocked out three Canadian tanks. Three tanks remained at the former location of the Maintenance Company at Aubry-le-Pantheou.

The towing duo of Rosowsky and Streng reached Brionne on 23 August 1944, after passing a column of vehicles—including medical vehicles—that had been shot-up by fighter-bombers. The commander of the 1st Company, *SS-Obersturmführer* Kalss, was awarded the Knight's Cross that day.

On 24 August 1944, Rosowsky and Streng linked up with the 2nd Company with both of their tanks. Streng's *Tiger* got as far as Elbeuf and had to be blown up there on 25 August 1944. The company commander's tank of the 1st Company was already on a ferry there, but the ferry sank (the crew was not on board).

Elements assembled at Fleury and made their way east towards the rally point of the battalion west of Amiens. *Tiger 223* was abandoned at Tostes.

Tiger 001 sank in the harbor at Rouen during a crossing attempt on 28 August 1944. That same day, a rail transport with three damaged *Tigers* was stopped by the U.S. 486th Anti-Aircraft Artillery Battalion at Braine, when the gunners shot up the locomotive with their 37mm antiaircraft cannon. Later on, Free French forces set the tanks alight.

The battalion was alerted at its rally point near Amiens and assembled for further movement. The road march started on 29 August with wheeled vehicles. It left from the area north of Albert (not far from Bapaume) for Arras, where personnel availed themselves of items from the abandoned supply depots. Moving through Vimy, Lens was reached in the evening.

The majority of the remaining *Tigers* on the Seine had to be blown up (a total of five in all).

On 1 September 1944, the march continued from Roubaix through Ath and Enghien and into the area around Leeuw. It then proceeded through the outer districts of Brussels, past Mechelen and continued to Diest.

A single *Tiger* engaged the lead elements of the 3rd Royal Tank Regiment outside of Seclin and just before the Belgian border. It got as far as Genval, where it was left by its crew after the main gun had been rendered unserviceable by means of explosives.

On 3 September 1944, the remaining crews —all without tanks—moved to Limburg (near Maastricht).

✠

Some of the remaining elements of *schwere Panzer-Abteilung 503* had even farther distances to move to get to the supposed safe harbor of the Seine.

13 August 1944: Elements of the 1st Company —*Tigers 112, 113* and *124*—were at Trun. *Tiger 100* was abandoned in St. Pierre-la-Rivière.

16 August 1944: Several tanks reached Ticheville.

18 August 1944: *Tiger 111* was abandoned in Le Billot; *Tiger 113* in Ommoy; and an unidentified *Tiger II* at the entrance to Vimoutiers.

20 August 1944: *Tigers 112* and *124* were blown up at Orville. Two tanks of the 2nd Company were abandoned in the vicinity of the *Ferme du Bois Belloir* near Montrieul-l'Argillé. *Tiger 213* got as far as Bourgtheroulde.

24 August 1944: Two more *Tigers* were abandoned in Bernay and in the vicinity of Menneval (near the *Chateau Danger*). Three *Tigers*—including *224* and *II*—had to be abandoned at the Caudebec ferry site at Elbeuf.

25 August 1944: *Tiger 222* was able to cross the Seine at Poses. However, it had to be abandoned at Saussay la Champagne (northeast of Les Andelys).

28 August 1944: The tankless crews moved from Pontoise to Germany for the battalion to be reconstituted.

30 August 1944: *Tiger 324* was destroyed and then abandoned between Goincourt and Aux Marais (west of Beauvais).

One *Tiger II* of the 1st Company also made it out of the Normandy area on rail transport. It traveled via Orleans to as far as the area of Gien. In 1947, it was transported to Sweden, where it was then tested. It was later used for firing experiments, before it was unfortunately sold for scrap sometime in the 1970's.

✠

These sketches demonstrate that individual tanks were still involved in combat activities; some even contributed significantly to the fighting to break out of the encirclement east of Falaise. Also characteristic is the unshakeable determination of the crews not to abandon their tanks, if at all possible. It represented not only a means to fight but also a means of transportation. It allowed them to escape from the possibility of being captured.

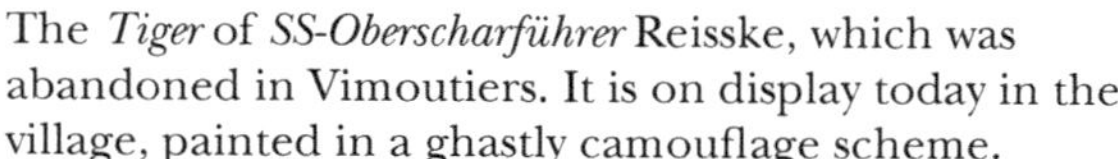

The *Tiger* of *SS-Oberscharführer* Reisske, which was abandoned in Vimoutiers. It is on display today in the village, painted in a ghastly camouflage scheme.

What remained of the *Tiger* destroyed in Saint-Lambert-sur-Dive.

One of the *Tigers* abandoned at the maintenance facility in Aubrey-le-Pantheou.

Below and the next page: Most of the *Tigers* attempted to make their way back to the Seine individually. Most had to be abandoned due to a lack of fuel or mechanical problems.

One of the *Tigers* that was left behind at Montormel.

The precise location of this *Tiger* is unknown.

The train that was stopped at Braine with the three damaged *Tigers* can be seen on this page and the next.

Tiger 223, abandoned at Tostes, is seen in this image and the next. (NAC)

One of the *Tigers* of the battalion making its way through Enghien. (de Meyer)

This *Tiger II* was moved to a maintenance facility at Tron, where it is awaiting evaluation.

Tiger 100 was abandoned in St. Pierre-la-Rivière. (Bovington Tank Museum)

One of the two *Tigers* of the 2nd Company abandoned at the Ferme du Bois Belloir (near Montrieul-l'Argillé).

Tiger 111, seen on this page and the next, was abandoned at Le Billot. (NAC)

Tiger 113 was abandoned in Ommoy after it had track problems on the right side. A piece of track can be seen on the front slope. Apparently, the crew attempted to repair the damaged track. The mounted tow hooks also indicate an effort to tow the vehicle. Prior to leaving the vehicle, the front part of the main gun was blown up.

There is a series of photographs of the *Tiger II* that was left outside of Vimoutiers, still attached to its tow vehicle, a *Bergepanther*. Vehicles from the Canadian Regiment Maisonneuve move past the two German vehicles on this and the next two pages. (NAC)

13

The *Tiger* abandoned at Bernay. (Wirton)

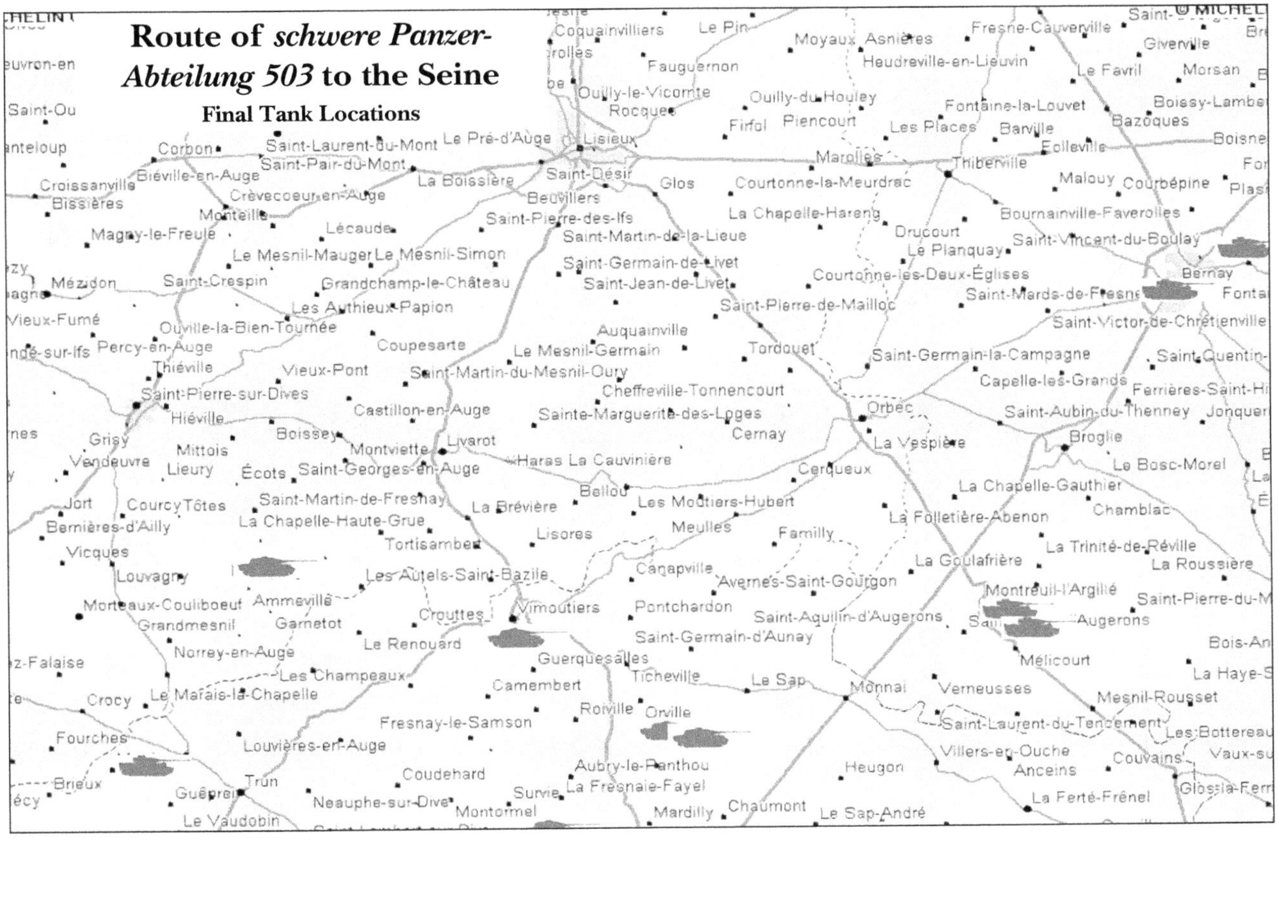

Route of *schwere Panzer-Abteilung 503* to the Seine

Final Tank Locations

Tiger 222 was abandoned at Saussay la Champagne. It appears that a demolition charge was placed above the third roadwheel.

A former tank of the 3rd Company—*Tiger 324*—was redesignated as *121*. It made it the farthest to the east, being lost just beyond Goincourt outside of Beauvais on 30 August 1944. (GEMOB).

One *Tiger II* of the battalion was discovered in the village of Gien. Apparently, it was a disabled tank that was supposed to have been transported there by rail. The "combat" tracks have been reinstalled, but the track guards were not.

The tank was transported to Sweden by ship, arriving in Stockholm on 27 November 1947. The tank was later transported to the Swedish armor school at Skövde and underwent extensive tests. During the trials, an unexploded hand grenade was found in the tank's interior.

Especially noticeable on this particular tank were the large noise dampeners that had been welded on the exhaust stacks in France. The round opening at the bottom of the rear hull is for insertion of the hand starter, which enabled the tank to be started whenever battery power was not strong enough. (SPHF)

Tiger 03, along with the five *Tiger II's* of *schwere Panzer-Kompanie (Fkl) 316*, was assigned to *Panzer-Lehr-Regiment 130* of the *Panzer-Lehr-Division*, which was originally earmarked to receive an entire battalion of *Tigers*. This tank was found in Nogent-le-Rotrou; no other details are known.

A "hybrid" is seen here in this *Tiger* that was discovered near Semousy (between Avesnes-sur-Elpes and Beaumont in Belgium). It has a new hull with steel-rimmed roadwheels, but an older turret with a submachine-gun opening on the left rear. This unusual combination is indicative of a *Tiger* that came from depot-level repair. Three of those "used" *Tigers* were also issued to *Panzer-Lehr-Regiment 130*.

After leaving behind its remaining *Tiger I's*, the 3rd Company was transported to Camp Mailly right after Operation "Goodwood," where it received fourteen new *Tiger II's*. The company then had a few days to get ready before moving back to the front.

Compared to operations around Caen, the time spent at the training area was a time of pure relaxation for the tankers. They were able to do things that they had only dreamed of for a long time. Apparently, there was no danger of being attacked from the air there.

Since the tanks were delivered in *goldoliv* (gold-olive) color, the crews had the obligation of applying camouflage to them. To that end, air guns were connected to the tire air compressor on a truck (in the background).

With the exception of the company command group and one other tank, the remaining eleven *Tiger II's* of the company were all equipped with the Porsche turret. *Tiger II's 300* (below) and *301* had the mass-produced Henschel (series) turrets.

Especially important in the case of new tanks is the justification and calibration of the new main gun and machine guns. To that end, the tanks fired at calibration targets at precisely 500 and 1,000 meters. Depending on the fall of the rounds, the gun sight optics were adjusted to bring the rounds closer to the center of mass of the target.

Gunnery training with the main gun and machine guns was also part of the program.

Towards the end of the stay at Camp Mailly, a live-fire exercise was conducted for war correspondents. Two of the tanks broke down and had to be left behind when the company moved out.

The tanks are still factory fresh and have no scrapes or dings. On 11 August 1944, the companies were loaded on trains and sent to Paris.

The crews still seem relaxed; even the air guard does not appear to take his duties too seriously.

One of the rail transports was attacked by fighter-bombers outside of Esternay on 12 August 1944. *Tiger 311* was knocked off its rail car, landing on its turret. Although it was later turned upright, it fell into the hands of the advancing Americans.

For propaganda purposes, the company marched down the Champs d'Elysées in Paris. One crewmember took a series of photographs form his tank. On the previous page, the company is on the Boulevard de la Chapelle on its way to the Saint-Lazare train station.

After detraining, the company seemed to march somewhat aimlessly through Paris. With the Allies approaching, it was an effective propaganda move. Initially, it was unclear what mission the company would receive.

The column along the Porte Vilette. The column stops on the Rue de la Chapelle. Since Paris was spared Allied aerial attack, the Germans were able to move about freely without fear of being attacked.

Hauptmann Scherf, the company commander, and his company spent several idle days in Paris.

The crews hid their tanks in Parisian parks and waited for a mission.

The company spent considerable time in the Bois de Vincennes.

300

ATTACKS AGAINST THE SEINE BRIDGEHEAD

The reconstituted *3./schwere Panzer-Abteilung 503* and the *1./schwere SS-Panzer-Abteilung 101* attempted to reduce the American bridgehead across the Seine at Mantes for about a week (22–29 August 1944). These engagements are not a part of the "Normandy" area of operations, of course, but they are closely related to it. For this reason, we will review them briefly.

✠

The *1./schwere SS-Panzer-Abteilung 101* had turned over its last three *Tiger I's* to the battalion's 3rd Company on 4 July 1944. The 1st Company arrived in Paderborn on 9 July 1944 and started its training on the *Tiger II.* From 12 to 19 July 1944, the tank commanders and drivers were trained at the Henschel factory in Kassel. From 28 July to 1 August 1944, fourteen *Tiger II's* were accepted by the company at Camp Senne. The company was loaded on trains at Camp Senne on 5 August 1944 started to head west.

It was not until 18 August 1944 that the company detrained thirty kilometers northeast of Paris. The Normandy front had collapsed, and the Falaise Pocket was starting to form. The original employment for which the company was intended was overcome by events.

On 23 August 1944, the company received the mission of moving to the area south of Magny-en-Vexin in order to be employed against the US bridgeheads over the Seine. On the way there, seven tanks fell out due to mechanical problems. There were several air attacks against the company in the area of St. Souplettes on 25 August 1944, with the company suffering several soldiers killed and wounded. The remaining tanks reached Arthies and bivouacked there.

On 26 August 1944, the company moved forward to Drocourt and then supported the counterattack of the *18. Luftwaffen-Feld-Division* west of Sielly against the U.S. 79th Infantry Division at Limay. The *3./schwere Panzer-Abteilung 503* was employed farther to the southeast.

✠

The *3./schwere Panzer-Abteilung 503* had been moved to the French Training Area of Mailly le Camp at the end of July. On 31 July 1944, fourteen *Tiger II's* arrived. Starting on 11 August 1944, the company was loaded on trains; two of the tanks that had mechanical problems during a demonstration for a propaganda company were left behind.

The company's train was attacked by fighter-bombers between Sezanne and Esternay on 12 August 1944. In attempting to conduct an emergency detraining, *Leutnant Freiherr* von Rosen's tank—*Tiger 311*—came off the rail car and flipped onto its turret. Although it was later righted, it fell into U.S. hands on 13 August 1944.

The company was detrained a few days later in Paris. In accordance with directives received from the local area commander, the company bivouacked in the Bois de Vincennes and was "forgotten" there.

On 21 August 1944, *Hauptmann* Scherf, on his own initiative, decided to move the company to the right bank of the Seine. It marched along the Boulevard de la Chapelle to the St. Lazare train station. From there, it proceeded along the Madeleine to the Place de la Concorde. (*Tiger 334* was left behind at the Porte Maillot, where it suffered transmission problems. A few days later, it had to be blown up.) The company then marched along the Champs Elysées, the Place de l'Etoile, Maillot and to the Pont de Neuilly, where it crossed to the righthand side of the Seine in the direction of Pontoise.

Another tank remained behind at Thermicourt. *Hauptmann* Scherf tried to contact the battalion and went ahead to the command post of *Gruppe*

Schwerin at Magny-en-Vexin in order to get oriented on the overall situation. (*Gruppe Schwerin* had been formed on 20 August 1944 to combat the American bridgeheads over the Seine.)

The company was immediately "impressed into service" and directed to support the *18. Luftwaffen-Feld-Division.* The march column was turned around and reached a bivouac site at Gaillonet (east of Oinville) late in the evening. The company had its own supply elements and was therefore self-sufficient for operations for a few days. The company was directed to bring *Luftwaffen-Jäger-Regiment 35* forward across the wooded and barely accessible Bois des Blancs Soleils Hill in the direction of Limay. Following that, it was intended for the company to support the attack of *Luftwaffen-Jäger-Regiment 36* at Fontenay.

On 22 August 1944, the terrain between Fontenay, Guitrancourt and Garganville was reconnoitered by *Luftwaffen-Jäger-Regiment 33* and *Luftwaffen-Jäger-Regiment 36.* That same evening, around 2040 hours, the first battalion-size attack was supported by five *Tigers* against the U.S. 314th Infantry at Fontenay. The attack was turned back.

Starting at 0700 hours on 23 August 1944, *Luftwaffen-Jäger-Regiment 33* attacked across the Bois des Blancs Soleils Hill in the direction of Limay. Two platoons of *Tigers* supported this effort by moving on both sides of the light infantry. The platoon attacking on the right reached the Melier Estate, where it received heavy defensive fire from American tank destroyers that had a magnificent position on the rise at Les Rues.

The four tanks of the lefthand platoon reached the Bois des Blancs Soleils Hill, where they knocked out an M10 tank destroyer. They then went into position along the southern edge of the wood line, where they received heavy defensive fire from tank destroyers posted along the outskirts of Limay. The Americans were pushed back to Limay.

At the same time, the *I./Luftwaffen-Jäger-Regiment 33* attacked from Guitrancourt through the Vallée aux Cailloux in the direction of the RN 190. It was supported by one *Tiger.* Once there, it swung to the west and reached the eastern outskirts of Limay after knocking out an M4.

In the meantime, all of the available U.S. artillery was firing at the *Tigers* in their positions on the hill and damaged almost all of them. Around noon, the righthand platoon received the mission of supporting the attack of *Luftwaffen-Jäger-Regiment 36* at Fontenay. Around 1610 hours, the remaining *Tigers* were withdrawn. As if by miracle, the company did not suffer a single wounded soldier. All of the attacks described above were also greeted with massed fighter-bomber attacks.

On 24 August 1944, the operational *Tigers* screened at Guitrancourt and Fontenay. All of the forces in position were again subjected to continuous fighter-bomber attacks. The company finally established contact with the battalion; superfluous crews were sent there.

The company continued to screen on 25 August 1944 at Guitrancourt and Fontenay. In the meantime, the *1./schwere SS-Panzer-Abteilung 101* also arrived.

On 26 August 1944, both of the *Tiger* companies —a total of fifteen tanks—attacked together through the woods at Montgison towards Fontenay. The *Tigers* of the *3./schwere Panzer-Abteilung 503* formed the left-hand group and attacked the Le Moucel section of Fontenay at the water tower. Around 1625 hours, fighter-bombers attacked this group. The *Tiger* of *Feldwebel* Weiland was damaged; while dismounting, the tank commander was mortally wounded by a burst from a submachine gun. It was later possible to evacuate the tank.

Tiger 332 of *Unteroffizier* Schmidt was lost at the water tower; *Tiger 112* of the *1./schwere SS-Panzer-Abteilung 101*, which came to its aid, was not able to recover the tank. Snipers constantly took the crews under fire, so it became impossible to attach the tow cables.

Tiger 301 of *Feldwebel* Neeb received five direct hits, of which none penetrated. After darkness had fallen, the attack was called off and the immobilized tanks were recovered. The Army company bivouacked in Gaillonat.

The *Tigers* of the *1./schwere SS-Panzer-Abteilung 101* moved out as the right-hand group via Montgison in the direction of Fontenay St. Pere. The attack was conducted together with two battalions of *Luftwaffe* field soldiers. The attack proceeded across the Maison Blanche crossing near the Du Mesnil castle, where it turned left. It also moved along the road from Montgison to Fontenay St. Pere.

The tanks had to pull back, because the friendly infantry suffered heavy casualties. There was another attack in the evening. The *Tiger* of *SS-Untersturmführer* Stamm was hit by an antitank gun and set alight as it moved on the D 193 in the direction of Maison Blanche. It was hit in the flank as it crossed the roadside ditch; the tank commander was killed.

A Sherman was knocked out at the Bois Clair. Farther to the northeast, *Tiger 124* of *SS-Oberscharführer* Zahner, which was bringing up the rear of the column along the Sailly–Fontenay road, was attacked by fighter-bombers. After two near misses by bombs, it crashed into a roadside ditch and landed on its righthand side.

✠

From alternating positions on 28 August 1944, the operational tanks supported the forces in position. Starting at 0145 hours, artillery fire was already pouring down on the German positions. When it dawned, the fighter-bombers joined in and fired at everything that moved. There were signs that the American offensive to break out of the bridgehead was starting. The operational tanks of the *3./schwere Panzer-Abteilung 503* were in ready positions at Sailly.

At 1600 hours, the entire front exploded. Concealed by artificial smoke, the Americans stormed the German positions. American bombers attacked at 1700 ours. The attacking Americans suffered heavy casualties, and it was only at Guitrancourt that they made progress towards evening. Two *Tigers* were badly damaged by the continuous artillery fire. The *Tigers* resupplied in Sailly during the night.

✠

The defensive positions were reoccupied during the morning of 28 August 1944. The Americans continued their attacks in the morning. A counterattack in the direction of Montgison was launched; the lead *Tiger* was a total loss after it received several hits. *Tiger 123* of *SS-Hauptscharführer* Hibbeler was separated from its company and joined up with the *3./schwere Panzer-Abteilung 503*. It received two hits at Sailly. Together with *Tiger 301* of the *3./schwere Panzer-Abteilung 503*, it was set alight and had to be abandoned. (*Tiger 123* is presently in the French armor museum at Saumur, where it can move under its own power.)

In the meantime, *Hauptmann* Scherf in *Tiger 300* and three other *Tigers* were employed in the area between Fontenay and Sailly. The tanks had to pull back through the woods under heavy enemy pressure, where they finally got to the main road. *Tiger 300* fell out due to running gear problems at the entrance to Oinville. Probably as a result of knocking down numerous trees, the final drive on the lefthand side got blocked and broke the track. The tank was destroyed in the face of the advancing enemy.

On 28 August 1944, the remaining operational tanks of the *1./schwere SS-Panzer-Abteilung 101* under *SS-Hauptsturmführer* Möbius were counterattacking west of Magny-en-Vexin with the *18. Luftwaffen-Feld-Division.* An enemy antitank-gun belt that was not recognized in time fired into the right flank of the tanks, and several *Tiger II's* were immobilized. Because two of the tanks could not be recovered, they were blown up.

Tiger 104 of *SS-Oberscharführer* Franzl received slight damage to its running gear west of Magny-en-Vexin after engaging in a firefight with Shermans. From a beet field, the tank engaged enemy in a farmhouse. When it started to pull back, it took a curve too sharply and the final drive broke. The tank was destroyed by its crew. While dismounting, the crew was engaged by French partisans and two of the crew killed. Sergeant Roberts of "A" Squadron of the 23rd Hussars engaged the abandoned tank after the fact and report the "kill." The tank currently resides at Shrivenham in Great Britain.

In the sector of the *3./schwere Panzer-Abteilung 503, Leutnant* Rambow was involved in defensive fighting with three tanks along the road from Vigny towards Gadancourt around 1800 hours. One of the tanks was hit so badly outside of Avernes that it had to be abandoned.

The company's logistics elements were located in the park of the castle at Marines. The tank of *Feldwebel* Müller had to be blown up there, because it could no longer be repaired. The same fate was shared by a tank near the village of Santieuil, which had broken down during the march.

Three *Tigers* that only had limited amounts of fuel and ammunition supported a counterattack of *Fallschirmjäger-Bataillon Reiter* at Gadancourt around 2030 hours. There they engaged Shermans of the U.S. 743rd Tank Battalion. Following this, they fell back to the Bois de L'Aunaie when they started to be engaged from the air. When a bomb detonated next to a tank, the crew left the tank and set it on fire. The two remaining *Tigers* broke down during the march between Marines and Auneuil and had to be abandoned the following morning.

✠

Two *Tigers* of the *1./schwere SS-Panzer-Abteilung 101* under *SS-Oberscharführer* Brandt were in action along the D 981 in the direction of Gisors on 30 August 1944. They knocked out three enemy tanks and prevented the *Kampfgruppe* from being outflanked. After Gisors was lost, the tanks pulled back to Trie-Chateau. *Tiger II 111* was knocked out by several British Shermans outside of Beauvais near Goincourt. *Tiger 324*—one of the few *Tiger I's* to make it over the Seine—was also knocked out in the vicinity.

The right track on a *Tiger II* of the *3./schwere Panzer-Abteilung 503* broke in Beauvais in front of the courthouse on the *Rue Antoine Caron.* The crew was working frantically to repair the damage, when the first tanks of the 4th/7th Dragoons penetrated into the town. A few minutes later, the tank was knocked out by a Firefly.

Several *Tigers* of the *1./schwere SS-Panzer-Abteilung 101* were employed at Lamecourt on 31 August 1944.

During the evening of 2 September 1944, *Tiger 113* was abandoned at Jemappes on the *Avenue Foch.*

Two *Tiger II's* knocked out several U.S. tanks at Brunehamel, some seven kilometers northeast of Rozoy. The remaining U.S. tanks pulled back.

SS-Hauptsturmführer Möbius succeeded in getting to the Meuse at Huy on 4 September 1944 with two *Tiger II's.* They had to be left behind there.

Tiger 121 of *SS-Oberscharführer* Zahner was stranded without fuel on the embankment at La Capelle on 5 September 1944. The crew damaged the main gun, placed charges in the engine compartment and abandoned the tank. U.S. Army forces pushed the obstacle off to the side of the road, where the tank flipped over. The tank is now located in the Armor Museum at Münster (Germany.)

Only one *Tiger II* succeeded in getting back. *SS-Unterscharführer* Salomon's tank was later loaded on a train at Siegburg and sent to the *SS* tank replacement battalion at Augustdorf. Two *Tiger II's* of the *3./schwere Panzer-Abteilung 503* were able to be evacuated to Reims thanks to the initiative of *Leutnant Freiherr* von Rosen. The *Tiger* of *Leutnant* Rambow got as far as Amiens, where it had to be abandoned due to a lack of fuel.

The reconstituted company's first loss: *Tiger 322* at the Fontenay water tower. Heavy enemy fire prevented its recovery.

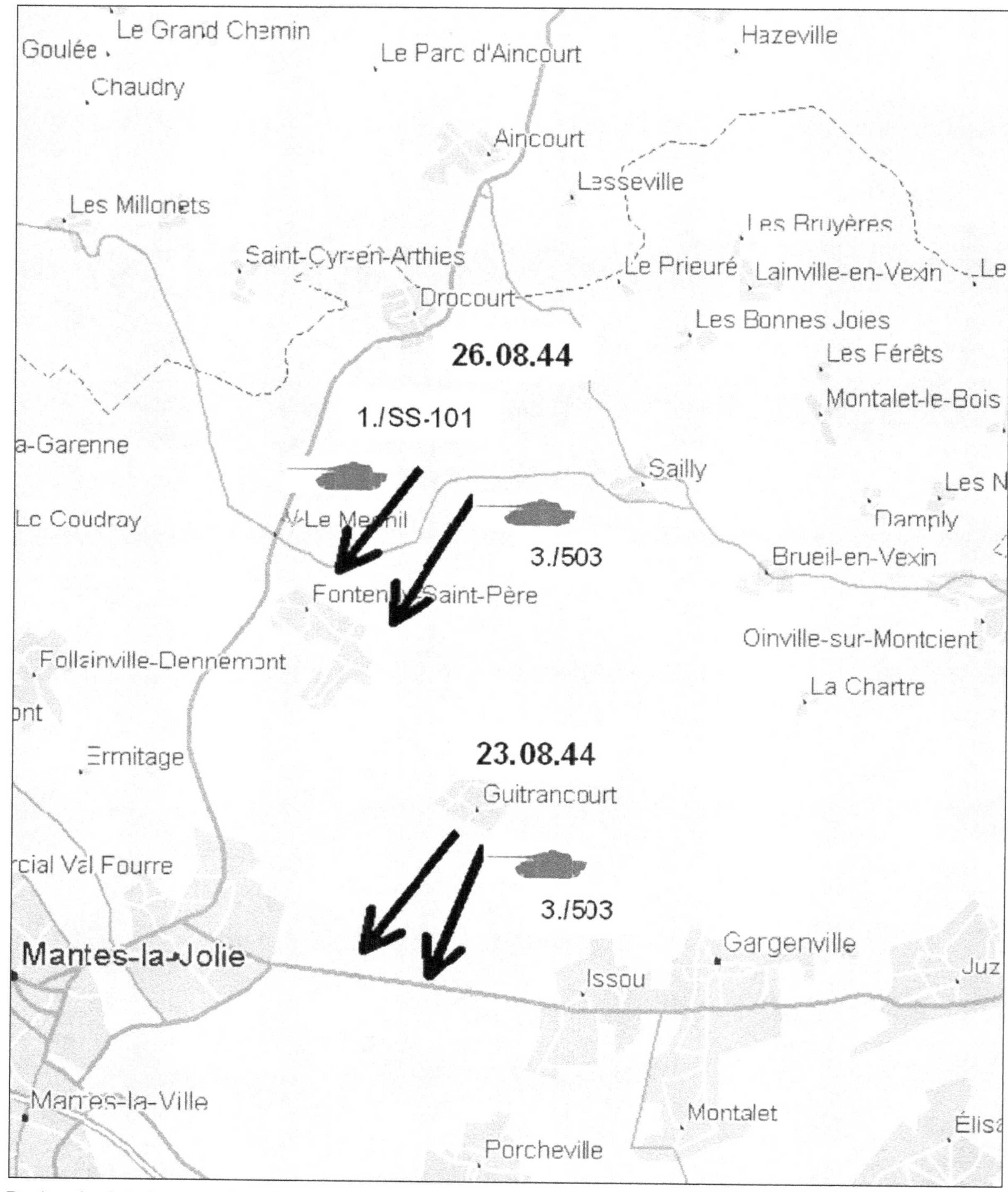

During the failed attempt by German forces to reduce the American bridgehead over the Seine at Mantes, there was the rare occurrence of two *Königstiger* companies being employed at the same time. From *schwere Panzer-Abteilung 503*, it was the reconstituted 3rd Company; from *schwere SS-Panzer-Abteilung 101*, it was the reformed 1st Company.

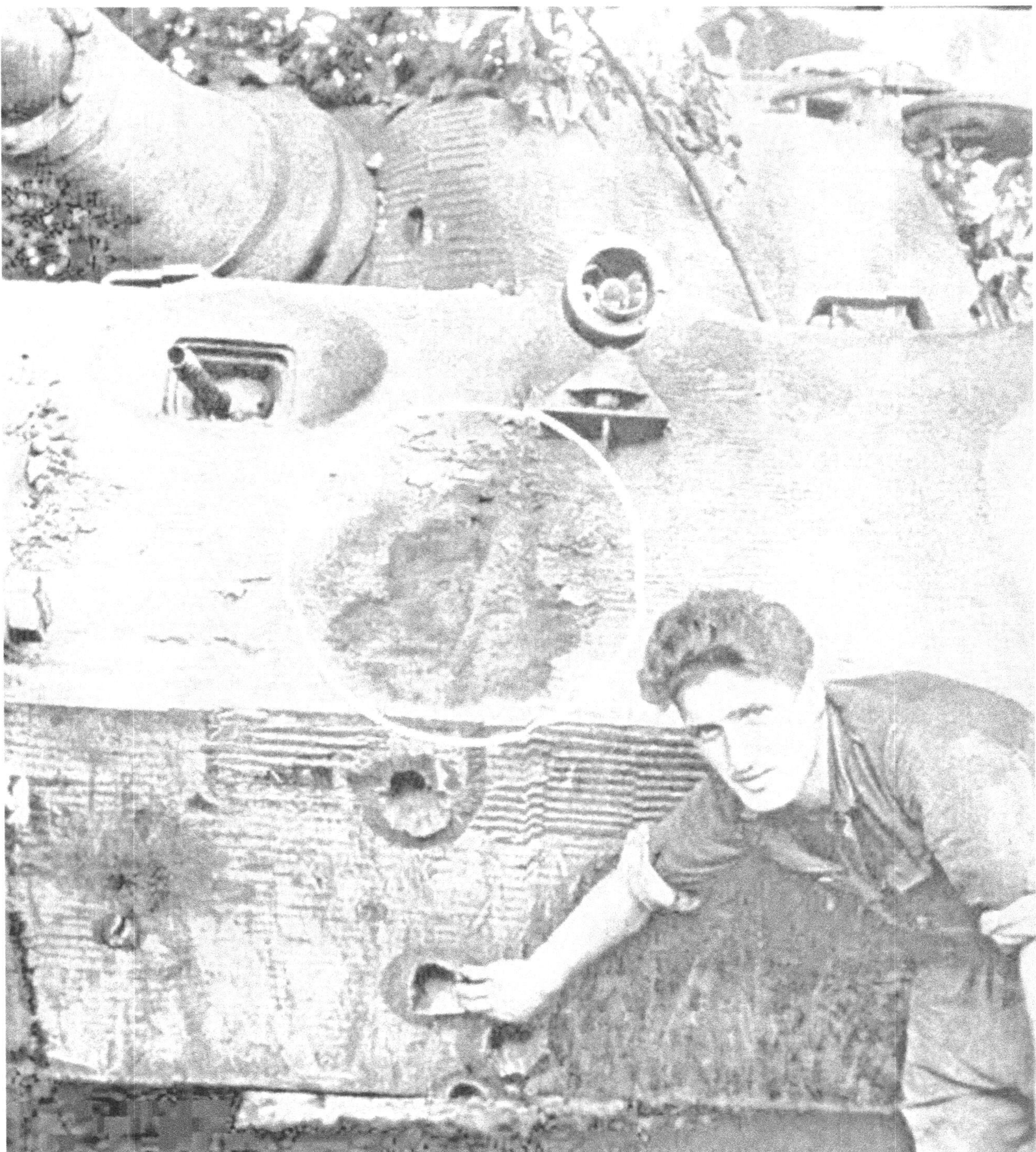

Gefreiter Jung, the driver on *Tiger 301*, points out the hits his tank suffered during the attack on the American bridgehead. None were sufficient to penetrate the thick frontal armor of the hull. This photograph was taken while the company was in its assembly area near Sailly after the fighting.

The three photographs on these two pages show *SS-Untersturmführer* Stamm's *Tiger,* which was knocked out by an antitank gun on the D 913 near Maison Blanche. The hit to the flank set the vehicle on fire.

Tiger 124 was knocked into a roadside ditch during a fighter-bomber attack and remained on its side. Remnants of this tank were found by the French amateur historian, Bruno Renoult, in 2001.

Tiger 123, which got separated from the *1./schwere SS-Panzer-Abteilung 101*, and temporarily joined *schwere Panzer-Abteilung 503*, had to be abandoned after receiving two hits at Sailly. The same fate befell *Tiger 301* of the Army battalion (right page).

Tiger 300, the command tank of *Hauptmann* Scherf, at the entrance to the village of Oinville. Hoping to be recovered, the crew mounted tow cables.

104

SS-Oberscharführer Franzis's *Tiger 104* had to be left behind west of Magny-en-Vexin after developing running-gear problems. It was recovered by the British. Today, it is on display at the Royal College of Military Science at Shrivenham (Chassis number 280093).

These poor-quality images date from a periodical published in 1947 and show *Tiger 104* being loaded on a seventy-ton trailer of the Royal Engineers.

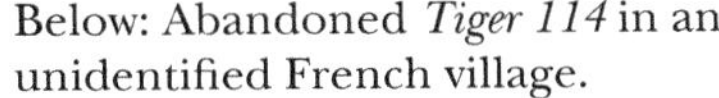

Below: Abandoned *Tiger 114* in an unidentified French village.

Feldwebel Müller's non-operational *Tiger* had to be abandoned by logistical elements on the palace grounds at Marines. It was one of the few tanks in the company to be equipped with the Henschel-production turret.

The tank on this pages and the previous is *Tiger 111*, which was knocked out by several Shermans near Goincourt.

This tank from the 3rd Company of *schwere Panzer-Abteilung 503* was knocked out by a Sherman Firefly shortly after it had lost its track in front of the court building on the Rue Antoin Caron in Beauvais and was immobilized. The main gun was apparently blown out of the turret by the force of the hit. (GEMOB)

Tiger 113 moves through Beauvais, but it had to be abandoned by its crew on 2 September 1944 in Jemappes when it ran out of fuel.

Later on, the righthand track was cut—it may have been frozen in place—to facilitate the removal of the tank from the road, which was blocking traffic. In the end, the main gun barrel was also cut off.

Leutnant Rambow's *Tiger* was also stranded for a lack of fuel, in this case at Saint-Pol-en-Ternoise, north of Amiens. The crew had optimistically traversed the turret to one side to allow faster access to the fuel tanks. Apparently, no more fuel could be found.

These two images also show Rambow's tank. The tanks were often left abandoned and in place for long periods of time. With ammunition and, potentially, weapons on board, they were not the ideal playground for children.

Despite their terrible quality, these photographs are of interest because they show the recovery of *Tiger 121* of the *1./schwere SS-Panzer-Abteilung 101*, which was abandoned without fuel on 5 September 1944 at La Chapelle. Since it was blocking the road, it was pushed aside, rolling down the roadside embankment and landing on its turret. The crew had placed demolition charges in both the main gun (front portion blown off) and in the hull. Later on, the tank was turned over to the U.S. Army. Today, this tank is on display at the German armor museum at Munster. These photographs were also taken from a Royal Engineer publication (1946).

The terrain in Normandy is marked by innumerable hedges and clumps of vegetation, which only rarely allowed extensive fields of vision. Consequently, well-camouflaged close-in weapons, such as the antitank gun in the lower photograph, had a distinct advantage.

CHAPTER 12

Overall Conclusions

In the fighting around the greater area of Caen there were a total of 134 *Tigers* employed—12 of them being the *Tiger II.* They were hardly ever employed in a strength greater than that of two platoons, however. The single largest cohesive operation took place on 11 July 1944 with the 21 tanks of *schwere SS-Panzer-Abteilung 102* on both sides of Hill 112. These were joined by several vehicles of *schwere SS-Panzer-Abteilung 101.* The *Tigers* were predominately employed in the smallest of groups. To a certain extent, they represented stationary antitank-gun positions as a backstop for the forces in position or led immediate counterattacks at the local level to stabilize situations. A classical employment of armor was impossible due to the difficult terrain—diminished fields of view caused by countless folds in the ground and hedgerows—as well as the oppressive air supremacy of the Allies.

It was not possible to pull forces out of the line and regroup them for an attack at the formation level—as has been shown—due to the rapid succession of British offensives. Only the newly arrived *II. SS-Panzer-Korps* was able to accomplish this. This happened on 29 June 1944 just north of the Odon with a larger-scale counterattack southeast of Rauray, where it was able to stabilize a critical situation in conjunction with several *Tigers* of *schwere SS-Panzer-Abteilung 101.*

By the middle of August 1944, the *Tigers* were credited with knocking out more than 500 tanks. It is generally known, however, that the Allies could replace those losses within the span of several days, in contrast to the Germans. For example, German tank losses up to 23 July 1944 numbered 406. Added to this were 75 assault guns. Of those losses, only 17 were replaced by new vehicles. In the same period of time, the Allies lost some 2,395 tanks. The majority of these losses were caused by hand-held antitank weapons as well as *PaK* and *Flak.*

Wherever the *Tigers* went into action, they usually brought the Germans some stability for a limited period of time. Because the operational count of the battalions was usually very low—see the table in the appendices—they could exert no lasting effect at the operational level. When they were only employed individually towards the end of the breakout fighting, their success was limited. The question asked at the beginning—what contribution the *Tiger* made to the weeks-long defensive fighting in Normandy—can be answered as follows:

They contributed significantly to the fact that the July offensives of the British on both sides of Caen ended disastrously with heavy casualties, even though terrain was gained. The exhaustive, bloody fighting was otherwise borne on the shoulders of the infantry, since the terrain dictated the terms of employment. This was true for both sides.

The *Tiger* tank itself was generally vastly superior to its opponents in tank-on-tank engagements. It also proved to be quite capable of standing up to artillery fire and weapons employed on fighter-bombers. The table listing the reasons for vehicular losses proves this. Only the British Sherman armed with the 17-pounder main gun—the "Firefly"—which was firing a sub-caliber kinetic-energy round, was dangerous to the *Tiger*. This was demonstrated during the last engagement of *SS-Hauptsturmführer* Wittmann on 8 August 1944.

The German evaluations of the Allies were mixed. The British infantry and artillery enjoyed universal respect. That was less so the case when it came to British armored forces. Probably as a result of their own inferiority in terms of materiel, they operated cautiously and, almost without exception, in support of their heavily burdened infantry. There were just too few of the capable Firefly tanks available. The majority of the British antitank guns were also basically ineffective against the *Tiger*. The Canadian also enjoyed a solid reputation among the Germans, the Polish contingent less so. The *Tiger* battalions did not engage U.S. forces until the fighting for the Seine bridgeheads. In tank-on-tank engagements, the *Tiger* crews had little to worry about, but the Germans had enormous respect of the sheer materiel superiority the Americans enjoyed.

There were amazingly few losses caused by aerial attack. This stands in stark contrast to the dubious "kill lists" compiled by Allied fighter-bomber wings.

The *Tiger* crews often employed a simple trick whenever they were attacked by fighter-bombers: They set off smoke pots and grenades to simulate a vehicle on fire. Out of the forty-five tanks in each battalion, the following were confirmed losses from aerial attacks: eight by *schwere Panzer-Abteilung 503*; three by *schwere SS-Panzer-Abteilung 101*; and two by *schwere SS-Panzer-Abteilung 102*. The fighter-bomber personnel claimed they destroyed enemy vehicles every other mission. An actual analysis of loses on the ground tells a different story. For instance, of the 133 tanks destroyed in the Falaise Pocket, only 33 were knocked out from the air. Of the 82 armored vehicles knocked out around Chambois—the so-called "Shambles Area"—only two had been hit by aerial rockets (none *Tigers*). Along the Seine—the "Chase" Area—not a single one of the 98 destroyed armored vehicles was destroyed from the air.

The logistics and maintenance services played a decisive role in the successful fighting of the *Tiger* battalions. This has been emphasized over and over again in many conversations with tank crewmembers. In many cases, the German tanks had to conduct long road marches, which placed a lot of wear and tear on the vehicles even before they entered combat. The tables showing the operational readiness of the battalions indicate that there were rarely more than half a dozen vehicles in each battalion operational, even though the maintenance companies worked around the clock.

Less successful were the twelve *Tiger II's* of *schwere Panzer-Abteilung 503*. They suffered a number of "teething problems" and were a nightmare for logistics personnel (different main-gun ammunition, different replacement parts).

With regard to logistics, the Germans suffered from a continuous shortage of repair and replacement parts and a lack of fuel. Occasionally, no operations were conducted because the fuel tanks were practically empty.

Divorced from the actual theme of this book, I would like to briefly address the question that often surfaces: How did it come about that the Allies, who enjoyed massive numerical superiority starting from about the middle of July 1944, needed so much time to bring about the decisive breakthrough?

The superiority of the Allies—in absolute numbers—was a given, but they were not without their worries, especially the British. Great Britain had stopped universal conscription between the two world wars and, as a consequence, did not have a large number of reservists. The number of formations that needed to be activated starting in 1939—including those for overseas obligations—was immense. In addition, there were not inconsiderable casualties in France in 1940 and in North Africa starting in 1941. As a result, no British formations were ever completely full through the very end of the war. This also applied to a certain extent to the Canadians.

The situation was always especially critical with regard to infantry, since their training takes considerably more time than, for instance, the artillery or logistics personnel. The heavy personnel losses in dead and wounded in June 1944 resulted in formations being replaced only partially with completely trained personnel. This fact was driven home to Montgomery on numerous occasions, including once by Winston Churchill himself.

As a result, the preparedness of the British to allow themselves to be engaged in a do-or-die fashion in casualty-intensive fighting was limited. In the final analysis, this was understandably also not considered necessary in the face of their own superiority on land and in the air. The issues involving the infantry had as a consequence that British armored formations were almost always without exception employed to directly support the infantry, usually in company-size elements.

At best, the British armored forces only had opportunity in North Africa to gather experience in the execution of wide-ranging, independent operations at the large-formation level. There were few aggressive armor commanders in the style of the Germans among their ranks.

Another aspect that bears examination is the quality of the major items of equipment. The post-war literature universally and constantly laments the fact that a nation of engineers such as the United Kingdom was incapable of constructing combat-effective tanks. In contrast to their artillery, which was also considered to be very effective by the Germans, the Cromwells and the Churchills that were developed were only moderately armored, underpowered and only lightly armed. In direct tank-versus-tank engagements against German counterparts, they were considerably inferior to some extent. Due to a lack of sufficient numbers of their own designs, approximately half of the British armored formations were equipped with the American Sherman tank. Although the American tank was less prone to mechanical failure, it was also inadequate in terms of combat power. Of course, this had a lasting psychological effect on the crews and put a brake on any type of boldness.

Finally, the terrain was decisive in Normandy. It was anything but "tank country." It only permitted wide-ranging operations in isolated instances and, as a result, especially favored the defender.

Despite this, starting in British publications in the 1970's and later, there were also very critical positions taken on leadership performance at the operational level. It is not without justification when it is claimed that a decision on the ground could have been forced earlier with a bit more decisiveness on the part of the leaders. In the long run, it is actually more likely that larger numbers of casualties were taken as a result of the long duration of the battles of attrition. The suffering and the death within the bravely fighting German formations also lasted longer as a result.

Only the Sherman "Firefly," armed with a 17-pounder main gun, was capable of taking on the *Tiger* on equal terms. But there was only one "Firefly" in each platoon of four Shermans. The typical employment of tanks in Normandy is seen below, where a Churchill provides firepower and moral support to the slowly advancing infantry.

Largely ineffective against the *Tiger* was the British handheld antitank weapon, the PIAT. It consisted of a small-caliber hollow-shaped charge that was propelled against its target by means of a powerful spring. It often missed its target, and the charge was not very reliable.

British tanks were markedly inferior to the *Tiger*. Efforts to provide additional protection by means of expedient measures were largely moral in nature. On the other hand, the British artillery was demonstrably effective. It hit its targets reliably and reacted quickly.

APPENDIX 1

British Forces Orders of Battle

Operation "Epsom"

VIII Corps

- 15th Scottish Infantry Division (reinforced with the 31st Tank Brigade)
- 43rd Wessex Infantry Division
- 11th Armoured Division (reinforced with the 4th Armoured Brigade)
- Corps Troops
  - 91st Anti-Tank Regiment Royal Artillery
  - 121st Anti-Aircraft Regiment Royal Artillery

21st Army Group Forces:

- 8th Army Group Royal Artillery
- 141st Regimental RAC (Crocodile flamethrower tanks of the 79th Armoured Division)

XXX Corps

- 49th West Riding Infantry Division
- 8th Armoured Division

Operation "Jupiter"

43rd Wessex Infantry Division (reinforced with the 4th Armoured Brigade and 31st Tank Brigade)

XII Corps Troops

- 86th Anti-Tank Regiment Royal Artillery

21st Army Group Forces:

- 3rd Army Group Royal Artillery
- 8th Army Group Royal Artillery
- 141st Regimental RAC (Crocodile flamethrower tanks of the 79th Armoured Division)

Operation "Goodwood"

I Corps

- 3rd Infantry Division (reinforced with the 27th Armoured Brigade)
- 6th Airborne Division
- 51st Highland Infantry Division

VIII Corps

- Guards Armoured Division
- 7th Armoured Division
- 11th Armoured Division

II Canadian Corps
- 2nd Infantry Division
- 3rd Infantry Division

Operation "Bluecoat"

XXX Corps
- 43rd Wessex Infantry Division
- 50th Northumbrian Infantry Division
- 7th Armoured Division

VIII Corps
- 15th Scottish Infantry Division (reinforced with the 6th Guards Tank Brigade)
- 11th Armoured Division
- Guards Armoured Division

Operation "Totalize"

2nd Infantry Division (Canadian)
4th Armoured Division (Canadian)
51st Highland Infantry Division
1st Armoured Division (Polish)

Order of Battle of Allied Division (Combat Formations)

15th Scottish Infantry Division
- 44th Lowland Infantry Brigade
  - 8th Royal Scots
  - 6th King's Own Scottish Border Regiment
  - 6th Royal Scots Fusiliers
- 46th Highland Infantry Brigade
  - 2nd Glasgow Highlanders
  - 7th Seaforth Highlanders
  - 9th Cameronian Highlanders
- 227th Highland Infantry Brigade
  - 10th Highland Light Infantry
  - 2nd Argyll & Sutherland Highlanders
  - 2nd Gordon Highlanders

43rd Wessex Infantry Division
- 129th Infantry Brigade
  - 4th Somerset Light Infantry
  - 4th Wiltshire Regiment
  - 5th Wiltshire Regiment
- 130th Infantry Brigade
  - 7th Hampshire Regiment
  - 4th Dorsetshire Regiment
  - 5th Dorsetshire Regiment
- 214th Infantry Brigade
  - 7th Somerset Light Infantry
  - 1st Worcestershire Regiment
  - 5th Duke of Cornwall's Light Infantry

50th Northumbrian Infantry Division
- 69th Infantry Brigade
  - 5th East Yorkshire
  - 6th The Green Howards
  - 7th The Green Howards
- 151st Infantry Brigade
  - 6th Durham Light Infantry
  - 8th Durham Light Infantry
  - 9th Durham Light Infantry
- 231st Infantry Brigade
  - 2nd Devonshire Regiment
  - 1st Hampshire Regiment
  - 1st Dorsetshire Regiment

51st Highland Infantry Division
- 152nd Infantry Brigade
  - 2nd Seaforth Highlanders
  - 5th Seaforth Highlanders
  - 5th Queen's Own Cameron Highlanders
- 153rd Infantry Brigade
  - 5th The Black Watch
  - 1st Gordon Highlanders
  - 5/7th Gordon Highlanders
- 154th Infantry Brigade
  - 1st The Black Watch
  - 7th The Black Watch
  - 7th Argyll & Sutherland Highlanders

7th Armoured Division
- 22nd Armoured Brigade
  - 5th Royal Inniskilling Dragoon Guards
  - 1st Royal Tank Regiment
  - 5th Royal Tank Regiment
- 1st Rifle Brigade
- 131st Infantry Brigade
  - 1/5th Queen's Royal Regiment
  - 1/6th Queen's Royal Regiment
  - 1/7th Queen's Royal Regiment

11th Armoured Division
- 29th Armoured Brigade
  - 23rd Hussars
  - 3rd Royal Tank Regiment
  - 2nd Fife and Forfar Yeomanry
- 8th Rifle Brigade
- 159th Infantry Brigade
  - 4th Kings Shropshire Light Infantry
  - 3rd Monmouthshire Regiment
  - 1st Herefordshire Regiment

Guards Armoured Division
- 5th Guards Armoured Brigade
  - 2nd (Armoured) Grenadier Guards
  - 1st (Armoured) Grenadier Guards
  - 1st Coldstream Guards
  - 2nd Irish Guards
  - 1st (Motor) Grenadier Guards
- 32nd Guards Armoured Brigade
  - 5th Coldstream Guards
  - 3rd Irish Guards
  - 1st Welsh Guards

Additional attached formations:

4th Armoured Brigade
- The Royal Scots Greys
- 3rd County of London Yeomanry
- 44th Royal Tank Regiment
- 2nd The King's Royal Rifle Corps

31st Tank Brigade
- 7th Royal Tank Regiment
- 9th Royal Tank Regiment

2nd Infantry Division (Canadian)
- 4th Infantry Brigade
  - The Royal Regiment of Canada
  - The Royal Hamilton Light Infantry
  - The Essex Scottish Regiment
- 5th Infantry Brigade
  - Royal Highland Regiment of Canada
  - Régiment de Maisonneuve
  - The Calgary Highlanders
- 6th Infantry Brigade
  - Les Fusilers Mont-Royal
  - Queen's Own Cameron Highlanders of Canada
  - South Saskatchewan Regiment

4th Armoured Division (Canadian)
- 4th Armoured Brigade
  - 21st Armoured Regiment
  - 22nd Armoured Regiment
  - 28th Armoured Regiment
  - The Lake Superior Regiment
- 10th Infantry Brigade
  - The Lincoln & Welland Regiment
  - The Algonquin Regiment
  - The Argyll & Sutherland Highlanders of Canada

1st Armoured Division (Polish)
- 10th Armoured Cavalry Brigade
  - 1st Armoured Regiment
  - 2nd Armoured Regiment
  - 24th Lancers
  - 10th Dragoons
- 3rd Rifle Brigade
  - Highland Rifle Battalion
  - 8th Rifle Battalion
  - 9th Rifle Battalion

APPENDIX 2

Composition of Tiger Units

Schwere SS-Panzer-Abteilung 101 (1 May 1944)

007 008 009

1.

105 104

111 112 113 114

121 122 123 124

131 132 133 134

2.

205 204

211 212 213 214

221 222 223 224

231 232 233 234

3.

305 304

311 312 313 314

321 322 323 324

331 332 333 334

Schwere SS-Panzer-Abteilung 102 (1 June 1944)

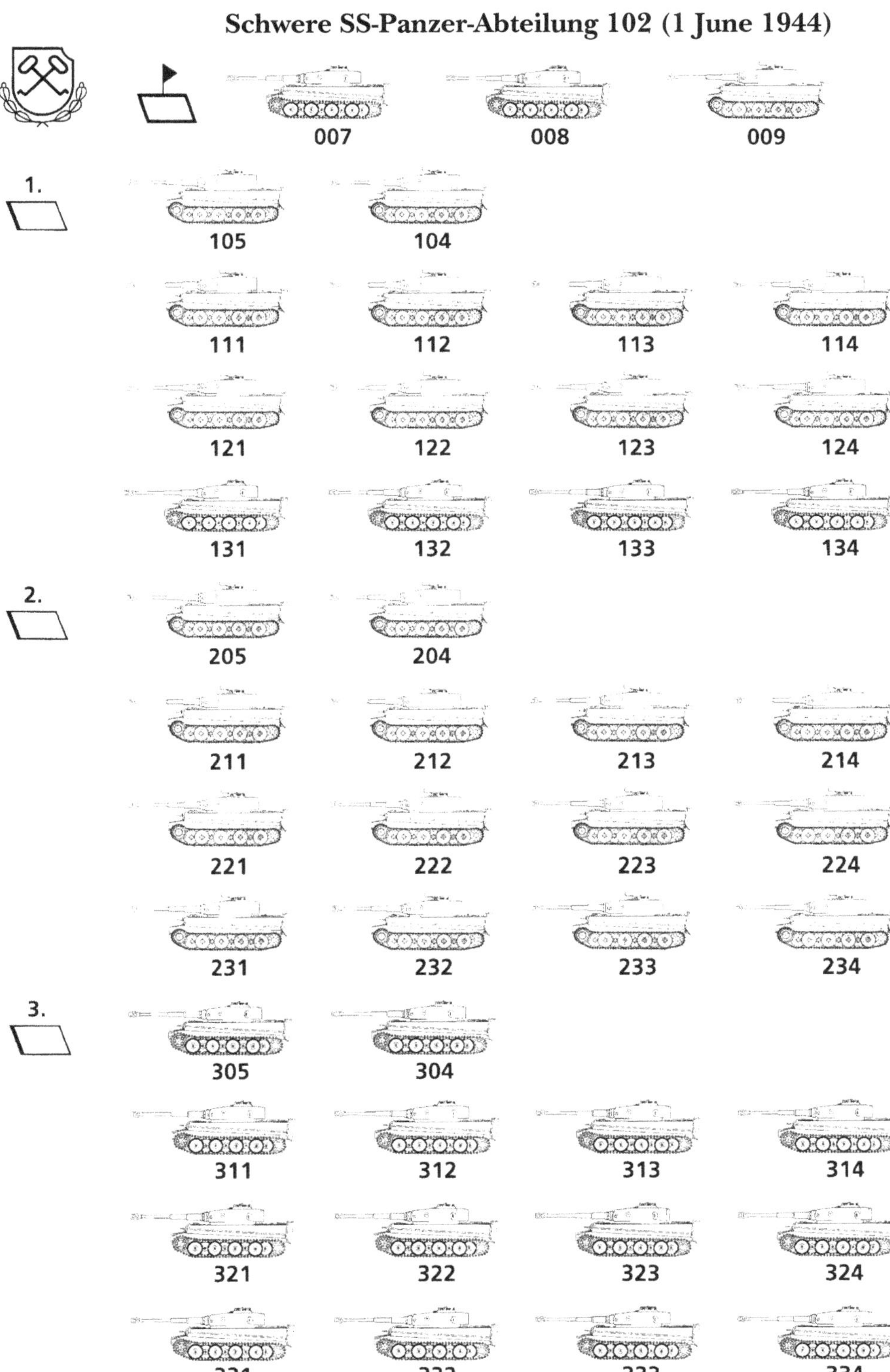

Schwere Panzer-Abteilung 503 (1 July 1944)

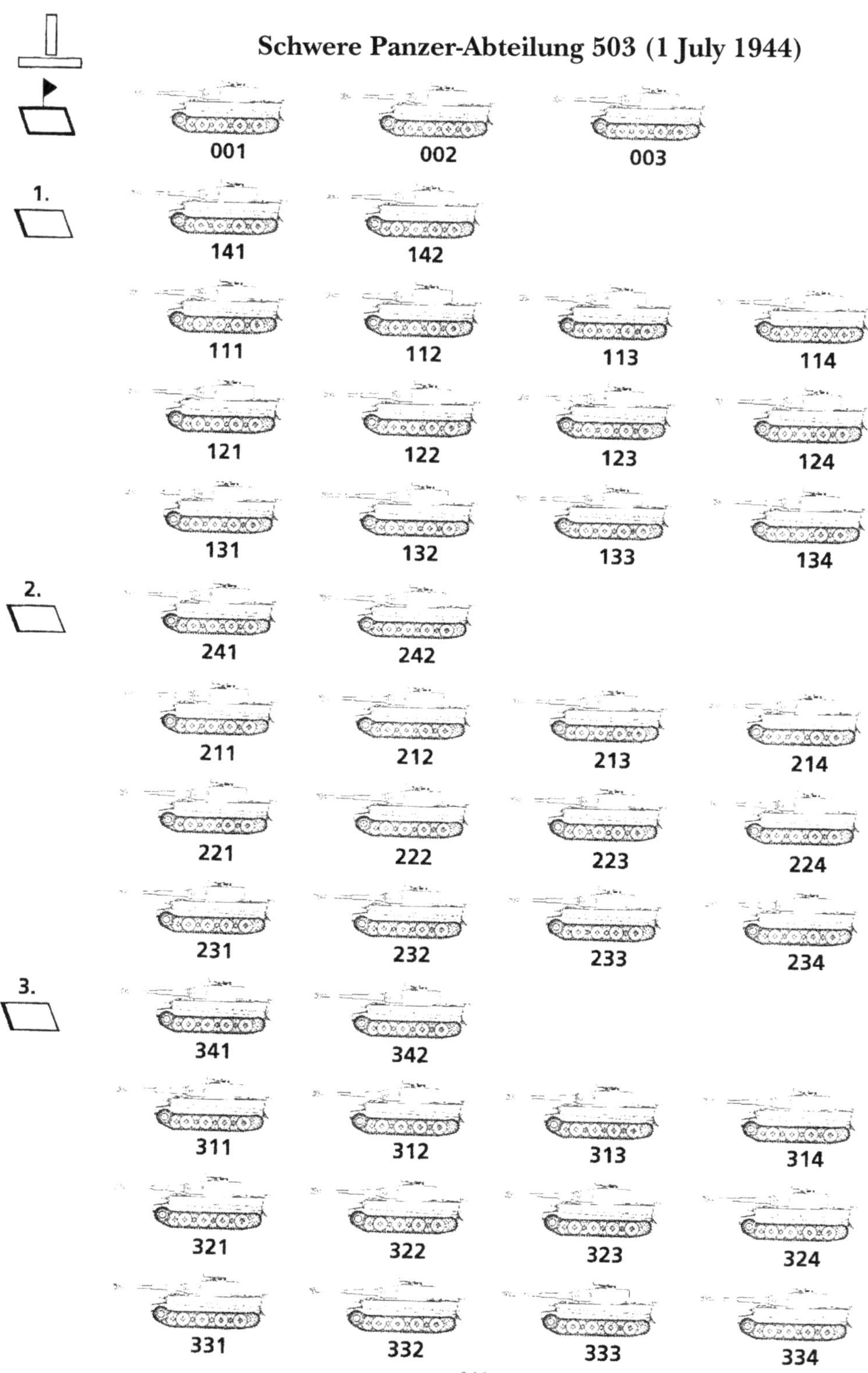

APPENDIX 3

Tiger Markings

In General

In general, it is not difficult to determine what formations the vehicles belonged to when looking at photographs, since the turrets had differing styles of markings and the color camouflage schemes were different. There were also considerable differences in the types of vehicles that were issued to each of the formations. It is considerably more difficult, however, to determine formations when the vehicles have been badly damaged or have burned out.

Schwere Panzer-Abteilung 503

Of note within this battalion is the fact that its 1st Company was issued differing versions of the *Tiger*: twelve *Tiger II's* and two *Tiger I's*. All of the *Tiger II's* had the so-called Porsche turret. This was the only battalion unit to have *Tiger II's* employed in Normandy. All of the remaining *Tigers* were late versions with steel roadwheels and reinforced turret roofs.

The numbering employed black numerals bordered in white. They were on both sides of the turret and on the turret rear as well. The numbers used were the standard German practice of three digits: Company — Platoon — Individual tank within the platoon. The two tanks in the company headquarters section had the company number, followed by a zero and then the number of the tank within the section, with a zero usually indicating the company commander's vehicle, e.g., 300 = The *Tiger* of the 3rd Company commander. The three tanks assigned to the battalion headquarters had Roman numerals: I, II and III.

The *Tiger II's* of the reconstituted 3rd Company, which was employed against the American bridgehead at Mantes, had the normal 300-series of numbers.

Schwere SS-Panzer-Abteilung 101

This battalion had a number of different identifiers with regard to the coloring of the tactical numbers as well as other markings. In addition, a portion of the *Tiger I's* still had the older-style running gear with the rubber-rimmed roadwheels, because the battalion had taken deliveries of ten tanks each in October 1943 and January 1944. All of the 3rd Company (fourteen tanks) had that version of the *Tiger*, while the 1st Company had four. Only the 2nd Company was completely equipped with steel-rimmed roadwheels.

The color of the turret numbers differed from company to company and at battalion headquarters. The 1st Company had olive-colored numerals, bordered in white; the 2nd, red with white; the 3rd, blue with yellow; and the battalion headquarters, pure white. The numbers were painted on the turret sides and rear.

All of the tanks had the corps tactical insignia on the front slope: two crossed skeleton keys above two oak leaves. Within the tanks of the 1st and 3rd Companies and the battalion headquarters section, the corps insignia was on the left side of the vehicle; the 2nd Company sported its insignia on the righthand side. In addition, the 1st Company placed the tactical insignia for tanks on the opposite of the corps insignia. Underneath it was a small "s", which stood for *schwer* (heavy). These insignia were either painted directly on the *Zimmerit* anti-magnetic coating or in a small field that was left free for that purpose.

Another peculiarity was, in part, the numbering system. The tanks of the company command sections all end with a 5, e.g., 105. The battalion's tanks were numbered 009, 008 and 007.

The reconstituted 1st Company, which was issued in its entirety with *Tiger II's* with standard-production turrets, had yellow turret numbers, which were painted under the *Balkenkreuz* (German cross) on the turret sides.

Schwere SS-Panzer-Abteilung 102

All of the *Tigers* of this battalion had steel roadwheels and, for the most part, normal numbering. The exceptions, once again, were the command and control tanks. The company command tanks had "4's", e.g., 141 and 142 in the 1st Company (analogous in the other two companies). The battalion command tanks were numbered 001, 002 and 003. The numerals were painted in outline form in white. On the stowage boxes on the back of the turrets, the numerals were in black with white borders. A peculiarity was a pink lightning rune (*Blitzrune*), which was painted on the left front hull and the left rear of the vehicles.

Schwere Panzer-Kompanie 316 (Fkl)

This company had five *Tiger II's* with the Porsche turret and three older-version *Tiger I's*. The tanks had large white numerals painted on the front part of either side of the turrets. The numbers of several of the *Tiger II's* have been verified: 02, 10 and 13.

APPENDIX 4

Tiger Availability and Losses

Tiger Operational Readiness in Normandy

Date	SS101	Inv.	Date	SS101	Inv.	SS102	Inv.	503	Inv.	Date	SS101	Inv.	SS102	Inv.	503	Inv.
			1.7	11	30					1.8	20	25		38	13	29
			2.7		30					2.8	19	25		37		29
			3.7		30					3.8	20	25		34		29
			4.7	0	30					4.8	20	25		33		29
			5.7	0	30					5.8		25	20	32		29
			6.7	0	28				44	6.8		25		32	11	28
			7.7	0	28	28	45		44	7.8	21	25		32		28
			8.7	21	28	15	45		44	8.8		18	21	32		28
			9.7	19	28	27	45		44	9.8	8	18		32		28
			10.7	15	28		40		44	10.8	17	18		32		28
			11.7	13	28	16	39	23	44	11.8	11	18	7	32		26
			12.7	13	28	12	39		44	12.8		18		32		26
13.6	12	32	13.7	14	28	12	39	32	44	13.8		18	13	31		25
14.6	4	32	14.7		28	22	39		44	14.8		17	13	29		25
15.6	15	32	15.7	20	28	8	39		44	15.8	8	17	7	29		25
16.6	15	32	16.7	19	28	7	39	40	44	16.8		16	2	27		25
17.6		32	17.7	1	28		39	39	44	17.8		16	5	26		25
18.6	0	32	18.7		27	5	39	9	32	18.8		15		25		21
19.6	0	32	19.7		26	8	39		32	19.8	8	14		19		21
20.6	0	32	20.7		25	11	39		32	20.8	6	14		18		19
21.6	0	32	21.7	6	25		39		32	21.8		14		14		
22.6	0	32	22.7	7	25	14	39		32	22.8		14		10		
23.6		32	23.7	10	25	8	39		32	23.8		14		10		
24.6		32	24.7	14	25		39		32	24.8		13		10		
25.6		32	25.7	14	25		39	20	32	25.8	10	11		7		3
26.6		32	26.7	14	25	7	38		32	26.8		8		7		
27.6	18	32	27.7	14	25	7	38	15	32	27.8	14	6		7		
28.6		32	28.7	20	25	9	38	14	32	28.8	2	6		6		
29.6		32	29.7	21	25	10	38	15	32	29.8	3	5				
30.6		32	30.7	20	25	10	38		32	30.8	2	3		1		
		32	31.7	19	25	11	38		32	31.8		3				

Inv. = Inventory–total numbers of Tigers on hand.

Operational Tigers of *schwere SS-Panzer-Abteilung 101*

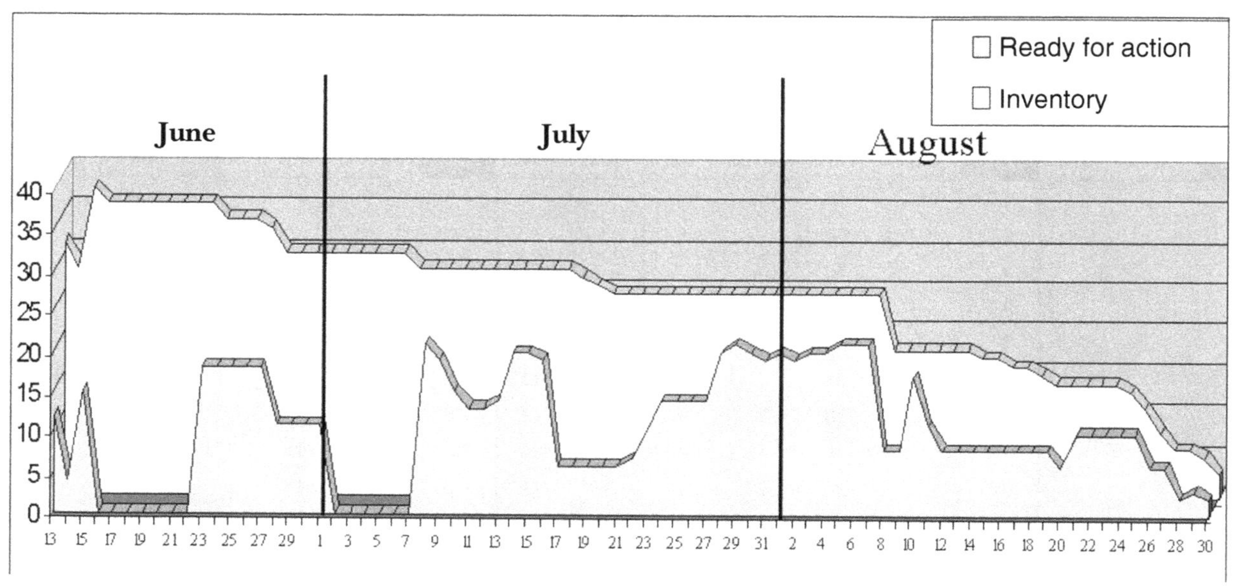

Operational Tigers of *schwere SS-Panzer-Abteilung 102*

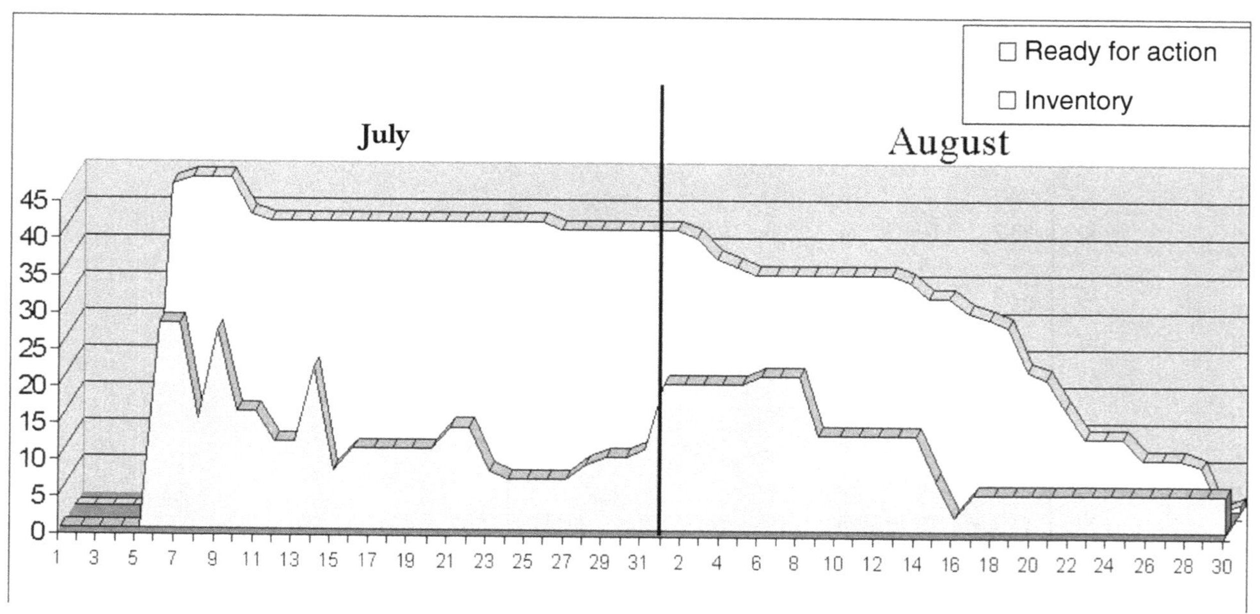

Operational Tigers of *schwere Panzer-Abteilung 503*

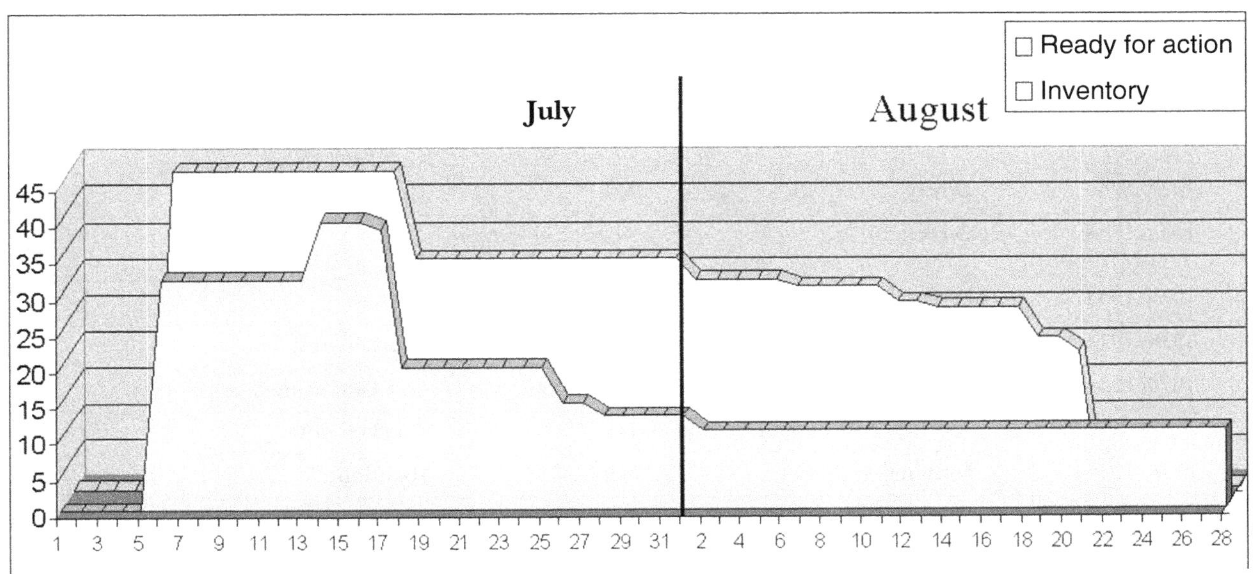

Losses of *schwere SS-Panzer-Abteilung 101*

Date	Location	Number	Cause
13.06.1944	Villers-Bocage	112	Firefly
13.06.1944	Villers-Bocage	121	Firefly
13.06.1944	Villers-Bocage	1xx	Anti-Tank Gun
13.06.1944	Villers-Bocage	1xx	Anti-Tank Gun
13.06.1944	Villers-Bocage	222	Anti-Tank Gun
15.06.1944	Evrecy	311	Aircraft
15.06.1944	Evrecy	3xx	Aircraft
15.06.1944	Evrecy	3xx	Aircraft
15.06.1944	Greland	132	Knocked out
16.06.1944	Cahagnes	111	Anti-Tank Gun
		1xx	Knocked out
26.06.1944	Fontenay-le-Pesnel	3xx	Abandoned
27.06.1944	Mouen	1xx	Knocked out
27.06.1944	Colleville	1xx	Knocked out
27.06.1944	Cheux	2xx	Anti-Tank Gun
28.06.1944	Grainville	331	Knocked out
28.06.1944	Grainville	1xx	Knocked out
28.06.1944	Rauray	334	Abandoned
29.06.1944	Gavrus	1xx	Anti-Tank Gun
18.07.1944	Soliers		Firefly
19.07.1944	Chicheboville	305	Friendly fire - AT Gun
20.07.1944	Bras	2xx	Knocked out
20.07.1944	Bouguébus	231	Knocked out
08.08.1944	Gausmesnil	2xx	Sherman
08.08.1944	Gausmesnil	ex1xx	Sherman
08.08.1944	Gausmesnil	314	Sherman
08.08.1944	Gausmesnil		Sherman
08.08.1944	Gausmesnil	007	Firefly
08.08.1944	Bois-de-Quesnay	2xx	Knocked out
14.08.1944	Maizieres	ex1xx	Sherman
14.08.1944	Potigny	211	Abandoned

15.08.1944	Hill 160/Falaise	304	Abandoned
16.08.1944	Rouen	324	Abandoned
18.08.1944	Livarot		Abandoned
	Elbeuf	321	Abandoned
	Elbeuf	332	Abandoned
24.08.1944	Montfort-sur-Risle		M10
27.08.1944	Gisors	221	Anti-Tank Gun
27.08.1944	Gisors		Abandoned
29.08.1944	Tilly		Knocked out
30.08.1944	Gisors	2xx	Abandoned
30.08.1944	Gisors	2xx	Abandoned
	St. Quentin	3xx	Sherman
	Marles	ex1xx	Abandoned
	Genval	3xx	Abandoned

Losses of *schwere SS-Panzer-Abteilung 102*

Date	Location	Number	Cause
10.07.1944	St. Martin		Aircraft
10.07.1944	St. Martin		Aircraft
10.07.1944	Hill 112	221	Missing
10.07.1944	Hill 112	311	Knocked out
10.07.1944	Hill 112	312	Knocked out
10.07.1944	Hill 112	3xx	Knocked out
02.08.1944	Le Hauts Vents	1xx	Knocked out
03.08.1944	La Bistierre	233	Knocked out
04.08.1944	Chenedollé	2xx	Burned out
14.08.1944	Tournebu	212	Knocked out
14.08.1944	Ussy	231	Knocked out
17.08.1944	Damblainville	1xx	Knocked out
18.08.1944	Abbaye	124	Blown up
19.08.1944	Brieux	2xx	
19.08.1944	Brieux	2xx	
	St. Lambert-sur-Dive	1xx	Infantry

	Nécy		
	Nécy		
	Nécy		
20.08.1944	Vimoutiers	2xx	Frozen Pistons
	Aubry-le-Panthou	1xx	Blown up
	Aubry-le-Panthou	1xx	Blown up
	Montormel		Burned out
22.08.1944	Brogliel	3xx	Blown up
	Mandeville	3xx	Immobilized
	Aubry-le Panthou		
	Aubry-le Panthou		
	Aubry-le Panthou		
25.08.1944	Elbeuf		
	Tostes	223	Abandoned
28.08.1944	Rouen	001	Sunk
28.08.1944	Braine		Captured on Train
28.08.1944	Braine		Captured on Train
28.08.1944	Braine		Captured on Train
28.08.1944	Bois Bourdon		Abandoned
	Enghien		Abandoned

Losses of *schwere Panzer-Abteilung 503*

Date	Location	Number	Cause/Vehicle
06.07.1944	Cannon	323	Total loss
18.07.1944	Manneville	313	Hit by bombs
18.07.1944	Manneville	332	Hit by bombs
18.07.1944	Manneville	3xx	Hit by bombs
18.07.1944	Manneville	3xx	Hit by bombs
18.07.1944	Emieville	213	Hit by bombs
18.07.1944	Cagny	3xx	Friendly Flak
18.07.1944	Cagny	3xx	Friendly Flak
18.07.1944	Demouville	1xx	Blown up—Tiger II
18.07.1944	Demouville	101	Knocked out—Tiger II

18.07.1944		122	Friendly fire—AT gun—Tiger II
01.08.1944	La Bigne		Abandoned
01.08.1944	La Bigne	123	Abandoned—Tiger II
02.08.1944	Jurcques		Fighter Bomber
03.08.1944	St. Pierre-du-Fresne		Knocked out
08.08.1944	Le Plessis-Grimoult	133	Nearby explosion—Tiger II
02.08.1944	St. Pierre-la-Vieille		Abandoned
09.08.1944	St. Pierre-la-Vieille		Abandoned
09.08.1944	St. Pierre-la-Vieille		Abandoned
09.08.1944	St. Pierre-la-Vieille		Abandoned
09.08.1944	St. Pierre-la-Vieille		Abandoned
09.08.1944	St. Pierre-la-Vieille		Abandoned
11.08.1944	St. Pierre-la-Vieille		Fighter Bomber
11.08.1944	St. Pierre-la-Vieille		Fighter Bomber
13.08.1944	Proussy		Mechanically disabled
13.08.1944	Proussy		Mechanically disabled
18.08.1944	Le Billot	111	Abandoned—Tiger II
18.08.1944	Vimoutiers	1xx	Abandoned—Tiger II
18.08.1944	Ommoy	113	Abandoned
18.08.1944	St. Pierre-la-Riviére	100	Abandoned—Tiger II
20.08.1944	Orville	112	Abandoned—Tiger II
	Orville	124	Abandoned—Tiger II
	Montreuil-L'Argillé	2xx	Abandoned
	Montreuil-L'Argillé	2xx	Abandoned
	Broughteroulde	213n	Abandoned
24.08.1944	Bernay		Abandoned
	Caudebec	II	Abandoned
	Caudebec	224	Abandoned
	Caudebec		Abandoned
24.08.1944	Menneval		Abandoned
25.08.1944	Saussy la Champagne	222	Abandoned
	Gien	1xx	Tiger II
30.08.1944	Goincourt	324/121	Abandoned

BIBLIOGRAPHY

Allsuo, John. *Hedgerow Hell.*

Baverstock, Kevin. *Breaking the Panzers.*

Beale, Peter. *Tank Tracks.*

Benamou, Jean-Pierre. *Bataille de Caen.*

Bernage, Georges. *Les Panzers dans la Bataille de Normandie.*

—. *Normandie Album Memorial.*

—. *Normandie: Aout 1944.*

Bernage/Cadel. *Cobra.*

Bernage/Leteinturer. *La Garde contre la Hohenstaufen.*

Berbage et al. *Bataille de Normandie.*

Blumenson, Martin. *The Duel for France 1944.*

Brisset, Jean. *Charge of the Bull.*

Bryan, Tony. *Operation Cobra 1944.*

Buffetaut, Yves. *La poche de Falaise.*

—. *Operation Goodwood.*

Close, Bill. *A View from the Turret.*

Copp, Terry. *Fields of Fire.*

Daglish, Ian. *Operation Bluecoat.*

Delaforce, Patrick. *The Black Bull.*

—. *Churchill's Desert Rats.*

—. *Churchill's Secret Weapons.*

—. *The Fighting Wessex Wyverns.*

—. *Monty's Marauders.*

—. *Taming the Panzers.*

Dunphie, Christopher. *The Pendulum of Battle.*

Fey et al. *Panzer im Brennpunkt der Fronten.*

Ford, Ken. *Assault Crossing.*

Furbringer, Herbert. *9. SS-Panzerdivision "Hohenstaufen."*

Van Greelen, Lothar. *Verkauft und verraten.*

Guderian, Heinz Günther. *Das letzte Kriegsjahr im Westen.*

Gudgin, Peter. *With Churchill to War.*

Hastings, Max. *Overlord.*

Hills, Stuart. *By Tank into Normandy.*

How, J. J. *Hill 112.*

Hunt, Eric. *Mont Pincon.*

Keegan, John. *Six Armies in Normandy.*

Klapdor, Ewald. *Die Entscheidung.*

Kortenhaus, Werner. *Die Schlacht um Caen 1944* (manuscript).

Lannoy, Francois de. *21st Army Group.*

Lefevre, Eric. *Normandie 1944—Les Panzers.*

—. *Panzers in Normandy—Then and Now.*

Lehmann/Tiemann. *Die Leibstandarte.*

Leleu, Jean-Luc. *Falaise.*

Lodieu, Didier. *D'Argentan à la Seine.*

Lodieu, Didier. *45 Tiger en Normandie.*

Ludewig, Joachim. *Der deutsche Rückzug aus Frankreich 1944.*

Mace, Paul. *Forrard.*

Marie, Henri. *Villers-Bocage Normandy 1944.*

Maule, Henry. *Caen: The Brutal Battle.*

McKee, Alexander. *Caen: Anvil of Victory.*

McNair, Ronald. *Repli sur la Seine.*

Meyer, Hubert. *Kriegsgeschichte der 12. SS-Panzerdivision "Hitlerjugend."*

Münch, Karlheinz. *Schwere Panzerjägerabteilung 654.*

Official History of the Canadian Army in WW II.

Paget, Julian. *Second to None.*

Reardon, Mark. *Victory at Mortain.*

Renoult/Havelange. *La Tete de Pont de Mantes.*

Restayn, Jean. *Tiger I on the Western Front.*

Reynolds, Michael. *Sons of the Reich.*

—. *Steel Inferno.*

Ritgen, Helmut. *Panzerlehrdivision im Westen 1944–45.*

Saunders, Tim. *Hill 112.*

—. *Operation Epsom.*

Schneider, Wolfgang. *Tiger im Kampf (Volumes 1 and 2).*

Stimpel, Hans-Martin. *Die deutsche Fallschirmjägertruppe 1942–1945.*

Sweet, John. *Mounting the Threat.*

Taylor, Daniel. *Villers-Bocage, Through the Lens.*

Tieke, Wilhelm. *Im Feuersturm der letzten Kriegsjahre.*

Tout, Ken. *The Bloody Battle for Tilly.*

Verney, G.L. *The Desert Rats.*

Weidinger, Otto. *Division Das Reich.*

Wilson, Edward. *Press On, Regardless.*

Zetterling, Niklas. *Normandy 1944.*

Periodicals: *"Der Freiwillige", "39-45"* and *"Panzer voran!"*

Numerous firsthand accounts from members of the former heavy tank battalions.

Despite the fear that the *Tiger* inspired in Normandy among the Allied soldiers, its actual influence on the course of operations was small. Usually abandoned by the crews themselves, the vehicles often spent a desolate existence for years as wrecks scattered across all of northern France. Here, the commander-in-chief of the Allied forces, General Eisenhower, views a destroyed *Tiger II*, which has been pushed to the side to clear a road.

www.ingramcontent.com/pod-product-compliance
Lightning Source LLC
Chambersburg PA
CBHW081925221224
19390CB00003B/4

9 780811 776950